Boeing Commercial Crew Transportation Capability Contract

TABLE OF CONTENTS

Contents

SECTION B. SUPPLIES OR SERVICES AND PRICES/COSTS 8
   B.1   NFS 1852.216-78 FIRM FIXED PRICE (DEC 1988) 8
   B.2   SUPPLIES AND/OR SERVICES TO BE PROVIDED / ITEMS ISSUED 8
      Table B.2 Services To Be Provided 8
   B.3   DESIGN, DEVELOPMENT, TEST AND EVALUATION (DDTE)/CERTIFICATION (CORE CONTRACT) (CLIN 001) 8
      Table B.3 DDTE/Certification SubCLINs (CLIN 001) 9
   B.4   POST CERTIFICATION MISSIONS (IDIQ) (CLIN 002) 9
      Table B.4.1 Post Certification Mission Prices (CLIN 002) 10
      Table B.4.2 Post Certification Mission Task Order List (CLIN 002) 10
   B.5   SPECIAL STUDIES SERVICES (IDIQ) (CLIN 003) 10
      Table B.5.1 Special Studies Labor Rates 11
      Table B.5.2 Special Studies Task Order List (CLIN 003) 11

SECTION C. DESCRIPTION/SPECIFICATIONS/STATEMENT OF WORK 12
   C.1   SPECIFICATION/STATEMENT OF WORK 12

SECTION D. PACKAGING AND MARKING 13
   D.1   CLAUSES INCORPORATED BY REFERENCE -- SECTION D 13
      NFS 1852.211-70   PACKAGING, HANDLING, AND TRANSPORTATION. (SEP 2005) 13
   D.2   NFS 1852.245-74 IDENTIFICATION AND MARKING OF GOVERNMENT EQUIPMENT (JAN 2011)   13

SECTION E. INSPECTION AND ACCEPTANCE 15
   E.1   CLAUSES INCORPORATED BY REFERENCE -- SECTION E 15
      NFS 1852.246-73   HUMAN SPACE FLIGHT ITEM (MAR 1997) 15
   E.2   52.246-4 INSPECTION OF SERVICES AND RESEARCH AND DEVELOPMENT WORK - FIXED-PRICE (AUG 1996) (DEVIATION) 15

SECTION F. DELIVERIES OR PERFORMANCE 17
   F.1   CLAUSES INCORPORATED BY REFERENCE -- SECTION F 17
      52.242-15   STOP-WORK ORDER. (AUG 1989) 17
      52.242-17   GOVERNMENT DELAY OF WORK. (APR 1984) 17
   F.2   DELIVERY AND/OR COMPLETION SCHEDULE 17
   F.3   PLACE OF PERFORMANCE 17

SECTION G. CONTRACT ADMINISTRATION DATA 18
   G.1   CLAUSES INCORPORATED BY REFERENCE -- SECTION G 18
      NFS 1852.227-70 NEW TECHNOLOGY. (MAY 2002) 18
   G.2   NFS 1852.227-72 DESIGNATION OF NEW TECHNOLOGY REPRESENTATIVE AND PATENT REPRESENTATIVE. (JUL 1997) 18
   G.3   APPOINTMENT OF CONTRACTING OFFICER REPRESENTATIVE 19
   G.4   NFS 1852.245-73 FINANCIAL REPORTING OF NASA PROPERTY IN THE CUSTODY OF CONTRACTORS. (JAN 2011) 20
   G.5   NFS 1852.245-75 PROPERTY MANAGEMENT CHANGES. (JAN 2011) 21
   G.6   NFS 1852.245-76 LIST OF GOVERNMENT PROPERTY FURNISHED PURSUANT TO FAR 52.245-1. (JAN 2011) 21
   G.7   NFS 1852.245-78 PHYSICAL INVENTORY OF CAPITAL PERSONAL PROPERTY. (JAN 2011) 22

G.8	SUBMISSION OF INVOICES FOR PAYMENT	24
G.9	REQUIREMENTS FOR DATA OTHER THAN CERTIFIED COST OR PRICING DATA	24

SECTION H. SPECIAL CONTRACT REQUIREMENTS 26

H.1	CLAUSES INCORPORATED BY REFERENCE -- SECTION H	26
	NFS 1852.223-75 MAJOR BREACH OF SAFETY OR SECURITY. (FEB 2002)	*26*
	NFS 1852.225-70 EXPORT LICENSES. (FEB 2000) -- ALTERNATE I (FEB 2000)	*26*
	NFS 1852.244-70 GEOGRAPHIC PARTICIPATION IN THE AEROSPACE PROGRAM. (APR 1985)	*26*
	NFS 1852.246-70 MISSION CRITICAL SPACE SYSTEM PERSONNEL RELIABILITY PROGRAM. (MAR 1997)	*26*
H.2	NFS 1852.216-80 TASK ORDERING PROCEDURE. (OCT 1996) (DEVIATION)	26
H.3	NFS 1852.223-72 SAFETY AND HEALTH (SHORT FORM). (APR 2002)	28
H.4	NFS 1852.232-77 LIMITATION OF FUNDS (FIXED- PRICE CONTRACT). (MAR 1989)	28
H.5	NFS 1852.228-76 CROSS-WAIVER OF LIABILITY FOR INTERNATIONAL SPACE STATION ACTIVITIES. (OCT 2012) (DEVIATION)	30
H.6	NFS 1852.223-74 DRUG- AND ALCOHOL-FREE WORKFORCE (MARCH 1996)	35
H.7	SPECIAL STUDIES TASK ORDERING PROCEDURES (APPLICABLE TO CLIN 003 ONLY)	37
H.8	POST CERTIFICATION MISSION TASK ORDERING PROCEDURES (APPLICABLE TO CLIN 002)	37
H.9	REPRESENTATIONS, CERTIFICATIONS AND OTHER STATEMENTS OF OFFEROR	39
H.10	[RESERVED]	39
H.11	UNITED STATES COMMERCIAL PROVIDER AND DOMESTIC SOURCE CRITERIA	39
H.12	GOVERNMENT FURNISHED SERVICES AND DATA	40
H.13	REMOTELY SENSED DATA	41
H.14	USE OF GOVERNMENT PROPERTY, FACILITIES, ASSETS, OR SERVICES	41
H.15	GOVERNMENT INSIGHT	43
H.16	NEW ENTRANT	46
H.17	PUBLIC AFFAIRS	46
H.18	LICENSES, PERMITS, AND OTHER AUTHORIZATIONS FOR A LAUNCH OR REENTRY SERVICE OPERATOR	48
H.19	POST CERTIFICATION MISSION PAYMENTS, MILESTONES AND AUTHORITY TO PROCEED (ATP) CRITERIA	48
	Table H.19.1: ATP Criteria	*49*
	Table H.19.2 (a): Mission Milestone Review Payment Schedule	*50*
	Table H.19.2 (b): Mission Milestone Review Payment Schedule	*51*
H.20	ADJUSTMENTS TO POST CERTIFICATION MISSION SCHEDULE	52
	Table H.20.1: Launch Windows for PCM ATP Prior to ISS DCR*	*53*
	Table H.20.2: Launch Windows for PCM ATP After ISS DCR*	*53*
H.21	POST CERTIFICATION MISSION SUCCESS DETERMINATION	55
H.22	LIABILITY FOR THIRD PARTY CLAIMS	57
H.23	NON-NASA PASSENGERS, CARGO AND PAYLOADS	62
H.24	STATEMENT ON WAIVER OF RIGHTS TO INVENTIONS	65
H.25	SAE AS9100	65
H.26	MISHAP REPORTING	66
H.27	GOVERNMENT-INDUSTRY DATA EXCHANGE PROGRAM (GIDEP)	68
H.28	ENVIRONMENTAL COMPLIANCE AND NATIONAL ENVIRONMENTAL POLICY ACT (NEPA) DOCUMENTATION	69
H.29	ANOMALY INVESTIGATION AND CORRECTIVE ACTION	69
H.30	HAZARDOUS OPERATIONS	70
H.31	INTERIM PERFORMANCE-BASED MILESTONE PAYMENTS (APPLICABLE TO CLIN 001)	71
H.32	SUBCONTRACTING WITH RUSSIAN ENTITIES FOR GOODS OR SERVICES	72

SECTION I. CONTRACT CLAUSES 75

I.1	52.252-2 CLAUSES INCORPORATED BY REFERENCE (FEB 1998)	75
I.2	CLAUSES INCORPORATED BY REFERENCE -- SECTION I	75
52.202-1	DEFINITIONS. (JUL 2012)	75
52.203-3	GRATUITIES. (APR 1984)	75
52.203-5	COVENANT AGAINST CONTINGENT FEES. (APR 1984)	75
52.203-6	RESTRICTIONS ON SUBCONTRACTOR SALES TO THE GOVERNMENT. (SEP 2006)	75
52.203-7	ANTI-KICKBACK PROCEDURES. (OCT 2010)	75
52.203-8	CANCELLATION, RESCISSION, AND RECOVERY OF FUNDS FOR ILLEGAL OR IMPROPER ACTIVITY. (JAN 1997)	75
52.203-10	PRICE OR FEE ADJUSTMENT FOR ILLEGAL OR IMPROPER ACTIVITY. (JAN 1997)	75
52.203-12	LIMITATION ON PAYMENTS TO INFLUENCE CERTAIN FEDERAL TRANSACTIONS. (OCT 2010)	75
52.203-13	CONTRACTOR CODE OF BUSINESS ETHICS AND CONDUCT. (APR 2010)	76
52.203-14	DISPLAY OF HOTLINE POSTER(S). (DEC 2007)	76
52.204-2	SECURITY REQUIREMENTS. (AUG 1996)	76
52.204-4	PRINTED OR COPIED DOUBLE-SIDED ON POSTCONSUMER FIBER CONTENT PAPER. (MAY 2011)	76
52.204-9	PERSONAL IDENTITY VERIFICATION OF CONTRACTOR PERSONNEL. (JAN 2011)	76
52.204-10	REPORTING EXECUTIVE COMPENSATION AND FIRST-TIER SUBCONTRACT AWARDS. (JUL 2013)	76
52.204-13	SYSTEM FOR AWARD MANAGEMENT MAINTENANCE (JUL 2013)	76
52.209-6	PROTECTING THE GOVERNMENT'S INTEREST WHEN SUBCONTRACTING WITH CONTRACTORS DEBARRED, SUSPENDED, OR PROPOSED FOR DEBARMENT. (AUG 2013)	76
52.210-1	MARKET RESEARCH. (APR 2011)	76
52.211-15	DEFENSE PRIORITY AND ALLOCATION REQUIREMENTS. (APR 2008)	76
52.215-2	AUDIT AND RECORDS - NEGOTIATION. (OCT 2010)	76
52.215-11	PRICE REDUCTION FOR DEFECTIVE CERTIFIED COST OR PRICING DATA – MODIFICATIONS. (AUG 2011)	76
52.215-13	SUBCONTRACTOR CERTIFIED COST OR PRICING DATA – MODIFICATIONS. (OCT 2010)	76
52.215-8	ORDER OF PRECEDENCE - UNIFORM CONTRACT FORMAT. (OCT 1997)	76
52.217-8	OPTION TO EXTEND SERVICES. (NOV 1999)	76
52.219-4	NOTICE OF PRICE EVALUATION PREFERENCE FOR HUBZONE SMALL BUSINESS CONCERNS. (JAN 2011)	77
52.219-8	UTILIZATION OF SMALL BUSINESS CONCERNS. (JUL 2013)	77
52.219-9	SMALL BUSINESS SUBCONTRACTING PLAN. (Deviation per PIC 13-06 (www.hq.nasa.gov/office/procurement/regs/pic.html)) – ALTERNATE II (OCT 2001)	77
52.219-16	LIQUIDATED DAMAGES - SUBCONTRACTING PLAN. (JAN 1999)	77
52.219-28	POST-AWARD SMALL BUSINESS PROGRAM REREPRESENTATION. (JUL 2013)	77
52.222-1	NOTICE TO THE GOVERNMENT OF LABOR DISPUTES. (FEB 1997)	77
52.222-3	CONVICT LABOR. (JUN 2003)	77
52.222-21	PROHIBITION OF SEGREGATED FACILITIES. (FEB 1999)	77
52.222-26	EQUAL OPPORTUNITY. (MAR 2007)	77
52.222-35	EQUAL OPPORTUNITY FOR VETERANS. (SEP 2010)	77
52.222-36	AFFIRMATIVE ACTION FOR WORKERS WITH DISABILITIES. (OCT 2010)	77
52.222-37	EMPLOYMENT REPORTS ON VETERANS. (SEP 2010)	77
52.222-40	NOTIFICATION OF EMPLOYEE RIGHTS UNDER THE NATIONAL LABOR RELATIONS ACT. (DEC 2010)	77
52.222-50	COMBATING TRAFFICKING IN PERSONS. (FEB 2009)	77
52.222-54	EMPLOYMENT ELIGIBILITY VERIFICATION. (AUG 2013)	77
52.223-6	DRUG-FREE WORKPLACE. (MAY 2001)	77
52.223-18	ENCOURAGING CONTRACTOR POLICIES TO BAN TEXT MESSAGING WHILE DRIVING. (AUG 2011)	77
52.225-13	RESTRICTIONS ON CERTAIN FOREIGN PURCHASES. (JUN 2008)	77

52.227-1	AUTHORIZATION AND CONSENT. (DEC 2007)	78
52.227-2	NOTICE AND ASSISTANCE REGARDING PATENT AND COPYRIGHT INFRINGEMENT. (DEC 2007)	78
52.227-3	PATENT INDEMNITY. (APR 1984)	78
52.227-16	ADDITIONAL DATA REQUIREMENTS. (JUN 1987)	78
52.229-3	FEDERAL, STATE, AND LOCAL TAXES. (FEB 2013)	78
52.232-1	PAYMENTS. (APR 1984) (Applicable to CLIN 002 and any appropriate task orders per CLIN 003)	78
52.232-2	PAYMENTS UNDER FIXED-PRICE RESEARCH AND DEVELOPMENT CONTRACTS. (APR 1984) (Applicable to CLIN 001 and any appropriate task orders per CLIN 003)	78
52.232-8	DISCOUNTS FOR PROMPT PAYMENT. (FEB 2002)	78
52.232-9	LIMITATION ON WITHHOLDING OF PAYMENTS. (APR 1984)	78
52.232-11	EXTRAS. (APR 1984)	78
52.232-17	INTEREST. (OCT 2010)	78
52.232-18	AVAILABILITY OF FUNDS. (APR 1984)	78
52.232-23	ASSIGNMENT OF CLAIMS. (JAN 1986)	78
52.232-25	PROMPT PAYMENT. (JUL 2013)	78
52.232-33	PAYMENT BY ELECTRONIC FUNDS TRANSFER- SYSTEM FOR AWARD MANAGEMENT. (JUL 2013)	78
52.233-1	DISPUTES. (JUL 2002) - ALTERNATE I (DEC 1991)	78
52.233-3	PROTEST AFTER AWARD. (AUG 1996)	78
52.233-4	APPLICABLE LAW FOR BREACH OF CONTRACT CLAIM. (OCT 2004)	78
52.242-13	BANKRUPTCY. (JUL 1995)	78
52.243-1	CHANGES - FIXED-PRICE. (AUG 1987) - ALTERNATE I (APR 1984) (Applicable to CLIN 002 and any appropriate task orders per CLIN 003)	79
52.243-1	CHANGES - FIXED-PRICE. (AUG 1987) - ALTERNATE V (APR 1984) (Applicable to CLIN 001 and any appropriate task orders per CLIN 003)	79
52.243-7	NOTIFICATION OF CHANGES. (APR 1984)	79
52.244-2	SUBCONTRACTS. (OCT 2010)	79
52.244-6	SUBCONTRACTS FOR COMMERCIAL ITEMS. (JUL 2013)	79
52.245-1	GOVERNMENT PROPERTY. (APR 2012) -- Alternate I (APR 2012)	79
52.245-9	USE AND CHARGES. (APR 2012)	79
52.246-25	LIMITATION OF LIABILITY - SERVICES. (FEB 1997)	79
52.249-2	TERMINATION FOR CONVENIENCE OF THE GOVERNMENT (FIXED-PRICE). (APRIL 2012)	79
52.253-1	COMPUTER GENERATED FORMS. (JAN 1991)	79
NFS 1852.203-70	DISPLAY OF INSPECTOR GENERAL HOTLINE POSTERS. (JUN 2001)	79
NFS 1852.204-76	SECURITY REQUIREMENTS FOR UNCLASSIFIED INFORMATION TECHNOLOGY RESOURCES (JAN 2011)	79
NFS 1852.209-72	COMPOSITION OF THE CONTRACTOR. (DEC 1988)	79
NFS 1852.219-74	USE OF RURAL AREA SMALL BUSINESSES. (SEP 1990)	79
NFS 1852.219-76	NASA 8 PERCENT GOAL. (JUL 1997)	79
NFS 1852.219-77	NASA MENTOR-PROTEGE PROGRAM. (MAY 2009)	79
NFS 1852.243-71	SHARED SAVINGS. (MAR 1997)	79
NFS 1852.235-70	CENTER FOR AEROSPACE INFORMATION. (DEC 2006)	79
I.3	52.209-9 UPDATES OF PUBLICLY AVAILABLE INFORMATION REGARDING RESPONSIBILITY MATTERS (JUL 2013)	80
I.4	52.215-21 REQUIREMENTS FOR CERTIFIED COST OR PRICING DATA AND DATA OTHER THAN CERTIFIED COST OR PRICING DATA – MODIFICATIONS. (OCT 2010) (THIS CLAUSE IS APPLICABLE TO THE EXTENT THAT ONLY SUBCONTRACTORS ARE REQUIRED TO SUBMIT CERTIFIED COST OR PRICING DATA)	81
I.5	52.215-21 REQUIREMENTS FOR CERTIFIED COST OR PRICING DATA AND DATA OTHER THAN CERTIFIED COST OR PRICING DATA - MODIFICATIONS. (OCT 2010) - ALTERNATE IV (OCT 2010) (THIS CLAUSE IS NOT APPLICABLE TO SUBCONTRACTORS)	83

I.6	52.216-18 ORDERING (OCT 1995) (APPLICABLE TO IDIQ CLINs 002 AND 003)	83
I.7	52.216-19 ORDER LIMITATIONS (OCT 1995) (APPLICABLE TO IDIQ CLINs 002 AND 003)	83
I.8	52.216-22 INDEFINITE QUANTITY (OCT 1995) (APPLICABLE TO IDIQ CLINs 002 AND 003)	84
I.9	52.227-11 PATENT RIGHTS--OWNERSHIP BY THE CONTRACTOR. (DEC 2007) / AS MODIFIED PER 1852.227-11 PATENT RIGHTS - RETENTION BY THE CONTRACTOR (SHORT FORM).	85
I.10	52.227-14 RIGHTS IN DATA – GENERAL, (DEC 2007) (DEVIATION) / ALTERNATE I, (DEC 2007) (DEVIATION) / ALTERNATE II, (DEC 2007) (DEVIATION) / ALTERNATE III (DEC 2007) (DEVIATION) / AS MODIFIED PER 1852.227-14 RIGHTS IN DATA - GENERAL	91
I.11	52.232-32 PERFORMANCE-BASED PAYMENTS (APR 2012) (DEVIATION), (APPLICABLE TO INTERIM PERFORMANCE-BASED PAYMENTS EVENTS)	99
I.12	52.232-99 PROVIDING ACCELERATED PAYMENT TO SMALL BUSINESS SUBCONTRACTORS (AUG 2012) (DEVIATION)	103
I.13	52.249-8 DEFAULT (FIXED-PRICE SUPPLY AND SERVICE) (APR 1984) (APPLICABLE TO CLIN 002 AND ANY APPROPRIATE TASK ORDERS PER CLIN 003) (DEVIATION)	103
I.14	52.249-9 DEFAULT (FIXED-PRICE RESEARCH AND DEVELOPMENT) (APR 1984) (APPLICABLE TO CLIN 001 AND ANY APPROPRIATE TASK ORDERS PER CLIN 003) (DEVIATION)	106
I.15	52.252-6 AUTHORIZED DEVIATIONS IN CLAUSES (APR 1984)	108
I.16	NFS 1852.215-84 OMBUDSMAN. (NOV 2011) -- ALTERNATE I (JUN 2000)	108
I.17	NFS 1852.225-71 RESTRICTION ON FUNDING ACTIVITY WITH CHINA (FEB 2012)	109
I.18	NFS 1852.237-72 ACCESS TO SENSITIVE INFORMATION (JUN 2005)	109
I.19	NFS 1852.237-73 RELEASE OF SENSITIVE INFORMATION (JUN 2005)	111

SECTION J. LIST OF DOCUMENTS, EXHIBITS, AND OTHER ATTACHMENTS 114

J.1	LIST OF ATTACHMENTS	114

SECTION B. SUPPLIES OR SERVICES AND PRICES/COSTS

B.1 NFS 1852.216-78 FIRM FIXED PRICE (DEC 1988)

The total firm fixed price of this contract is the total amount shown in Table B.2, *Services To Be Provided*.

(End of Clause)

B.2 SUPPLIES AND/OR SERVICES TO BE PROVIDED / ITEMS ISSUED

The Contractor shall provide all resources necessary to deliver and/or perform the requirements of the contract in accordance with the following table and per clause C.1, *Specification/Statement of Work*, except for resources provided by the Government under clause G.6, *NFS 1852.245-76 List of Government Property Furnished Pursuant to FAR 52.245-1 (Jan 2011)* and clause H.12 *Government Furnished Services and Data*.

Table B.2 Services To Be Provided

CLIN Category	CLIN	Title	Price
Fixed Price Core Contract	001	Design, Development, Test, and Evaluation (DDTE)/Certification	■
Fixed Price IDIQ	002	Post Certification Missions (PCM)	TBD
Fixed Price IDIQ	003	Special Studies	TBD
		Total:	■

TBP: To Be Proposed / TBD: To Be Determined / IDIQ: Indefinite Delivery Indefinite Quantity / CLIN: Contract Line Item Number

(End of Clause)

B.3 Design, Development, Test and Evaluation (DDTE)/Certification (Core Contract) (CLIN 001)

NASA Certification under CLIN 001 is complete when the Contractor's Crew Transportation System (CTS) has met NASA's requirements for safely transporting crew to and from the International Space Station (ISS) in accordance with documents identified in Section C.1, *Specifications/Statement of Work*. SubCLINS 001A and 001B, identified in Table B.3, *DDTE/Certification SubCLINs*, are delivery milestones that represent completion of required work necessary to achieve NASA Certification. Delivery payment for the ISS Design Certification Review (DCR) for the crewed flight to the ISS includes all work under this CLIN that occurs from the contract effective date through the ISS DCR completion. The delivery payment for the Certification Review (CR) will include all work that occurs from the ISS DCR delivery date through the end of the DDTE/Certification CLIN 001.

Table B.3 DDTE/Certification SubCLINs (CLIN 001)

CLIN Category	CLIN	Title	Price
Fixed Price	001A	ISS Design Certification Review (ISS DCR)*	▮
Fixed Price	001B	Certification Review (CR)	▮
		Sub-Total (CLIN 001 Firm Fixed Price (FFP))	▮

*ISS DCR is the DCR for the crewed flight to ISS

(End of Clause)

B.4 POST CERTIFICATION MISSIONS (IDIQ) (CLIN 002)

In accordance with clause C.1, *Specification/Statement of Work*, the task ordering procedures and other terms and conditions in the contract, the Contracting Officer may issue Post Certification Mission (PCM) task orders. The Contractor shall use the Mission pricing rates shown in Table B.4.1, *Post Certification Mission Prices*. The per mission prices are for a single order at the price stated per the Calendar Year (CY) based on the number of missions ordered. CTS full mission capability prices shall be based on (1) fulfillment of the design reference mission to the ISS found in CCT-DRM-1110, *Crew Transportation System Design Reference Missions*, Attachment J-03, *Contract Performance Work Statement*, and other terms and conditions in the contract and (2) all inherent CTS capabilities that are within the proposed mission prices.

Post Certification Missions require at least ▮ months prior to launch to account for lead times.

The minimum quantity of Post Certification Missions in this contract is two (2). PCM task orders will not be issued until the Contractor has accomplished the criteria shown in clause H.19, *Post Certification Mission Payments, Milestones and ATP Criteria*, paragraph (a).

The maximum potential number of Post Certification Missions which may be ordered under this contract is six (6).

Table B.4.1 Post Certification Mission Prices (CLIN 002)

Calendar Year Ordered	Price ($M) Per Mission Based on order quantity of One (1)	Unit Price ($M) Per Mission Based on order quantity of Two (2)	Unit Price ($M) Per Mission Based on order quantity of Three (3)	Unit Price ($M) Per Mission Based on order quantity of Four (4)
2015				
2016				
2017				
2018				
2019				
2020				

Table B.4.2 Post Certification Mission Task Order List (CLIN 002)

Task Order Number	Description	Firm Fixed Price Amount
*To be filled in by Government as Task Orders are issued during contract performance	TBD	TBD
	TOTAL	TBD

(End of Clause)

B.5 SPECIAL STUDIES SERVICES (IDIQ) (CLIN 003)

In accordance with Attachment J-03, *Contract Performance Work Statement*, the task ordering procedures and other terms and conditions in the contract, the Contractor shall perform special studies, test and analyses, as initiated by written direction from the Contracting Officer. IDIQ tasks may include performing technical, cost, schedule and risk assessments for potential new or changes to existing requirements, as identified by the Government, for their impact on the Contractor's design, schedule and cost/price as it relates to CCtCap or life cycle activities; performing additional analyses, modeling, and/or tests of hardware or software to provide further confidence and understanding of robustness of design and advance planning, feasibility or trade studies for development or certification activities. These IDIQ tasks do not include any work necessary to accomplish the requirements under CLIN 001 and CLIN 002. The Contractor shall utilize the fully burdened labor rates shown in Table B.5.1, *Special Studies Labor Rates* when proposing to a Government Request for Task Order Proposal. The maximum potential total value of all Special Studies IDIQ tasks which may be ordered under this contract is $150 million.

Table B.5.1 Special Studies Labor Rates

Labor Category	Labor Rates						
	CY14	CY15	CY16	CY17	CY18	CY19	CY20
Professional / Technical (Exempt)							
Ops./Mfg. (Non-Exempt)							

Table B.5.2 Special Studies Task Order List (CLIN 003)

Task Order Number	Description	Firm Fixed Price Amount
*To be filled in by Government as Task Orders are issued during contract performance	TBD	TBD
	TOTAL	**TBD**

(End of Clause)

SECTION C. DESCRIPTION/SPECIFICATIONS/STATEMENT OF WORK

C.1 SPECIFICATION/STATEMENT OF WORK

The purpose of the Commercial Crew Program (CCP) is to facilitate the development of a U.S. commercial crew space transportation capability with the goal of achieving safe, reliable and cost effective access to and from low Earth orbit (LEO) including the International Space Station (ISS) no later than 2017. Once the capability is matured and available, NASA intends to purchase commercial crew transportation services to meet its ISS crew rotation and emergency return needs.

NASA is using a two-phased acquisition to certify fully integrated Crew Transportation Systems (CTS) that meet specified NASA safety and ISS requirements and standards, and begin missions to the ISS. Phase 1, the Certification Products Contract (CPC), requires delivery and disposition of specified early lifecycle plans and products that address CTS compliance with NASA's standards and requirements for an ISS design reference mission. The CPC deliverables mature in parallel with the maturation of the CTS design. Phase 2, the Commercial Crew Transportation Capability (CCtCap), is the requirement of this contract as described below.

Requirements:
The Contractor shall complete the design, development, test, evaluation, and certification of an integrated CTS capable of transporting NASA crew to and from the ISS, in accordance with the design reference missions and the certification standards and requirements specified in this contract. Certification of the CTS shall be determined by NASA. The Contractor shall provide special studies for risk reduction and other purposes related to its CTS, to the extent ordered under CLIN 003 of this contract. The Contractor shall also provide complete, initial Post Certification Missions to and from ISS including ground, launch, on-orbit, return and recovery operations, as ordered by IDIQ tasks under this contract.

(a) The Contractor shall provide all facilities, resources, personnel, items or services necessary to perform the requirements specified in Section B, *Supplies or Services and Prices/Costs* (except for Government furnished property as listed in clause G.6, NFS 1852.245-76, *List Of Government Property Furnished Pursuant To FAR 52.245-1* and *Government Furnished Services and Data* as listed in clause H.12) in accordance with the following:

Attachment J-01, *Integrated Crew Transportation System Requirements*
Attachment J-02, *Data Requirement Deliverables (DRDs)*
Attachment J-03, *Contract Performance Work Statement (PWS)* – To be proposed by Offeror
    Attachment J-03, Appendix A, *Milestone Acceptance Criteria and Payment Schedule* – To be proposed by Offeror

(b) Section C incorporates Attachments J-01, J-02 and J-03 into the Schedule. In case of a conflict, Attachment J-01 shall take precedence over Attachments J-02, and J-03. Attachment J-03 shall take precedence over Attachment J-02.

(End of Clause)

SECTION D. PACKAGING AND MARKING

D.1 CLAUSES INCORPORATED BY REFERENCE -- SECTION D

Clause(s) at the beginning of this Section are incorporated by reference, with the same force and effect as if they were given in full text. Clauses incorporated by reference which require a fill-in by the Government include the text of the affected paragraph(s) only. This does not limit the clause to the affected paragraph(s). The Contractor is responsible for understanding and complying with the entire clause. The full text of the clause is available at the addresses contained in clause I.1 52.252-2, *Clauses Incorporated by Reference*, of this contract.

NFS 1852.211-70   PACKAGING, HANDLING, AND TRANSPORTATION. (SEP 2005)

(End of Clause)

D.2   NFS 1852.245-74   IDENTIFICATION AND MARKING OF GOVERNMENT EQUIPMENT (JAN 2011)

(a) The Contractor shall identify all equipment to be delivered to the Government using NASA Technical Handbook (NASA-HDBK) 6003, *Application of Data Matrix Identification Symbols to Aerospace Parts Using Direct Part Marking Methods/Techniques*, and NASA Standard (NASA-STD) 6002, *Applying Data Matrix Identification Symbols on Aerospace Parts* or through the use of commercial marking techniques that: (1) are sufficiently durable to remain intact through the typical lifespan of the property: and, (2) contain the data and data format required by the standards. This requirement includes deliverable equipment listed in the schedule and other equipment when no longer required for contract performance and NASA directs physical transfer to NASA or a third party. The Contractor shall identify property in both machine and human readable form unless the use of a machine readable-only format is approved by the NASA Industrial Property Officer.

(b) Equipment shall be marked in a location that will be human readable, without disassembly or movement of the equipment, when the items are placed in service unless such placement would have a deleterious effect on safety or on the item's operation.

(c) Concurrent with equipment delivery or transfer, the Contractor shall provide the following data in an electronic spreadsheet format:

   (1) Item Description.

   (2) Unique Identification Number (License Tag).

   (3) Unit Price.

   (4) An explanation of the data used to make the unique identification number.

(d) For equipment no longer needed for contract performance and physically transferred under paragraph (a) of this clause, the following additional data is required:

    (1) Date originally placed in service.

    (2) Item condition.

(e) The data required in paragraphs (c) and (d) of this clause shall be delivered to the NASA center receiving activity listed below:

    Transportation Officer, NASA
    C/O ISC Warehouse, Building M6-744
    Kennedy Space Center, FL 32899

(f) The Contractor shall include the substance of this clause, including this paragraph (f), in all subcontracts that require delivery of equipment.

                      (End of Clause)

SECTION E. INSPECTION AND ACCEPTANCE

E.1 CLAUSES INCORPORATED BY REFERENCE -- SECTION E

Clause(s) at the beginning of this Section are incorporated by reference, with the same force and effect as if they were given in full text. Clauses incorporated by reference which require a fill-in by the Government include the text of the affected paragraph(s) only. This does not limit the clause to the affected paragraph(s). The Contractor is responsible for understanding and complying with the entire clause. The full text of the clause is available at the addresses contained in clause I.1 52.252-2, *Clauses Incorporated by Reference*, of this contract.

NFS 1852.246-73 HUMAN SPACE FLIGHT ITEM (MAR 1997)

(End of Clause)

E.2 52.246-4 INSPECTION OF SERVICES AND RESEARCH AND DEVELOPMENT WORK - FIXED-PRICE (AUG 1996) (Deviation)

(a) Definition: "Services," as used in this clause, includes services performed, workmanship, and material furnished or utilized in the performance of services.

(b) The Contractor shall provide and maintain an inspection system acceptable to the Government covering the services and Research and Development (R&D) work under this contract. Complete records of all inspection work performed by the Contractor shall be maintained and made available to the Government during contract performance and for as long afterwards as the contract requires.

(c) The Government has the right to inspect and test all services and R&D work called for by the contract, to the extent practicable at all times and places during the term of the contract. The Government may also inspect on the premises of the Contractor or any subcontractor engaged in contract performance. The Government shall perform inspections and tests in a manner that will not unduly delay the work.

(d) If the Government performs inspections or tests on the premises of the Contractor or a subcontractor, the Contractor shall furnish, and shall require subcontractors to furnish, at no increase in contract price, all reasonable facilities and assistance for the safe and convenient performance of these duties.

(e) Inspection and test by the Government does not relieve the Contractor from responsibility for failures to meet the contract requirements that may be discovered before acceptance. Government failure to inspect and accept or reject the services or R&D work shall not relieve the Contractor from responsibility, nor impose liability on the Government, for nonconforming services or R&D work. Acceptance shall be conclusive, except for latent defects, fraud, gross mistakes amounting to fraud, or as otherwise specified in the contract.

(f) The Government has the right to reject nonconforming services or R&D work. Nonconforming services or R&D work is when it is defective in material or workmanship or is otherwise not in conformity with contract requirements.

(g) If any of the services or R&D work do not conform with contract requirements, the Government may require the Contractor to perform the services or R&D work again in conformity with contract requirements, at no increase in contract amount. If acceptance is not conclusive for any of the causes in paragraph (e), in addition to any other rights and remedies provided by law, or under other provisions of this contract, or when the defects in services or R&D work cannot be corrected by reperformance, the Government may -

   (1)   Require the Contractor to take necessary action to ensure that future performance conforms to contract requirements; and

   (2)   Reduce the contract price to reflect the reduced value of the services or R&D work performed.

(h) If the Contractor fails to promptly perform the services again or to take the necessary action to ensure future performance in conformity with contract requirements, the Government may –

   (1)   By contract or otherwise, perform the services and charge to the Contractor any cost incurred by the Government that is directly related to the performance of such service; or

   (2)   Terminate the contract for default.

(i) The rights in paragraph (g) and (h) of this clause are superseded by the conditions in clause H.21, *Post Certification Mission Success Determination*, specific only to the Post Certification Mission (PCM) flights. For these flights, the rights in clause H.21 regarding acceptance (mission success determination), payment procedures in the event of a determination for other than full mission success and waiver of the Government requirement's to re-perform the final PCM flight, shall apply.

(End of Clause)

SECTION F. DELIVERIES OR PERFORMANCE

F.1   CLAUSES INCORPORATED BY REFERENCE -- SECTION F

Clause(s) at the beginning of this Section are incorporated by reference, with the same force and effect as if they were given in full text. Clauses incorporated by reference which require a fill-in by the Government include the text of the affected paragraph(s) only. This does not limit the clause to the affected paragraph(s). The Contractor is responsible for understanding and complying with the entire clause. The full text of the clause is available at the addresses contained in clause I.1 52.252-2, *Clauses Incorporated by Reference*, of this contract.

52.242-15   STOP-WORK ORDER. (AUG 1989)

52.242-17   GOVERNMENT DELAY OF WORK. (APR 1984)

(End of Clause)

F.2   DELIVERY AND/OR COMPLETION SCHEDULE

The Contractor shall deliver and/or complete performance of the items required under this contract as follows:

(a) CLIN 001, *DDTE/Certification*: The date of delivery for work performed under this contract is from date of award through completion of the last required milestone in Attachment J-03, Appendix A, *Milestone Acceptance Criteria and Payment Schedule*.

Milestone delivery and completion dates are defined in Attachment J-03, Appendix A for CLIN 001.

(End of Clause)

F.3   PLACE OF PERFORMANCE

The principal place of performance shall be The United States Of America.

(End of Clause)

SECTION G. CONTRACT ADMINISTRATION DATA

G.1 CLAUSES INCORPORATED BY REFERENCE -- SECTION G

Clause(s) at the beginning of this Section are incorporated by reference, with the same force and effect as if they were given in full text. Clauses incorporated by reference which require a fill-in by the Government include the text of the affected paragraph(s) only. This does not limit the clause to the affected paragraph(s). The Contractor is responsible for understanding and complying with the entire clause. The full text of the clause is available at the addresses contained in clause I.1 52.252-2, *Clauses Incorporated by Reference*, of this contract.

NFS 1852.227-70   NEW TECHNOLOGY. (MAY 2002)

(End of Clause)

G.2   NFS 1852.227-72   DESIGNATION OF NEW TECHNOLOGY REPRESENTATIVE AND PATENT REPRESENTATIVE. (JUL 1997)

(a) For purposes of administration of the clause of this contract entitled "New Technology" or "Patent Rights - Retention by the Contractor (Short Form)," whichever is included, the following named representatives are hereby designated by the Contracting Officer to administer such clause:

New Technology Representative
Technology and Integration Office, Mail Code: KSC-NET
NASA, John F. Kennedy Space Center
Kennedy Space Center, FL 32899

Patent Representative
Office of Chief Counsel, Mail Code: KSC-CC
NASA, John F. Kennedy Space Center
Kennedy Space Center, FL 32899

(b) Reports of reportable items, and disclosure of subject inventions, interim reports, final reports, utilization reports, and other reports required by the clause, as well as any correspondence with respect to such matters, should be directed to the New Technology Representative unless transmitted in response to correspondence or request from the Patent Representative. Inquires or requests regarding disposition of rights, election of rights, or related matters should be directed to the Patent Representative. This clause shall be included in any subcontract hereunder requiring a "New Technology" clause or "Patent Rights - Retention by the Contractor (Short Form)" clause, unless otherwise authorized or directed by the Contracting Officer. The respective responsibilities and authorities of the above-named representatives are set forth in 1827.305-370 of the NASA FAR Supplement.

(End of Clause)

G.3 APPOINTMENT OF CONTRACTING OFFICER REPRESENTATIVE

(a) Performance of the work under this contract is subject to the functions of the Contracting Officer Representative (COR), who shall be specifically appointed by the Contracting Officer in writing in accordance with NASA FAR Supplement (NFS) 1842.270. The COR will serve as the Contracting Officer's technical liaison with the Contractor by providing performance monitoring; review of Contractor's progress; support to Government Insight activities as defined in clause H.15, *Government Insight*; or furnishing similar monitoring for work within the scope of the contract.

(b) The COR does not have the authority to, and shall not, issue any instruction or direction that:

   (1) Constitutes an assignment of additional work outside the statement of work;

   (2) Constitutes a change as defined in the changes clauses in I.2, *Clauses Incorporated by Reference*;

   (3) Constitutes a basis for any increase or decrease in contract requirements; or any contract price; or the time required for contract performance;

   (4) Changes any of the expressed terms, conditions, or specifications of the contract; or

   (5) Interferes with the Contractor's rights to perform the terms and conditions of the contract.

(c) If, in the Contractor's opinion, any communication by the COR is deemed to be an instruction or direction that falls within any of the categories defined in paragraph (b) of this clause, the Contractor shall not proceed but shall notify the Contracting Officer in writing within five (5) working days after receiving it and shall request the Contracting Officer to take action as described in this clause. Upon receiving this notification, the Contracting Officer shall either issue an appropriate contract modification within a reasonable time or advise the Contractor in writing within fifteen (15) days that the communication is -

   (1) Rescinded in its entirety; or

   (2) Within the functions of the COR and does not constitute a change under the changes clauses of the contract, and that the Contractor should continue to proceed with contract performance.

(d) A failure of the Contractor and Contracting Officer to agree that the communication by the COR does not constitute a change under the changes clauses in I.2, or a failure to agree upon the contract action to be taken with respect to the communication, shall be subject to the Disputes clause of this contract.

(e) Any action(s) taken by the Contractor in response to any instruction or direction given by any person other than the Contracting Officer shall be at the Contractor's risk.

(End of Clause)

G.4 NFS 1852.245-73 FINANCIAL REPORTING OF NASA PROPERTY IN THE CUSTODY OF CONTRACTORS. (JAN 2011)

(a) The Contractor shall submit annually a NASA Form (NF) 1018, NASA Property in the Custody of Contractors, in accordance with this clause, the instructions on the form and NFS subpart 1845.71, and any supplemental instructions for the current reporting period issued by NASA.

(b) (1) Subcontractor use of NF 1018 is not required by this clause; however, the Contractor shall include data on property in the possession of subcontractors in the annual NF 1018.

(2) The Contractor shall mail the original signed NF 1018 directly to the cognizant NASA Center Deputy Chief Financial Officer, Finance, unless the Contractor uses the NF 1018 Electronic Submission System (NESS) for report preparation and submission.

(3) One copy shall be submitted (through the Department of Defense (DOD) Property Administrator if contract administration has been delegated to DOD) to the following address: NASA, John F. Kennedy Space Center, Attn: OP-OS-IP, Industrial Property Officer, Kennedy Space Center, unless the Contractor uses the NF 1018 Electronic Submission System (NESS) for report preparation and submission.

(c) (1) The annual reporting period shall be from October 1 of each year through September 30 of the following year. The report shall be submitted in time to be received by October 15. The information contained in these reports is entered into the NASA accounting system to reflect current asset values for agency financial statement purposes. Therefore, it is essential that required reports be received no later than October 15. Some activity may be estimated for the month of September, if necessary, to ensure the NF 1018 is received when due. However, Contractors' procedures must document the process for developing these estimates based on planned activity such as planned purchases or NASA Form 533 (NF 533 Contractor Financial Management Report) cost estimates. It should be supported and documented by historical experience or other corroborating evidence, and be retained in accordance with FAR Subpart 4.7, Contractor Records Retention. Contractors shall validate the reasonableness of the estimates and associated methodology by comparing them to the actual activity once that data is available, and adjust them accordingly. In addition, differences between the estimated cost and actual cost must be adjusted during the next reporting period. Contractors shall have formal policies and procedures, which address the validation of NF 1018 data, including data from subcontractors, and the identification and timely reporting of errors. The objective of this validation is to ensure that information reported is accurate and in compliance with the NASA FAR Supplement. If errors are discovered on NF 1018 after submission, the Contractor shall contact the cognizant NASA

Center Industrial Property Officer (IPO) within 30 days after discovery of the error to discuss corrective action.

(2) The Contracting Officer may, in NASA's interest, withhold payment until a reserve not exceeding $25,000 or 5 percent of the amount of the contract, whichever is less, has been set aside, if the Contractor fails to submit annual NF 1018 reports in accordance with NFS subpart 1845.71 and any supplemental instructions for the current reporting period issued by NASA. Such reserve shall be withheld until the Contracting Officer has determined that NASA has received the required reports. The withholding of any amount or the subsequent payment thereof shall not be construed as a waiver of any Government right.

(d) A final report shall be submitted within 30 days after disposition of all property subject to reporting when the contract performance period is complete in accordance with paragraph (b)(1) through (3) of this clause.

(End of Clause)

G.5   NFS 1852.245-75   PROPERTY MANAGEMENT CHANGES. (JAN 2011)

(a) The Contractor shall submit any changes to standards and practices used for management and control of Government property under this contract to the assigned property administrator prior to making the change whenever the change -

(1) Employs a standard that allows increase in thresholds or changes the timing for reporting loss, damage, or destruction of property;

(2) Alters physical inventory timing or procedures;

(3) Alters recordkeeping practices;

(4) Alters practices for recording the transport or delivery of Government property; or

(5) Alters practices for disposition of Government property.

(End of Clause)

G.6   NFS 1852.245-76 LIST OF GOVERNMENT PROPERTY FURNISHED PURSUANT TO FAR 52.245-1. (JAN 2011)

For performance of work under this contract, the Government will make available Government property identified below on a no charge-for-use basis pursuant to the clause at FAR 52.245-1, *Government Property (Alt I)*, as incorporated in this contract. The Contractor shall use this property in the performance of this contract at the Contractor's facility and at other location(s) as may be approved by the Contracting Officer. Under FAR 52.245-1 (Alt I), the Contractor is accountable for the identified property.

Description	Part Number (Docking Adapter Kit Docking Adapter Assembly)	Acquisition Value	Quantity	Available Date
NASA Docking System Block 1 (NDSB1) Flight Unit 1	683-100100-0001	$14,000,000	1	02/2016
	683-100000-0001			
NDSB1 Flight Unit 2	683-100100-0001	$14,000,000	1	04/2016
	683-100000-0001			
NDSB1 Flight Unit 3	683-100100-0001	$14,000,000	0	06/2016
	683-100000-0001			
NDSB1 Flight Unit 4	683-100100-0001	$14,000,000	0	08/2016
	683-100000-0001			

The Government understands that the NDSB1 Flight Units may be consumed in performance of this contract.

(End of Clause)

G.7 NFS 1852.245-78 PHYSICAL INVENTORY OF CAPITAL PERSONAL PROPERTY. (JAN 2011)

(a) In addition to physical inventory requirements under the clause at FAR 52.245-1, *Government Property*, as incorporated in this contract, the Contractor shall conduct annual physical inventories for individual property items with an acquisition cost exceeding $100,000.

(1) The Contractor shall inventory -

(i) Items of property furnished by the Government;

(ii) Items acquired by the Contractor and titled to the Government under the clause at FAR 52.245-1;

(iii) Items constructed by the Contractor and not included in the deliverable, but titled to the Government under the clause at FAR 52.245-1; and

(iv) Complete but undelivered deliverables.

(2) The Contractor shall use the physical inventory results to validate the property record data, specifically location and use status, and to prepare summary reports of inventory as described in paragraph (c) of this clause.

(b) Unless specifically authorized in writing by the Property Administrator, the inventory shall be performed and posted by individuals other than those assigned custody of the items, responsibility for maintenance, or responsibility for posting to the property record. The Contractor may request a waiver from this separation of duties requirement from the Property Administrator, when all of the conditions in either (1) or (2) of this paragraph are met.

   (1) The Contractor utilizes an electronic system for property identification, such as a laser bar-code reader or radio frequency identification reader, and

      (i) The programs or software preclude manual data entry of inventory identification data by the individual performing the inventory; and

      (ii) The inventory and property management systems contain sufficient management controls to prevent tampering and assure proper posting of collected inventory data.

   (2) The Contractor has limited quantities of property, limited personnel, or limited property systems; and the Contractor provides written confirmation that the Government property exists in the recorded condition and location;

   (3) The Contractor shall submit the request to the cognizant property administrator and obtain approval from the property administrator prior to implementation of the practice.

(c) The Contractor shall report the results of the physical inventory to the property administrator within 10 calendar days of completion of the physical inventory. The report shall -

   (1) Provide a summary showing number and value of items inventoried; and

   (2) Include additional supporting reports of -

      (i) Loss in accordance with the clause at 52.245-1, Government Property;

      (ii) Idle property available for reuse or disposition; and

      (iii) A summary of adjustments made to location, condition, status, or user as a result of the physical inventory reconciliation.

(d) The Contractor shall retain auditable physical inventory records, including records supporting transactions associated with inventory reconciliation. All records shall be subject to Government review and/or audit.

(End of Clause)

G.8 SUBMISSION OF INVOICES FOR PAYMENT

(a) The Contractor shall submit invoices for the work completed in accordance with Attachment J-03, Appendix A, *Milestone Acceptance Criteria and Payment Schedule* and task orders issued under this contract. The designated billing office for invoices for purposes of clause FAR 52.232-25, *Prompt Payment*, in I.2, *Clauses Incorporated by Reference,* is indicated below. Invoices shall include a reference to the number of this contract.

(b) Original invoices shall be submitted to:

> NASA Shared Services Center
> Financial Management Division (FMD)
> Accounts Payable
> Building 1111, C Road
> Stennis Space Center, MS   39529-6000
> Phone: 1-877-677-2123
> Fax: 1-866-209-5415
> e-mail: NSSC-AccountsPayable@nasa.gov

(c) Additional copies shall be furnished to:

> Copy 1:
> Contracting Officer, Mail Code: OP-MS
> NASA, John F. Kennedy Space Center
> Kennedy Space Center, FL 32899
>
> Copy 2:
> Commercial Crew Program Office, Mail Code: FA-A
> NASA, John F. Kennedy Space Center
> Kennedy Space Center, FL 32899

(End of Clause)

G.9 REQUIREMENTS FOR DATA OTHER THAN CERTIFIED COST OR PRICING DATA

NASA has waived the Certified Cost or Pricing Data required per FAR 15.403-4 for contractors but not subcontractors. "Certified Cost or Pricing Data" means cost or pricing data that is required to be submitted in accordance with FAR 15.403-4 and 15.403-5 and have been certified, or are required to be certified, in accordance with 15.406-2. Certified Cost or Pricing Data will not be required for contract modifications and task orders of any amount under this contract. In lieu of Certified Cost or Pricing Data, the Contractor shall submit "Data Other Than Certified Cost or Pricing Data" as defined in FAR 2.101, if required by the Contracting Officer as part of the Contractor's proposal to support any contract price adjustments. This data may be requested such as in the case when the Contracting Officer issues a contract modification, a change order in accordance with the *Changes* clauses in I.2 or any Request for Task Order Proposal issued per CLIN 002 or CLIN 003 of this contract.

(End of Clause)

SECTION H. SPECIAL CONTRACT REQUIREMENTS

H.1 CLAUSES INCORPORATED BY REFERENCE -- SECTION H

Clause(s) at the beginning of this Section are incorporated by reference, with the same force and effect as if they were given in full text. Clauses incorporated by reference which require a fill-in by the Government include the text of the affected paragraph(s) only. This does not limit the clause to the affected paragraph(s). The Contractor is responsible for understanding and complying with the entire clause. The full text of the clause is available at the addresses contained in clause I.1 52.252-2, *Clauses Incorporated by Reference*, of this contract.

NFS 1852.223-75   MAJOR BREACH OF SAFETY OR SECURITY. (FEB 2002)

NFS 1852.225-70   EXPORT LICENSES. (FEB 2000) -- ALTERNATE I (FEB 2000)
    Paragraph (b): Any NASA installation

NFS 1852.244-70 GEOGRAPHIC PARTICIPATION IN THE AEROSPACE PROGRAM. (APR 1985)

NFS 1852.246-70   MISSION CRITICAL SPACE SYSTEM PERSONNEL RELIABILITY PROGRAM. (MAR 1997)

(End of Clause)

H.2   NFS 1852.216-80 TASK ORDERING PROCEDURE. (OCT 1996) (Deviation)

(a) Only the Contracting Officer may issue task orders to the Contractor, providing specific authorization or direction to perform work within the scope of the contract and as specified in the schedule. The Contractor may incur costs under this contract in performance of task orders and task order modifications issued in accordance with this clause. No other costs are authorized unless otherwise specified in the contract or expressly authorized by the Contracting Officer.

(b) Prior to issuing a task order, the Contracting Officer shall provide the Contractor with the following data:

    (1)   A functional description of the work identifying the objectives or results desired from the contemplated task order.

    (2)   Proposed performance standards to be used as criteria for determining whether the work requirements have been met.

    (3)   A request for a task plan from the Contractor to include the technical approach, period of performance, appropriate cost information, and any other information required to determine the

reasonableness of the Contractor's proposal.

(c) Within 30 calendar days after receipt of the Contracting Officer's request, the Contractor shall submit a task plan conforming to the request.

(d) After review and any necessary discussions, the Contracting Officer may issue a task order to the Contractor containing, as a minimum, the following:

    (1)   Date of the order.

    (2)   Contract number and order number.

    (3)   Functional description of the work identifying the objectives or results desired from the task order, including special instructions or other information necessary for performance of the task.

    (4)   Performance standards, and where appropriate, quality assurance standards.

    (5)   Maximum dollar amount authorized (cost and fee or price). This includes allocation of award fee among award fee periods, if applicable.

    (6)   Any other resources (travel, materials, equipment, facilities, etc.) authorized.

    (7)   Delivery/performance schedule including start and end dates.

    (8)   If contract funding is by individual task order, accounting and appropriation data.

(e) The Contractor shall provide acknowledgment of receipt to the Contracting Officer within 5 working days after receipt of the task order.

(f) If time constraints do not permit issuance of a fully defined task order in accordance with the procedures described in paragraphs (a) through (d), a task order which includes a ceiling price may be issued.

(g) The Contracting Officer may amend tasks in the same manner in which they were issued.

(h) In the event of a conflict between the requirements of the task order and the Contractor's approved task plan, the task order shall prevail.

(End of Clause)

H.3 NFS 1852.223-72 SAFETY AND HEALTH (SHORT FORM). (APR 2002)

(a) Safety is the freedom from those conditions that can cause death, injury, occupational illness; damage to or loss of equipment or property, or damage to the environment. NASA's safety priority is to protect: (1) the public, (2) astronauts and pilots, (3) the NASA workforce (including Contractor employees working on NASA contracts), and (4) high-value equipment and property.

(b) The Contractor shall take all reasonable safety and occupational health measures consistent with standard industry practice in performing this contract. The Contractor shall comply with all Federal, State, and local laws applicable to safety and occupational health and with the safety and occupational health standards, specifications, reporting requirements, and any other relevant requirements of this contract.

(c) The Contractor shall take, or cause to be taken, any other safety, and occupational health measures the Contracting Officer may reasonably direct. To the extent that the Contractor may be entitled to an equitable adjustment for those measures under the terms and conditions of this contract, the equitable adjustment shall be determined pursuant to the procedures of the Changes clause of this contract; provided, that no adjustment shall be made under this Safety and Health clause for any change for which an equitable adjustment is expressly provided under any other clause of the contract.

(d) The Contracting Officer may notify the Contractor in writing of any noncompliance with this clause and specify corrective actions to be taken. In situations where the Contracting Officer becomes aware of noncompliance that may pose a serious or imminent danger to safety and health of the public, astronauts and pilots, the NASA workforce (including Contractor employees working on NASA contracts), or high value mission critical equipment or property, the Contracting Officer shall notify the Contractor orally, with written confirmation. The Contractor shall promptly take and report any necessary corrective action. The Government may pursue appropriate remedies in the event the Contractor fails to promptly take the necessary corrective action.

(e) The Contractor (or subcontractor or supplier) shall insert the substance of this clause, including this paragraph (e) and any applicable Schedule provisions, with appropriate changes of designations of the parties, in subcontracts of every tier that exceed the micro-purchase threshold.

(End of Clause)

H.4 NFS 1852.232-77 LIMITATION OF FUNDS (FIXED- PRICE CONTRACT). (MAR 1989)

(a) Of the total price of all CLIN items identified in Section B, the sum of $129.3M is presently available for payment and allotted to this contract. It is anticipated that from time to time additional funds will be allocated to the contract as required by the payment schedules in Attachment J-03, Appendix A, *Milestone Acceptance Criteria and Payment Schedule* and task orders awarded under CLIN 002 and 003 (see table B.4.2 and B.5.2 respectively) until the total price of said items is allotted.

(b) The Contractor agrees to perform or have performed work on the items specified in paragraph (a) of this clause up to the point at which, if this contract is terminated pursuant to the Termination for Convenience of the Government clause of this contract, the total amount payable by the Government (including amounts payable for subcontracts and settlement costs) pursuant to paragraphs (f) and (g) of that clause would, in the exercise of reasonable judgment by the Contractor, approximate the total amount at the time allotted to the contract. The Contractor is not obligated to continue performance of the work beyond that point. The Government is not obligated in any event to pay or reimburse the Contractor more than the amount from time to time allotted to the contract, anything to the contrary in the Termination for Convenience of the Government clause notwithstanding.

(c) (1) It is contemplated that funds presently allotted to this contract will cover the work to be performed until October 15, 2014.

(2) If funds allotted are considered by the Contractor to be inadequate to cover the work to be performed until that date, or an agreed date substituted for it, the Contractor shall notify the Contracting Officer in writing when within the next 60 days the work will reach a point at which, if the contract is terminated pursuant to the Termination for Convenience of the Government clause of this contract, the total amount payable by the Government (including amounts payable for subcontracts and settlement costs) pursuant to paragraphs (f) and (g) of that clause will approximate 75 percent of the total amount then allotted to the contract.

(3) (i) The notice shall state the estimate when the point referred to in paragraph (c) (2) of this clause will be reached and the estimated amount of additional funds required to continue performance to the date specified in paragraph (c) (1) of this clause, or an agreed date substituted for it.

(ii) The Contractor shall, 60 days in advance of the date specified in paragraph (c) (1) of this clause, or an agreed date substituted for it, advise the Contracting Officer in writing as to the estimated amount of additional funds required for the timely performance of the contract for a further period as may be specified in the contract or otherwise agreed to by the parties.

(4) If, after the notification referred to in paragraph (c) (3) (ii) of this clause, additional funds are not allotted by the date specified in paragraph (c) (1) of this clause, or an agreed date substituted for it, the Contracting Officer shall, upon the Contractor's written request, terminate this contract on that date or on the date set forth in the request, whichever is later, pursuant to the Termination for Convenience of the Government clause.

(d) When additional funds are allotted from time to time for continued performance of the work under this contract, the parties shall agree on the applicable period of contract performance to be covered by these funds. The provisions of paragraphs (b) and (c) of this clause shall apply to

these additional allotted funds and the substituted date pertaining to them, and the contract shall be modified accordingly.

(e) If, solely by reason of the Government's failure to allot additional funds in amounts sufficient for the timely performance of this contract, the Contractor incurs additional costs or is delayed in the performance of the work under this contract, and if additional funds are allotted, an equitable adjustment shall be made in the price or prices (including appropriate target, billing, and ceiling prices where applicable) of the items to be delivered, or in the time of delivery, or both.

(f) The Government may at any time before termination, and, with the consent of the Contractor, after notice of termination, allot additional funds for this contract.

(g) The provisions of this clause with respect to termination shall in no way be deemed to limit the rights of the Government under the default clause of this contract. The provisions of this Limitation of Funds clause are limited to the work on and allotment of funds for the items set forth in paragraph (a) of this clause. This clause shall become inoperative upon the allotment of funds for the total price of said work except for rights and obligations then existing under this clause.

(h) Nothing in this clause shall affect the right of the Government to terminate this contract pursuant to the Termination for Convenience of the Government clause of this contract.

(End of Clause)

H.5 NFS 1852.228-76 CROSS-WAIVER OF LIABILITY FOR INTERNATIONAL SPACE STATION ACTIVITIES. (OCT 2012) (Deviation)

(a) The Intergovernmental Agreement for the International Space Station (ISS) contains a cross-waiver of liability provision to encourage participation in the exploration, exploitation, and use of outer space through the ISS. The cross-waiver of liability in this clause is intended to be broadly construed to achieve this objective.

(b) As used in this clause, the term:

(1) "Agreement" refers to any NASA Space Act agreement or contract that contains the cross-waiver of liability provision authorized by 14 CFR Part 1266.102.

(2) "Damage" means:

(i) Bodily injury to, or other impairment of health of, or death of, any person;

(ii) Damage to, loss of, or loss of use of any property;

(iii) Loss of revenue or profits; or

(iv) Other direct, indirect, or consequential Damage.

(3) "Launch" means the intentional ignition of the first-stage motor(s) of the Launch Vehicle intended to place or try to place a Launch Vehicle (which may or may not include any Transfer Vehicle, Payload or crew) from Earth:

(i) in a suborbital trajectory;

(ii) in Earth orbit in outer space; or

(iii) otherwise in outer space,

including activities involved in the preparation of a Launch Vehicle, Transfer Vehicle or Payload for launch.

(4) "Launch Services" means:

(i) Activities involved in the preparation of a Launch Vehicle, Transfer Vehicle, Payload, or crew (including crew training), if any, for launch; and

(ii) The conduct of a Launch.

(5) "Launch Vehicle" means an object, or any part thereof, intended for launch, launched from Earth, or returning to Earth which carries Payloads or persons, or both.

(6) "Partner State" includes each Contracting Party for which the Agreement Among the Government of Canada, Governments of Member States of the European Space Agency, the Government of Japan, The Government of the Russian Federation, and the Government of the United States of America concerning Cooperation on the Civil International Space Station (IGA) has entered into force, pursuant to Article 25 of the IGA or pursuant to any successor Agreement. A Partner State includes its Cooperating Agency. It also includes any entity specified in the Memorandum of Understanding (MOU) between NASA and the Government of Japan's Cooperating Agency in the implementation of that MOU.

(7) "Party" means a party to an Agreement involving activities in connection with the ISS, including this contract.

(8) "Payload" means all property to be flown or used on or in a Launch Vehicle or the ISS.

(9) "Protected Space Operations" means all Launch or Transfer Vehicle activities, ISS activities, and Payload activities on Earth, in outer space, or in transit between Earth and outer space performed in implementation of the IGA, MOUs concluded pursuant to the IGA, implementing arrangements, and contracts to perform work in support of NASA's obligations under these Agreements. It includes, but is not limited to:

(i) Research, design, development, test, manufacture, assembly, integration, operation, or use of Launch or Transfer Vehicles, the ISS, Payloads, or instruments, as well as related support equipment and facilities and services; and

(ii) All activities related to ground support, test, training, simulation, or guidance and control equipment and related facilities or services. "Protected Space Operations" also includes all activities related to evolution of the ISS, as provided for in Article 14 of the IGA. "Protected Space Operations" excludes activities on Earth which are conducted on return from the ISS to develop further a Payload's product or process for use other than for ISS-related activities in implementation of the IGA.

(10) "Reentry" means to return or attempt to return, purposefully, a Transfer Vehicle, Payload, or crew from the ISS, Earth orbit, or outer space to Earth.

(11) "Reentry Services" means:

(i) Activities involved in the preparation of a Transfer Vehicle, Payload, or crew (including crew training), if any, for Reentry; and

(ii) The conduct of a Reentry.

(12) "Related Entity" means:

(i) A contractor or subcontractor of a Party or a Partner State at any tier;

(ii) A user or customer of a Party or a Partner State at any tier; or

(iii) A contractor or subcontractor of a user or customer of a Party or a Partner State at any tier.

The terms "contractor" and "subcontractor" include suppliers of any kind.

(13) "Transfer Vehicle" means any vehicle that operates in space and transfers Payloads or persons or both between two different space objects, between two different locations on the same space object, or between a space object and the surface of a celestial body. A Transfer Vehicle also includes a vehicle that departs from and returns to the same location on a space object.

(c) Cross-waiver of liability:

(1) The Contractor agrees to a cross-waiver of liability pursuant to which it waives all claims against any of the entities or persons listed in paragraphs (c)(1)(i) through (c)(1)(iv) of this clause based on Damage arising out of Protected Space Operations. This cross-waiver shall apply only if the person, entity, or property causing the Damage is involved in Protected Space Operations and the person, entity, or property damaged is damaged by virtue of its involvement in Protected

Space Operations. The cross-waiver shall apply to any claims for Damage, whatever the legal basis for such claims, against:

(i) A Party as defined in (b)(7) of this clause;

(ii) A Partner State, including the United States of America;

(iii) A Related Entity of any entity identified in paragraph (c)(1)(i) or (c)(1)(ii) of this clause; or

(iv) The employees of any of the entities identified in paragraphs (c)(1)(i) through (c)(1)(iii) of this clause.

(2) In addition, the contractor shall, by contract or otherwise, extend the cross-waiver of liability set forth in paragraph (c)(1) of this clause, to its Related Entities by requiring them, by contract or otherwise, to:

(i) Waive all claims against the entities or persons identified in paragraphs (c)(1)(i) through (c)(1)(iv) of this clause; and

(ii) Require that their Related Entities waive all claims against the entities or persons identified in paragraphs (c)(1)(i) through (c)(1)(iv) of this clause.

(3) For avoidance of doubt, this cross-waiver of liability includes a cross-waiver of claims arising from the *Convention on International Liability for Damage Caused by Space Objects*, which entered into force on September 1, 1972, where the person, entity, or property causing the Damage is involved in Protected Space Operations and the person, entity, or property damaged is damaged by virtue of its involvement in Protected Space Operations.

(4) Notwithstanding the other provisions of this clause, this cross-waiver of liability shall not be applicable to:

(i) Claims between the Contractor and its own Related Entities or between its Related Entities;

(ii) Claims made by a natural person (with the exception of Passengers and Commercial Cargo Customers as defined in clause H.23 of this contract), his/her estate, survivors or subrogees (except when a subrogee is a Party to an Agreement or is otherwise bound by the terms of this cross-waiver) for bodily injury to, or other impairment of health of, or death of, such person;

(iii) Claims for Damage caused by willful misconduct;

(iv) Intellectual property claims;

(v) Claims for Damage resulting from a failure of the contractor to extend the cross-waiver of liability to its subcontractors or related entities, pursuant to paragraph (c)(2) of this clause;

(vi) Claims by the Government arising out of or relating to the contractor's failure to perform its obligations under this contract.

(vii) Claims against Passengers or Commercial Cargo Customers as defined in clause H.23 of this contract.

(5) Nothing in this clause shall be construed to create the basis for a claim or suit where none would otherwise exist.

(d) Waiver of claims Between the Government and Contractor:

(1) This clause provides for a reciprocal waiver of claims between the Government and the Contractor and their Related Entities as described in paragraph (c) above, except that the Government shall waive such claims only to the extent such claims exceed the maximum amount of the Contractor's insurance or financial capability required under paragraph (f) below. This reciprocal waiver of claims shall not apply to rights and obligations arising from the application of any of the other clauses in the contract or to rights and obligations arising from activities that are not within the scope of this contract.

(2) Pursuant to paragraph (c)(2), the Contractor shall extend this waiver of claims to its Related Entities by requiring them, by contract or otherwise, to waive all claims against the Government and its Related Entities. For avoidance of doubt, the Contractor shall require its Passengers and Commercial Cargo Customers, as defined in clause H.23 of this contract, to waive claims against the Government and the Government's Related Entities; however, the Government does not waive such claims against Passengers or Commercial Cargo Customers.

(e) Clause H.18 of this contract requires the Contractor to obtain a Federal Aviation Administration (FAA) license, in accordance with 51 U.S.C. 50901 *et seq.*, for Launch and Reentry Services performed under CLIN 002 missions. The waivers of claims in this clause H.5 shall apply to CLIN 001 activities. The waivers of claims also shall apply to CLIN 002 activities, except that the waiver of claims between the Government and the Contractor under paragraph (d) shall not be applicable for CLIN 002 Launch Services and Reentry Services that are subject to the FAA license.

(f) The Contractor shall maintain insurance, or demonstrate financial capability to compensate, for damages (as defined in paragraph (b)(2)(ii)) to U.S. Government property, except for: (a) damage to all on orbit ISS structures, modules, and systems required for functionality of the ISS, during Launch Services, Reentry Services, or transportation to, from, in proximity of, or docking with the ISS under this contract; and (b) damage or loss resulting from the willful misconduct of the Government or its employees. For purposes of this paragraph (f), "preparation" of a Launch Vehicle or Transfer Vehicle includes test, assembly, integration or operations of the Launch

Vehicle, Transfer Vehicle or their Payloads on a Government installation. Such insurance shall be an amount up to $100 million, or the maximum amount available in the market at reasonable cost, subject to approval by the Contracting Officer. Financial capability, if authorized by the Contracting Officer, shall be in the amount of $100 million. The Contractor shall provide acceptable evidence of the insurance or financial capability to the Contracting Officer, subject to Contracting Officer approval. Insurance policies shall name the United States Government as an additional insured party. Once approved by the Contracting Officer, insurance policies may not be modified or canceled without the prior, written approval of the Contracting Officer.

(End of Clause)

H.6   NFS 1852.223-74 DRUG- AND ALCOHOL-FREE WORKFORCE (MARCH 1996)

(a) **Definitions.** As used in this clause the terms **"employee," "controlled substance," "employee in a sensitive position,"** and **"use, in violation of applicable law or Federal regulation, of alcohol"** are as defined in 48 CFR 1823.570-2.

(b) (1) The Contractor shall institute and maintain a program for achieving a drug-and alcohol-free workforce. As a minimum, the program shall provide for preemployment, reasonable suspicion, random, post-accident, and periodic recurring (follow-up) testing of Contractor employees in sensitive positions for use, in violation of applicable law or Federal regulation, of alcohol or a controlled substance. The Contractor may establish its testing or rehabilitation program in cooperation with other Contractors or organizations.

   (2) This clause neither prohibits nor requires the Contractor to test employees in a foreign country. If the Contractor chooses to conduct such testing, this clause does not authorize the Contractor to violate foreign law in conducting such testing.

   (3) The Contractor's program shall test for the use of marijuana and cocaine. The Contractor's program may test for the use of other controlled substances.

   (4) The Contractor's program shall conform to the "Mandatory Guidelines for Federal Workplace Drug Testing Programs" published by the Department of Health and Human Services (59 FR 29908, June 9, 1994) and the procedures in 49 CFR part 40, "Procedures for Transportation Workplace Drug Testing Programs," in which references to "DOT" shall be read as "NASA", and the split sample method of collection shall be used.

(c) (1) The Contractor's program shall provide, where appropriate, for the suspension, disqualification, or dismissal of any employee in a sensitive position in any instance where a test conducted and confirmed under the Contractor's program indicates that such individual has used, in violation of applicable law or Federal regulation, alcohol or a controlled substance.

(2) The Contractor's program shall further prohibit any such individual from working in a sensitive position on a NASA contract, unless such individual has completed a program of rehabilitation described in paragraph (d) of this clause.

(3) The Contractor's program shall further prohibit any such individual from working in any sensitive position on a NASA contract if the individual is determined under the Contractor's program to have used, in violation of applicable law or Federal regulation, alcohol or a controlled substance and the individual meets any of the following criteria:

(i) The individual had undertaken or completed a rehabilitation program described in paragraph (d) of this clause prior to such use;

(ii) Following such determination, the individual refuses to undertake such a rehabilitation program;

(iii) Following such determination, the individual fails to complete such a rehabilitation program; or

(iv) The individual used a controlled substance or alcohol while on duty.

(d) The Contractor shall institute and maintain an appropriate rehabilitation program which shall, as a minimum, provide for the identification and opportunity for treatment of employees whose duties include responsibility for safety-sensitive, security, or National security functions who are in need of assistance in resolving problems with the use of alcohol or controlled substances.

(e) The requirements of this clause shall take precedence over any state or local Government laws, rules, regulations, ordinances, standards, or orders that are inconsistent with the requirements of this clause.

(f) For any collective bargaining agreement, the Contractor will negotiate the terms of its program with employee representatives, as appropriate, under labor relations laws or negotiated agreements. Such negotiation, however, cannot change the requirements of this clause. Employees covered under collective bargaining agreements will not be subject to the requirements of this clause until those agreements have been modified, as necessary; provided, however, that if one year after commencement of negotiation the parties have failed to reach agreement, an impasse will be determined to have been reached and the Contractor will unilaterally implement the requirements of this clause.

(g) The Contractor shall insert a clause containing all the terms of this clause, including this paragraph (g), in all subcontracts in which work is performed by an employee in a sensitive position, except subcontracts for commercial items (see FAR Parts 2 and 12).

(End of Clause)

H.7 SPECIAL STUDIES TASK ORDERING PROCEDURES (APPLICABLE TO CLIN 003 ONLY)

If the Government issues a Request for Special Studies Task Order Proposal or a modification to a task order, the Contractor shall utilize the fully burdened labor rates shown in Table B.5.1, *Special Studies Labor Rates*, and other data defined in clause G.9, *Requirements for Data Other than Certified Cost or Pricing Data*, as required per the Contracting Officer, for pricing task orders. The Contracting Officer will use this data to determine if the proposed prices for any task orders are fair and reasonable in accordance with FAR 15.4. The types of data other than certified cost and pricing data that may be required to be included in the proposal associated with these task orders could include:

(a) Prior sales, catalog pricing and discounts.

(b) Other information such as: hours by labor category, historical, current and projected labor hours and rates, prime Contractor and subcontractor cost/price analyses, or historical material (non-labor) purchases.

(c) Additional data not included in (a) or (b) that is considered Other Than Certified Cost or Pricing Data.

(End of Clause)

H.8 POST CERTIFICATION MISSION TASK ORDERING PROCEDURES (APPLICABLE TO CLIN 002)

(a) Requirements for Competition.
In the event that two (2) or more commercial crew transportation contracts are awarded, a fair opportunity to be considered for task orders issued under this contract based upon the specific task order requirements will be provided, unless the Contracting Officer determines that one of the following apply:

(1) The Agency need is of such urgency that competing the requirements among Contractors would result in unacceptable delays;

(2) Only one Contractor is capable of providing the service at the level of quality required because the service ordered is unique or highly specialized;

(3) The order must be issued on a sole-source basis in the interest of economy and efficiency because it is a logical follow-on to an order issued under the contract, provided that all Contractors were given a fair opportunity to be considered for the original order; or

(4) It is necessary to place an order to satisfy the minimum guarantee per clause B.4, *Post Certification Missions (IDIQ) (CLIN 002)*.

(b) Task Ordering Information Applicable to Post Certification Mission Task Orders.

(1) Prior to the issuance of a request for proposal applicable to a Post Certification Mission Task Order, exchanges and fact-finding may take place with Contractor(s). The request for a task order proposal will provide any special instructions regarding the level of detail required in the proposal. The request will include a date and time for submission of the proposal. Proposals will be due within thirty (30) calendar days from the date of the proposal request unless stated otherwise.

(2) The Contractor, when submitting a Post Certification Mission Task Order Proposal, shall indicate that the proposal is compliant with the contract terms, statement of work, and the specific requirements contained in the Task Order Request for Proposal, and shall include the following at a minimum:

(i) A **DRD 202 Post Certification Mission (PCM) Work Plan** anchored to the PCM mission launch date and landing date specified by the Government.

(ii) A **DRD 201 Mission Integration and Operations Management Plan (MIOMP).**

(iii) Any feedback to the NASA proposed mission success criteria and specific percentages of the final payment (reference clause H.21, *Post Certification Mission Success Determination*).

(iv) Any Contractor proposed mission objectives above PCM objectives and manifesting requirements specified by the Government.

(3) Mandatory Proposal Submission.
Unless otherwise agreed to by the Contracting Officer, it is mandatory for contract holders under multiple award to respond to each Request for Post Certification Mission Task Order Proposal provided these requirements are identified in the schedule and do not conflict with the contract ordering limitations.

(4) All competitive Post Certification Mission Task Order Proposals shall be submitted by the date and time specified in the request, or it will be treated as a late proposal in accordance with FAR 52.215-1(C)(3), *Instructions to Offerors – Competitive Acquisition*. The Contracting Officer will evaluate a Task Order proposal per the evaluation criteria stated in the Request for Task Order Proposal. Each Request for Task Order Proposal will use evaluation criteria tailored for the specific mission, but will at a minimum include technical approach and price.

(5) Award of Task Orders.
Each of the Contractors will be notified of NASA's award of a Task Order. Pursuant to FAR 16.505(a)(10), no protest under Subpart 33.1 is authorized in connection with the issuance or proposed issuance of an order under a task-order contract or delivery-order contract, except for—(A) A protest on the grounds that the order increases the scope, period, or maximum value of

the contract; or (B) A protest of an order valued in excess of $10 million. Protests of orders in excess of $10 million may only be filed with the Government Accountability Office, in accordance with the procedures at Subpart 33.104.

Pursuant to FAR 16.505(b)(1)(iv), for task or delivery orders in excess of $5 million, the requirement to provide all awardees a fair opportunity to be considered for each order shall include an opportunity for a post-award debriefing in accordance with FAR 16.505(b)(6).

(End of Clause)

H.9 REPRESENTATIONS, CERTIFICATIONS AND OTHER STATEMENTS OF OFFEROR

The completed provision FAR 52.204-8, *Annual Representations and Certifications*, including any amended representation(s) made at paragraph (b) of the provision; and other representations, certifications and other statements contained in Section K completed and submitted as part of the offer dated July 7, 2014 are hereby incorporated by reference in this resulting contract.

(End of Clause)

H.10 [RESERVED]

H.11 UNITED STATES COMMERCIAL PROVIDER AND DOMESTIC SOURCE CRITERIA

The Contractor shall perform as a United States Commercial Provider per paragraph (a) and meet the domestic source criteria per paragraph (b). Failure to comply with these criteria during the performance of this contract may be grounds for termination in accordance with the Default clauses in I.2.

(a) "United States commercial provider" means a commercial provider, organized under the laws of the United States or of a State, which is—

(1) more than 50 percent owned by United States nationals; or

(2) a subsidiary of a foreign company and the Secretary of Transportation finds that—

(i) such subsidiary has in the past evidenced a substantial commitment to the United States market through—

(A) investments in the United States in long-term research, development, and manufacturing (including the manufacture of major components and subassemblies); and

(B) significant contributions to employment in the United States; and

(ii) the country or countries in which such foreign company is incorporated or organized, and, if appropriate, in which it principally conducts its business, affords reciprocal treatment to companies described in subparagraph (a)(1) comparable to that afforded to such foreign company's subsidiary in the United States, as evidenced by—

(A) providing comparable opportunities for companies described in subparagraph (a)(1) to participate in Government sponsored research and development similar to that authorized under this Act;

(B) providing no barriers, to companies described in subparagraph (a)(1) with respect to local investment opportunities, that are not provided to foreign companies in the United States; and

(C) providing adequate and effective protection for the intellectual property rights of companies described in subparagraph (a)(1).

(b) The Contractor shall produce in performance of this contract a Crew Transportation System (CTS) that is a domestic end product. The CTS intended for this contract, as carried through production for the provision of service missions, shall be a domestic end product only if the cost of its components, mined, produced or manufactured in the United States exceeds 50 percent of the cost of all its components. The cost of each component includes transportation costs to the place of incorporation into the CTS and any applicable duty (whether or not a duty-free entry certificate is issued). "Components" as used in this clause, means those articles, materials and supplies directly incorporated into the design of the end product.

(End of Clause)

H.12 GOVERNMENT FURNISHED SERVICES AND DATA

The Government will furnish the following services and data to the Contractor on a no-charge-for-use basis to the extent reasonably necessary for the Contractor to fulfill its contractual obligations:

(a) The Government will provide Tracking and Data Relay Satellite System (TDRSS) and NASA Integrated Services Network (NISN) support over existing assets for tracking and recovery during the performance of flight tests and Post Certification Missions. The Contractor shall optimize the use of TDRSS and limit the Single Access (SA) to critical operations such as system check-out, critical maneuvers, and proximity rendezvous operations. The Contractor shall identify, with reasonable notice, their request for this service with rationale describing the required usage within their mission profile. Standard routing of data will be at NASA's discretion depending on the location of the customer control center in order to achieve the most efficient and cost effective routing.

(b) The Government will make available the NASA Docking System (NDS) data per the schedule below:

(1) The preliminary build-to-print package will be available by November 2014.

(2) The final build-to-print package will be available by June 2016.

(3) The Mass Simulator build-to-print will be available by August 2014.

(End of Clause)

H.13 REMOTELY SENSED DATA

The Contractor consents to the U.S. Government collecting remotely sensed data related to its CTS vehicles and to use such data for U.S. Government purposes. The remotely sensed data may be used, modified, reproduced, released, performed, displayed, or disclosed within the Government under suitable protective conditions. The Government may not, without written permission, of the Contractor, release or disclose the data outside the Government, except as otherwise required by law, use the technical data for manufacture, or authorize the technical data to be used by a party outside the Government. The remotely sensed data may be shared with, released to, or otherwise disclosed to the Contractor.

(End of Clause)

H.14 USE OF GOVERNMENT PROPERTY, FACILITIES, ASSETS, OR SERVICES

This clause applies to any Government support, including property, facilities, assets, or services, not otherwise provided for under this contract whether obtained from NASA or another Government Agency.

(a) Support obtained from a Government Agency other than NASA.

(1) The Contractor shall obtain and maintain any necessary contracts or agreements between the Contractor and any Government Agency authorizing the use of Government property, facilities, assets or services in performance of this contract (except as may be expressly stated in this contract as furnished by the Government). The Contractor shall be responsible to arrange any contracts or agreements outside of this contract as it deems appropriate. The terms and conditions of such contracts or agreements will govern the use of those Government resources. Any costs associated with such contracts or agreements shall result in no increase in the price of this contract. All remedies to disputes or performance issues shall be resolved in accordance with the terms and conditions of those contracts or agreements. The Contractor shall notify the Contracting Officer

Representative (COR), or designee, of any contracts or agreements between the Contractor and any Government Agency under this paragraph (a).

(2)   NASA makes no warranty whatsoever as to the availability or suitability for use of Government property, facilities, assets, or services made available by another Government Agency under the terms and conditions of other contracts or agreements.   The Contractor assumes all responsibility for determining the suitability for use of all property, facilities, assets, or services acquired or made available to the Contractor by a Government Agency under other contracts or agreements.   The Contractor further acknowledges and agrees that any use of such Government property, facilities, assets, or services shall not relieve the Contractor of full performance responsibility under the contract.

(b) Support obtained from a NASA Center or Component Facility.

(1)   Except as may be expressly stated in this contract as furnished by the Government, the Contractor shall obtain use of any Government property, facilities, assets or services available from a NASA Center or Component Facility (a "Performing Organization") for performance of this contract through the use of an appropriate Task Plan.   For Task Plan reference instructions, the Contractor shall contact the Performing Organization Point of Contact (POC).   The Contractor shall be responsible for obtaining, negotiating and documenting all Task Plans with the Performing Organization.   The Contractor shall be responsible for any costs associated with property, facilities, assets, or services provided by a Performing Organization under a Task Plan and such costs shall result in no increase in the price of this contract.   The Contractor shall notify the Contracting Officer Representative (COR), or designee, of any Task Plans between the Contractor and a Performing Organization under this paragraph (b).

(2)   NASA makes no warranty whatsoever as to the availability or suitability for use of property, facilities, assets, or services made available by a Performing Organization under a Task Plan.   The Contractor assumes all responsibility for determining the suitability for use of all such property, facilities, assets, or services, including technical suitability, schedule availability and cost.   The Contractor further acknowledges and agrees that any use of Government property, facilities, assets, or services under a Task Plan shall not relieve the Contractor of full performance responsibility under the contract.

(3)   Any implementation issues or disputes arising under a Task Plan shall be referred for resolution to the Points of Contact, or if necessary the signatories, identified in the Task Plan.

(End of Clause)

H.15 GOVERNMENT INSIGHT

(a) Introduction

(1) Government insight provides NASA Commercial Crew Program (CCP) and ISS Program Management an understanding of the Contractor's activities to assess the status, critical paths, and risk associated with successfully completing contract requirements, achieving final certification, and successfully completing Post Certification Missions. Government insight will include: Insight, Quality Assurance function, and Joint Test Team (JTT) participation as defined below.

(2) Government insight is defined as gaining an understanding of the Contractor's activities and data through an effective working relationship, inspections and interactions, without approval or disapproval authority, and provides information for the eventual certification approval.

(i) This clause describes the intended primary working-level interface between the Contractor and the Government during execution of this contract. It is intended to facilitate an exchange of information adequate for nominal activities.

(ii) The Government reserves the right to implement remedies for nonconforming services or work. These remedies are described in clause E.2 52.246-4 *Inspection of Services and Research and Development Work - Fixed-Price (Deviation)*.

(3) The Contractor shall ensure the Government has insight, into all subcontractors and suppliers performing or supporting any critical work associated with this contract.

(4) Details of the Contractor's approach to insight to accomplish items (a)(1), (a)(2) and (a)(3) above shall be implemented in accordance with **DRD 001 Insight Implementation Plan.**

(b) Notification
The Contractor shall notify the Commercial Crew Program designee of technical meetings, control boards, reviews, tests, and areas identified for Government Quality Assurance associated with certification and Post Certification Mission activities in the mutually agreed timeframe to permit meaningful Government participation through the entire event, in accordance **with DRD 001 Insight Implementation Plan.**

(c) Access

(1) The Contractor shall provide the Government and its support services contractor(s), under suitable protective conditions, access to all Contractor activities associated with certification and Post Certification Mission activities under this contract. Activities include, but are not limited to CCT-PLN-1100, *Crew Transportation Plan,* Appendix C, *Insight Areas*.

(2) The Contractor shall provide the Government and its support services contractor access to all data used in performance of this contract, including but not limited to, data associated with

areas of insight identified in CCT-PLN-1100 Appendix C and supporting data/information, and administrative and management information with the exception of financial information; and any other information, not used in performance of the contract, related to the Crew Transportation System (CTS) design, production, and operations to include technical data, supporting data/information, and administrative and management information with the exception of financial information.

(3) At a minimum, access to data is the ability for Government and its support services contractor personnel, both remotely and on-site at the Contractor's facilities, to locate and review all data (as defined in (4) directly below) in a useable and readable format.

(4) The Government may use the data to which it has access under this provision solely for the purposes specified in paragraph (a)(1).

(5) The Contractor shall provide office space co-located on-site, badging, furniture, telephones, and use of easily accessible fax, data lines, and copy machines, for full-time and temporary Government personnel and its support services contractor performing insight activities, in accordance with **DRD 001 Insight Implementation Plan.**

(d) Joint Test Team Activities

(1) The JTT-related activities will be Contractor-led (reference CCT-PLN-1120, *Crew Transportation Technical Processes,* Section 5.3, *Flight Test*), and shall include active and steady state Government participation both on site and remotely. The Contractor shall accommodate Government personnel who will provide embedded insight during the activities identified in (d)(2). Government JTT members will not provide direction to Contractor personnel on design changes or procedures, or any other aspect of CTS development, production, or operation. Government JTT members provide insight only, and will not approve or disapprove any aspect of the Contractor's CTS design or performance of the contract. Any action(s) taken by the Contractor in response to any direction given by any person other than the Contracting Officer shall be at the Contractor's risk. The JTT will provide a formal, unambiguous, programmatic structure for Government operationally focused input to the Contractor. In addition, the Government lead on the JTT will provide integrated, consolidated operations insight to the CCP. By its structure, the JTT will prevent unintended, informal Government inputs to the Contractor. To the maximum extent possible, the JTT will work together and strive to resolve operational issues at the lowest level.

(2) The Government's JTT insight activities will focus on qualitative assessments of crew operational interfaces with the vehicle and human-in-the-loop assessments of operational suitability. These assessments will include, but are not limited to vehicle handling qualities, situational awareness, workload and operational complexity, usability, cockpit layout, displays and controls, and flight crew suits. In addition, insight will occur through participation during the planning and build up phase of ground testing (e.g., simulator training and evaluations, mockup demonstrations, etc.), during test flights, and during the post-test flight evaluation process. Insight gained through integrated operations assessments will ultimately feed into NASA's

verification approval decisions (before test flight) and validation approval decisions (post test flight).

(e) Government Quality Assurance (GQA) Functions

(1) The Government will perform the following quality assurance functions: Product Examination, Process Witnessing, Record Review, Surveillance, and Audit.

(2) GQA functions will be performed for all safety-critical items/processes/products identified by a risk based analysis (RBA). A RBA is an iterative analysis based on a comprehensive understanding of the design, development, testing, critical manufacturing / assembly processes, and operations used to identify areas of risk. The Contractor shall support the RBA, by providing technical expertise, as required. The definition of safety critical is found in CCT-REQ-1130, *ISS Crew Transportation and Services Requirements Document,* and SSP 50808, *ISS to Commercial Orbital Transportation Services (COTS) Interface Requirements Document (IRD).*

(f) Result of Insight

(1) Insight should result in an effective working relationship between the Government and the Contractor leading to a NASA certification of the Contractor's CTS. Should insight and/or JTT participation identify non-compliance with CCT-REQ-1130, CCT-PLN-1120, and/or SSP 50808; the terms and conditions of the contract; or a difference in interpretation of test results; or disagreement with the Contractor's technical approach; the Government insight team will elevate the issue through the appropriate CCP boards. Through an effective, functioning relationship, the Government and Contractor should strive to resolve issues at the lowest working level and minimize issues elevated to program boards. Program boards will disposition recommendations in a timely manner and provide oversight resolution if necessary. Resulting board decisions and direction will be transmitted to the Contractor through the Contracting Officer. If disposition results in a requirement change, the change clause (I.2, FAR 52.243-1, *Changes-Fixed Price*) would take effect. If the Contractor and Contracting Officer disagree on whether the board disposition provided is within the requirements of the contract, the disputes clause (I.2, FAR 52-233-1, *Disputes-Alternate I*) is applicable.

(2) The data generated as a result of Government insight may be used, modified, reproduced, released, performed, displayed, or disclosed within the Government and its support service contractors under suitable protected conditions. The Government may not, without written permission of the Contractor, release or disclose the data outside the Government, except as otherwise required by law, use the technical data for manufacture, or authorize the technical data to be used by a party outside the Government.

(g) Contractor Responsibility

Notwithstanding the insight set forth in this Clause, the Contractor assumes full performance responsibility as set forth in this contract. The Government's insight or JTT participation under this clause shall not be construed as authorization, endorsement or approval of milestones, certification or final acceptance or rejection of Post Certification Mission success.

(End of Clause)

H.16   NEW ENTRANT

(a) The purpose of this clause is to notify the Contractor that NASA may conduct a subsequent competition due to the loss of an existing CTS provider or if there are additional future NASA requirements for certified crew transportation. NASA will determine if these conditions are met prior to synopsizing and conducting a New Entrant competition. New entrants may compete for all task orders under this contract.

(b) The Government reserves the right to issue a solicitation in the future to seek an additional source(s) for the same or similar efforts/services.

(End of Clause)

H.17   PUBLIC AFFAIRS

(a) It is anticipated that the Contractor will execute media events to cover major contract activities. The Contractor may, consistent with Federal law and this Contract, release general information regarding its activities conducted within the scope of the Contract:

   (1)   The Contractor will coordinate with the NASA Public Affairs Office (PAO) at Kennedy Space Center in a timely manner prior to major media releases, media interviews, news conferences, contingency statements, media scouts, photo opportunities and film crew activities regarding NASA CCtCap-related efforts.

   (2)   The use of any direct quote by a NASA official shall be submitted for NASA concurrence to ensure accuracy prior to its release.

   (3)   NASA will coordinate, with the Contractor, public releases of information to obtain comments and technical corrections related to the Contractor's CCtCap-related efforts prior to NASA's release of information to the public. The Contractor shall use its best efforts to provide its review and comments back to NASA within five (5) days of the request. If comments are not provided within the five (5) day time period, the submitted content will be considered acceptable for release. For breaking news items, there may be a need for more timely release of information to the public in which case the Government PAO team will coordinate with the Contractor for imminent release.

   (4)   The Contractor shall assist the NASA PAO in developing the mission commentary for NASA Television by furnishing CTS background material.

(5) The Contractor may also be requested to provide information to support the development of press kit documents and NASA news conferences.

(6) At a minimum of forty-five (45) days in advance, the Contractor shall work with the COR to coordinate any public affairs requirements for any launches, landings, major milestones and tests under this contract.

(7) If the Contractor has knowledge that the press is inquiring about an event that meets criteria in paragraph (b) of clause H.26, *Mishap Reporting*, the Contractor shall promptly notify the Contracting Officer, or designee, of the event. The Contracting Officer, or designee, will facilitate access to NASA Public Affairs. NASA Public Affairs will work with the Contractor to generate a coordinated response to the Press and the public.

(b) The Contractor shall protect NASA crew member's audio and imagery for all contract activities in accordance with SSP 50521, *Return, Processing, Distribution and Archiving of Imagery Products from the ISS*, to protect NASA crew member privacy. For downlinked audio and imagery, the Contractor shall route the data in real-time to the NASA Mission Control Center. NASA will monitor feed(s) and instruct the Contractor to remove the feed-from release to the public in the event of a privacy concern. For imagery and audio recorded during flight operations and recovered post-flight, the Contractor shall send a copy of the data to NASA for review. The Contractor shall not release any video and/or audio with NASA crew members in view until the NASA review is complete. NASA will inform the Contractor if any data is restricted. Restricted data cannot be released by the Contractor, either internally or externally, or used in any way. Data that does not contain NASA crew members may be used by the Contractor after proper coordination in accordance with paragraph (a) above.

(c) The Contractor shall not use the words "National Aeronautics and Space Administration" or the letters "NASA" in connection with a product or service in a manner reasonably calculated to convey any impression that such product or service has the authorization, support, sponsorship, or endorsement of NASA, which does not, in fact, exist. In addition, the Contractor shall submit in advance any proposed public use of the NASA name or initials for NASA review and approval. NASA approval shall be based on applicable law and policy governing the use of the NASA name and initials. NASA's approval will not be unreasonably withheld. Use of NASA emblems/devices (i.e., NASA Seal, NASA Insignia, NASA logotype, NASA Program Identifiers, and the NASA Flag) is governed by 14 C.F.R. Part 1221. The Contractor shall not publicly use such emblems/devices without prior NASA review and approval in accordance with such regulations.

(d) NASA does not endorse or sponsor any commercial product, service, or activity. NASA's certification of the CTS under this Contract does not constitute certification or endorsement by NASA that the CTS is safe for public transportation of humans to Low Earth Orbit. NASA's CTS certification means the Contractor's CTS has met NASA's safety requirements for transporting NASA or NASA-sponsored crew to the ISS. The Contractor agrees that nothing in this Contract will be construed to imply that NASA authorizes supports, endorses, or sponsors any product or service of the Contractor resulting from activities conducted under this Contract.

(End of Clause)

H.18   LICENSES, PERMITS, AND OTHER AUTHORIZATIONS FOR A LAUNCH OR REENTRY SERVICE OPERATOR

The Contractor shall obtain and maintain the necessary licenses, permits and clearances that may be required by the Department of Transportation, Department of Commerce, Department of Defense, NASA, or other Governmental agencies in order to provide flight tests and Post Certification Missions under this contract. The Contractor shall obtain a Federal Aviation Administration license, in accordance with 51 U.S.C. Section 50901 *et seq.*, for launch and reentry operations performed under CLIN 002, *Post Certification Missions (PCM)*, of this contract. All costs and fees associated with obtaining licenses, permits and clearances are included in the standard prices identified for CLIN 001, *DDTE/Certification,* in Table B.3, *DDTE/Certification SubCLINs (CLIN 001),* and for CLIN 002 in Table B.4.1, *Post Certification Mission Prices (CLIN 002).*

The Contractor shall meet all contract requirements, in addition to all requirements necessary to obtain and maintain licenses, permits and clearances. In the event conflicts arise, the Contractor is responsible for resolving the conflict and shall immediately notify the Contracting Officer of the conflict and shall describe the methods the Contractor used to try to resolve the conflict.

(End of Clause)

H.19   POST CERTIFICATION MISSION PAYMENTS, MILESTONES AND AUTHORITY TO PROCEED (ATP) CRITERIA

(a) Post Certification Mission (PCM) task orders may be awarded prior to completion of CLIN 001, *DDTE/Certification.* However, the Contractor shall meet the following development-related criteria before NASA will grant Authority to Proceed (ATP) with such missions. ATP for PCMs is at NASA's sole discretion and is dependent on meeting the criteria. Specific mission objectives and target launch date are provided by NASA.

Table H.19.1: ATP Criteria

Post Certification Mission Number	ATP Criteria
1	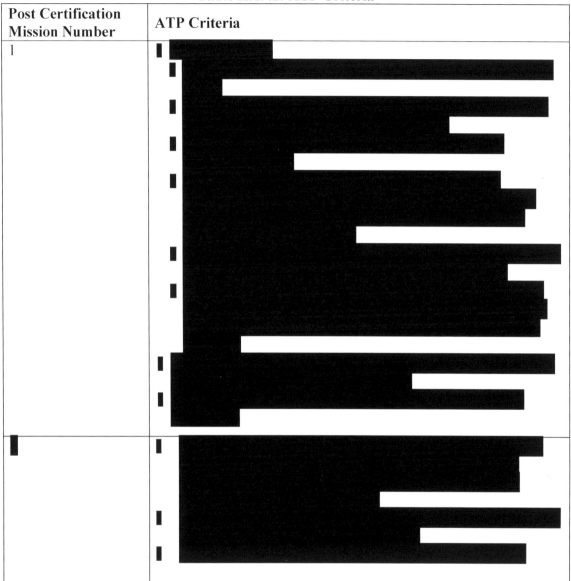

The following constraints apply to ATP criteria:

(1) A maximum of two (2) PCMs can be ordered prior to completion of the ISS Design Certification Review (ISS DCR).

(2) Prior to the first PCM ATP, the Certification Baseline Review (CBR) and one or more interim milestones, from Attachment J-03, Appendix A, *Milestone Acceptance Criteria and Payment Schedule,* representing work culminating in a significant design review between CBR and the first DCR must be successfully completed. These interim milestones ensure the detailed design will satisfy the requirements with adequate margins, are sufficiently mature to proceed with

fabrication, assembly, integration, and test, and the product verification and product validation plans are complete.

(b) Post certification mission payments will be based upon successful completion of approved milestone schedule and acceptance criteria defined in the Contract PWS and developed per the **DRD 202 Post Certification Mission (PCM) Work Plan**. NASA has up to thirty (30) calendar days to determine whether the performance of the Mission Milestone Review (per Table H.19.2, *Mission Milestone Review Payment Schedule*) satisfies the approved criteria.

(c) All Post Certification Mission milestone payments are performance-based interim financing payments made in accordance with FAR 52.232-32, *Performance Based Payments*. Milestone payments once made are subject to repayment by the Contractor if the conditions defined in FAR 52.232-32 (j), *Special terms regarding default*, apply.

(d) Table H.19.2 (a) and Table H.19.2 (b) identify the Mission Milestone Reviews required under the contract which are to be included by the Contractor in the **DRD 202 Post Certification Mission Work Plan**.

Table H.19.2 (a): Mission Milestone Review Payment Schedule

Mission Level Milestone	Mission Milestone Reviews	Amount (% of Standard Mission Price)
■	■	■
■	■	■
■	■	■
■	■	■
■	■	■
■	■	■
■	■	■
■	■	■
■	■	■
■	■	■

Table H.19.2 (b): Mission Milestone Review Payment Schedule

Mission Level Milestone	Mission Milestone Reviews	Amount (% of Standard Mission Price)
■	■	■
■	■	■
■	■	■
■	■	■
■	■	■
■	■	■
■	■	■
■	■	■
■	■	■
■	■	■
■	■	■
■	■	■

(e) PCM task order payment constraints: The total PCM task order payments made prior to and including:

(1) The completion of the SubCLIN 001A, *ISS Design Certification Review (ISS DCR)*, (associated with the required crewed flight test to ISS; see Attachment J-03, Appendix A) shall not exceed 20% of the total price of the mission.

(2) The completion of the Vehicle Baseline Review (VBR) shall not exceed 30% of the total price of the mission.

(3) The completion of the Mission Integration Review (MIR) shall not exceed 50% of the total price of the mission.

(4) The completion of the SubCLIN 001B, *Certification Review (CR)*, (see Attachment J-03, Appendix A) shall not exceed 60% of the total price of the mission.

(5) The completion of the NASA Flight Readiness Review (FRR) shall not exceed 75% of the total price of the mission.

(6) The final milestone payment must equal at least 10% of the price of the mission.

(f) Payment schedules may be deferred or canceled by NASA if the Contractor fails to make substantial progress in accomplishing DDTE/Certification and Post Certification Mission major milestone events.

(g) In the event of a mission schedule adjustment by NASA or Contractor in accordance with clause H.20, *Adjustments to Post Certification Mission Schedule*, the payment schedule for the applicable mission shall be postponed for the length of the delay, if necessary, to correspond with the new delivery date and the milestone events in the **DRD 202 Post Certification Mission (PCM) Work Plan**. The requirement to make substantial progress in general conformance with the Post Certification Mission Work Plan, however, is not waived for any postponement of the mission.

(End of Clause)

H.20 ADJUSTMENTS TO POST CERTIFICATION MISSION SCHEDULE

(a) This clause covers launch delays at the convenience of NASA and the Contractor. The provisions of this clause do not apply to circumstances arising under clause H.23 (d), *Non-NASA Passengers, Cargo and Payloads,* related to requested delays to accommodate Contractor's passengers or non-NASA cargo or payloads.

(b) Task orders issued to Contractors are intended to require Post Certification Missions to ISS with limited flexibility to adjust launch dates. To provide flexibility to both the Contractor and NASA, a standard launch window will be established for each planned Post Certification Mission. Authorization to Proceed (ATP) is formal written direction from the Contracting Officer that authorizes the Contractor to proceed with the work detailed within a DRD 202 Post Certification

Mission Work Plan. The standard launch window will be created by NASA establishing an initial window for each mission at ATP. Thereafter, with mutual agreement between the Contractor and NASA, the launch window will be reduced according to the table below.

Table H.20.1: Launch Windows for PCM ATP Prior to ISS DCR*

Months Prior to Launch Date – First Day to Last Day	Standard Launch Window (Days)
ATP through L-13m	90d
L-13m through L-4m	30d
L-4m through Launch	7d

Table H.20.2: Launch Windows for PCM ATP After ISS DCR*

Months Prior to Launch Date – First Day to Last Day	Standard Launch Window (Days)
ATP through L-13m	30d
L-13m through Launch	7d

*ISS DCR is the DCR for the crewed flight to ISS

(c) At each major review referenced in Table H.19.2 (a) and Table H.19.2 (b), *Mission Milestone Review Payment Schedule*, NASA and the Contractor shall review the window established and mutually agree on the next reduced launch window corresponding to the Tables H.20.1 and H.20.2.

(d) For PCM(s) ordered prior to completion of SubCLIN 001A, *ISS DCR*, Table H.20.1, *Launch Windows for PCM ATP Prior to ISS DCR*, each party, NASA or Contractor, may request a cumulative maximum delay of thirty (30) calendar days per mission regardless of fault without a change in the fixed price of the mission.

(e) If either NASA or Contractor desires a change to the launch date, NASA or the Contractor will give written notice of the desired change. Any request for changes to the launch date should be submitted within twenty-four (24) hours of identifying the need to request a change in the launch date. For any request for changes to launch date submitted greater than one month prior to launch, NASA and the Contractor shall reach mutual agreement on a new launch date within fourteen (14) days of the request. Any requests for changes to the launch date submitted between one (1) month prior to launch and launch day shall be a priority and resolved as soon as possible. If mutual agreement on the revised launch date cannot be reached, the Contracting Officer shall have the right to unilaterally establish a new schedule.

(f) In the event of a NASA- or Contractor-requested delay of the launch window beyond the days allowable in Table H.20.1 and paragraph (d) or Table H.20.2, *Launch Windows for PCM ATP After ISS DCR*, the Contracting Officer shall direct the Contractor, in writing, of the revised launch window. For a NASA requested delay, the Government will allow the Contractor to submit a proposal for the effect of any delay beyond the days allowable on the task order price of all affected PCMs, launch schedule, or other terms of the contract except for conditions defined in clause H.23, *Commercial Passengers, Cargo, and Payloads*. For a Contractor requested delay,

NASA reserves the right to seek an equitable adjustment. Upon failure to agree to an adjustment, the Contracting Officer shall have the right to unilaterally adjust the task order.

(g) There will be no basis for an equitable adjustment when the delay in delivery or performance arises solely out of causes beyond the control of NASA or Contractor and not due to the fault or negligence of NASA or Contractor. Such causes include, but are not limited to the following:

(1) Delays resulting from:
- Range Mission Rules and Range Launch Requirements (Mandatory and Required Assets),
- acts of God,
- acts (including delay or failure to act) of any Governmental authority (De Jure or De Facto),
- wars (declared or undeclared),
- riots,
- revolution,
- hijacking,
- fires,
- freight embargoes,
- sabotage,
- epidemics,
- strikes and
- interruptions of essential services such as electricity, natural gases, fuels and water,

(2) or any condition which jeopardizes the safety of the employees of the Contractor, NASA, or its subcontractors;

(3) or a CTS failure investigation, provided NASA retains its original position in the order of the queue sequence and that all data related to the failure investigation is made available to NASA without restriction.

(End of Clause)

H.21 POST CERTIFICATION MISSION SUCCESS DETERMINATION

(a) Mission Success Criteria

(1) The Mission Success criteria will be defined on a per mission basis and agreed to by NASA and the Contractor during the Task Ordering process.

(2) NASA will provide the initial mission success criteria and specific percentages of the final payment earned for mission performance during the Task Ordering process. The final payment is defined in clause H.19, *Post Certification Mission Payments, Milestones and ATP Criteria*. Any revision to the criteria and payment percentage shall be agreed to at the Mission Certification Review (MCR). In the event that an agreement cannot be reached, the Contracting Officer will establish the criteria and payment percentage by the Flight Readiness Review. The revised criteria will be incorporated into a Task Order revision. The MCR shall include Contractor plans for providing data to confirm mission success as part of the post flight report.

(3) Mission Success Criteria will be established per the following guidelines:

  (i) Criteria will consider the Contractor's mission capabilities.

  (ii) Criteria will consider the Contractor's performance, independent of NASA's.

  (iii) Criteria will consider ascent aborts or earlier than pre-launch planned End-Of-Mission timeframe, contingency spacecraft crew support, and inability to dock with the ISS.

(4) Definitions.

  (i) Full Mission Success - meeting all primary objectives and secondary objectives;

  (ii) Mission Failure – loss of one or more primary objectives, serious injury or fatality as defined in H.26, *Mishap Reporting*, or damage to the ISS;

  (iii) Partial mission success – all primary mission objectives satisfied but loss of one or more secondary mission objectives.

(b) Mission Success Determination

(1) Mission Success Determination will be made using the mission success criteria and the corresponding data and parameters that are jointly agreed to by NASA and the Contractor.

(2) The Contractor shall submit the relevant data and parameters that provide the most accurate information on performance of the mission success criteria, at the Mission Integration Review (MIR). The types of data NASA would consider as relevant information include:

(i) Vehicle data that represents critical systems for all flight phases (such as ascent, approach, docking, mating, and entry).

(ii) Available launch and orbital vehicle data verifying **DRD 203 Vehicle Interface Definition Document (IDD)** environments.

(iii) Closeout photos both on the ground and on orbit documenting CTS configuration at launch and prior to landing per **DRD 214 Imagery and Associated Cataloging**.

(iv) Any supplemental data that may support the Contractor's performance.

(3) If there is data that the Contractor requests NASA to provide (on orbit attached telemetry, on orbit photos, etc.), the Contractor shall identify that prior to the MCR.

(c) Procedures

(1) The Contracting Officer determines unilaterally whether a mission is considered a Mission Success, Partial Mission Success, or a Failed Mission. For partial mission success, the percentage of the final payment earned is based on the agreed to mission success criteria defined in section (a)(2) of this clause. Within fifteen (15) calendar days from receipt of the preliminary **DRD 209 Post-Flight Assessment Report**, the Contracting Officer will either make the Mission Success determination or inform the Contractor of NASA's intent to partially withhold final payment in the event of Partial Mission success, or withhold final payment in the event of a Failed Mission. In the event of a failed mission determination, an additional 15% of the Post Certification Mission (PCM) price shall be applied as a credit to another PCM, other in-kind considerations determined by the parties, or be returned to the Government if it cannot be applied to a subsequent PCM at the Government's discretion. In the event of a Partial Mission Success or a Failed Mission determination, the rights and remedies contained in this Clause are in lieu of any rights and remedies in case of default applicable to this PCM only, including the rights and remedies in clause 52.249-8 *Default (Fixed-Price Supply and Service)* and clause E.2, *Inspection of Services and Research and Development Work - Fixed-Price (Aug 1996) (Proposed Deviation)*, paragraphs (g) and (h); FAR 52.232-32 (j) *Special terms regarding default,* and; NFS 1852.223-75 *Major Breach of Safety or Security* For all other activities under the contract not part of this PCM task order, the Government reserves the right to terminate the contract for default in accordance with FAR 52.249-8 *Default (Fixed-Price Supply and Service)*. Remedies described in this paragraph are available at Launch. Launch is defined as the intentional ignition of the first-stage motor(s) of the launch vehicle intended to place or try to place a launch vehicle (which may or may not include any payload or crew) from Earth:

(i) in a suborbital trajectory;

(ii) in Earth orbit in outer space;

(iii) or otherwise in outer space.

(2) If NASA informs the Contractor it will partially withhold or withhold the final payment, NASA will utilize the final **DRD 209 Post-Flight Assessment** and findings from the Contractor's investigation board to complete the NASA assessment. The Contracting Officer shall submit a final determination of either Partial Mission Success or Failed Mission within one (1) week of the NASA assessment. Any stop work order issued during a Mishap Investigation Board (MIB) or similar Partial Mission Success/Failed Mission investigation shall not be subject to an equitable adjustment by either party as provided for under clause H.20(g).

(d) Final Payment for Final Mission Success Determination
The amount of final payment will be based on mission success determination per the agreed criteria and percentage of final payment.

(e) Acceptance
Final acceptance for any unsuccessful mission objectives of the crew transportation service will be accomplished following the Contracting Officer's mission success determination. The Contracting Officer will notify the Contractor in writing of both Mission Success Determination and Acceptance.

(End of Clause)

H.22 LIABILITY FOR THIRD PARTY CLAIMS

This contract clause applies to Third Party claims that arise out of the conduct of hazardous launch, on-orbit, reentry, landing, recovery, and rescue activities under this contract which are not subject to an FAA license pursuant to 51 U.S.C. Section 50901 *et seq.*. More specifically, this contract clause allocates between the Government and the Contractor the risk of Third Party claims for damage to or loss of property or personal injury or death arising from the burning, explosion, detonation, combustion or impact of a launch vehicle, its payloads, spacecraft, or any components thereof, from the time of preparation of a launch vehicle until landing and recovery.

(a) *Definitions.*

(1) Covered Activities: Any and all Hazardous Activities involved in the preparation of a launch vehicle for launch and conduct of the launch, when those activities take place at a launch site in the United States; any and all Hazardous Activities involved in on-orbit operations during transportation to, from or in proximity with the International Space Station (ISS); any and all Hazardous Activities involved in reentry of the spacecraft into the Earth's atmosphere; any and all Hazardous Activities involved in landing and recovery of the crew and spacecraft; and any and all Hazardous Activities involved in rescue operations.

(2) Damages:

(i) Bodily injury or death; or

(ii) Damage to or loss of any real or personal property;

(3) Hazardous Activities: any operation or other work activity that, without implementation of proper mitigations, has a high potential to result in loss of life, serious injury to personnel or public, or damage to property due to the burning, explosion, detonation, combustion or impact of a launch vehicle, its payloads, spacecraft, or any components thereof, from the time of launch until landing and recovery, or during rescue operations.

(4) Launch: The intentional ignition of the first-stage motor(s) of the launch vehicle intended to place or try to place a launch vehicle (which may or may not include any payload or crew) from Earth:

(i) in a suborbital trajectory;

(ii) in Earth orbit in outer space; or

(iii) otherwise in outer space.

(5) Launch Vehicle: a vehicle built to place a payload or human beings in outer space.

(6) Party or Parties: The Contractor or NASA, or both.

(7) Payload: All equipment that has been or will be integrated with the launch vehicle for transportation into Earth orbit or escape trajectories.

(8) Preparation of a Launch Vehicle: begins with the arrival of a launch vehicle or payload at a U.S. launch site, and entails critical steps preparatory to initiating launch.

(9) Reentry: The return or attempt to return a spacecraft and its payload and crew, if any, from Earth orbit or from outer space to Earth.

(10) Related Party:

(iv) Any of the Parties' directors, officers, agents, or employees

(v) Any of the Parties' Contractors, subcontractors, or suppliers at any tier involved directly or indirectly in the performance of this Contract

(vi) Any entity having any right, title or interest, whether through sale, lease or service arrangement or otherwise, directly or indirectly, in the payload, the launch vehicle, the spacecraft, or services related to launch, mission, landing, recovery or rescue operations.

A Related Party does not include Passengers and Commercial Cargo Customers, as defined in clause H.23 of this contract.

(11) Spacecraft: A vehicle built to operate in outer space which transports or plans to transport payloads or human beings to/from Earth orbit or escape trajectories.

(12) Third Party: Any person or entity other than the Government, the Contractor and Related Parties, but not including Passengers or Commercial Cargo Customers, as defined in clause H.23 of this contract.

(b) Required Insurance or Demonstration of Financial Capability for Liability to Third Parties

(1) The Contractor shall continue in effect or acquire insurance, or demonstrate financial capability to compensate, for claims by Third Parties for Damages arising in connection with the Covered Activities under this contract. The amount of the insurance or financial capability shall be the maximum amount available in the commercial marketplace at reasonable cost, but shall not exceed $500 million for each test flight or mission, subject to approval by the Contracting Officer.

(2) The Contractor shall provide acceptable evidence to the Contracting Officer of required insurance or financial capability no later than thirty (30) days prior to the beginning of the covered activities. The amount of required insurance or financial capability, and the terms and conditions for the insurance or financial capability, shall be subject to approval by the Contracting Officer. Once approved, insurance policies and terms and conditions for maintaining financial capability may not be modified or canceled without the prior, written approval of the Contracting Officer.

(3) Insurance policies shall name the United States Government and the Related Parties as additional insured parties. Insurance policies shall attach no later than the arrival of the launch vehicle at the launch site and shall remain in force for preparation of a launch vehicle until thirty (30) days after landing and recovery.

(4) The foregoing requirement does not preclude the Contractor from acquiring or continuing in effect any additional insurance to protect the interests of the Contractor, its Related Parties or customers.

(c) Third Party Claims in Excess of Required Insurance or Demonstrated Financial Capability

(1) NASA has determined that activities under this contract are conducted in performance of its functions, as specified in 51 U.S.C. Section 20112(a). As a result, once the Contractor or its insurers have paid out for Third Party claims up to the amount of insurance or financial capability under paragraph (b), NASA will consider any additional Third Party claims for Damages arising from Covered Activities in performance of this contract as claims against the United States under the authority of 51 U.S.C. Section 20113(m). Such claims must be presented to NASA within two (2) years after the incident out of which the claim arises.

(2) The Contractor or its insurers shall adjust, settle and pay meritorious and reasonable Third Party claims against the Contractor and its Related Parties for Damages arising from Covered Activities in performance of this contract up to the amount of insurance or financial capability required in paragraph (b). If a Third Party claim (or multiple Third Party claims

resulting from a single event) exceeds the amount of insurance or financial capability required in paragraph (b), the Contractor shall provide timely written notification along with all documentation of the Third Party claim(s) to the Contracting Officer. To the extent NASA determines that such Third Party claim(s) is meritorious, reasonable, and the cumulative costs of all such claims arising from a single incident is $25,000 or less, NASA shall reimburse the Contractor. To the extent NASA determines that such Third Party claim(s) is meritorious, reasonable, and the cumulative cost of all such claims arising from a single incident exceeds $25,000, NASA will forward the claim(s) to the Secretary of Treasury for certification and payment pursuant to 31 U.S.C. § 1304(a). The costs of the Third Party claim(s) are subject to the availability of funds and the usual tests for allowability. The total of costs to pay for Third Party claims resulting from a single event may be paid up to a limit of $1.5 billion (plus additional amounts necessary to reflect inflation occurring after January 1, 1989) above the payments made by the Contractor or its insurers for such claims. Payment(s) for a claim or cumulative claims arising from a single event the sum total of which exceed the Contractor's insurance or financial capability amount, may be made only if the Contractor has provided notice to the Government with the opportunity to participate or assist in the defense of the claim(s) or action. The NASA Administrator must approve any part of a settlement to be paid out of appropriations of the Government.

(3) In evaluating Third Party claims paid by the Contractor under this clause, NASA will consider such a claim to be meritorious unless the claim represents:

(i) Liabilities for which the Contractor is otherwise responsible under the express terms or conditions of the contract or a task order issued under this contract;

(ii) Liabilities for which the Contractor has failed to insure or has failed to maintain insurance or financial capability as required by the Contracting Officer;

(iii) Liabilities for which the Contractor has not reasonably adjusted, settled, or paid on a meritorious and reasonable basis;

(iv) Liabilities that result from willful misconduct, gross negligence, or lack of good faith on the part of any of the Contractor's directors, officers, managers, superintendents, or other representatives who have supervision or direction of:

(A) All or substantially all of the Contractor's business;

(B) All or substantially all of the Contractor's operations at any one plant or separate location in which this contract is being performed; or

(C) A separate and complete major industrial operation in connection with the performance of this contract;

(v) Liabilities that arise from the willful misconduct or gross negligence of the Claimant or, in the case of a claim based on death, the claimant's estate;

(vi) Liabilities that arise from the conduct, negligence, or failure to act of Passengers, as defined in clause H.23 of this contract; or.

(vii) Liabilities that arise from Non-NASA Cargo or Payloads, as defined in clause H.23 of this contract.

(End of Clause)

H.23 NON-NASA PASSENGERS, CARGO AND PAYLOADS

This clause is applicable to CLIN 002 Post Certification Mission (PCM) task orders. The requirements of a specific PCM will be established by NASA in the task order in accordance with clause H.8, *Post Certification Mission Task Ordering Procedures (Applicable to CLIN 002)*. If NASA determines, in its sole discretion, that its requirements can be met without using the full capacity of the CTS, NASA may notify the Contractor of the opportunity to propose to manifest a Passenger or non-NASA Cargo or Payload on a flight conducted under this contract as part of the task proposal process. NASA will only authorize manifesting a Passenger or non-NASA Cargo or Payload if it can be accommodated consistent with NASA's obligations to its International Partners under the Intergovernmental Agreement for the International Space Station (ISS), all applicable FAA regulations or requirements, and other applicable laws, regulations or requirements, without interference to NASA's mission or cost to NASA, and pursuant to the terms and conditions of the contract and the PCM task order.

(a) Definitions, for the purpose of this clause:

(1) NASA or NASA-sponsored crew: Personnel assigned by NASA to be transported between Earth and the ISS in the CTS.

(2) Contractor crew: Employees or subcontractors of the Contractor who perform activities in the course of employment directly relating to the operation of the CTS while on board the CTS.

(3) Passenger: Any person proposed by the Contractor to be transported on the CTS who is not NASA or NASA-sponsored crew, or Contractor crew.

(4) Non-NASA Cargo or Payload: Any property proposed by the Contractor to be flown or used on the CTS which is not the primary payload of a Post Certification Mission, nor required for certification of the CTS.

(5) Commercial Cargo Customer: Any person or entity that provides non-NASA cargo or payloads to the Contractor.

(b) NASA Unilateral Determination; NASA Right to Revoke; Costs.

The Contractor acknowledges and agrees that any decision to authorize the manifest of a Passenger(s) or non-NASA Cargo or Payload in response to a task order proposal shall be a unilateral determination at NASA's sole discretion. NASA retains the right to revoke its prior approval of a Passenger(s) or non-NASA Cargo or Payload at any time prior to launch of the Post Certification Mission. NASA shall not be responsible for any costs, liabilities or obligations incurred by the Contractor to manifest a Passenger(s) or non-NASA Cargo or Payload; NASA shall not be responsible for any costs, liabilities or obligations incurred by the Contractor should NASA revoke its prior approval of Passenger(s) or non-NASA Cargo or Payload.

If for any reason, the Contractor is unable to transport a Passenger(s), the Passenger(s) is not ready or available for the Post Certification Mission, there is insufficient time to complete Passenger training for the Post Certification Mission before the launch date, or the Contractor is unable to meet applicable FAA or NASA requirements, the Contractor shall bear the cost of and be responsible for any related impacts or delays to the mission. If the Contractor is unable to provide the non-NASA cargo or payload for CTS integration, or there is insufficient time to complete a new mission analysis before the launch date, the Contractor shall bear the cost and shall be responsible for designing, fabricating, and installing a cargo or payload mass simulator in lieu of the non-NASA cargo or payload.

(c) Procedures.

If applicable, NASA will identify any opportunities to propose to manifest a Passenger or non-NASA cargo or payloads in the request for a task order proposal under clause H.8 (b). The Contractor shall propose at no cost to NASA the non-NASA mission requirements, if any, and price adjustment or other consideration to be received by NASA, to be included with the task order proposal for the Post Certification Mission. NASA may request task order proposals with and without Passengers or non-NASA Cargo or Payloads.

(1) Passengers.

(i) Task Order Proposal

For any task order proposal involving Passenger(s), the Contractor shall submit to NASA a detailed description of the purpose and activities of the Passenger(s), a training plan for the Passenger(s), plans for compliance with any FAA license requirements, the *ISS Medical Operations Requirements Document* (SSP 50260) and, as applicable, the *Medical Evaluation Document, Volumes A-C* (SSP 50667), the liability waiver required in paragraph (c)(1)(ii), and any additional documentation or analyses requested by NASA. The Contractor shall be responsible for the costs of and ensuring completion of all necessary training in accordance with FAA license requirements and NASA requirements, including all training required for the CTS and for the ISS, even if such training is provided by NASA.

(ii) Liability and Insurance

The Contractor shall extend section (c) of clause H.5, NFS 1852.228-76 *Cross-Waiver Of Liability For International Space Station Activities (Oct 2012) (Deviation)*, to Passengers by requiring them to waive any and all claims against the entities listed in section (c)(1) of that clause, except that Passengers are not required to waive such claims against the Contractor unless the Contractor so requires. The Contractor shall inform Passengers that the entities listed in section (c)(1) have not waived any claims against Passengers. The Contractor shall obtain a written waiver of claims from the Passenger for all activities related to the mission, including acknowledgment by the Passenger that the entities listed in section (c)(1) have not waived any claims against Passengers, and shall provide such documentation to NASA for NASA's approval with the proposal to manifest the Passenger. The Contractor shall require Passengers to maintain insurance covering damage to or loss of any property or injury or death of any person on the ISS or in the CTS resulting from any action, negligence, or failure to act by the Passenger. The

Contractor shall provide acceptable evidence to the Contracting Officer of required insurance no later than thirty (30) days prior to the launch on which the Passenger is manifested. The amount of required insurance and the terms and conditions for the policy or policies shall be subject to review by the Contracting Officer. Once reviewed, the policy or policies may not be modified or canceled without the prior, written approval of the Contracting Officer.

    (2)   Non-NASA Cargo or Payloads

        (i)   Task Order Proposal

For any task order proposal involving a Non-NASA Cargo or Payload, the Contractor shall submit to NASA a description of the purpose of the Non-NASA Cargo or Payload, a detailed cargo or payload description, a cargo or payload compatibility assessment, plans for compliance with any FAA license requirements, the liability waiver required in paragraph (c)(2)(ii), and any additional documentation or analyses requested by NASA. The Contractor shall be responsible for the costs of and ensuring completion of all FAA license requirements and all NASA requirements for the CTS and for the ISS relating to the Non-NASA Cargo or Payload, even if the Contractor requires support from NASA.

        (ii)   Liability and Insurance.

The Contractor shall extend section (c) of clause H.5, NFS 1852.228-76 *Cross-Waiver Of Liability For International Space Station Activities (Oct 2012) (Deviation)*, to Commercial Cargo Customers by requiring them to waive any and all claims against the entities listed in section (c)(1) of that clause, except that Commercial Cargo Customers are not required to waive such claims against the Contractor unless the Contractor so requires. The Contractor shall inform Commercial Cargo Customers that the entities listed in section (c)(1) have not waived any claims against Commercial Cargo Customers. The Contractor shall obtain a written waiver of claims from the Commercial Cargo Customer for all activities related to the mission, including acknowledgment by the Commercial Cargo Customer that the entities listed in section (c)(1) have not waived any claims against Commercial Cargo Customers, and shall provide such documentation to NASA for NASA's approval with the proposal to manifest the non-NASA cargo or payload. The Contractor shall require Commercial Cargo Customers to maintain insurance covering damage to or loss of any property or injury or death of any person on the ISS or in the CTS resulting from the flight of the non-NASA Cargo or Payload. The Contractor shall provide acceptable evidence to the Contracting Officer of required insurance no later than thirty (30) days prior to the launch on which the non-NASA Cargo or Payload is manifested. The amount of required insurance and the terms and conditions for the policy or policies shall be subject to review by the Contracting Officer. Once reviewed, the policy or policies may not be modified or canceled without the prior, written approval of the Contracting Officer.

(d) Delays

The launch and mission schedule will not be changed to accommodate Passengers or Non-NASA Cargo or Payloads, except at NASA's sole discretion. If NASA chooses to reschedule the launch or mission, NASA shall not be responsible for any costs, liabilities or obligations associated with rescheduling. The provisions of clause H.20, *Adjustments To Post Certification Mission*

Schedule, do not apply to circumstances arising under this clause H.23 related to requested delays to accommodate Passengers or non-NASA Cargo or Payloads. If for any reason, the Contractor is unable to transport the Passenger(s) or Non-NASA Cargo or Payload, the Passenger(s) or Non-NASA Cargo or Payload are not ready or available in time for the Post Certification Mission, the Contractor is unable to meet applicable FAA or NASA requirements, or there is insufficient time to complete Passenger training for the Post Certification Mission before the launch date, the Contractor shall bear all costs and be responsible for any related impacts or delays to the launch or mission. In no case shall NASA be liable for any costs or expenses incurred by Commercial Cargo Customers, Passengers or by the Contractor on behalf of its Commercial Cargo Customers or Passengers.

(End of Clause)

H.24 STATEMENT ON WAIVER OF RIGHTS TO INVENTIONS

The crew transportation systems certified and used under this contract will be commercially developed, and the developers may pursue other commercial uses of their systems outside of this contract. NASA has determined that the interest of the United States would be served by waiving to the Contractor, in accordance with 51 U.S.C. 20135(g), rights to inventions or class of inventions made by the Contractor in the performance of this contract. Therefore, upon petition submitted by the Contractor, as set forth in NFS 1852.227-70, *New Technology*, NASA will waive such rights to the Contractor.

(End of Clause)

H.25 SAE AS9100

The Contractor shall have a quality program that complies with International Organization for Standardization document SAE AS9100, *Quality Management Systems – Requirements for Aviation, Space and Defense Organizations* by the Certification Baseline Review.

(a) Third party certification is not required. However, if the Government has accepted the Contractor's SAE AS9100 certification and the Contractor subsequently changes registrars, loses its registration status, or is put on notice of losing its registration status, the Contractor shall notify the Contracting Officer within three days of receiving such notice from its registrar. The Contractor shall coordinate with any Certification Registrars or Databases, or Certifying Organizations to allow NASA access to certification documentation and audit information pertinent to this contract.

(b) If the Contractor is not SAE AS9100 certified, the Government will perform, or have a third party perform, an SAE AS9100 compliance audit no earlier than six (6) months after contract award. Compliance audits will normally be re-accomplished every thirty-six (36) months, but the

Government may conduct annual surveillance audits. The Contractor shall support the audits as required.

(End of Clause)

H.26 MISHAP REPORTING

(a) Definitions, as used in this clause,

(1) NASA Personnel: any person employed by NASA, or other Government personnel performing services on behalf of NASA.

(2) NASA Operations: any activity or process that is under NASA direct control or includes major NASA involvement.

(3) NASA Mishap: is an unplanned event that results in at least one of the following:

(i) Injury to non-NASA personnel, caused by NASA operations.

(ii) Damage to public or private property (including foreign property) not under the ownership or control of the Contractor and/or its subcontractors under this contract, caused by NASA operations or NASA-funded development or research projects.

(iii) Damage to Property (including foreign property) under the ownership or control of the Contractor and/or its subcontractors under this contract, caused by NASA operations.

(iv) Occupational injury or occupational illness to NASA personnel.

(v) Mission failure of any Flight Test or PCM before the scheduled completion of the planned primary mission.

(vi) Destruction of, or damage to, NASA property or NASA equipment.

(4) Close Call: an event in which there is no injury, or only minor injury requiring first aid, and/or no equipment/property damage or minor equipment/property damage (less than $20,000), but which possesses a potential to cause a mishap.

(5) Exposure:

(i) Vulnerability of population, property, or other value system to a given activity or hazard; or

(ii) Other measure of the opportunity for failure or mishap events to occur.

(6) Lost Time Injury/Illness: a nonfatal traumatic injury that causes any loss of time from work beyond the day or shift it occurred; or a nonfatal nontraumatic illness/disease that causes disability at anytime.

(7) Mission Failure: a mishap of whatever intrinsic severity that prevents the achievement of the success criteria or objectives as identified in the applicable Flight Test Plan or determined by clause H.21 *Post Certification Mission Success Determination*.

(8) Serious Injury: any injury resulting from a mishap in which any one or more of the following apply:

(i) Requires hospitalization for more than forty-eight (48) hours, commencing within seven (7) days from the date the injury was received.

(ii) Results in a fracture of any bone (except simple fractures of fingers, toes, or nose).

(iii) Causes severe hemorrhages or nerve, muscle, or tendon damage.

(iv) Involves any internal organ.

(v) Involves second- or third-degree burns, or any burns affecting more than five (5) percent of the body surface.

(9) Substantial Damage to property or equipment: damage or failure which adversely affects the structural strength, performance, or operational characteristics of the property or equipment, and which would normally require major repair or replacement of the affected component(s).

(b) The Contractor shall notify and promptly report to the Contracting Officer, or a designee, any of the following associated with any work performed under this Contract:

(1) Close Calls involving NASA personnel, NASA property, or NASA equipment.

(2) Exposures involving NASA personnel, NASA property, or NASA equipment, which could result in fatality; lost-time occupational injury; or occupational disease.

(3) NASA Mishaps, which result in serious injury; fatality; lost-time occupational injury; occupational disease; any environmental damage; any mission failure; or substantial damage to or loss of equipment or property damage of at least $50,000.

(c) The Contractor shall conduct a mishap investigation for any event that meets paragraph (b) requirements. The Contractor shall allow NASA participation in the investigation, and make all data and resulting reports available to NASA. The Contractor is not required to include in any report an expression of opinion as to the fault or negligence of any employee.

(1) If the Contractor conducts a mishap investigation in the performance of activities not under this contract, but relevant to the CTS design, production and operations, the Contractor shall make available to NASA all data and resulting reports.

(d) The Contractor shall maintain the data of any mishap investigation referenced above for the term of this Contract plus three (3) years.

(e) NASA may investigate any NASA mishaps or close calls that involve NASA personnel, equipment, or property, that occur in the performance of this contract in accordance with CCT-PLN-1010, *Mishap Preparedness and Contingency Plan for Commercial Crew Program*. The Contractor shall provide personnel support and data, as necessary, to support a NASA investigation.

(f) When applicable, the Contractor shall support a Commission appointed by the President per 51 U.S.C Section 70701 *et seq.*.

(End of Clause)

H.27 GOVERNMENT-INDUSTRY DATA EXCHANGE PROGRAM (GIDEP)

(a) Definitions, as used in this clause

(1) Close-loop reporting: providing a written response of no impact, no usage or impact with rationale at program milestone and readiness reviews or according to contract or other specified reporting times/events for each GIDEP Notice and NASA Advisory.

(2) GIDEP Notices: means "GIDEP Alerts, GIDEP Safe-Alerts, GIDEP Problem Advisories, and GIDEP Agency Action Notices." Life-cycle logistics should be addressed per contractual requirements identified by the Program/Project.

(b) The Contractor shall participate in the GIDEP in accordance with the requirements of the GIDEP Operations Manual (GIDEP SO300-BT-PRO-101) and the GIDEP Requirements Guide (SO300-BU-GYD-010), available from the GIDEP Operations Center, PO Box 8000, Corona, California 92878-8000.

(c) The Contractor shall review all GIDEP Notices and designated NASA Advisories to determine if they affect the Contractor's products/and or services provided to the Government.

(d) The Contractor shall respond by stating, in writing, whether or not each GIDEP Notice and NASA Advisory affects the Contractor's products and services provided to the Government. The Contractor is responsible for stating whether or not each GIDEP Notice and NASA Advisories affects the subcontractor's products and services provided to the Government.

(e) For GIDEP Notices and NASA Advisories that affect the Contractor's products and services provided to the Government, the Contractor shall take action to eliminate or mitigate any negative effect and inform the Government of such actions to ensure GIDEP Notices and NASA Advisories adhere to close-loop reporting.

(f) The Contractor shall generate applicable GIDEP Alerts in accordance with the requirements of GIDEP SO300-BT-PRO-101 and SO300-BU-GYD-010 whenever failed or nonconforming items, available to other buyers, are discovered during the course of the Contract.

(End of Clause)

H.28 ENVIRONMENTAL COMPLIANCE AND NATIONAL ENVIRONMENTAL POLICY ACT (NEPA) DOCUMENTATION

(a) Environmental Compliance. The Contractor shall ensure that all operations, activities, equipment, and facilities under this contract are in compliance with all applicable Federal, state, and local environmental laws, statutes, regulations, and ordnances. Unless otherwise stated in this contract, the Contractor shall be solely responsible for compliance with aforementioned environmental requirements including environmental permits. The Contractor shall be considered an independent entity responsible for its own actions for the purposes of environmental compliance and permitting matters.

(b) National Environmental Policy Act (NEPA). Should Contractor activities trigger the need for NEPA documentation during the performance of the contract, the Contractor shall be responsible for complying with NPR 8580.1, *NASA National Environmental Policy Act Management Requirements*, and providing documentation and supporting rationale to NASA throughout the NEPA process, as required by the Contracting Officer.

(End of Clause)

H.29 ANOMALY INVESTIGATION AND CORRECTIVE ACTION

(a) For the purposes of this clause, an anomaly is an unexpected event, hardware or software damage, departure from established procedures or performance, or a deviation of system, subsystem, or hardware or software performance outside intended design or expected performance specification limits.

(b) For the purposes of this clause, data includes, but is not limited to data associated with areas of insight identified in CCT-PLN-1100, *Crew Transportation Plan*, Appendix C, *Insight Areas*, and data relevant to the Crew Transportation System (CTS) design, production and operations.

(c) The Contractor shall notify the Government of reportable CTS anomalies. For reportable anomalies that occur during the period prior to Flight Readiness Review (FRR) for the next mission of any affected CTS vehicle, notification shall be within thirty (30) days, but no later than at FRR. Anomalies that occur after FRR shall be reported to the Government, as soon as is practical. Reportable anomalies are those that:

   (1)   After resolution, negatively affect CTS certification, post certification performance, hazards, hazard controls, or verifications; or

   (2)   Are unexplained or could not be duplicated; or

   (3)   Occur during standard repairs or nominal processing tasks and indicate an unexpected trend in one or more CTS vehicles.

(d) The Contractor shall determine the scope of the investigation and shall conduct and control the investigation. The Government may designate representatives to observe and participate in the Contractor's investigation. The Contractor shall accommodate Government representation to the Contractor's investigation.

(e) The Contractor shall be responsible for identifying the cause(s) of the anomaly, and implementing corrective action(s). The Contractor shall provide the Government access to any findings and any proposed corrective actions. If the Contractor implements any changes to the CTS design that could negatively affect certification, post certification performance, hazards, controls, or verifications of the CTS, the Contractor shall notify the Government of the change.

(f) The Government may conduct its own investigation of any anomaly or failed mission. The Contractor shall provide personnel support and data, as necessary, to support a Government investigation.

(End of Clause)

H.30   HAZARDOUS OPERATIONS

(a) Definitions, as used in this clause

   (1)   Hazardous Operations: any operation or other work activity that, without implementation of proper mitigations, has a high potential to result in loss of life, serious injury to personnel or public, or damage to property due to the material or equipment involved or the nature of the operation/activity.

   (2) Hazardous Flight Operations: any Hazardous Operations performed on this contract that affect the CTS or its elements; and occur between initiation of tanking of the CTS, and post-detanking or post-flight safing. Hazardous Flight Operations may be initiated by Government or Contractor Flight Crew, Government or Contractor Ground Controllers, Government or Contractor Closeout Crew, Government or Contractor Recovery Personnel, or software.

(3) Hazardous Ground Operations: any Hazardous Operations performed on this contract, other than Hazardous Flight Operations.

(b) All Hazardous Flight Operations conducted in the performance of this contract shall be reviewed and approved through the Commercial Crew Program and/or International Space Station Program safety review processes.

(c) All Hazardous Ground Operations under control of the Contractor or Subcontractor(s) in performance of this contract shall comply with all Federal, State, and Local requirements intended to mitigate risk to personnel, equipment, and property.

(End of Clause)

H.31 INTERIM PERFORMANCE-BASED MILESTONE PAYMENTS (APPLICABLE TO CLIN 001)

SubCLINS 001A and 001B listed in CLIN 001, *DDTE/Certification*, are delivery milestones (delivery items). For each delivery milestone, the Contractor may request interim-milestone financing payments in accordance with FAR 52.232-32, *Performance Based Payments*. Milestone events, schedule, price and acceptance criteria are identified in Attachment J-03, Appendix A, *Milestone Acceptance Criteria and Payment Schedule*. The sum of interim-milestone financing payments with each delivery item shall not exceed 90% of that delivery item price in accordance with FAR 32.1004(b)(2)(ii). Liquidation of performance-based financing payments will occur once the Government accepts each delivery item.

The ISS DCR associated with the delivery milestone (SubCLIN 001A) will be the DCR associated with the crewed flight test to ISS. The ISS DCR delivery milestone shall include all work under CLIN 001 that occurs from contract start date through this milestone completion. The delivery payment for the Certification Review associated with the delivery milestone (SubCLIN 001B) will include all work under CLIN 001 that occurs from this ISS DCR delivery milestone through the end of the DDTE/Certification.

The Contracting Officer will unilaterally determine the Contractor's successful accomplishment of each milestone event. The Contracting Officer's determination of milestone accomplishment will be based on the criteria listed in Attachment J-03, Appendix A, *Milestone Acceptance Criteria and Payment Schedule*, as well as the Contractor's compliance with the terms of the contract, including performance of PWS and deliverable requirements. The delivery-milestone payments are not financing payments and unlike interim-milestone payments, once made, are not subject to repayment by the Contractor if the conditions defined in FAR 52.232-32 (j), *Special terms regarding default*, apply.

Generally, milestone payment will be paid in succession. All preceding payment events shall be successfully accomplished before payment will be made for the next payment event, unless the prior written consent of the Contracting Officer is obtained.

(End of Clause)

H.32 SUBCONTRACTING WITH RUSSIAN ENTITIES FOR GOODS OR SERVICES

(a) Definitions: In this clause:

(1) The term "Russian entities" means:

(i) Russian persons, or

(ii) Entities created under Russian law or owned, in whole or in part, by Russian persons or companies including, but not limited to, the following:

(A) The Russian Federal Space Agency (Roscosmos),

(B) Any organization or entity under the jurisdiction or control of Roscosmos, or

(C) Any other organization, entity or element of the Government of the Russian Federation.

(2) The term "extraordinary payments" means payments in cash or in kind made or to be made by the United States Government prior to December 31, 2020, for work to be performed or services to be rendered prior to that date necessary to meet United States obligations under the Agreement Concerning Cooperation on the Civil International Space Station, with annex, signed at Washington January 29, 1998, and entered into force March 27, 2001, or any protocol, agreement, memorandum of understanding, or contract related thereto.

(b) This clause implements the reporting requirement in section 6(i) of the Iran, North Korea, and Syria Nonproliferation Act, as amended (INKSNA). This clause also implements section 6(a) and the exception in section 7(1)(B) of INKSNA that is applicable through December 31, 2020. NASA has applied the restrictions in INKSNA to include funding of Russian entities via U.S. Contractors.

(c) (1) The Contractor shall not subcontract with Russian entities without first receiving written approval from the Contracting Officer. In order to obtain this written approval to subcontract with any Russian entity as defined in paragraphs (a), the Contractor shall provide the Contracting Officer with the following information related to each planned new subcontract and any change to an existing subcontract with entities that fit the description in paragraph (a):

(i) A detailed description of the subcontracting entity, including its name, address, and a point of contact, as well as a detailed description of the proposed subcontract including the specific purpose of payments that will made under the subcontract.

(ii) The Contractor shall provide certification that the subcontracting entity is not, at the date of the subcontract approval request, on any of the lists of proscribed denied parties, specially designated nationals and entities of concern found at:

> BIS's Listing of Entities of Concern (see http://www.access.gpo.gov/bis/ear/pdf/744spir.pdf)

> BIS's List of Denied Parties (see http://www.bis.doc.gov/index.php/policy-guidance/lists-of-parties-of-concern/denied-persons-list)

> OFAC's List of Specially Designated Nationals (Adobe® PDF format) (see http://www.bis.doc.gov/index.php/policy-guidance/lists-of-parties-of-concern/unverified-list)

> List of Unverified Persons in Foreign Countries (see http://www.bis.doc.gov/index.php/policy-guidance/lists-of-parties-of-concern/unverified-list)

> State Department's List of Parties Statutorily Debarred for Arms Export Control Act Convictions (see http://pmddtc.state.gov/compliance/debar.html)

> State Department's Lists of Proliferating Entities (see http://www.state.gov/t/isn/c15231.htm)

(2) Unless relief is granted by the Contracting Officer, the information necessary to obtain approval to subcontract shall be provided to the Contracting Officer thirty (30) business days prior to executing any planned subcontract with entities defined in paragraph (a).

(d) After receiving approval to subcontract, the Contractor shall provide the Contracting Officer with a report every six (6) months that documents the individual payments made to an entity in paragraph (a). The reports are due on July 15th and January 15th. The July 15th report shall document all of the individual payments made from the previous January through June. The January 15th report shall document all of the individual payments made from the previous July through December. The content of the report shall provide the following information for each time a payment is made to an entity in paragraph (a):

(1) The name of the entity

(2) The subcontract number

(3) The amount of the payment

(4) The date of the payment

(e) The Contracting Officer may direct the Contractor to provide additional information for any other prospective or existing subcontract at any tier. The Contracting Officer may direct the Contractor to terminate for the convenience of the Government any subcontract at any tier with an entity defined in paragraph (a), subject to an equitable adjustment.

(f) All work subcontracted to the Russian Federal Space Agency, any organization or entity under the jurisdiction or control of the Russian Federal Space Agency, or any other organization, entity or element of the Government of the Russian Federation must be completed on or before December 31, 2020. No payments for such work may be made by the Contractor to the subcontractor, or by NASA to the Contractor, after December 31, 2020. The Contractor is responsible for ensuring the completion of and payment for such subcontracted work in sufficient time to enable payment by NASA to the Contractor on or before December 31, 2020.

(g) The Contractor shall include the substance of this clause in all its subcontracts, and shall require such inclusion in all other subcontracts of any tier. The Contractor shall be responsible to obtain written approval from the Contracting Officer to enter into any tier subcontract that involves entities defined in paragraph (a).

(h) Performance of this contract after December 31, 2020 may be subject to prohibitions on payments to Russian entities under INKSNA.

(End of Clause)

SECTION I. CONTRACT CLAUSES

I.1   52.252-2   CLAUSES INCORPORATED BY REFERENCE (FEB 1998)

This contract incorporates one or more clauses by reference, with the same force and effect as if they were given in full text. Upon request, the Contracting Officer will make their full text available. Also, the full text of a clause may be accessed electronically at this/these address(es):

For Federal Acquisition Regulation (FAR) clauses, see
https://www.acquisition.gov/far/

For NASA FAR Supplement (NFS) clauses, see
http://www.hq.nasa.gov/office/procurement/regs/nfstoc.htm

(End of Clause)

I.2   CLAUSES INCORPORATED BY REFERENCE -- SECTION I

Clause(s) at the beginning of this Section are incorporated by reference, with the same force and effect as if they were given in full text. Clauses incorporated by reference which require a fill-in by the Government include the text of the affected paragraph(s) only. This does not limit the clause to the affected paragraph(s). The Contractor is responsible for understanding and complying with the entire clause. The full text of the clause is available at the addresses contained in clause I.1 52.252-2, *Clauses Incorporated by Reference*, of this contract.

Clause	Title
52.202-1	DEFINITIONS. (JUL 2012)
52.203-3	GRATUITIES. (APR 1984)
52.203-5	COVENANT AGAINST CONTINGENT FEES. (APR 1984)
52.203-6	RESTRICTIONS ON SUBCONTRACTOR SALES TO THE GOVERNMENT. (SEP 2006)
52.203-7	ANTI-KICKBACK PROCEDURES. (OCT 2010)
52.203-8	CANCELLATION, RESCISSION, AND RECOVERY OF FUNDS FOR ILLEGAL OR IMPROPER ACTIVITY. (JAN 1997)
52.203-10	PRICE OR FEE ADJUSTMENT FOR ILLEGAL OR IMPROPER ACTIVITY. (JAN 1997)
52.203-12	LIMITATION ON PAYMENTS TO INFLUENCE CERTAIN FEDERAL TRANSACTIONS. (OCT 2010)

52.203-13	CONTRACTOR CODE OF BUSINESS ETHICS AND CONDUCT. (APR 2010)
52.203-14	DISPLAY OF HOTLINE POSTER(S). (DEC 2007) [NASA Office of Inspector General, Code W, Washington, DC, 20546-0001, (202) 358-1220. http://oig.nasa.gov/hotline.html]
52.204-2	SECURITY REQUIREMENTS. (AUG 1996)
52.204-4	PRINTED OR COPIED DOUBLE-SIDED ON POSTCONSUMER FIBER CONTENT PAPER. (MAY 2011)
52.204-9	PERSONAL IDENTITY VERIFICATION OF CONTRACTOR PERSONNEL. (JAN 2011)
52.204-10	REPORTING EXECUTIVE COMPENSATION AND FIRST-TIER SUBCONTRACT AWARDS. (JUL 2013)
52.204-13	SYSTEM FOR AWARD MANAGEMENT MAINTENANCE (JUL 2013)
52.209-6	PROTECTING THE GOVERNMENT'S INTEREST WHEN SUBCONTRACTING WITH CONTRACTORS DEBARRED, SUSPENDED, OR PROPOSED FOR DEBARMENT. (AUG 2013)
52.210-1	MARKET RESEARCH. (APR 2011)
52.211-15	DEFENSE PRIORITY AND ALLOCATION REQUIREMENTS. (APR 2008)
52.215-2	AUDIT AND RECORDS - NEGOTIATION. (OCT 2010)
52.215-11	PRICE REDUCTION FOR DEFECTIVE CERTIFIED COST OR PRICING DATA – MODIFICATIONS. (AUG 2011)
52.215-13	SUBCONTRACTOR CERTIFIED COST OR PRICING DATA – MODIFICATIONS. (OCT 2010)
52.215-8	ORDER OF PRECEDENCE - UNIFORM CONTRACT FORMAT. (OCT 1997)
52.217-8	OPTION TO EXTEND SERVICES. (NOV 1999) [the sixty (60) days prior to completion of the last required milestone or delivery date].

52.219-4	NOTICE OF PRICE EVALUATION PREFERENCE FOR HUBZONE SMALL BUSINESS CONCERNS. (JAN 2011)
52.219-8	UTILIZATION OF SMALL BUSINESS CONCERNS. (JUL 2013)
52.219-9	SMALL BUSINESS SUBCONTRACTING PLAN. (Deviation per PIC 13-06 (www.hq.nasa.gov/office/procurement/regs/pic.html)) – ALTERNATE II (OCT 2001)
52.219-16	LIQUIDATED DAMAGES - SUBCONTRACTING PLAN. (JAN 1999)
52.219-28	POST-AWARD SMALL BUSINESS PROGRAM REREPRESENTATION. (JUL 2013) The Contractor represents that it ___ is, _X_ is not a small business concern under NAICS Code 336414 assigned to contract number TBD. (*Contractor to sign and date and insert authorized signer's name and title*).
52.222-1	NOTICE TO THE GOVERNMENT OF LABOR DISPUTES. (FEB 1997)
52.222-3	CONVICT LABOR. (JUN 2003)
52.222-21	PROHIBITION OF SEGREGATED FACILITIES. (FEB 1999)
52.222-26	EQUAL OPPORTUNITY. (MAR 2007)
52.222-35	EQUAL OPPORTUNITY FOR VETERANS. (SEP 2010)
52.222-36	AFFIRMATIVE ACTION FOR WORKERS WITH DISABILITIES. (OCT 2010)
52.222-37	EMPLOYMENT REPORTS ON VETERANS. (SEP 2010)
52.222-40	NOTIFICATION OF EMPLOYEE RIGHTS UNDER THE NATIONAL LABOR RELATIONS ACT. (DEC 2010)
52.222-50	COMBATING TRAFFICKING IN PERSONS. (FEB 2009)
52.222-54	EMPLOYMENT ELIGIBILITY VERIFICATION. (AUG 2013)
52.223-6	DRUG-FREE WORKPLACE. (MAY 2001)
52.223-18	ENCOURAGING CONTRACTOR POLICIES TO BAN TEXT MESSAGING WHILE DRIVING. (AUG 2011)
52.225-13	RESTRICTIONS ON CERTAIN FOREIGN PURCHASES. (JUN 2008)

52.227-1	AUTHORIZATION AND CONSENT. (DEC 2007)
52.227-2	NOTICE AND ASSISTANCE REGARDING PATENT AND COPYRIGHT INFRINGEMENT. (DEC 2007)
52.227-3	PATENT INDEMNITY. (APR 1984)
52.227-16	ADDITIONAL DATA REQUIREMENTS. (JUN 1987)
52.229-3	FEDERAL, STATE, AND LOCAL TAXES. (FEB 2013)
52.232-1	PAYMENTS. (APR 1984) (Applicable to CLIN 002 and any appropriate task orders per CLIN 003)
52.232-2	PAYMENTS UNDER FIXED-PRICE RESEARCH AND DEVELOPMENT CONTRACTS. (APR 1984) (Applicable to CLIN 001 and any appropriate task orders per CLIN 003)
52.232-8	DISCOUNTS FOR PROMPT PAYMENT. (FEB 2002)
52.232-9	LIMITATION ON WITHHOLDING OF PAYMENTS. (APR 1984)
52.232-11	EXTRAS. (APR 1984)
52.232-17	INTEREST. (OCT 2010)
52.232-18	AVAILABILITY OF FUNDS. (APR 1984)
52.232-23	ASSIGNMENT OF CLAIMS. (JAN 1986)
52.232-25	PROMPT PAYMENT. (JUL 2013)
52.232-33	PAYMENT BY ELECTRONIC FUNDS TRANSFER- SYSTEM FOR AWARD MANAGEMENT. (JUL 2013)
52.233-1	DISPUTES. (JUL 2002) - ALTERNATE I (DEC 1991)
52.233-3	PROTEST AFTER AWARD. (AUG 1996)
52.233-4	APPLICABLE LAW FOR BREACH OF CONTRACT CLAIM. (OCT 2004)
52.242-13	BANKRUPTCY. (JUL 1995)

52.243-1	CHANGES - FIXED-PRICE. (AUG 1987) - ALTERNATE I (APR 1984) (Applicable to CLIN 002 and any appropriate task orders per CLIN 003)
52.243-1	CHANGES - FIXED-PRICE. (AUG 1987) - ALTERNATE V (APR 1984) (Applicable to CLIN 001 and any appropriate task orders per CLIN 003)
52.243-7	NOTIFICATION OF CHANGES. (APR 1984) Fill in (b) seven (7) calendar days Fill in (d) seven (7) calendar days
52.244-2	SUBCONTRACTS. (OCT 2010)
52.244-6	SUBCONTRACTS FOR COMMERCIAL ITEMS. (JUL 2013)
52.245-1	GOVERNMENT PROPERTY. (APR 2012) -- Alternate I (APR 2012)
52.245-9	USE AND CHARGES. (APR 2012)
52.246-25	LIMITATION OF LIABILITY - SERVICES. (FEB 1997)
52.249-2	TERMINATION FOR CONVENIENCE OF THE GOVERNMENT (FIXED-PRICE). (APRIL 2012)
52.253-1	COMPUTER GENERATED FORMS. (JAN 1991)
NFS 1852.203-70	DISPLAY OF INSPECTOR GENERAL HOTLINE POSTERS. (JUN 2001)
NFS 1852.204-76	SECURITY REQUIREMENTS FOR UNCLASSIFIED INFORMATION TECHNOLOGY RESOURCES (JAN 2011)
NFS 1852.209-72	COMPOSITION OF THE CONTRACTOR. (DEC 1988)
NFS 1852.219-74	USE OF RURAL AREA SMALL BUSINESSES. (SEP 1990)
NFS 1852.219-76	NASA 8 PERCENT GOAL. (JUL 1997)
NFS 1852.219-77	NASA MENTOR-PROTEGE PROGRAM. (MAY 2009)
NFS 1852.243-71	SHARED SAVINGS. (MAR 1997)
NFS 1852.235-70	CENTER FOR AEROSPACE INFORMATION. (DEC 2006)

(End of Clause)

I.3   52.209-9   UPDATES OF PUBLICLY AVAILABLE INFORMATION REGARDING RESPONSIBILITY MATTERS (JUL 2013)

(a) The Contractor shall update the information in the Federal Awardee Performance and Integrity Information System (FAPIIS) on a semi-annual basis, throughout the life of the contract, by posting the required information in the System for Award Management database via *https://www.acquisition.gov*.

(b) As required by section 3010 of the Supplemental Appropriations Act, 2010 (Pub. L. 111-212), all information posted in FAPIIS on or after April 15, 2011, except past performance reviews, will be publicly available.   FAPIIS consist of two segments—

   (1) The non-public segment, into which Government officials and the Contractor post information, which can only be viewed by—

      (i) Government personnel and authorized users performing business on behalf of the Government; or

      (ii) The Contractor, when viewing data on itself; and

   (2) The publicly-available segment, to which all data in the non-public segment of FAPIIS is automatically transferred after a waiting period of 14 calendar days, except for--

      (i) Past performance reviews required by subpart 42.15;

      (ii) Information that was entered prior to April 15, 2011; or

      (iii) Information that is withdrawn during the 14-calendar-day waiting period by the Government official who posted it in accordance with paragraph (c)(1) of this clause.

(c) The Contractor will receive notification when the Government posts new information to the Contractor's record.

   (1) If the Contractor asserts in writing within 7 calendar days, to the Government official who posted the information, that some of the information posted to the non-public segment of FAPIIS is covered by a disclosure exemption under the Freedom of Information Act, the Government official who posted the information must within 7 calendar days remove the posting from FAPIIS and resolve the issue in accordance with agency Freedom of Information procedures, prior to reposting the releasable information. The Contractor must cite 52.209-9 and request removal within 7 calendar days of the posting to FAPIIS.

   (2) The Contractor will also have an opportunity to post comments regarding information that has been posted by the Government.   The comments will be retained as long as the associated

information is retained, i.e., for a total period of 6 years. Contractor comments will remain a part of the record unless the Contractor revises them.

(3) As required by section 3010 of Pub. L. 111-212, all information posted in FAPIIS on or after April 15, 2011, except past performance reviews, will be publicly available.

(d) Public requests for system information posted prior to April 15, 2011, will be handled under Freedom of Information Act procedures, including, where appropriate, procedures promulgated under E.O. 12600.

(End of Clause)

I.4   52.215-21   REQUIREMENTS FOR CERTIFIED COST OR PRICING DATA AND DATA OTHER THAN CERTIFIED COST OR PRICING DATA – MODIFICATIONS. (OCT 2010) (This Clause Is Applicable To The Extent That Only Subcontractors Are Required To Submit Certified Cost Or Pricing Data)

(a) *Exceptions from certified cost or pricing data.*

(1) In lieu of submitting certified cost or pricing data for modifications under this contract, for price adjustments expected to exceed the threshold set forth at FAR 15.403-4 on the date of the agreement on price or the date of the award, whichever is later, the Contractor may submit a written request for exception by submitting the information described in the following subparagraphs. The Contracting Officer may require additional supporting information, but only to the extent necessary to determine whether an exception should be granted, and whether the price is fair and reasonable –

(i) *Identification of the law or regulation establishing the price offered.* If the price is controlled under law by periodic rulings, reviews, or similar actions of a governmental body, attach a copy of the controlling document, unless it was previously submitted to the contracting office.

(ii) *Information on modifications of contracts or subcontracts for commercial items.*

(A) If --
(1) The original contract or subcontract was granted an exception from certified cost or pricing data requirements because the price agreed upon was based on adequate price competition or prices set by law or regulation, or was a contract or subcontract for the acquisition of a commercial item; and

(2) The modification (to the contract or subcontract) is not exempted based on one of these exceptions, then the Contractor may provide information to establish that the modification would not change the contract or subcontract from a contract or subcontract for the

acquisition of a commercial item to a contract or subcontract for the acquisition of an item other than a commercial item.

        (B) For a commercial item exception, the Contractor shall provide, at a minimum, information on prices at which the same item or similar items have previously been sold that is adequate for evaluating the reasonableness of the price of the modification. Such information may include –

        (1) For catalog items, a copy of or identification of the catalog and its date, or the appropriate pages for the offered items, or a statement that the catalog is on file in the buying office to which the proposal is being submitted. Provide a copy or describe current discount policies and price lists (published or unpublished), e.g., wholesale, original equipment manufacturer, or reseller. Also explain the basis of each offered price and its relationship to the established catalog price, including how the proposed price relates to the price of recent sales in quantities similar to the proposed quantities.

        (2) For market-priced items, the source and date or period of the market quotation or other basis for market price, the base amount, and applicable discounts. In addition, describe the nature of the market.

        (3) For items included on an active Federal Supply Service Multiple Award Schedule contract, proof that an exception has been granted for the schedule item.

    (2) The Contractor grants the Contracting Officer or an authorized representative the right to examine, at any time before award, books, records, documents, or other directly pertinent records to verify any request for an exception under this clause, and the reasonableness of price. For items priced using catalog or market prices, or law or regulation, access does not extend to cost or profit information or other data relevant solely to the Contractor's determination of the prices to be offered in the catalog or marketplace.

(b) *Requirements for certified cost or pricing data.* If the Contractor is not granted an exception from the requirement to submit certified cost or pricing data, the following applies:

    (1) The Contractor shall submit certified cost or pricing data, data other than certified cost or pricing data, and supporting attachments in accordance with the instruction contained in Table 15-2 of FAR 15.408, which is incorporated by reference with the same force and effect as though it were inserted here in full text. The instructions in Table 15-2 are incorporated as a mandatory format to be used in this contract, unless the Contracting Officer and the Contractor agree to a different format and change this clause to use Alternate I.

    (2) As soon as practicable after agreement on price, but before award (except for unpriced actions), the Contractor shall submit a Certificate of Current Cost or Pricing Data, as prescribed by FAR 15.406-2.

(End of Clause)

I.5   52.215-21   REQUIREMENTS FOR CERTIFIED COST OR PRICING   DATA AND DATA OTHER THAN CERTIFIED COST OR PRICING DATA - MODIFICATIONS. (OCT 2010) - Alternate IV (OCT 2010) (This Clause Is Not Applicable To Subcontractors)

(a) Submission of certified cost or pricing data is not required.

(b) Provide information described below: [If required by the Government, the Contractor(s) shall submit *Data Other than Certified Cost or Pricing Data* as defined in Clause G.9, *Requirements for Data Other than Certified Cost or Pricing Data* to permit an adequate evaluation of the proposed price in accordance with 15.403-3.]

(End of Clause)

I.6   52.216-18   ORDERING (OCT 1995) (Applicable to IDIQ CLINs 002 and 003)

(a) Any supplies and services to be furnished under this contract shall be ordered by issuance of delivery orders or task orders by the individuals or activities designated in the Schedule.   Such orders may be issued up to 5-years from the effective date of the contract.

(b) All delivery orders or task orders are subject to the terms and conditions of this contract.   In the event of conflict between a delivery order or task order and this contract, the contract shall control.

(c) If mailed, a delivery order or task order is considered "issued" when the Government deposits the order in the mail.   Orders may be issued orally, by facsimile, or by electronic commerce methods only if authorized in the Schedule.

(End of Clause)

I.7   52.216-19   ORDER LIMITATIONS (OCT 1995) (Applicable to IDIQ CLINs 002 and 003)

(a) Minimum order.   When the Government requires supplies or services covered by this contract in an amount of less than

   (a) One (1) Post Certification Mission, pursuant to CLIN 002 or

   (b) A Special Studies Task order valued at $5,000, pursuant to CLIN 003, or

The Government is not obligated to purchase, nor is the Contractor obligated to furnish, those supplies or services under the contract.

(b) Maximum order. The Contractor is not obligated to honor

(1) Any order for CLIN 002 for a single item in excess of the ▓▓▓▓▓▓▓▓▓▓▓▓▓▓

(2) Any order for CLIN 002 for a combination of items in excess of ▓▓▓▓▓ or

(3) A series of orders from the same ordering office within 10 days that together call for quantities exceeding the limitation in subparagraph (b)(1) or (2) of this section.

(4) Any order for a single item for CLIN 003 is ▓▓▓▓▓

(5) Any order for CLIN 003 for a combination of items is ▓▓▓▓▓

(c) If this is a requirements contract (i.e., includes the Requirements clause at subsection 52.216-21 of the Federal Acquisition Regulation (FAR)), the Government is not required to order a part of any one requirement from the Contractor if that requirement exceeds the maximum-order limitations in paragraph (b) of this section.

(d) Notwithstanding paragraphs (b) and (c) of this section, the Contractor shall honor any order exceeding the maximum order limitations in paragraph (b), unless that order (or orders) is returned to the ordering office within 15 days after issuance, with written notice stating the Contractor's intent not to ship the item (or items) called for and the reasons. Upon receiving this notice, the Government may acquire the supplies or services from another source.

(End of Clause)

I.8   52.216-22   INDEFINITE QUANTITY (OCT 1995) (Applicable to IDIQ CLINs 002 and 003)

(a) This is an indefinite-quantity contract for the supplies or services specified, and effective for the period stated, in the Schedule. The quantities of supplies and services specified in the Schedule are estimates only and are not purchased by this contract.

(b) Delivery or performance shall be made only as authorized by orders issued in accordance with the Ordering clause. The Contractor shall furnish to the Government, when and if ordered, the supplies or services specified in the Schedule up to and including the quantity designated in the Schedule as the "maximum." The Government shall order at least the quantity of supplies or services designated in the Schedule as the "minimum."

(c) Except for any limitations on quantities in the Order Limitations clause or in the Schedule, there is no limit on the number of orders that may be issued. The Government may issue orders requiring delivery to multiple destinations or performance at multiple locations.

(d) Any order issued during the effective period of this contract and not completed within that period shall be completed by the Contractor within the time specified in the order. The contract shall govern the Contractor's and Government's rights and obligations with respect to that order to the same extent as if the order were completed during the contract's effective period; provided, that the Contractor shall not be required to make any deliveries under this contract three years after the end of the ordering period.

(End of Clause)

I.9   52.227-11   PATENT RIGHTS--OWNERSHIP BY THE CONTRACTOR. (DEC 2007) / AS MODIFIED PER 1852.227-11 PATENT RIGHTS - RETENTION BY THE CONTRACTOR (SHORT FORM).

(a) As used in this clause -
"Invention" means any invention or discovery that is or may be patentable or otherwise protectable under title 35 of the U.S. Code, or any variety of plant that is or may be protectable under the Plant Variety Protection Act (7 U.S.C. 2321, *et seq.*)

"Made" means –

(1) When used in relation to any invention other than a plant variety, the conception or first actual reduction to practice of the invention; or

(2) When used in relation to a plant variety, that the Contractor has at least tentatively determined that the variety has been reproduced with recognized characteristics.

"Nonprofit organization" means a university or other institution of higher education or an organization of the type described in section 501(c)(3) of the Internal Revenue Code of 1954 (26 U.S.C. 501(c)) and exempt from taxation under section 501(a) of the Internal Revenue Code (26 U.S.C. 501(a)), or any nonprofit scientific or educational organization qualified under a State nonprofit organization statute.

"Practical application" means to manufacture, in the case of a composition of product; to practice, in the case of a process or method; or to operate, in the case of a machine or system; and, in each case, under such conditions as to establish that the invention is being utilized and that its benefits are, to the extent permitted by law or Government regulations, available to the public on reasonable terms.

"Subject invention" means any invention of the Contractor made in the performance of work under this contract.

(b) Contractor's rights.

(1) Ownership. The Contractor may retain ownership of each subject invention throughout the world in accordance with the provisions of this clause.

(2) License.

(i) The Contractor shall retain a nonexclusive royalty-free license throughout the world in each subject invention to which the Government obtains title, unless the Contractor fails to disclose the invention within the times specified in paragraph (c) of this clause. The Contractor's license extends to any domestic subsidiaries and affiliates within the corporate structure of which the Contractor is a part, and includes the right to grant sublicenses to the extent the Contractor was legally obligated to do so at contract award. The license is transferable only with the written approval of the agency, except when transferred to the successor of that part of the Contractor's business to which the invention pertains.

(ii) The Contractor's license may be revoked or modified by the agency to the extent necessary to achieve expeditious practical application of the subject invention in a particular country in accordance with the procedures in FAR 27.302(i)(2) and 27.304-1(f).

(c) Contractor's obligations.

(1) The Contractor shall disclose in writing each subject invention to the Contracting Officer within 2 months after the inventor discloses it in writing to Contractor personnel responsible for patent matters. The disclosure shall identify the inventor(s) and this contract under which the subject invention was made. It shall be sufficiently complete in technical detail to convey a clear understanding of the subject invention. The disclosure shall also identify any publication, on sale (i.e., sale or offer for sale), or public use of the subject invention, or whether a manuscript describing the subject invention has been submitted for publication and, if so, whether it has been accepted for publication. In addition, after disclosure to the agency, the Contractor shall promptly notify the Contracting Officer of the acceptance of any manuscript describing the subject invention for publication and any on sale or public use.

(2) The Contractor shall elect in writing whether or not to retain ownership of any subject invention by notifying the Contracting Officer within 2 years of disclosure to the agency. However, in any case where publication, on sale, or public use has initiated the 1-year statutory period during which valid patent protection can be obtained in the United States, the period for election of title may be shortened by the agency to a date that is no more than 60 days prior to the end of the statutory period.

(3) The Contractor shall file either a provisional or a nonprovisional patent application or a Plant Variety Protection Application on an elected subject invention within 1 year after election. However, in any case where a publication, on sale, or public use has initiated the 1-year statutory period during which valid patent protection can be obtained in the United States, the Contractor

shall file the application prior to the end of that statutory period. If the Contractor files a provisional application, it shall file a nonprovisional application within 10 months of the filing of the provisional application. The Contractor shall file patent applications in additional countries or international patent offices within either 10 months of the first filed patent application (whether provisional or nonprovisional) or 6 months from the date permission is granted by the Commissioner of Patents to file foreign patent applications where such filing has been prohibited by a Secrecy Order.

(4)   The Contractor may request extensions of time for disclosure, election, or filing under paragraphs (c)(1), (c)(2), and (c)(3) of this clause.

(5)   The Contractor may use whatever format is convenient to disclose subject inventions required in subparagraph (c)(1). NASA prefers that the Contractor use either the electronic or paper version of NASA Form 1679, *Disclosure of Invention and New Technology (Including Software)* to disclose subject inventions. Both the electronic and paper versions of NASA Form 1679 may be accessed at the electronic New Technology Reporting Web site http://invention.nasa.gov.

(d) Government's rights –

(1)   Ownership. The Contractor shall assign to the agency, on written request, title to any subject invention –

(i)   If the Contractor fails to disclose or elect ownership to the subject invention within the times specified in paragraph (c) of this clause, or elects not to retain ownership; provided, that the agency may request title only within 60 days after learning of the Contractor's failure to disclose or elect within the specified times.

(ii)   In those countries in which the Contractor fails to file patent applications within the times specified in paragraph (c) of this clause; provided, however, that if the Contractor has filed a patent application in a country after the times specified in paragraph (c) of this clause, but prior to its receipt of the written request of the agency, the Contractor shall continue to retain ownership in that country.

(iii)   In any country in which the Contractor decides not to continue the prosecution of any application for, to pay the maintenance fees on, or defend in reexamination or opposition proceeding on, a patent on a subject invention.

(2)   License. If the Contractor retains ownership of any subject invention, the Government shall have a nonexclusive, nontransferable, irrevocable, paid-up license to practice, or have practiced for or on its behalf, the subject invention throughout the world.

(e) Contractor action to protect the Government's interest.

(1) The Contractor shall execute or have executed and promptly deliver to the agency all instruments necessary to –

(i) Establish or confirm the rights the Government has throughout the world in those subject inventions in which the Contractor elects to retain ownership; and

(ii) Assign title to the agency when requested under paragraph (d) of this clause and to enable the Government to obtain patent protection and plant variety protection for that subject invention in any country.

(2) The Contractor shall require, by written agreement, its employees, other than clerical and nontechnical employees, to disclose promptly in writing to personnel identified as responsible for the administration of patent matters and in the Contractor's format, each subject invention in order that the Contractor can comply with the disclosure provisions of paragraph (c) of this clause, and to execute all papers necessary to file patent applications on subject inventions and to establish the Government's rights in the subject inventions. The disclosure format should require, as a minimum, the information required by paragraph (c)(1) of this clause. The Contractor shall instruct such employees, through employee agreements or other suitable educational programs, as to the importance of reporting inventions in sufficient time to permit the filing of patent applications prior to U.S. or foreign statutory bars.

(3) The Contractor shall notify the Contracting Officer of any decisions not to file a nonprovisional patent application, continue the prosecution of a patent application, pay maintenance fees, or defend in a reexamination or opposition proceeding on a patent, in any country, not less than 30 days before the expiration of the response or filing period required by the relevant patent office.

(4) The Contractor shall include, within the specification of any United States nonprovisional patent or plant variety protection application and any patent or plant variety protection certificate issuing thereon covering a subject invention, the following statement, "This invention was made with Government support under (identify the contract) awarded by (identify the agency). The Government has certain rights in the invention."

(5) The Contractor shall provide the Contracting Officer the following:

(i) A listing every 12 months (or such longer period as the Contracting Officer may specify) from the date of the contract, of all subject inventions required to be disclosed during the period.

(ii) A final report prior to closeout of the contract listing all subject inventions or certifying that there were none.

(iii) Upon request, the filing date, serial number and title, a copy of the patent application, and patent number and issue date for any subject invention in any country in which the Contractor has applied for patents.

(iv) An irrevocable power to inspect and make copies of the patent application file, by the Government, when a Federal Government employee is a coinventor.

(f) Reporting on utilization of subject inventions. The Contractor shall submit, on request, periodic reports no more frequently than annually on the utilization of a subject invention or on efforts at obtaining utilization of the subject invention that are being made by the Contractor or its licensees or assignees. The reports shall include information regarding the status of development, date of first commercial sale or use, gross royalties received by the Contractor, and other data and information as the agency may reasonably specify. The Contractor also shall provide additional reports as may be requested by the agency in connection with any march-in proceeding undertaken by the agency in accordance with paragraph (h) of this clause. The Contractor also shall mark any utilization report as confidential/proprietary to help prevent inadvertent release outside the Government. As required by 35 U.S.C. 202(c)(5), the agency will not disclose that information to persons outside the Government without the Contractor's permission.

(g) Preference for United States industry. Notwithstanding any other provision of this clause, neither the Contractor nor any assignee shall grant to any person the exclusive right to use or sell any subject invention in the United States unless the person agrees that any products embodying the subject invention or produced through the use of the subject invention will be manufactured substantially in the United States. However, in individual cases, the requirement for an agreement may be waived by the agency upon a showing by the Contractor or its assignee that reasonable but unsuccessful efforts have been made to grant licenses on similar terms to potential licensees that would be likely to manufacture substantially in the United States, or that under the circumstances domestic manufacture is not commercially feasible.

(h) March-in rights. The Contractor acknowledges that, with respect to any subject invention in which it has retained ownership, the agency has the right to require licensing pursuant to 35 U.S.C. 203 and 210(c), and in accordance with the procedures in 37 CFR 401.6 and any supplemental regulations of the agency in effect on the date of contract award.

(i) Special provisions for contracts with nonprofit organizations. If the Contractor is a nonprofit organization, it shall –

(1) Not assign rights to a subject invention in the United States without the written approval of the agency, except where an assignment is made to an organization that has as one of its primary functions the management of inventions, provided, that the assignee shall be subject to the same provisions as the Contractor;

(2) Share royalties collected on a subject invention with the inventor, including Federal employee co-inventors (but through their agency if the agency deems it appropriate) when the subject invention is assigned in accordance with 35 U.S.C. 202(e) and 37 CFR 401.10;

(3) Use the balance of any royalties or income earned by the Contractor with respect to subject inventions, after payment of expenses (including payments to inventors) incidental to the administration of subject inventions for the support of scientific research or education; and

(4) Make efforts that are reasonable under the circumstances to attract licensees of subject inventions that are small business concerns, and give a preference to a small business concern when licensing a subject invention if the Contractor determines that the small business concern has a plan or proposal for marketing the invention which, if executed, is equally as likely to bring the invention to practical application as any plans or proposals from applicants that are not small business concerns; provided, that the Contractor is also satisfied that the small business concern has the capability and resources to carry out its plan or proposal. The decision whether to give a preference in any specific case will be at the discretion of the Contractor.

(5) Allow the Secretary of Commerce to review the Contractor's licensing program and decisions regarding small business applicants, and negotiate changes to its licensing policies, procedures, or practices with the Secretary of Commerce when the Secretary's review discloses that the Contractor could take reasonable steps to more effectively implement the requirements of paragraph (i)(4) of this clause.

(j) Communications. The Contractor shall contact the Contracting Officer for any communications regarding this clause.

(k) Subcontracts.

(1) The Contractor shall include the substance of this clause, including this paragraph (k), in all subcontracts for experimental, developmental, or research work to be performed by a small business concern or nonprofit organization.

(2) The Contractor shall include the clause in the NASA FAR Supplement at 1852.227-70, New Technology, suitably modified to identify the parties, in all subcontracts, regardless of tier, for experimental, developmental, research, design, or engineering work to be performed by other than a small business firm or nonprofit organization.

(3) At all tiers, the patent rights clause must be modified to identify the parties as follows: references to the Government are not changed, and the subcontractor has all rights and obligations of the Contractor in the clause. The Contractor shall not, as part of the consideration for awarding the subcontract, obtain rights in the subcontractor's subject inventions.

(4) In subcontracts, at any tier, the agency, the subcontractor, and the Contractor agree that the mutual obligations of the parties created by this clause constitute a contract between the subcontractor and the agency with respect to the matters covered by the clause; provided, however, that nothing in this paragraph is intended to confer any jurisdiction under the Contract Disputes Act in connection with proceedings under paragraph (h) of this clause.

(End of Clause)

I.10 52.227-14 RIGHTS IN DATA – GENERAL, (DEC 2007) (Deviation) / ALTERNATE I, (DEC 2007) (Deviation) / ALTERNATE II, (DEC 2007) (Deviation) / ALTERNATE III (DEC 2007) (Deviation) / AS MODIFIED PER 1852.227-14 RIGHTS IN DATA - GENERAL

(a) *Definitions.* As used in this clause—

"Computer database" or "database" means a collection of recorded information in a form capable of, and for the purpose of, being stored in, processed, and operated on by a computer. The term does not include computer software.

"Computer software"—

(1) Means

(i) Computer programs that comprise a series of instructions, rules, routines, or statements, regardless of the media in which recorded, that allow or cause a computer to perform a specific operation or series of operations; and

(ii) Recorded information comprising source code listings, design details, algorithms, processes, flow charts, formulas, and related material that would enable the computer program to be produced, created, or compiled.

(2) Does not include computer databases or computer software documentation.

"Computer software documentation" means owner's manuals, user's manuals, installation instructions, operating instructions, and other similar items, regardless of storage medium, that explain the capabilities of the computer software or provide instructions for using the software.

"Data" means recorded information, regardless of form or the media on which it may be recorded. The term includes technical data and computer software. The term does not include information incidental to contract administration, such as financial, administrative, cost or pricing, or management information.

"Form, fit, and function data" means data relating to items, components, or processes that are sufficient to enable physical and functional interchangeability, and data identifying source, size, configuration, mating and attachment characteristics, functional characteristics, and performance requirements. For computer software it means data identifying source, functional characteristics, and performance requirements but specifically excludes the source code, algorithms, processes, formulas, and flow charts of the software.

"Government purpose" means any activity in which the United States Government is a party, including, but not limited to, cooperative activities with international or multi-national defense organizations, or sales or transfers by the United States Government to foreign governments or international organizations. Government purposes include competitive procurement.

"Government purpose rights" means the rights to (i) Use, modify, reproduce, manufacture, release, perform, display, or disclose data within the Government without restriction; and (ii) Release or disclose data outside the Government and authorize persons to whom release or disclosure has been made to use, modify, reproduce, manufacture, release, perform, display, or disclose that data for United States Government purposes.

"Limited rights" means the rights of the Government in limited rights data as set forth in the Limited Rights Notice of paragraph (g)(3) if included in this clause.

"Limited rights data" means data, other than computer software, developed wholly or in part at private expense that embody trade secrets or are commercial or financial and confidential or privileged.

"Restricted computer software" means computer software developed wholly or in part at private expense and that is a trade secret, is commercial or financial and confidential or privileged, or is copyrighted computer software, including minor modifications of the computer software.

"Restricted rights," as used in this clause, means the rights of the Government in restricted computer software, as set forth in a Restricted Rights Notice of paragraph (g) if included in this clause, or as otherwise may be provided in a collateral agreement incorporated in and made part of this contract, including minor modifications of such computer software.

"Technical data" means recorded information (regardless of the form or method of the recording) of a scientific or technical nature (including computer databases and computer software documentation). This term does not include computer software or financial, administrative, cost or pricing, or management data or other information incidental to contract administration. The term includes recorded information of a scientific or technical nature that is included in computer databases (See 41 U.S.C. 403(8)).

"Unlimited rights" means the rights of the Government to use, disclose, reproduce, prepare derivative works, distribute copies to the public, and perform publicly and display publicly, in any manner and for any purpose, and to have or permit others to do so.

(b) Allocation of rights.

    (1) Except as provided in paragraph (c) of this clause, the Government shall have unlimited rights in—

        (i) Data first produced in the performance of this contract exclusively at Government expense;

        (ii) Form, fit, and function data delivered under this contract;

        (iii) Data delivered under this contract (except for restricted computer software) that constitute manuals or instructional and training material for installation, operation, or routine maintenance and repair of items, components, or processes delivered or furnished for use under this contract; and

       (iv) All other data delivered under this contract unless provided otherwise for limited rights data or restricted computer software in accordance with paragraph (g) of this clause.

(2) The Contractor shall have the right to—

       (i) Assert copyright in data first produced in the performance of this contract to the extent provided in paragraph (c)(1) of this clause;

       (ii) Use, release to others, reproduce, distribute, or publish any data first produced or specifically used by the Contractor in the performance of this contract, unless provided otherwise in paragraph (d) of this clause;

       (iii) Substantiate the use of, add, or correct limited rights, restricted rights, or copyright notices and to take other appropriate action, in accordance with paragraphs (e) and (f) of this clause; and

       (iv) Protect from unauthorized disclosure and use those data that are limited rights data or restricted computer software to the extent provided in paragraph (g) of this clause.

(3) There shall be a presumption that modifications to data identified in FAR 52.227-15 comprise limited rights data or restricted computer software.

(4) Data delivered under this contract, in which the Government previously obtained less than limited or restricted rights, as defined in paragraph (g) of this clause, pursuant to the terms of another contract or agreement, comprises limited rights data or restricted computer software under this contract.

(5) In the event this contract is terminated for default, the Government shall have Government purpose rights in all data first produced, and all software first developed, wholly or in part at private expense in performance of this contract.

(c) Copyright—

(1) Data first produced in the performance of this contract.

       (i) Unless provided otherwise in paragraph (d) of this clause, the Contractor may, without prior approval of the Contracting Officer, assert copyright in scientific and technical articles based on or containing data first produced in the performance of this contract and published in academic, technical or professional journals, symposia proceedings, or similar works. The prior, express written permission of the Contracting Officer is required to assert copyright in all other data first produced in the performance of this contract.

(ii) When authorized to assert copyright to the data, the Contractor shall affix the applicable copyright notices of 17 U.S.C. 401 or 402, and an acknowledgment of Government sponsorship (including contract number).

(iii) For data other than computer software, the Contractor grants to the Government, and others acting on its behalf, a paid-up, nonexclusive, irrevocable, worldwide license in such copyrighted data to reproduce, prepare derivative works, distribute copies to the public, and perform publicly and display publicly by or on behalf of the Government.   For computer software, the Contractor grants to the Government, and others acting on its behalf, a paid-up, nonexclusive, irrevocable, worldwide license in such copyrighted computer software to reproduce, prepare derivative works, and perform publicly and display publicly (but not to distribute copies to the public) by or on behalf of the Government.

(2) *Data not first produced in the performance of this contract.* The Contractor shall not, without the prior written permission of the Contracting Officer, incorporate in data delivered under this contract any data not first produced in the performance of this contract unless the Contractor—

(i) Identifies the data; and

(ii) Grants to the Government, or acquires on its behalf, a license of the same scope as set forth in paragraph (c)(1) of this clause or, if such data are restricted computer software, the Government shall acquire a copyright license as set forth in paragraph (g)(4) of this clause (if included in this contract) or as otherwise provided in a collateral agreement incorporated in or made part of this contract.

(3)   (i) The Contractor agrees not to establish claim to copyright, publish or release to others any computer software first produced in the performance of this contract without the Contracting Officer's prior written permission.

(ii) If the Government desires to obtain copyright in computer software first produced in the performance of this contract and permission has not been granted as set forth in paragraph (d)(3)(i) of this clause, the Contracting Officer may direct the Contractor to assert, or authorize the assertion of, claim to copyright in such data and to assign, or obtain the assignment of, such copyright to the Government or its designated assignee.

(iii) Whenever the word "establish" is used in this clause, with reference to a claim to copyright, it shall be construed to mean "assert".

(4) *Removal of copyright notices.* The Government will not remove any authorized copyright notices placed on data pursuant to this paragraph (c), and will include such notices on all reproductions of the data.

(d) *Release, publication, and use of data.* The Contractor shall have the right to use, release to others, reproduce, distribute, or publish any data first produced or specifically used by the Contractor in the performance of this contract, except—

(1) As prohibited by Federal law or regulation (*e.g.*, export control or national security laws or regulations);

(2) As expressly set forth in this contract; or

(3) If the Contractor receives or is given access to data necessary for the performance of this contract that contain restrictive markings, the Contractor shall treat the data in accordance with such markings unless specifically authorized otherwise in writing by the Contracting Officer.

(e) Unauthorized marking of data.

(1) Notwithstanding any other provisions of this contract concerning inspection or acceptance, if any data delivered under this contract are marked with the notices specified in paragraph (g)(3) or (g) (4) if included in this clause, and use of the notices is not authorized by this clause, or if the data bears any other restrictive or limiting markings not authorized by this contract, the Contracting Officer may at any time either return the data to the Contractor, or cancel or ignore the markings. However, pursuant to 41 U.S.C. 253d, the following procedures shall apply prior to canceling or ignoring the markings.

(i) The Contracting Officer will make written inquiry to the Contractor affording the Contractor 60 days from receipt of the inquiry to provide written justification to substantiate the propriety of the markings;

(ii) If the Contractor fails to respond or fails to provide written justification to substantiate the propriety of the markings within the 60-day period (or a longer time approved in writing by the Contracting Officer for good cause shown), the Government shall have the right to cancel or ignore the markings at any time after said period and the data will no longer be made subject to any disclosure prohibitions.

(iii) If the Contractor provides written justification to substantiate the propriety of the markings within the period set in paragraph (e)(1)(i) of this clause, the Contracting Officer will consider such written justification and determine whether or not the markings are to be cancelled or ignored. If the Contracting Officer determines that the markings are authorized, the Contractor will be so notified in writing. If the Contracting Officer determines, with concurrence of the head of the contracting activity, that the markings are not authorized, the Contracting Officer will furnish the Contractor a written determination, which determination will become the final agency decision regarding the appropriateness of the markings unless the Contractor files suit in a court of competent jurisdiction within 90 days of receipt of the Contracting Officer's decision. The Government will continue to abide by the markings under this paragraph (e)(1)(iii) until final resolution of the matter either by the Contracting Officer's determination becoming final (in which instance the Government will thereafter have the right to cancel or ignore the markings at any time and the data will no longer be made subject to any disclosure prohibitions), or by final disposition of the matter by court decision if suit is filed.

(2) The time limits in the procedures set forth in paragraph (e)(1) of this clause may be modified in accordance with agency regulations implementing the Freedom of Information Act (5 U.S.C. 552) if necessary to respond to a request thereunder.

(3) Except to the extent the Government's action occurs as the result of final disposition of the matter by a court of competent jurisdiction, the Contractor is not precluded by paragraph (e) of the clause from bringing a claim, in accordance with the Disputes clause of this contract, that may arise as the result of the Government removing or ignoring authorized markings on data delivered under this contract.

(f) Omitted or incorrect markings.

(1) Data delivered to the Government without any restrictive markings shall be deemed to have been furnished with unlimited rights. The Government is not liable for the disclosure, use, or reproduction of such data.

(2) If the unmarked data has not been disclosed without restriction outside the Government, the Contractor may request, within 6 months (or a longer time approved by the Contracting Officer in writing for good cause shown) after delivery of the data, permission to have authorized notices placed on the data at the Contractor's expense. The Contracting Officer may agree to do so if the Contractor—

(i) Identifies the data to which the omitted notice is to be applied;

(ii) Demonstrates that the omission of the notice was inadvertent;

(iii) Establishes that the proposed notice is authorized; and

(iv) Acknowledges that the Government has no liability for the disclosure, use, or reproduction of any data made prior to the addition of the notice or resulting from the omission of the notice.

(3) If data has been marked with an incorrect notice, the Contracting Officer may—

(i) Permit correction of the notice at the Contractor's expense if the Contractor identifies the data and demonstrates that the correct notice is authorized; or

(ii) Correct any incorrect notices.

(g) Protection of limited rights data and restricted computer software.

(1) The Contractor may withhold from delivery qualifying limited rights data or restricted computer software that are not data identified in paragraphs (b)(1)(i), (ii), and (iii) of this clause. As a condition to this withholding, the Contractor shall—

(i) Identify the data being withheld; and

(ii) Furnish form, fit, and function data instead.

(2) Limited rights data that are formatted as a computer database for delivery to the Government shall be treated as limited rights data and not restricted computer software.

(3) Notwithstanding paragraph (g)(1) of this clause, the contract may identify and specify the delivery of limited rights data, or the Contracting Officer may require by written request the delivery of limited rights data that has been withheld or would otherwise be entitled to be withheld. If delivery of that data is required, the Contractor shall affix the following "Limited Rights Notice" to the data and the Government will treat the data, subject to the provisions of paragraphs (e) and (f) of this clause, in accordance with the notice:

Limited Rights Notice (Dec 2007) (Deviation)

(a) These data are submitted with limited rights under Government Contract No. _____ (and subcontract _____, if appropriate). These data may be reproduced and used by the Government with the express limitation that they will not, without written permission of the Contractor, be used for purposes of manufacture nor disclosed outside the Government; except that the Government may disclose these data outside the Government to support service contractors and/or pursuant to agreements and contracts related to the International Space Station; provided that the Government makes such disclosure subject to prohibition against further use and disclosure.

(b) In the event this contract is terminated for Contractor default, the Government shall have Government purpose rights in all data first produced wholly or in part at private expense in performance of this contract.

(c) This notice shall be marked on any reproduction of these data, in whole or in part.

(End of notice)

(4) (i) Notwithstanding paragraph (g)(1) of this clause, the contract may identify and specify the delivery of restricted computer software, or the Contracting Officer may require by written request the delivery of restricted computer software that has been withheld or would otherwise be entitled to be withheld. If delivery of that computer software is required, the Contractor shall affix the following "Restricted Rights Notice" to the computer software and the Government will treat the computer software, subject to paragraphs (e) and (f) of this clause, in accordance with the notice:

Restricted Rights Notice (Dec 2007) (Deviation)

(a) This computer software is submitted with restricted rights under Government Contract No. _____ (and subcontract _____, if appropriate). It may not be used, reproduced, or

disclosed by the Government except as provided in paragraph (b) of this notice or as otherwise expressly stated in the contract.

(b) This computer software may be—

(1) Used or copied for use with the computer(s) for which it was acquired, including use at any Government installation to which the computer(s) may be transferred;

(2) Used or copied for use with a backup computer if any computer for which it was acquired is inoperative;

(3) Reproduced for safekeeping (archives) or backup purposes;

(4) Modified, adapted, or combined with other computer software, provided that the modified, adapted, or combined portions of the derivative software incorporating any of the delivered, restricted computer software shall be subject to the same restricted rights;

(5) Disclosed to and reproduced for use by support service Contractors or their subcontractors in accordance with paragraphs (b)(1) through (4) of this notice; and

(6) Used or copied for use with a replacement computer.

(c) Notwithstanding the foregoing, if this computer software is copyrighted computer software, it is licensed to the Government with the minimum rights set forth in paragraph (b) of this notice.

(d) Any other rights or limitations regarding the use, duplication, or disclosure of this computer software are to be expressly stated in, or incorporated in, the contract.

(e) In the event this contract is terminated for Contractor default, the Government shall have Government purpose rights in all computer software first developed wholly or in part at private expense in performance of this contract.

(f) This notice shall be marked on any reproduction of this computer software, in whole or in part.

(End of notice)

(ii) Where it is impractical to include the Restricted Rights Notice on restricted computer software, the following short-form notice may be used instead:

Restricted Rights Notice Short Form (Jun 1987)

Use, reproduction, or disclosure is subject to restrictions set forth in Contract No. _____ (and subcontract, if appropriate) with _____ (name of Contractor and subcontractor).

(End of notice)

(iii) If restricted computer software is delivered with the copyright notice of 17 U.S.C. 401, it will be presumed to be licensed to the Government without disclosure prohibitions, with the minimum rights set forth in paragraph (b) of this clause.

(h) *Subcontracting.* The Contractor shall obtain from its subcontractors all data and rights therein necessary to fulfill the Contractor's obligations to the Government under this contract. If a subcontractor refuses to accept terms affording the Government those rights, the Contractor shall promptly notify the Contracting Officer of the refusal and shall not proceed with the subcontract award without authorization in writing from the Contracting Officer.

(i) *Relationship to patents or other rights.* Nothing contained in this clause shall imply a license to the Government under any patent or be construed as affecting the scope of any license or other right otherwise granted to the Government except as specifically set forth in paragraph (b) of this clause.

(End of Clause)

I.11   52.232-32   PERFORMANCE-BASED PAYMENTS (APR 2012) (Deviation), (Applicable to Interim Performance-Based Payments Events)

(a) *Amount of payments and limitations on payments.* Subject to such other limitations and conditions as are specified in this contract and this clause, the amount of payments and limitations on payments shall be specified in the contract's description of the basis for payment.

(b) *Contractor request for performance-based payment.* The Contractor may submit requests for payment of performance-based payments not more frequently than monthly, in a form and manner acceptable to the Contracting Officer. Unless otherwise authorized by the Contracting Officer, all performance-based payments in any period for which payment is being requested shall be included in a single request, appropriately itemized and totaled. The Contractor's request shall contain the information and certification detailed in paragraphs (l) and (m) of this clause.

(c) *Approval and payment of requests.*

(1) The Contractor shall not be entitled to payment of a request for performance-based payment prior to successful accomplishment of the event or performance criterion for which payment is requested. The Contracting Officer shall determine whether the event or performance criterion for which payment is requested has been successfully accomplished in accordance with the terms of the contract. The Contracting Officer may, at any time, require the Contractor to substantiate the successful performance of any event or performance criterion which has been or is represented as being payable.

(2) A payment under this performance-based payment clause is a contract financing payment under the Prompt Payment clause of this contract and not subject to the interest penalty provisions of the Prompt Payment Act. The designated payment office will pay approved requests on the

15th day after receipt of the request for performance-based payment by the designated payment office. However, the designated payment office is not required to provide payment if the Contracting Officer requires substantiation as provided in paragraph (c)(1) of this clause, or inquires into the status of an event or performance criterion, or into any of the conditions listed in paragraph (e) of this clause, or into the Contractor certification. The payment period will not begin until the Contracting Officer approves the request.

(3) The approval by the Contracting Officer of a request for performance-based payment does not constitute an acceptance by the Government and does not excuse the Contractor from performance of obligations under this contract.

(d) *Liquidation of performance-based payments.*

(1) Performance-based finance amounts paid prior to payment for delivery of an item shall be liquidated by deducting a percentage or a designated dollar amount from the delivery payment. If the performance-based finance payments are on a delivery item basis, the liquidation amount for each such line item shall be the percent of that delivery item price that was previously paid under performance-based finance payments or the designated dollar amount. If the performance-based finance payments are on a whole contract basis, liquidation shall be by either predesignated liquidation amounts or a liquidation percentage.

(2) If at any time the amount of payments under this contract exceeds any limitation in this contract, the Contractor shall repay to the Government the excess. Unless otherwise determined by the Contracting Officer, such excess shall be credited as a reduction in the unliquidated performance-based payment balance(s), after adjustment of invoice payments and balances for any retroactive price adjustments.

(e) *Reduction or suspension of performance-based payments.* The Contracting Officer may reduce or suspend performance-based payments, liquidate performance-based payments by deduction from any payment under the contract, or take a combination of these actions after finding upon substantial evidence any of the following conditions:

(1) The Contractor failed to comply with any material requirement of this contract (which includes paragraphs (h) and (i) of this clause).

(2) Performance of this contract is endangered by the Contractor's -

(i) Failure to make progress; or

(ii) Unsatisfactory financial condition.

(3) The Contractor is delinquent in payment of any subcontractor or supplier under this contract in the ordinary course of business.

(f) *Reserved.*

(g) *Risk of loss.* Before delivery to and acceptance by the Government, the Contractor shall bear the risk of loss for property, the title to which vests in the Government under this clause, except to the extent the Government expressly assumes the risk. If any property is lost (see 45.101), the basis of payment (the events or performance criteria) to which the property is related shall be deemed to be not in compliance with the terms of the contract and not payable (if the property is part of or needed for performance), and the Contractor shall refund the related performance-based payments in accordance with paragraph (d) of this clause.

(h) *Records and controls.* The Contractor shall maintain records and controls adequate for administration of this clause. The Contractor shall have no entitlement to performance-based payments during any time the Contractor's records or controls are determined by the Contracting Officer to be inadequate for administration of this clause.

(i) *Reports and Government access.* The Contractor shall promptly furnish reports, certificates, financial statements, and other pertinent information requested by the Contracting Officer for the administration of this clause and to determine that an event or other criterion prompting a financing payment has been successfully accomplished. The Contractor shall give the Government reasonable opportunity to examine and verify the Contractor's records and to examine and verify the Contractor's performance of this contract for administration of this clause.

(j) *Special terms regarding default.* If this contract is terminated under the Default clause, (1) the Contractor shall, on demand, repay to the Government the amount of unliquidated performance-based payments, and (2) title shall vest in the Contractor, on full liquidation of all performance-based payments, for all property for which the Government elects not to require delivery under the Default clause of this contract. The Government shall be liable for no payment except as provided by the Default clause.

(k) *Reservation of rights.*
    (1) No payment or vesting of title under this clause shall -

        (i) Excuse the Contractor from performance of obligations under this contract; or

        (ii) Constitute a waiver of any of the rights or remedies of the parties under the contract.

    (2) The Government's rights and remedies under this clause -

        (i) Shall not be exclusive, but rather shall be in addition to any other rights and remedies provided by law or this contract; and

        (ii) Shall not be affected by delayed, partial, or omitted exercise of any right, remedy, power, or privilege, nor shall such exercise or any single exercise preclude or impair any further exercise under this clause or the exercise of any other right, power, or privilege of the Government.

(l) *Content of Contractor's request for performance-based payment.* The Contractor's request for performance-based payment shall contain the following:

    (1) The name and address of the Contractor;

    (2) The date of the request for performance-based payment;

    (3) The contract number and/or other identifier of the contract or order under which the request is made;

    (4) Such information and documentation as is required by the contract's description of the basis for payment; and

    (5) A certification by a Contractor official authorized to bind the Contractor, as specified in paragraph (m) of this clause.

(m) *Content of Contractor's certification.* As required in paragraph (l)(5) of this clause, the Contractor shall make the following certification in each request for performance-based payment:

I certify to the best of my knowledge and belief that -

    (1) This request for performance-based payment is true and correct; this request (and attachments) has been prepared from the books and records of the Contractor, in accordance with the contract and the instructions of the Contracting Officer;

    (2) (Except as reported in writing on _____), all payments to subcontractors and suppliers under this contract have been paid, or will be paid, currently, when due in the ordinary course of business;

    (3) There are no encumbrances (except as reported in writing on _____) against the property acquired or produced for, and allocated or properly chargeable to, the contract which would affect or impair the Government's title;

    (4) There has been no materially adverse change in the financial condition of the Contractor since the submission by the Contractor to the Government of the most recent written information dated _____; and

    (5) After the making of this requested performance-based payment, the amount of all payments for each deliverable item for which performance-based payments have been requested will not exceed any limitation in the contract, and the amount of all payments under the contract will not exceed any limitation in the contract.

                                (End of Clause)

I.12   52.232-99   PROVIDING ACCELERATED PAYMENT TO SMALL BUSINESS SUBCONTRACTORS (AUG 2012) (DEVIATION)

This clause implements the temporary policy provided by OMB Policy Memorandum M-12-16, Providing Prompt Payment to Small Business Subcontractors, dated July 11, 2012.

(a) Upon receipt of accelerated payments from the Government, the Contractor is required to make accelerated payments to small business subcontractors to the maximum extent practicable after receipt of a proper invoice and all proper documentation from the small business subcontractor.

(b) Include the substance of this clause, including this paragraph (b), in all subcontracts with small business concerns.

(c) The acceleration of payments under this clause does not provide any new rights under the Prompt Payment Act.

(End of Clause)

I.13   52.249-8   DEFAULT (FIXED-PRICE SUPPLY AND SERVICE) (APR 1984) (Applicable To CLIN 002 And Any Appropriate Task Orders Per CLIN 003) (DEVIATION)

(a) (1) The Government may, subject to paragraphs (c) and (d) and (i) of this clause, by written notice of default to the Contractor, terminate this contract in whole or in part if the Contractor fails to --

   (i) Deliver the supplies or to perform the services within the time specified in this contract or any extension;

   (ii) Make progress, so as to endanger performance of this contract (but see subparagraph (a)(2) of this clause); or

   (iii) Perform any of the other provisions of this contract (but see subparagraph (a)(2) of this clause).

(2) The Government's right to terminate this contract under subdivisions (a)(1)(ii) and (1)(iii) of this clause, may be exercised if the Contractor does not cure such failure within 10 days (or more if authorized in writing by the Contracting Officer) after receipt of the notice from the Contracting Officer specifying the failure.

(b) If the Government terminates this contract in whole or in part, it may acquire, under the terms and in the manner the Contracting Officer considers appropriate, supplies or services similar to those terminated, and the Contractor will be liable to the Government for any excess costs for those supplies or services limited to $200 million for all task orders ordered and not accepted under CLIN 002 and CLIN 003. The $200 million is a cumulative total to include any excess re-procurement costs assessed under FAR 52.249-9, *Default (Fixed-Price Research and Development)* as modified within this contract. However, the Contractor shall continue the work not terminated.

(c) Except for defaults of subcontractors at any tier, the Contractor shall not be liable for any excess costs if the failure to perform the contract arises from causes beyond the control and without the fault or negligence of the Contractor. Examples of such causes include

   (1) acts of God or of the public enemy,

   (2) acts of the Government in either its sovereign or contractual capacity,

   (3) fires,

   (4) floods,

   (5) epidemics,

   (6) quarantine restrictions,

   (7) strikes,

   (8) freight embargoes, and

   (9) unusually severe weather.

In each instance the failure to perform must be beyond the control and without the fault or negligence of the Contractor.

(d) If the failure to perform is caused by the default of a subcontractor at any tier, and if the cause of the default is beyond the control of both the Contractor and subcontractor, and without the fault or negligence of either, the Contractor shall not be liable for any excess costs for failure to perform, unless the subcontracted supplies or services were obtainable from other sources in sufficient time for the Contractor to meet the required delivery schedule.

(e) If this contract is terminated for default, the Government may require the Contractor to transfer title and deliver to the Government, as directed by the Contracting Officer, any

   (1) completed supplies, and

   (2) partially completed supplies and materials, parts, tools, dies, jigs, fixtures, plans, drawings, information, and contract rights (collectively referred to as "manufacturing materials" in this

clause) that the Contractor has specifically produced or acquired for the terminated portion of this contract.

Upon direction of the Contracting Officer, the Contractor shall also protect and preserve property in its possession in which the Government has an interest.

(f) The Government shall pay contract price for completed supplies delivered and accepted. The Contractor and Contracting Officer shall agree on the amount of payment for manufacturing materials delivered and accepted and for the protection and preservation of the property. Failure to agree will be a dispute under the Disputes clause. The Government may withhold from these amounts any sum the Contracting Officer determines to be necessary to protect the Government against loss because of outstanding liens or claims of former lien holders.

(g) If, after termination, it is determined that the Contractor was not in default, or that the default was excusable, the rights and obligations of the parties shall be the same as if the termination had been issued for the convenience of the Government.

(h) The rights and remedies of the Government in this clause are in addition to any other rights and remedies provided by law or under this contract.

(i) The rights and remedies of the Government under this clause are superseded by the conditions in clause H.21 *Post Certification Mission Success Determination*, specific to the Post Certification Mission (PCM) flights that end in a mission failure or partial mission success. A mission failure or partial mission success determination pursuant to clause H.21 for a PCM shall not be the basis for a default termination for that PCM task order under this clause. For all other activities under the contract not part of this PCM task order, the Government reserves the right to terminate the contract for default.

(End of Clause)

I.14   52.249-9   **DEFAULT (FIXED-PRICE RESEARCH AND DEVELOPMENT) (APR 1984) (Applicable To CLIN 001 And Any Appropriate Task Orders Per CLIN 003) (DEVIATION)**

(a) (1) The Government may, subject to paragraphs (c) and (d) of this clause, by written Notice of Default to the Contractor, terminate this contract in whole or in part if the Contractor fails to --

   (i) Perform the work under the contract within the time specified in this contract or any extension;

   (ii) Prosecute the work so as to endanger performance of this contract (but see subparagraph (a)(2) of this clause); or

   (iii) Perform any of the other provisions of this contract (but see subparagraph (a)(2) of this clause).

   (2) The Government's right to terminate this contract under subdivisions (a)(1)(ii) and (iii) of this clause may be exercised if the Contractor does not cure such failure within 10 days (or more, if authorized in writing by the Contracting Officer) after receipt of the notice from the Contracting Officer specifying the failure.

(b) If the Government terminates this contract in whole or in part, it may acquire, under the terms and in the manner the Contracting Officer considers appropriate, work similar to the work terminated, and the Contractor will be liable to the Government for any excess costs for the similar work limited to 200 million dollars, for work under CLIN 001 and for all task orders ordered and not accepted under CLIN 003. The 200 million dollars is a cumulative total to include any excess re-procurement costs assessed under FAR 52.249-8, *Default (Fixed-Price Supply and Service)* as modified within this contract. However, the Contractor shall continue the work not terminated.

(c) Except for defaults of subcontractors at any tier, the Contractor shall not be liable for any excess costs if the failure to perform the contract arises from causes beyond the control and without the fault or negligence of the Contractor. Examples of such causes include

   (1) acts of God or of the public enemy,

   (2) acts of the Government in either its sovereign or contractual capacity,

   (3) fires,

   (4) floods,

   (5) epidemics,

   (6) quarantine restrictions,

(7) strikes,

(8) freight embargoes, and

(9) unusually severe weather.

In each instance the failure to perform must be beyond the control and without the fault or negligence of the Contractor.

(d) If the failure to perform is caused by the default of a subcontractor at any tier, and if the cause of the default is beyond the control of both the Contractor and subcontractor, and without the fault or negligence of either, the Contractor shall not be liable for any excess costs for failure to perform, unless the subcontracted supplies or services were obtainable from other sources in sufficient time for the Contractor to meet the required delivery schedule or other performance requirements.

(e) If this contract is terminated for default, the Government may require the Contractor to transfer title and deliver to the Government, as directed by the Contracting Officer, any

(1) completed or partially completed work not previously delivered to, and accepted by, the Government and

(2) other property, including contract rights, specifically produced or acquired for the terminated portion of this contract.

Upon direction of the Contracting Officer, the Contractor shall also protect and preserve property in its possession in which the Government has an interest.

(f) The Government shall pay the contract price, if separately stated, for completed work it has accepted and the amount agreed upon by the Contractor and the Contracting Officer for

(1) completed work for which no separate price is stated,

(2) partially completed work,

(3) other property described above that it accepts, and

(4) the protection and preservation of the property.

Failure to agree will be a dispute under the Disputes clause. The Government may withhold from these amounts any sum the Contracting Officer determines to be necessary to protect the Government against loss from outstanding liens or claims of former lien holders.

(g) If, after termination, it is determined that the Contractor was not in default, or that the default was excusable, the rights and obligations of the parties shall be the same as if the termination had been issued for the convenience of the Government.

(h) The rights and remedies of the Government in this clause are in addition to any other rights and remedies provided by law or under this contract.

(End of Clause)

I.15   52.252-6 AUTHORIZED DEVIATIONS IN CLAUSES (APR 1984)

(a) The use in this solicitation or contract of any Federal Acquisition Regulation (48 CFR Chapter 1) clause with an authorized deviation is indicated by the addition of "(DEVIATION)" after the date of the clause.

(b) The use in this solicitation or contract of any NFS (48 CFR Chapter 18) clause with an authorized deviation is indicated by the addition of "(DEVIATION)" after the name of the regulation.

(End of Clause)

I.16   NFS 1852.215-84   OMBUDSMAN. (NOV 2011) -- Alternate I (JUN 2000)

(a) An ombudsman has been appointed to hear and facilitate the resolution of concerns from Offerors, potential Offerors, and Contractors during the preaward and postaward phases of this acquisition. When requested, the ombudsman will maintain strict confidentiality as to the source of the concern. The existence of the ombudsman is not to diminish the authority of the contracting officer, the Source Evaluation Board, or the selection official. Further, the ombudsman does not participate in the evaluation of proposals, the source selection process, or the adjudication of formal contract disputes. Therefore, before consulting with an ombudsman, interested parties must first address their concerns, issues, disagreements, and/or recommendations to the contracting officer for resolution.

(b) If resolution cannot be made by the contracting officer, interested parties may contact the installation ombudsman, whose name, address, telephone number, facsimile number, and email address may be found at: http://prod.nais.nasa.gov/pub/pub_library/Omb.html. Concerns, issues, disagreements, and recommendations which cannot be resolved at the installation may be referred to the Agency ombudsman identified at the above URL. Please do not contact the ombudsman to request copies of the solicitation, verify offer due date, or clarify technical requirements. Such inquiries shall be directed to the Contracting Officer or as specified elsewhere in this document.

(c) If this is a task or delivery order contract, the ombudsman shall review complaints from Contractors and ensure they are afforded a fair opportunity to be considered, consistent with the procedures of the contract.

(End of Clause)

I.17 NFS 1852.225-71 RESTRICTION ON FUNDING ACTIVITY WITH CHINA (FEB 2012)

(a) Definition - "China" or "Chinese-owned company" means the People's Republic of China, any company owned by the People's Republic of China or any company incorporated under the laws of the People's Republic of China.

(b) Public Laws 112-10, Section 1340(a) and 112-55, Section 539, restrict NASA from contracting to participate, collaborate, coordinate bilaterally in any way with China or a Chinese-owned company using funds appropriated on or after April 25, 2011. Contracts for commercial and non developmental items are exempted from the prohibition because they constitute purchase of goods or services that would not involve participation, collaboration, or coordination between the parties.

(c) This contract may use restricted funding that was appropriated on or after April 25, 2011. The Contractor shall not contract with China or Chinese-owned companies for any effort related to this contract except for acquisition of commercial and non-developmental items. If the Contractor anticipates making an award to China or Chinese-owned companies, the Contractor must contact the contracting officer to determine if funding on this contract can be used for that purpose.

(d) Subcontracts - The Contractor shall include the substance of this clause in all subcontracts made hereunder.

(End of Clause)

I.18 NFS 1852.237-72 ACCESS TO SENSITIVE INFORMATION (JUN 2005)

(a) As used in this clause, "sensitive information'" refers to information that a Contractor has developed at private expense, or that the Government has generated that qualifies for an exception to the Freedom of Information Act, which is not currently in the public domain, and which may embody trade secrets or commercial or financial information, and which may be sensitive or privileged.

(b) To assist NASA in accomplishing management activities and administrative functions, the Contractor shall provide the services specified elsewhere in this contract.

(c) If performing this contract entails access to sensitive information, as defined above, the Contractor agrees to--

(1) Utilize any sensitive information coming into its possession only for the purposes of performing the services specified in this contract, and not to improve its own competitive position in another procurement.

(2) Safeguard sensitive information coming into its possession from unauthorized use and disclosure.

(3) Allow access to sensitive information only to those employees that need it to perform services under this contract.

(4) Preclude access and disclosure of sensitive information to persons and entities outside of the Contractor's organization.

(5) Train employees who may require access to sensitive information about their obligations to utilize it only to perform the services specified in this contract and to safeguard it from unauthorized use and disclosure.

(6) Obtain a written affirmation from each employee that he/she has received and will comply with training on the authorized uses and mandatory protections of sensitive information needed in performing this contract.

(7) Administer a monitoring process to ensure that employees comply with all reasonable security procedures, report any breaches to the Contracting Officer, and implement any necessary corrective actions.

(d) The Contractor will comply with all procedures and obligations specified in its Organizational Conflicts of Interest Avoidance Plan, which this contract incorporates as a compliance document.

(e) The nature of the work on this contract may subject the Contractor and its employees to a variety of laws and regulations relating to ethics, conflicts of interest, corruption, and other criminal or civil matters relating to the award and administration of government contracts. Recognizing that this contract establishes a high standard of accountability and trust, the Government will carefully review the Contractor's performance in relation to the mandates and restrictions found in these laws and regulations. Unauthorized uses or disclosures of sensitive information may result in termination of this contract for default, or in debarment of the Contractor for serious misconduct affecting present responsibility as a Government Contractor.

(f) The Contractor shall include the substance of this clause, including this paragraph (f), suitably modified to reflect the relationship of the parties, in all subcontracts that may involve access to sensitive information

(End of Clause)

I.19   NFS 1852.237-73   RELEASE OF SENSITIVE INFORMATION (JUN 2005)

(a) As used in this clause, "Sensitive information" refers to information, not currently in the public domain, that the Contractor has developed at private expense, that may embody trade secrets or commercial or financial information, and that may be sensitive or privileged.

(b) In accomplishing management activities and administrative functions, NASA relies heavily on the support of various service providers. To support NASA activities and functions, these service providers, as well as their subcontractors and their individual employees, may need access to sensitive information submitted by the Contractor under this contract. By submitting this proposal or performing this contract, the Contractor agrees that NASA may release to its service providers, their subcontractors, and their individual employees, sensitive information submitted during the course of this procurement, subject to the enumerated protections mandated by the clause at 1852.237-72, *Access to Sensitive Information*.

(c) (1)   The Contractor shall identify any sensitive information submitted in support of this proposal or in performing this contract. For purposes of identifying sensitive information, the Contractor may, in addition to any other notice or legend otherwise required, use a notice similar to the following:

Mark the title page with the following legend:

This proposal or document includes sensitive information that NASA shall not disclose outside the Agency and its service providers that support management activities and administrative functions. To gain access to this sensitive information, a service provider's contract must contain the clause at NFS 1852.237-72, *Access to Sensitive Information*. Consistent with this clause, the service provider shall not duplicate, use, or disclose the information in whole or in part for any purpose other than to perform the services specified in its contract. This restriction does not limit the Government's right to use this information if it is obtained from another source without restriction. The information subject to this restriction is contained in pages [*insert page numbers or other identification of pages*]. Mark each page of sensitive information the Contractor wishes to restrict with the following legend:

Use or disclosure of sensitive information contained on this page is subject to the restriction on the title page of this proposal or document.

(2)   The Contracting Officer shall evaluate the facts supporting any claim that particular information is "sensitive." This evaluation shall consider the time and resources necessary to protect the information in accordance with the detailed safeguards mandated by the clause at 1852.237-72, *Access to Sensitive Information*. However, unless the Contracting Officer decides, with the advice of Center counsel, that reasonable grounds exist to challenge the Contractor's claim that particular information is sensitive, NASA and its service providers and their employees shall comply with all of the safeguards contained in paragraph (d) of this clause.

(d) To receive access to sensitive information needed to assist NASA in accomplishing management activities and administrative functions, the service provider must be operating under a contract that contains the clause at 1852.237-72, *Access to Sensitive Information*. This clause obligates the service provider to do the following:

(1) Comply with all specified procedures and obligations, including the Organizational Conflicts of Interest Avoidance Plan, which the contract has incorporated as a compliance document.

(2) Utilize any sensitive information coming into its possession only for the purpose of performing the services specified in its contract.

(3) Safeguard sensitive information coming into its possession from unauthorized use and disclosure.

(4) Allow access to sensitive information only to those employees that need it to perform services under its contract.

(5) Preclude access and disclosure of sensitive information to persons and entities outside of the service provider's organization.

(6) Train employees who may require access to sensitive information about their obligations to utilize it only to perform the services specified in its contract and to safeguard it from unauthorized use and disclosure.

(7) Obtain a written affirmation from each employee that he/she has received and will comply with training on the authorized uses and mandatory protections of sensitive information needed in performing this contract.

(8) Administer a monitoring process to ensure that employees comply with all reasonable security procedures, report any breaches to the Contracting Officer, and implement any necessary corrective actions.

(e) When the service provider will have primary responsibility for operating an information technology system for NASA that contains sensitive information, the service provider's contract shall include the clause at 1852.204-76, *Security Requirements for Unclassified Information Technology Resources*. The Security Requirements clause requires the service provider to implement an Information Technology Security Plan to protect information processed, stored, or transmitted from unauthorized access, alteration, disclosure, or use. Service provider personnel requiring privileged access or limited privileged access to these information technology systems are subject to screening using the standard National Agency Check (NAC) forms appropriate to the level of risk for adverse impact to NASA missions. The Contracting Officer may allow the service provider to conduct its own screening, provided the service provider employs substantially equivalent screening procedures.

(f) This clause does not affect NASA's responsibilities under the Freedom of Information Act.

(g) The Contractor shall insert this clause, including this paragraph (g), suitably modified to reflect the relationship of the parties, in all subcontracts that may require the furnishing of sensitive information.

(End of Clause)

SECTION J. LIST OF DOCUMENTS, EXHIBITS, AND OTHER ATTACHMENTS

J.1 LIST OF ATTACHMENTS

The following documents are attached hereto and made a part of this contract:

Attachment	Document Revision Date
Attachment J-01, Integrated Crew Transportation System Requirements	See Attachment
Attachment J-02, Data Requirement Deliverables (DRDs)	See Attachment
Attachment J-03, Contract Performance Work Statement (PWS)	See Attachment
Attachment J-03, Appendix A, Milestone Acceptance Criteria and Payment Schedule	See Attachment
Attachment J-03, Appendix B, PCM Milestone Acceptance Criteria and Payment Schedule	See Attachment
Attachment J-04, Small Business Subcontracting Plan	See Attachment
Attachment J-05, Glossary and Acronym List	See Attachment
Attachment J-06, Personal Identity Verification (PIV) Card Issuance Procedure	See Attachment

(End of Clause)

Attachment J-02
Data Requirement Deliverables (DRDs)

Attachment J-02

1.0 DATA REQUIREMENTS LIST (DRL) DESCRIPTION
The DRL provides the Data Requirement Deliverable (DRD) number, title, data type, and submittal frequency for each data deliverable item.

2.0 ORGANIZATION OF DATA REQUIREMENTS LIST (DRL)

2.1 DRD Number
For the purpose of classification and control, the individual data deliverables in the DRL are grouped into the following categories:

- 0XX   series DRDs applicable to all contract activities
- 1XX   series DRDs applicable to Contract Line Item Number (CLIN) 001, applicable to CLIN 002 Post Certification Missions, Certification maintenance, and any re-Certification
- 2XX   series DRDs applicable to CLIN 002, applicable to CLIN 001 for crewed flight tests

2.2 Data Types
The types of data and their contractually applicable requirements for approval and delivery after contract award are:

TYPE	DESCRIPTION
1	All submittals of and interim changes to Type 1 DRDs require written approval from NASA before formal release for use or implementation. Type 1 DRDs shall be delivered by the Contractor into a NASA location as specified by the Contracting Officer (CO).
2	For Type 2 DRDs, NASA reserves a time-limited right to provide written disapproval of any submittal of and interim changes to those submittals. Type 2 DRDs shall be delivered by the Contractor into a NASA location as specified by the Contracting Officer not less than 45 calendar days prior to its release for use or implementation. The Contractor shall clearly identify the target release date in the "submitted for review" transmittal. If the Contractor has not been notified of any disapproval prior to the target release date, the data shall be considered approved. To be an acceptable DRD submission, disapproved data shall be revised to remove causes for the disapproval and re-submitted for approval before its release.
3	Type 3 DRDs shall be delivered either electronically or in hardcopy by the Contractor into a NASA location as specified by the Contracting Officer. Type 3 DRDs do not require NASA approval; however, the DRD must satisfy all applicable contractual requirements.

TYPE	DESCRIPTION
4	Type 4 DRDs shall be delivered by the Contractor within the Contractor's electronic system where NASA has been granted read and downloadable access through contract completion. The Contractor's act of placing the data within their system wherein NASA is provided the ability to read and download the data shall constitute delivery for purposes of defining NASA's rights in data as set forth in FAR 52.227-14, *Rights in Data – General (Deviation)*, as modified in this contract. Type 4 DRDs do not require NASA approval; however, the DRD must satisfy all applicable contractual requirements. For Type 4 DRDs, the Contractor shall notify the Contracting Officer or designated representatives when the data has been delivered into the Contractor system.

In the cases where the DRL classifies a DRD with two data type requirements, (e.g., DRD 002 is a Type 2/4), the DRD will clearly identify the data type requirements as well as the delivery requirement associated with each type.

2.3 Delivery Fidelity

In addition to the required frequency for data deliverable submittals, the DRL also defines the level of readiness/fidelity, which applies to the submission of DRDs:

Baseline (B) - A preliminary version of a delivery for NASA review. Baseline submittals may contain some To be Determined (TBDs). Baseline version fidelity shall reflect the Contractor's internally approved baseline of the product and be adequate to permit NASA disposition in accordance with the DRD Type or Attachment J-03, Appendix A, *Milestone Acceptance Criteria and Payment Schedule*. Baseline versions may be submitted periodically leading to a Final version.

Final (F) – A Final version of a delivery shall reflect the Contractor's internally approved final version of the product and is ready for NASA disposition in accordance with the DRD Type or Attachment J-03, Appendix A, *Milestone Acceptance Criteria and Payment Schedule*. No TBDs may be included. Unless otherwise specified within the DRD, after final version DRD has been dispositioned by NASA, the contractor shall submit any changes or additions for NASA review and disposition in accordance with the DRD Type.

Attachment J-02

3.0 DATA REQUIREMENT DOCUMENT
This section provides a description of the fields of the Data Requirement Documents (DRDs).

 A. DRD No.: Unique identifier for the DRD.
 B. DRD Title: Unique name for the DRD.
 C. Date: Date prepared.
 D. Purpose / Use: The purpose of and NASA's intended use for the DRD.
 E. Remarks: This field provides additional submittal information, if necessary.
 F. Data Requirements: This field provides the detailed description of the required and/or expected content and scope of the deliverable(s).

4.0 DATA TRANSMITTAL AND FORMAT
This section provides additional detail regarding the transmittal and format of the DRDs.

4.1 Data Transmittal
DRDs shall be transmitted to NASA via electronically, hardcopy, or by other mechanism agreed to by the Contracting Officer. The Contractor shall notify the Contracting Officer and the Contracting Officer Representative (COR) in writing of DRD delivery.

4.1.1 Data Transmittal Package
For each DRD, the transmittal package shall include:
 (a) Contractor transmittal memorandum that provides the following information:
  (1) Contract number.
  (2) Contractor name.
  (3) DRD number.
  (4) DRD data type (specified in "Type" column of the DRL).
  (5) Submission date or milestone being satisfied.
  (6) Document number and revision.
  (7) Document title.
  (8) File names of all files being delivered; multiple files per document must be clearly related to the document.
  (9) Distribution (Notification list as defined by the DRD distribution field and the Contracting Officer's letter).
  (10) Targeted release date.
 (b) Electronic files submitted to the appropriate NASA or Contractor site.
 (c) Hardcopy as required. (See Section 4.2.2, *Hardcopy Format*)

4.2 Data Format
Existing Contractor internal documents may be used to meet the data requirements of the DRD to the extent practicable. The DRD will call out any special format requirements, if they are required.

Attachment J-02

4.2.1 Electronic Format
The DRDs shall be provided in an electronic format that meets three basic requirements: "Readable", "Printable", and "Downloadable" (see Attachment J-05, *Glossary and Acronym List*) by NASA utilizing publicly available off-the-shelf software. If the electronic format is not supported by publicly available off-the-shelf software, the Contractor shall provide NASA with the necessary software and approach to support the three basic requirements.

4.2.2 Hardcopy Format
Hardcopy submission of DRDs is required by this contract for the Final version and subsequent updates to all Type 1 and Type 2 DRDs. One hardcopy of each DRD, shall be delivered to the Contracting Officer Representative at the following address:

> NASA/Kennedy Space Center (KSC)
> Attn: CCtCap Contracting Officer Representative/FA
> Kennedy Space Center, FL 32899

5.0 DRD MAINTENANCE PROCECURES
Throughout the performance of the contract, the DRL provides a listing by data category of the DRDs.

5.1 DRD Submittals

5.1.1 Configuration Management of DRD
The Contractor shall employ a system for organizing, identifying, and tracking all submittals of DRDs, to include any changes or revisions. At a minimum, this system shall include the mapping of Contractor documents and files submitted in response to each DRD, and shall include identification of the DRD Type per the DRL.

5.1.2 Reference to Other Documents and DRDs in Data Submittals
The Contractor's submittal of a DRD may make reference to other documents and/or other DRDs. At the time of submission of the DRD, any referenced document within the DRD shall be made available to NASA. The Contractor shall provide NASA with access to any referenced document and the location of that data within the referenced document. Any reference made to data associated with another DRD that is required separately by the contract shall include the DRL number of and location of the data within the referenced DRD.

5.1.3 Additional Information Regarding Type 1 and Type 2 DRD Submittals
All Type 1 and Type 2 submittals shall be marked as "Pending NASA Approval", and once approved shall be delivered and marked as "Approved by NASA". Type 1 and Type 2 DRDs shall be updated and delivered when, in the opinion of the Contractor and/or NASA, the document has been revised to the extent that it is unusable in its present state, or when directed by the Contracting Officer.

Attachment J-02

6.0 DATA REQUIREMENTS LIST (DRL)

DRD #	DRD Title	Type	Delivery	Update / Frequency
001	Insight Implementation Plan	2	With Proposal	F 45 days prior to Certification Baseline Review (CBR)
002	Integrated Master Plan (IMP) and Integrated Master Schedule (IMS)	2/4	See DRD	See DRD
003	IT Security Management Plan (ITSMP)	3	30 days after Contract Start	As Required
004	IT Security Plan (ITSP)	3	If required by the Government, based on ITSMP	As Required
005	Quarterly Program Review (QPR) Data Package	3	90 days after Contract Start	Quarterly
006	Export Control Plan	3	30 days after Contract Start	As Required

Attachment J-02

Delivery Dates & Frequency Requirements

DRD #	DRD Title	Type	CBR	DCR	FTRR	ORR	CR	ATP	VBR	MIR	MCR	SORR/FRR	PFR	Update / Frequency
101	Milestone Review Plan	2												See DRD
102	Certification Baseline Review (CBR) Data Package	3/2	See DRD											See DRD
103	Design Certification Review (DCR) Data Package	3		F 45 Days prior to DCR										
104	Flight Test Readiness Review (FTRR) Data Package	3			F NLT 45 Days prior to FTRR									
105	Operations Readiness Review (ORR) Data Package	3				F 45 Days prior to ORR								
106	Certification Review (CR) Milestone Data Package	3					F 45 Days prior to CR							
107	Certification Plan	1	B 45 Days prior to CBR											F 45 Days prior to Delta l-CDR

Attachment J-02

Delivery Dates & Frequency Requirements

DRD #	DRD Title	Type	CBR	DCR	FTRR	ORR	CR	ATP	VBR	MIR	MCR	SORR/FRR	PFR	Update/Frequency
108	Verification and Validation (V&V) Plan	1	B 45 Days prior to CBR											F 45 Days prior to Delta I-CDR
109	Flight Test Plan	2	B 45 Days prior to CBR	F NLT 45 Days prior to DCR										See DRD
110	Hazard Reports	2												See DRD
111	Verification Closure Notice (VCN)	1		F 45 Days prior to DCR							F 45 Days prior to MCR			Incremental delivery in support of the process leading up to DCR and MCR is required by DRD
112	Certification Data Package	1		F 45 Days prior to DCR							F 45 Days prior to MCR			
113	Range Safety Data Documentation	4		F 45 Days prior to DCR							F 45 Days prior to MCR			

Attachment J-02

Delivery Dates & Frequency Requirements

DRD #	DRD Title	Type	CBR	DCR	FTRR	ORR	CR	ATP	VBR	MIR	MCR	SORR/ FRR	PFR	Update / Frequency
114	CTS Data Input for NASA Integration and Independent Verification and Validation (IV&V)	3												See DRD
201	Mission Integration and Operations Management Plan (MIOMP)	2						F with task order proposal						See DRD For DDTE, DRD is 30 days prior to Delta I-CDR for OFT/CFT in support of the flight test to ISS.
202	Post Certification Mission (PCM) Work Plan	2						F with task order proposal						See DRD
203	Vehicle Interface Definition Document (IDD)	3		B					F 45 Days prior to VBR					

Attachment J-02

| 204 | Mission Resource Allocation Document (MRAD) | 3 | | | | | | | See DRD | See DRD | See DRD | For DDTE, DRD is L-10 months, L-3 months, and L-6 weeks for OFT and CFT in support of the flight test to ISS. |

Attachment J-02

Delivery Dates & Frequency Requirements

DRD #	DRD Title	Type	CBR	DCR	FTRR	ORR	CR	ATP	VBR	MIR	MCR	SORR/FRR	PFR	Update / Frequency
205	Spacecraft Computer Aided Design (CAD) Models	3							B	F				For DDTE, DRD requirement is L-18 and L-13 months and for maintenance 7 days of release using tools defined in Insight Implementation Plan (reference DRD 001) in support of the flight test to ISS.
206	Internal Cargo Interface Control Agreement (ICA)	2							B	F at L-8m				For DDTE, DRD is L-18 and L-8 months for OFT and CFT in support of the flight test to ISS.

Attachment J-02

Delivery Dates & Frequency Requirements

DRD #	DRD Title	Type	CBR	DCR	FTRR	ORR	CR	ATP	VBR	MIR	MCR	SORR/ FRR	PFR	Update / Frequency
207	Integrated Cargo Phase III Hazard Report	2									F NLT 45 Days prior to MCR			
208	Flight Readiness Review Data Package	3										F NLT 45 Days prior to SORR/ FRR		

Attachment J-02

Delivery Dates & Frequency Requirements

DRD #	DRD Title	Type	CBR	DCR	FTRR	ORR	CR	ATP	VBR	MIR	MCR	SORR/FRR	PFR	Update / Frequency
209	Post Flight Assessment Report	2											See DRD	For DDTE, DRD is Initial (Quick Look) NLT Docking +14 days, Update at Landing + 14 days, and Final NLT Landing + 60 days for OFT and CFT in support of the flight test.

Attachment J-02

Delivery Dates & Frequency Requirements

DRD #	DRD Title	Type	CBR	DCR	FTRR	ORR	CR	ATP	VBR	MIR	MCR	SORR/ FRR	PFR	Update / Frequency
210	Imagery Plan and Associated Cataloging	3/2									See DRD	See DRD		For DDTE, DRD is For Imagery Plan: NLT L-6 mnths, Pre-flight imagery will be posted to the NASA accessible site as defined in Insight Implementation Plan (reference DRD 001) between L-2 wks. and launch to accommodate late imagery from late cargo stowage for OFT and CFT in support of the flight test to ISS.

Attachment J-02

Data Requirement Document
(Note: Please see DRL for Data Deliverable Type and Submission Frequency)

A. DRD No.: 001

B. DRD Title: Insight Implementation Plan

C. Date: 12/20/13

D. Purpose / Use:

NASA will utilize the Contractor's Insight Implementation Plan to ensure NASA personnel and its support services contractors can perform their insight as defined in clause H.15, *Government Insight*, and consistent with the model in CCT-PLN-1100, *Crew Transportation Plan*, Section entitled *CCP Insight/Oversight* and Appendix entitled *Insight Areas*. In addition, NASA will utilize the Contractor's Insight Implementation Plan to ensure NASA personnel can perform Joint Test Team (JTT) participation role as defined in clause H.15, *Government Insight*, and consistent with CCT-PLN-1120, *Crew Transportation Technical Management Processes*.

E. Remarks: None

F. Data Requirements:

At a minimum, the Contractor's Insight Implementation Plan shall establish a cooperative environment that ensures an effective working relationship between NASA and the Contractor dedicated to successful CTS Certification and Post Certification Missions. The Contractor's Insight Implementation Plan shall describe the accommodations for providing Government personnel and its support services contractor(s) timely and open access necessary to obtain a working-level understanding into all Contractor's Certification and Post Certification Mission activities. These accommodations include facility access, data, and any other information including technical and management processes required to meet contract requirements, milestone acceptance criteria, and to support approval of Type 1 and 2 data deliverables. The Contractor's Insight Implementation Plan shall identify instructions or training required to allow for meaningful NASA insight and participation (e.g., facility and safety familiarization).

In addition, the Insight Plan shall address:
(a) Accommodating clause H.15, *Government Insight* and the following items:

(1) The transparency by which the Contractor will provide the Government on-going access into activities and data used for mutually achieving successful milestone acceptance, approval of Type 1 and 2 data deliverables and making progress toward NASA Certification and Post Certification Missions.

Continued on next page…

Attachment J-02

Data Requirement Document (Continuation Sheet)

A. **DRD No.:** 001

B. **DRD Title:** Insight Implementation Plan

F. **Data Requirements (continued):**

(a) continued:

(2) The transparency by which the Contractor will provide the Government on-going access to data, both remotely and on-site, in a useable and readable format; and provide the Government the ability to locate and review all data used in performance of this contract and any other information related to the Crew Transportation System (CTS), to include technical data, supporting data/information, and administrative and management information with the exception of financial information. Whether the data accessed includes the ability of the Government to download or copy data; the Contractor's proposed data restriction legends on accessed data; and mechanisms to ensure that access data is not confused with data delivered under the contract.

(3) The timeframe the Contractor shall notify the Commercial Crew Program designee of technical meetings, control boards, reviews, demonstrations and tests to permit meaningful Government participation through the entire event.

(4) The timeliness and ease by which the Contractor will provide access and make data available to mutually address risks associated with completing acceptance milestone review criteria, approving Type 1 and 2 data deliverables and making progress toward NASA Certification and Post Certification Missions. This includes the technical plans required in CCT-REQ-1130, *ISS Crew Transportation and Services Requirements Document*, and SSP 50808, *ISS to Commercial Orbital Transportation Services (COTS) Interface Requirements Document (IRD)*.

(b) Accommodating NASA's participation in the Joint Test Team in accordance with clause H.15, *Government Insight*. This shall include:

(1) The timeliness and ease by which the Contractor will accommodate NASA's participation in the JTT activities and make data available to mutually address risks associated with achieving successful demonstrations, tests, completing acceptance milestone review criteria and making progress toward NASA Certification and Post Certification Missions.

Continued on next page…

Attachment J-02

Data Requirement Document (Continuation Sheet)

A. DRD No.: 001

B. DRD Title: Insight Implementation Plan

F. Data Requirements (continued):

(b) continued:

(1) The timeliness and ease by which the Contractor will accommodate NASA's participation during the planning and build up phase of ground testing (e.g., simulator training and evaluations, mockup demonstrations, etc.), during test flights, and during the post-test flight evaluation process.

(2) The approach to implement a Joint Test Team (JTT) for the planning and execution of flight test activities, including how they are incorporating Government flight and ground personnel in qualitative assessments of crew operational interfaces with the vehicle and human-in-the-loop assessments of operational suitability; development of operations products; development of flight test objectives and plans; post-flight evaluation; and any other activities.

(c) Accommodating Government Quality Assurance (GQA) functions in accordance with clause H.15, *Government Insight*. This shall include:

(1) The timeliness and ease by which the Contractor will accommodate NASA and make data available for the Government to perform a successful risk based analysis that will facilitate the identification of high risk areas.

(2) The timeliness and ease by which the Contractor will accommodate NASA performing the GQA activities identified by the risk based analysis and make data available to achieve successful GQA activities.

(d) Establishing a cooperative environment between NASA and the contractor dedicated to successful Certification and Post Certification Missions. This shall include:

(1) Establishing excellent working relationships at every level of both organizations that enable both parties to solve problems as a team.

(2) Ensuring a level of candor that permits the parties to mutually avoid risk and enables a continuous dialogue.

Continued on next page…

Attachment J-02

Data Requirement Document (Continuation Sheet)

A. **DRD No.:** 001

B. **DRD Title:** Insight Implementation Plan

F. **Data Requirements (continued):**

(e) Resolving concerns and issues identified by NASA and its support services contractor's insight effort as well as from NASA's participation in the JTT activities. This shall include:

    (1) Permit timely elevation of issues to NASA.

    (2) The process of highlighting critical activities of interest (such as changes, decisions, key testing events, critical meetings) to NASA.

(f) Accommodating NASA's insight in the Contractor's development and successful fulfillment of operational requirements. This shall include:

    (1) The timeliness and ease by which the Contractor will accommodate NASA's insight in the operational activities and make data available to mutually address risks associated with achieving successful demonstrations, tests, completing acceptance milestone review criteria and making progress toward NASA Certification and Post Certification Missions.

    (2) Highlights critical activities of interest (such as changes, decisions, key events, critical meetings) to NASA.

    (3) The process to permit timely elevation of issues to NASA.

(g) In addition to access to Contractor facilities for insight, the Contractor shall describe the NASA provisions for office space co-located on-site, badging, furniture, telephones, and use of easily accessible fax, data lines, and copy machines, for full-time and temporary Government insight and support services contractor personnel in performance of this contract, including training. This shall include:

    (1) Co-located on site accommodations clearly identified.

    (2) Innovative use of technology that enables effective participation for completing milestone reviews acceptance criteria and making progress toward NASA Certification and Post Certification Missions.

Continued on next page…

Attachment J-02

Data Requirement Document (Continuation Sheet)

A. DRD No.: 001

B. DRD Title: Insight Implementation Plan

F. Data Requirements (continued):

(h) The process of providing the Government insight into all subcontractors and suppliers performing or supporting any critical work associated with this contract.

Attachment J-02

Data Requirement Document
(Note: Please see DRL for Data Deliverable Type and Submission Frequency)

A. DRD No.: 002

B. DRD Title: Integrated Master Plan (IMP) & Integrated Master Schedule (IMS)

C. Date: 11/19/13

D. Purpose / Use:

To provide NASA the Contractor's integrated program schedules using established standard processes, data structures and reporting conventions to plan, manage, and report the work required in the performance of this contract.

E. Remarks:

Schedule consistency as used in this DRD is defined as the degree to which the Contractor utilized standardized scheduling approaches between similar activities and flows. Scheduling accuracy as used in this DRD is defined as the accurate representation of work content and tasks duration (predicted vs. actuals). Schedule stability as used in this DRD refers to the degree to which daily schedule changes are minimized and limited to unforeseen hardware or software problems or NASA-directed changes.

The Contractor is encouraged to utilize modern manufacturing resource planning, industrial engineering techniques, and other approaches to ensure schedule stability, accuracy, reliability, predictability, and achievability. The Contractor may satisfy the requirements of the DRD by combining the requirements of the IMP and the IMS in a single format.

F. Data Requirements:

The IMP shall describe the significant activities, with the associated success criteria, as derived from the Contract Performance Work Statement (Attachment J-03, *Contract PWS*), DRDs, and other contract requirements.

The IMS is an integrated logically linked schedule and shall capture the activities described in the IMP and the lower level work necessary to support each of the IMP activities. The IMS will be used to verify attainability of contract objectives and requirements, and to evaluate progress.

The IMS shall include all contract milestones, activities, and tasks leading to the proposed date for CTS Certification and for work described in task orders, including those for Post Certification Missions (PCMs) and Special Studies. The IMS shall show percentage completion of all Design, Development, Testing and Evaluation (DDTE) and PCM milestones. The IMS Continued on next page…

Attachment J-02

Data Requirement Document (Continuation Sheet)

A. DRD No.: 002

B. DRD Title: Integrated Master Plan (IMP) & Integrated Master Schedule (IMS)

F. Data Requirements (continued):

shall provide the ability to fully identify, analyze, mitigate and control scheduling risks and impacts; accurately identify and analyze critical path activities; and allow its users to easily measure the progress towards achieving the IMP. At a minimum, the IMS shall identify tasks at the Subsystem level (whereas the Crew Transportation System (CTS) is a "System" and the spacecraft and launch vehicles are "Elements", the Subsystem level is a level lower than the Element) for major activities or products associated with DDTE and PCM(s). Additionally, at a minimum, the IMS shall be formatted with the largest increment of time being measured in units of months.

The IMS should identify priorities of tasks, order and sequence of tasks, primary and secondary critical path, schedule margin, and dependencies and relationships among tasks. The IMS should clearly identify tasks or activities which have a dependency on a NASA delivery or approval (for example, delivery of an NASA Docking System (NDS) unit), and should distinguish tasks or activities which are conducted jointly with NASA (for example, an integrated test with the ISS Program).

For both Type 2 and Type 4 deliveries of the IMP/IMS, the Contractor shall provide the DRDs in an electronic format.

The IMP/IMS shall be delivered for NASA approval on the following schedule (reference Type 2 DRD definition):

A. For the Certification Baseline Review (CBR), the Contractor shall deliver to NASA a final IMP/IMS, for approval, 45 days prior to the CBR. See Attachment J-03.

B. For a Design Certification Review (DCR), the Contractor shall deliver to NASA an updated IMP/IMS, for approval, 45 days prior to a DCR. Reference DRD 103, DCR Data Package and Attachment J-03.

C. For the Post Certification Missions (PCMs), the Contractor shall deliver to NASA an updated IMP/IMS, for approval, with the PCM Work Plan, DRD 202.

The IMS shall be maintained and delivered to NASA on a monthly basis (reference Type 4 DRD definition).

Attachment J-02

Data Requirement Document
(Note: Please see DRL for Data Deliverable Type and Submission Frequency)

A. **DRD No.:** 003

B. **DRD Title:** IT Security Management Plan (ITSMP)

C. **Date:** 11/19/13

D. **Purpose / Use:**

To provide Government insight into the Contractor's methodology for managing all aspects of information security and to ensure critical components are addressed.

E. **Remarks:**

The ITSMP will be in compliance with NFS 1852.204-76, *Security Requirements for Unclassified Information Technology Resources (Jan 2011)*. The Government, after review of the ITSMP, will notify the Contractor of the need for an IT Security Plan (ITSP) and the associated due date.

F. **Data Requirements:**

The Contractor shall describe the processes and procedures that will be followed to ensure appropriate security of information technology (IT) resources that are developed, processed, or used under this contract.

Unlike the IT security plan, which addresses the IT system and the security control implementations, the ITSMP addresses how the Contractor will manage personnel and processes associated with IT security on the contract.

The ITSMP shall include, at a minimum, the following:

(a) Contractor's information security Points of Contact (POC(s)) including roles and responsibilities.

(b) A description of policies, processes, and/or procedures for:

(1) Meeting all applicable security assessment & authorization requirements, including but not limited to development and maintenance of IT Security Plans (ITSPs), including external IT systems; implementation and validation of security controls, security assessment, authorization, and continuous monitoring in accordance to NASA directives and guidance.
Continued on next page…

Attachment J-02

Data Requirement Document (Continuation Sheet)

A. DRD No.: 003

B. DRD Title: IT Security Management Plan (ITSMP)

F. Data Requirements (continued):

(b) continued:

(2) Addressing all applicable information security requirements, including vulnerability scanning and mitigation, maintaining secure operating system configuration, patch/configuration management, contingency planning, and protection of sensitive data in transit and at rest.

(3) Information security, privacy, incident management and responses, including coordination with NASA Security Operations Center (SOC), Center Chief Information Security Officer (CISO), and Center Privacy Manager as required.

(4) Ensure the Contractor employees meet information security requirements, such as information security awareness, rules of behavior, and elevated privilege training as required. Users are knowledgeable of NASA information security policies and procedures when handling NASA data.

Attachment J-02

Data Requirement Document
(Note: Please see DRL for Data Deliverable Type and Submission Frequency)

A. DRD No.: 004

B. DRD Title: IT Security Plan (ITSP)

C. Date: 11/19/13

D. Purpose / Use:

To provide Government insight into the Contractor's methodology for managing all aspects of information security and to ensure critical components are addressed.

E. Remarks:

The **DRD 003 ITSMP** is required within thirty (30) days of contract start. The Government, after review of the ITSMP, will notify the Contractor of the need for an IT Security Plan (ITSP) and the associated due date. The ITSP will be in compliance with NFS 1852.204-76, *Security Requirements For Unclassified Information Technology Resources (Jan 2011)*.

F. Data Requirements:

The Contractor shall develop, implement and maintain an ITSP for all systems provided or operated in performance of this contract as required in clause I.12, NFS 1852.204-76, *Security Requirements for Unclassified Information Technology Resources*.

The ITSP provides an overview of the security requirements of the system and describes the implementation details of the management, operational, and technical security controls in place or planned, and responsibilities and expected behavior of all individuals who access the system.

The ITSP, at a minimum, shall include the following:

(a) Security categorization of the Information System

(b) A description of the detailed implementation of the following classes of control:

(1) Operational Controls - The security controls (i.e., safeguards or countermeasures) for an information system that are primarily implemented and executed by people (as opposed to systems).

Continued on next page…

Attachment J-02

Data Requirement Document (Continuation Sheet)

A. DRD No.: 004

B. DRD Title: IT Security Plan

F. Data Requirements (continued):

(b) Continued:

(2) Management Controls - Actions taken to manage the development, maintenance, and use of the system, including system-specific policies, procedures and rules of behavior, individual roles and responsibilities, individual accountability, and personnel security decisions.

(3) Technical Controls - Security controls (i.e., safeguards or countermeasures) for an information system that are primarily implemented and executed by the information system through mechanisms contained in the hardware, software, or firmware components of the system. The controls can provide automated protection for unauthorized access or misuse, facilitate detection of security violations, and support security requirements for applications and data.

Attachment J-02

Data Requirement Document
(Note: Please see DRL for Data Deliverable Type and Submission Frequency)

A. DRD No.: 005

B. DRD Title: Quarterly Program Review (QPR) Briefing Package

C. Date: 11/19/13

D. Purpose / Use:

QPRs provide an opportunity for discussions and technical interchange between NASA and the Contractor regarding progress of CCtCap objectives and scope. As a basis for the discussions and technical interchange, the QPR Briefing Package shall detail the Contractor's technical progress, risk assessment, schedule status, and cost assessment, and plans forward. Progress shall be estimated and reported in a quantifiable performance method. NASA will provide feedback, may assign actions and request action responses to be completed by jointly agreed upon dates.

E. Remarks:

The QPRs should occur, on average, every three (3) months. For the cases where a QPR coincides with a required milestone (Certification Baseline Review (CBR), Design Certification Review(s) (DCR), Operations Readiness Review (ORR), Flight Test Readiness Review(s) (FTRR), Certification Review (CR), Vehicle Baseline Review (VBR), Mission Integration Review (MIR), Mission Certification Review (MCR), Flight Readiness Review (FRR) or Post Flight Review (PFR)), the QPR may be combined with the required milestone.

F. Data Requirements:

The Quarterly Program Review (QPR) Briefing Package shall include the following items:

(a) A summary highlighting accomplishments.

(b) Identification of new challenges and opportunities and a status of those discussed or identified in the previous QPR.

(c) Status of the interim and completion milestones, with an emphasis on milestones occurring in the next six (6) months.

Continued on next page…

Attachment J-02

Data Requirement Document (Continuation Sheet)
i. **DRD No.:** 005

B. **DRD Title:** Quarterly Program Review (QPR) Briefing Package

F. **Data Requirements (continued):**

(d) The status, closure plan and schedule to demonstrate compliance to the contract requirements. This shall include:

(1) A status of the CTS design requirements, verifications activities, and Verification Closure Notice (VCN) closures.

(2) A summary of any tasks required to be repeated in the event of changes to the CTS Certification baseline.

(3) Master Equipment List (MEL) showing the categorized list of equipment related to the Crew Transportation System (CTS). The equipment items shall be identified at the Subsystem level (whereas the CTS is a "System" and the spacecraft and launch vehicles are "Elements", the Subsystem level is a level lower than the Element), organized by the Element level, and include the following for each item, as applicable:

   (i) Quantity

   (ii) Mass, contingency mass, and expected mass changes

   (iii) Power

   (iv) Center of Gravity (cg)

(e) Status of the Integrated Master Schedule (IMS) (ref. **DRD 002 IMP & IMS**) progress to date and schedule reserves. Identification of interdependencies among tasks associated with all CLINs, and associated risks, impacts and mitigation plans.

(f) A risk management status that includes a description of the top programmatic risks with a discussion of potential impacts to the CTS safety, technical, cost and schedule performance, and the associated mitigation strategies.

Continued on next page…

Attachment J-02

Data Requirement Document (Continuation Sheet)
(a) **DRD No.:** 005

B. DRD Title: Quarterly Program Review (QPR) Briefing Package

F. Data Requirements (continued):

(g) A cost assessment that provides updates to the expected costs through Certification and the associated costs for Post Certification Missions. The cost assessment shall:

(1) Clearly identify and forecast potential cost growth from the contract value, highlighting any changes since the previous QPR or milestone.

(2) Detail the contractor's risk mitigation strategies associated with potential cost growth, including planned methods of resolving potential cash flow needs and potential impacts to PCMs.

(3) Provide an integrated assessment of the cost growth and its impact(s) to the most current IMS.

(4) Provide details of progress of corporate commitments.

Attachment J-02

Data Requirement Document
(Note: Please see DRL for Data Deliverable Type and Submission Frequency)

A. DRD No.: 006

B. DRD Title: Export Control Plan

C. Date: 11/19/13

D. Purpose / Use: The plan shall describe all export control activities related to the performance of contract requirements.

E. Remarks: None

F. Data Requirements:

The Contractor shall prepare and submit an Export Control Plan (ECP), describing the Contractor's planned approach for accomplishing contract functions while adhering to export laws, regulations and directives.

The final export control plan shall be submitted within thirty (30) days after contract start. The plan shall be reviewed at least annually thereafter and updated as required.

Attachment J-02

Data Requirement Document
(Note: Please see DRL for Data Deliverable Type and Submission Frequency)

A. DRD No.: 101

B. DRD Title: Milestone Review Plan

C. Date: 11/19/13

D. Purpose / Use:

To establish an agreement between NASA and the Contractor on planning, preparing for, and conducting milestone reviews.

E. Remarks: None

F. Data Requirements:

The Contractor shall deliver a Milestone Review Plan for the reviews identified in the contract requirements, the Attachment J-03, Appendix A, *Milestone Acceptance Criteria and Payment Schedule,* including contractor defined interim milestones, and Attachment J-03, *Contract PWS*. Milestone reviews shall meet the requirements noted in CCT- PLN-1120, *Crew Transportation Technical Management Processes Document,* Attachment J-03 Appendix A, and Section F, *Data Requirements*, of **DRDs 102, 103, 104, 105 and 106**. For each milestone, including interim milestones, the milestone review plan shall describe: the review process (including any specific tools and tool training required to conduct the review), schedule, location, deliverables, delivery method, delivery dates, means and timing by which data will be made available to NASA, document review dates, presentation meetings, Technical Interchange Meetings (TIMs), pre-boards, boards, and other logistics related information.

The milestone review plan shall describe the approach for review input including comments and when the comments are due, disposition process, actions, action recording and tracking, configuration management and minutes. The plan shall ensure the Government has adequate time and access to data to perform meaningful technical reviews of the deliverables. The milestone review plan shall identify data/documentation subject to Review Item Dispositions (RIDs). The plan may be segregated into volumes for individual reviews or split up accordingly to optimize incremental updates. Upon NASA approval/concurrence of each iteration of the **DRD 101 Milestone Review Plan**, it will supersede the CCT-PLN-1120 data requirements for that specific review.

Continued on next page…

Attachment J-02

Data Requirement Document
(Note: Please see DRL for Data Deliverable Type and Submission Frequency)

A. **DRD No.:** 101

B. **DRD Title:** Milestone Review Plan

F. **Data Requirements (continued):**

The plan is due with proposal. The proposal submittal shall provide the detailed plan for Certification Baseline Review (CBR), estimated dates for remaining milestones, and the allocated time for NASA review and approval of milestone data. The proposal submittal shall describe when the plan will be updated to address the detailed content for future milestones. The final plan shall be submitted forty-five (45) days prior to CBR, for approval at CBR. The Contractor shall update the plan in accordance with the schedule identified in the CBR version to address the detailed content prior to the upcoming milestones.

Attachment J-02

Data Requirement Document
(Note: Please see DRL for Data Deliverable Type and Submission Frequency)

A. DRD No.: 102

B. DRD Title: Certification Baseline Review (CBR) Data Package

C. Date: 11/19/13

D. Purpose / Use: Identify the data required to baseline the Contractor's current state of design and development for the integrated CTS associated with the requirements defined in CCT-REQ-1130, *ISS Crew Transportation and Services Requirements Document*, SSP 50808, *ISS to Commercial Orbital Transportation Services (COTS) Interface Requirements Document*, and CCT-PLN-1120, *Crew Transportation Technical Management Processes,* and to define management plans and products.

E. Remarks: None

F. Data Requirements:

Unless otherwise specified in this DRD, the data delivered under this DRD is Type 3.

The Contractor shall deliver to NASA the CBR Data Package No Later Than (NLT) forty-five (45) days prior to the CBR milestone. The CBR Data Package shall contain:

(a) A Requirements Baseline that contains, at a minimum:

  (1) Documentation of requirements, including allocation to the Elements and Subsystems of the CTS traceable to CCT-REQ-1130 and SSP 50808. Identification of approved variances and alternate standards in the Contractor's CTS requirements baseline.

  (2) Joint ISS integration products (Interface Control Documents (ICDs), Joint Integrated Verification Test Plan (JiVTP), Bilateral Data Exchange Agreement List and Schedule (BDEALS), Bilateral Hardware Software Exchange Agreement List and Schedule (BSHEALS)) identified in SSP 50964, *Visiting Vehicle ISS Integration Plan.*

  (3) Concept of operations.

Continued on next page…

Attachment J-02

Data Requirement Document (Continuation Sheet)

A. **DRD No.:** 102

B. **DRD Title:** Certification Baseline Review (CBR) Data Package

F. **Data Requirements (continued):**

(b) A Design baseline that contains, at a minimum:

(1) Definition of proposed design baseline, including design analyses, drawings, models, software artifacts, system and cargo interface definition, and other artifacts to be proposed. Physical location and access details of design baseline artifacts to allow interrogation of design baseline through insight activities.

(2) Status of system safety process and analyses including a Human Error Analysis, integrated Probabilistic Safety Analysis, hazard identification, control and verification, fault tolerance assessment, top safety risks, and the crew survival strategy with capabilities required to support the strategy.

(3) Evidence of expected integrated vehicle performance margin and design margin as defined in CCT-PLN-1120.

(4) Crew training template to accommodate crew to ISS. Contractor and NASA will develop crew training templates for crewed test flight to ISS and for Post Certification Mission flights to ensure crew can perform required functions at ISS.

(5) Human Systems Integration Data Products as identified in CCT-PLN-1120 [Data Type 2].

(c) Final management plans and products

(1) The management and technical plans in CCT-PLN-1120, that support the design, development, test, evaluation, and Certification of the CTS, including:

(i) Program Management Plan [Data Type 2]

(ii) Configuration Management Plan [Data Type 2]

(iii) Risk Management Plan [Data Type 2]

(iv) Safety and Reliability Plan [Data Type 2]

(v) Requirements Management Plan [Data Type 2]

Continued on next page…

Attachment J-02

Data Requirement Document (Continuation Sheet)
A. DRD No.: 102
B. DRD Title: Certification Baseline Review (CBR) Data Package

F. Data Requirements (continued):

(c) (1) Final Management plans and products (continued)

      (vi)   Quality Management Plan [Data Type 2]

      (vii) Human System Integration Strategy [Data Type 2]

      (viii) Software Safety Plan

      (ix)   Radioactive Materials Usage Report

      (x)   Software Development Plan

      (xi)   Margin Management Plan

(1) Status and definition of Production and Operations Plans and Products as described in CCT-PLN-1120.

(d) Documentation demonstrating the top programmatic risks have been identified and assessed to include plans, processes, and appropriate resources necessary to effectively manage the risks.

(e) All Review Item Dispositions (RIDs), To be Determined (TBD) and To be Resolved (TBR) items clearly identified with acceptable plans and schedules for their disposition.

Attachment J-02

Data Requirement Document
(Note: Please see DRL for Data Deliverable Type and Submission Frequency)

A. DRD No.: 103

B. DRD Title: Design Certification Review (DCR) Data Package

C. Date: 12/20/13

D. Purpose / Use:

The DCR Data Package establishes the data required for a Design Certification Review of the integrated CTS and planned operations. DCR acceptance criteria in Attachment J-03, Appendix A, *Milestone Acceptance Criteria and Payment Schedule*, must be met prior to any crewed orbital test flights.

E. Remarks: None

F. Data Requirements:

The DCR Data Package shall address the following:

(a) DCR Presentation Package including summary of the Certification Data Package, integrated vehicle performance, margin and constraints, variances, and identification of open items with the plan for completion.

(b) Incremental tests required or conducted due to design or requirements changes made since test initiation, and resolution of issues have been identified and submitted.

(c) Evidence that configurations used for certification have been reconciled with the design configuration.

(d) All Review Item Dispositions (RIDs) and actions from design reviews, verification reviews and Certification Baseline Review (CBR) including status of To be Determined (TBD) and To be Resolved (TBR) items clearly identified with plans for disposition.

(e) Provide an assessment of the top cost schedule, and technical Programmatic risks to Crew Transportation System (CTS) Certification, an assessment of risks to contract performance, and management of residual risk acceptance.

Continued on next page…

Attachment J-02

Data Requirement Document (Continuation Sheet)

A. DRD No.: 103

B. DRD Title: Design Certification Review (DCR) Data Package

F. Data Requirements (continued):

(f) Facilities and processes to develop and execute operational plans, products, training and in-flight/post-flight anomaly resolution including joint processes for ISS integration that meets the operational requirements in CCT-PLN-1120, *Crew Transportation Technical Management Processes,* and SSP 50808, *ISS to Commercial Orbital Transportation (COTS) Interface Requirements Document (IRD)*. Operational controls, limitations and constraints of integrated vehicle have been incorporated.

(g) Operational products, personnel and crew are ready or are scheduled for completion prior to need date (to support crewed test flight).

(h) Status, constraints and interdependencies with crewed flight tests and Post Certification Missions.

Attachment J-02

Data Requirement Document
(Note: Please see DRL for Data Deliverable Type and Submission Frequency)

A. DRD No.: 104

B. DRD Title: Flight Test Readiness Review (FTRR) Data Package

C. Date: 12/20/13

D. Purpose / Use:

The FTRR Data Package establishes the data required to evaluate readiness and provide approval to conduct a crewed orbital flight test within the risk baseline accepted at a Design Certification Review (DCR).

E. Remarks: None

F. Data Requirements:
The Contractor shall deliver to NASA the following data:

(a) Flight Test Readiness Review Data Package in accordance with CCT-PLN-1120, *Crew Transportation Technical Management Processes*, Appendix F, *CTS FTRR/FRR Milestone Data*, clearly identifying any Crew Transportation System (CTS) changes from DCR.

(b) All changes, modifications and anomalies since DCR have been resolved.

(c) Status of all Review Item Dispositions (RIDs), actions, and open work from Interim Milestone Reviews, DCR, and Stage Operational Readiness Review (SORR).

(d) Documentation that Mission support team is defined, has been trained, and is in place.

(e) Evidence that all operational supporting and enabling capabilities necessary for nominal and contingency operations have been tested and delivered/installed at the site(s).

(f) Plans, procedures, and training for nominal and contingency operations for the CTS have been completed.

(g) Evidence that systems, hardware, software, personnel, and procedures are in place.

(h) Status of system safety process and analyses including a Human Error Analysis, integrated Probabilistic Safety Analysis, hazard identification, control and verification, fault tolerance assessment, top safety risks, and the crew survival strategy with capabilities required to support the strategy.
Continued on next page…

Attachment J-02

Data Requirement Document (Continuation Sheet)

A. DRD No.: 104

B. DRD Title: Flight Test Readiness Review (FTRR) Data Package

F. Data Requirements (continued):

(i) Documentation showing all acceptance, checkout and integration testing has been completed.

(j) Plan and schedule of preplanned forward work.

Attachment J-02

Data Requirement Document
(Note: Please see DRL for Data Deliverable Type and Submission Frequency)

A. DRD No.: 105

B. DRD Title: Operations Readiness Review (ORR) Data Package

C. Date: 11/19/13

D. Purpose / Use:

The ORR Data Package establishes the data required to evaluate that the actual Crew Transportation System (CTS) system characteristics and the procedures used in operations reflect the deployed state of the CTS. The ORR Data Package also establishes the data required to demonstrate that all program and support (flight and ground) hardware, software, personnel, and procedures to ensure flight and associated ground systems are in compliance with program requirements and constraints.

E. Remarks: None

F. Data Requirements:

The Operations Readiness Review Data Package shall address the following:

(a) ORR Presentation Package, including summary of ORR Data Package and constraints

(b) Closure of any remaining open requirements (**DRD 111 Verification Closure Notice**).

(c) Evidence that all validation testing has been completed (or planned for completion prior to Certification Review (CR)).

(d) Evidence that anomalies have been resolved and the results incorporated.

(e) Evidence that all operational supporting and enabling capabilities (e.g., facilities, equipment, documents, updated databases) necessary for nominal and contingency operations have been tested and delivered/installed at the site(s) necessary to support recurring operations.

(f) Evidence that plans, processes, procedures, personnel and training for nominal and contingency operations for the CTS have been completed to support recurring operations.

(g) Evidence that systems, hardware, and software, are in place to support recurring operations.

Continued on next page…

Attachment J-02

Data Requirement Document (Continuation Sheet)

A. **DRD No.:** 105

B. **DRD Title:** Operations Readiness Review (ORR) Data Package

F. **Data Requirements (continued):**

(h) Documentation demonstrating the top programmatic risks have been identified and assessed to include plans, processes, and appropriate resources necessary to effectively manage the risks.

(i) Status of system safety process and analyses including a Human Error Analysis, integrated Probabilistic Safety Analysis, hazard identification, control and verification, fault tolerance assessment, top safety risks, and the crew survival strategy with capabilities required to support the strategy.

(j) Documentation substantiating all Review Item Dispositions (RIDs) and actions from design reviews, verification reviews, Design Certification Review(s) (DCR(s)), and Flight Test Readiness Review(s) (FTRR(s)) are closed.

Attachment J-02

Data Requirement Document
(Note: Please see DRL for Data Deliverable Type and Submission Frequency)

A. DRD No.: 106

B. DRD Title: Certification Review (CR) Milestone Data Package

C. Date: 11/19/13

D. Purpose / Use:

The Certification Review Milestone Data Package establishes the data required for the review and approval of Certification by NASA of the CTS and planned implementation of ISS servicing missions at the Certification Review Milestone.

E. Remarks: None

F. Data Requirements:
The Certification Review Milestone Data Package shall address the following:

(a) Certification Review Milestone Presentation, including: integrated vehicle performance, margin and constraints, variances, a summary of Certification Data Package (**DRD 112 Certification Data Package**), and identification of open items with the plan for completion.

(b) Technical management processes have effectively controlled the design, been implemented for manufacturing and operations, and accepted by NASA.

(c) Any incremental tests conducted due to design or requirement changes made since ISS Design Certification Review (DCR) and resolution of issues have been identified and submitted.

(d) All actions from ISS DCR, Flight Test Readiness Review (FTRR) and Operations Readiness Review (ORR) are closed and have been submitted. Any updates required to plans and processes have been implemented and released.

(e) Provide an assessment of the top cost, schedule, and technical Programmatic risks; an assessment of risks to contract performance; and management of residual risk acceptance.

(f) Operational products and documentation are available and ready or are scheduled for completion prior to need date. Operational limits and constraints have been incorporated into the operational documentation. Operational roles, responsibilities, and procedures have been incorporated for crew, mission team and mission management into the operational products.

Continued on the next page…

Attachment J-02

Data Requirement Document (Continuation Sheet)

A. DRD No.: 106

B. DRD Title: Certification Review Milestone Data Package

F. Data Requirements (continued):

(g) Production plans and processes are in place, including verification plans and procedures.

(h) Facilities and processes to develop and execute operational plans, products, training and in-flight/post-flight anomaly resolution including joint processes for ISS integration that meets the operational requirements in CCT-PLN-1120, *Crew Transportation Technical Management Processes,* and SSP 50808, *ISS to Commercial Orbital Transportation Services (COTS) Interface Requirements Document (IRD)*. Operational controls, limitations and constraints of integrated vehicle have been incorporated.

(i) Operational personnel and crew are ready or are scheduled for completion prior to need date (to support crewed flight).

Attachment J-02

Data Requirement Document
(Note: Please see DRL for Data Deliverable Type and Submission Frequency)

A. DRD No.: 107

B. DRD Title: Certification Plan

C. Date: 11/19/13

D. Purpose / Use:

The Certification Plan will be used to approve the Contractor's approach for Certification of the Crew Transportation System (CTS).

E. Remarks:

The Certification Plan and any deliverables associated with its implementation may be submitted incrementally until the final version delivery date.

F. Data Requirements:

If the Contractor had a Certification Products Contract (CPC) during Phase 1 of this procurement, the CPC products that were delivered to and dispositioned by NASA as part of final delivery are approved for initial use during performance of CCtCap. Subsequent approvals of this DRD supersede the CPC approved version.

The Contractor shall deliver a Certification Plan that meets the requirements of CCT-PLN-1120, *Crew Transportation Technical Management Processes,* including Appendix C, *CTS Certification Plan.* The Contractor shall clearly define the order of execution, with a schedule and critical path clearly outlined.

The Contractor shall propose a final submittal, consistent with the Contractor system development, production, and Certification lifecycle.

Attachment J-02

Data Requirement Document
(Note: Please see DRL for Data Deliverable Type and Submission Frequency)

A. DRD No.: 108

B. DRD Title: Verification and Validation (V&V) Plan

C. Date: 11/19/13

D. Purpose / Use:

The Verification and Validation Plan will be used to approve the Contractor's detailed plans for completing Crew Transportation System (CTS) verification and validation tasks.

E. Remarks:

The Verification and Validation Plan and any deliverables associated with its implementation may be submitted incrementally until the final version delivery date

F. Data Requirements:

If the Contractor had a Certification Products Contract (CPC) during Phase 1 of this procurement, the CPC products that were delivered to and dispositioned by NASA as part of final delivery are approved for initial use and implementation during performance of CCtCap. Subsequent approvals of this DRD supersede the CPC approved version.

The Contractor shall deliver a Verification and Validation Plan that meets the requirements of CCT-PLN-1120, *Crew Transportation Technical Management Processes,* including Appendix D, *CTS Verification and Validation Plan.* The V&V Plan shall include at a minimum the Contractor's approach for verifying compliance with the requirements, including detailed verification methods and objectives and definition of necessary compliance data required for the Verification Closure Notice (VCN). Where CCT-REQ-1130, *ISS Crew Transportation and Services Requirements Document,* requirement calls out a specific verification plan as part of the requirement (e.g., Structural Verification Plan), the V&V Plan approval is contingent upon approval of that specific plan.

The V&V Plan shall also address the data and products for verification and validation of: manufacturing operations, hardware and software qualification, acceptance test programs, and environmental testing. It shall also address the data and products for the verification and validation of the models or simulations used to make critical decisions that may impact human safety and mission success.

The Contractor shall propose a final submittal, consistent with the Contractor system development, production, and Certification lifecycle.

Attachment J-02

Data Requirement Document
(Note: Please see DRL for Data Deliverable Type and Submission Frequency)

A. DRD No.: 109

B. DRD Title: Flight Test Plan

C. Date: 12/20/13

D. Purpose / Use:
The purpose is to baseline the plan for conducting the flight test program as part of Crew Transportation System (CTS) Certification. The Flight Test Plan will be used to approve the Contractor's flight test objectives and plan for accomplishing the flight.

E. Remarks: None

F. Data Requirements:
The Contractor shall deliver to NASA a flight test plan that meets the requirements of CCT-PLN-1120, *Crew Transportation Technical Management Processes*, the Attachment J-03, *Contract Performance Work Statement*, and this DRD.

The format for delivery may be a single plan that addresses the entire flight test program and each flight test, or separate plans for each flight test. The format and organization of the plan should accommodate NASA incremental approvals as described below.

The Data Requirements List (DRL) defines delivery of a Baseline version at Certification Baseline Review (CBR) and Final version to be proposed, but no later than the first Design Certification Review (DCR).

Baseline: The Baseline version delivered for CBR shall include information to evaluate the entire flight test program and the scope and objectives for each flight test, and information necessary for NASA participation and joint activities.

Final: The Contractor shall propose when the final version shall be delivered based on their development plan, milestones and the following constraints:

  (a) *Crewed Flight Tests* - Final approval no later than (NLT) the DCR associated with that Flight Test.

  (b) *Uncrewed Flight Tests* - Occurring prior to the first DCR, final approval of the plan content related to that flight test is prior to the applicable proposed interim milestones (e.g. Test Readiness Reviews (TRRs)) for that test. For uncrewed flight tests occurring after the first DCR, final approval NLT the first DCR.

Continued on next page…

Attachment J-02

Data Requirement Document (Continuation Sheet)

A. **DRD No.:** 109

B. **DRD Title:** Flight Test Plan

F. **Data Requirements (continued):**

Flight tests include flight test events performed to demonstrate design performance, validate models or used as substantiation data for verification or validation of a requirement. The following are examples of flight tests, although not an exhaustive list:

- Pad Abort Test
- Ascent Abort Test
- Stage Separation Flight Tests
- Atmospheric Drop Tests
- Powered Flight Tests
- Suborbital Flight Tests
- Orbital Flight Tests

The flight test plan shall include the following information:

CBR	DCR(s) – Update to CBR information including additional information provided below
<ul><li>Test Team Organization</li><li>Ground Team definition</li><li>Test Organizational Interfaces (such as range, ISSP, communications and tracking)</li><li>Review and Approval Authority</li><li>Linkages to Risk Management Plan</li></ul>	<ul><li>Test Team Roles and responsibilities</li><li>Test Organizational Interface agreements</li><li>Review and Approval Authority</li></ul>
<ul><li>Test Configuration</li><li>Test Objectives</li><li>Success Criteria</li><li>Linkage to V&V Plan</li><li>Identified test attributes to be used for validation, verification, or demonstration of design requirements, system performance, mission suitability, or accuracy of analytical models beyond that described in the Verification and Validation Plan</li><li>Post Certification Mission (PCM) DRDs applicable to the crewed flight test(s)</li></ul>	<ul><li>Test Configuration</li><li>Test Objectives</li><li>Success Criteria</li><li>Linkage to Verification & Validation (V&V) Plan</li><li>Identified test attributes to be used for validation, verification, or demonstration of design requirements, system performance, mission suitability, or accuracy of analytical models beyond that described in the Verification and Validation Plan</li><li>Development Flight Instrumentation list</li><li>Data collection and reconstruction</li></ul>
<ul><li>Integrated schedule</li><li>Test Duration</li></ul>	<ul><li>Schedule Updates</li><li>Test Duration</li></ul>

Continued on next page…

Attachment J-02

Data Requirement Document (Continuation Sheet)

A. DRD No.: 109

B. DRD Title: Flight Test Plan

F. Data Requirements (continued):

The flight test plan shall include the following information (continued):

CBR	DCR(s) – Update to CBR information including additional information provided below
• Test Locations	• Test Locations • Mission design
• Test Logistics organization • Procedure development Process • Progress and Approval Milestone • Flight Test requirements definition • Instrumentation Plan • Approach to flight test production, operations (control centers and launch/ recovery sites, mission planning, etc.)	• Test Logistics • Preflight Test Procedures • Flight Test Procedures • Launch Commit Criteria (LCC)/Flight Rules • Flight Test requirements verification • Planned Design departures • Training Status • Updates to approach to flight test production, operations (control centers and launch/ recovery sites, mission planning, etc.)

For Crewed Flight Tests, the flight test plan shall include the following additional information:

CBR	DCR(s)
• Joint Test Team (JTT) Integration • Crew Makeup • Ground Team Crew Handover Responsibilities	• JTT updates • Crew Makeup updates • Ground Team Crew Handover Agreements
• Crew Training Plan and template	

Attachment J-02

Data Requirement Document
(Note: Please see DRL for Data Deliverable Type and Submission Frequency)

A. DRD No.: 110

B. DRD Title: Hazard Reports

C. Date: 11/19/13

D. Purpose / Use:

The Hazard Reports (HRs) will be used to ensure that hazards inherent in the design have been identified, and that hazard controls and verification methods have been implemented and verified.

E. Remarks:

The description below encompasses both hardware and software activities.

F. Data Requirements:

The Contractor shall deliver Hazard Reports in accordance with CCT-PLN-1120, *Crew Transportation Technical Management Processes,* and SSP 30599, *Safety Review Process.* The Contractor shall make two (2) final deliveries of each Hazard Report:

(a) After completion of the NASA Phase II Safety Review

(b) After completion of the NASA Phase III Safety Review, but no later than (NLT) forty-five (45) days prior to a Design Certification Review (DCR).

Phase III final Hazard Reports shall be maintained current and shall reflect the configuration of the integrated CTS design, operations, and functional capabilities.

Attachment J-02

Data Requirement Document
(Note: Please see DRL for Data Deliverable Type and Submission Frequency)

A. DRD No.: 111

B. DRD Title: Verification Closure Notices (VCNs)

C. Date: 11/19/13

D. Purpose / Use:

Provide evidence of closure of each technical requirement within CCT-REQ-1130, Section 3, *ISS Crew Transportation and Services Requirements Document*, and SSP 50808, *ISS to Commercial Orbital Transportation Services (COTS) Interface Requirements Document (IRD)*. Verification Closure Notice (VCN) status will be designated as initial, interim (dated), and as final in the closure field.

E. Remarks: None

F. Data Requirements:

The Contractor shall provide verification evidence for each CCT-REQ-1130 and SSP 50808 requirement in accordance with the approved Verification and Validation (V&V) plan (**DRD 108 V&V Plan**).

One VCN per requirement shall be submitted in this DRD. Final submittals against a specific requirement shall be made only after dependent verifications are completed and submitted. Partial early submission is encouraged and the Contractor shall identify open work associated with the verification activity and identify as partial submittal in the VCN.

VCN closure rationale shall provide specific description and/or reference to specific evidence to verify and validate compliance to the requirement. Each VCN shall have a unique identifier associated with each "shall" statement in the CCT-REQ-1130 or SSP 50808 requirement it closes. Also, each VCN shall include the requirement statement; and associated V&V Plan method, objectives, and success criteria. The detailed verification methods for the VCN (Analysis, Inspection, Test, or Demonstration) shall be identified on the VCN. The decomposition and interdependencies of the V&V objectives with success criteria shall be identified.

Flowdown of requirements to indentured product baseline shall be identified, where applicable. These lower level requirements shall be identified with associated closure verification. VCN closure is not complete until the lower level requirements are satisfied.

Continued on next page…

Attachment J-02

Data Requirement Document (Continuation Sheet)

A. DRD No.: 111

B. DRD Title: Verification Closure Notices

F. Data Requirements (continued):

The evidence submitted with the VCN for final approval shall include analysis, test reports, demonstration reports, or inspection results with a concise summary. The evidence shall point to the location of clear evidence for verifying the requirement. All evidence shall be delivered as attachment to the VCN. Any associated reference or supporting data shall be made available to NASA during the contract period of performance.

Production and operational verifications associated with recurring verification activities, including acceptance testing, shall include reference to the released procedure or constraint.

Variances to the requirement shall be identified in the VCN.

Signature blocks for the Contractor and NASA shall be included.

Attachment J-02

Data Requirement Document
(Note: Please see DRL for Data Deliverable Type and Submission Frequency)

A. DRD No.: 112

B. DRD Title: Certification Data Package

C. Date: 11/19/13

D. Purpose / Use:

The package collectively illustrates, with supporting evidence, that the system has met the operational and design technical requirements.

E. Remarks: None

F. Data Requirements:

Certification Data Package shall include:

(a) Crew Transportation System (CTS) configuration for Certification, including product definition, such as Drawing Tree and Product Breakdown Structure.

(b) The requirements that the system is certified to, including any applicable system specification, and any variances or waivers.

(c) A description of the reference mission and operations plans for which CTS Certification is being requested.

(d) Vehicle interface definition for any crew or cargo interfaces.

(e) A summary of the end-to-end design certification process, with reference to the Certification Plan, and identification of any differences between the certification plan and the certification activities completed. The summary will identify Verification and Validation (V&V) methods employed, general implementation approach, and summary results.

(f) Management systems, including Quality Management and Configuration Management, and the related implementation and control process including identification and tracking of limited life items.

Continued on the next page...

Attachment J-02

Data Requirement Document (Continuation Sheet)

A. **DRD No.:** 112

B. **DRD Title:** Certification Data Package

F. **Data Requirements (continued):**

(g) **DRD 111 Verification Closure Notices**, which include the evidence necessary to substantiate that the requirement has been met

(h) System Safety assessment to include probabilistic safety analysis, hazard analysis, fault tolerance assessment, human error analysis, software safety analysis, top safety risks, and crew survival strategy assessment.

(i) Integrated risk management and analysis results.

(j) A summary of Operational elements that meet the requirements of CCT-PLN-1120 and SSP 50808, *ISS to Commercial Orbital Transportation Services (COTS) Interface Requirements Document (IRD)*. The summary will identify how facilities, plans, processes, governing standards, and documents will ensure safe execution of all mission phases. The summary shall include success and risks identified in simulated mission phases.

Attachment J-02

Data Requirement Document
(Note: Please see DRL for Data Deliverable Type and Submission Frequency)

A. DRD No.: 113

B. DRD Title: Range Safety Data Documentation

C. Date: 11/19/13

D. Purpose / Use:

This DRD covers the submission of Range Safety-related data and documentation required to be delivered to NASA. This DRD is in addition to the Contractor's responsibility to meet the Range requirements established by the applicable Federal or Range Safety Organizations.

E. Remarks:

NASA Procedural Requirement (NPR) 8715.5, *Range Flight Safety Program*, is applicable to all Crew Transportation System (CTS) flights not licensed by the Federal Aviation Administration (FAA).

F. Data Requirements:

The Contractor shall make all Range Safety non-conformance requests and associated documentation available to NASA as a Type 4 DRD. The Contractor shall notify NASA of Range Safety non-conformances, or other Range Safety related issues, at the same time the applicable Federal or Range Safety Organization is notified, or as soon afterwards as is practical.

Attachment J-02

Data Requirement Document
(Note: Please see DRL for Data Deliverable Type and Submission Frequency)

A. DRD No.: 114

B. DRD Title: Crew Transportation System (CTS) Data Input for NASA Integration and Independent Verification and Validation (IV&V)

C. Date: 11/19/13

D. Purpose / Use:
To establish data required for the Government to perform ISS integration, stage verification, and Independent Verification and Validation of select analyses used for verification of applicable requirements.

E. Remarks:
For ISS integration and stage verification, the requirement in this DRD may be superseded if the Contractor has a Bilateral Data Exchange Agreement List and Schedule (BDEALS) jointly developed with the ISS Program.

F. Data Requirements:
The Contractor shall provide the data, documentation, drawings, analytical models, and support services upon request as necessary to support the ISS integration, stage verification, and the Government independent verification and validation of the following integrated analyses to the extent that these analyses are used to verify the applicable requirements. Multiple deliveries may be required during design and development, and the deliveries may be independent of major milestones. The deliveries support Government analytical tool development and perform analyses for ISS integration, stage verification, and Government independent verification and validation. In the event the Contractor has data that is applicable to more than one area listed, the Contractor may combine the data in one delivery and shall specify which areas the data applies to. Applicable data is data developed by the contractor during performance of the nominal work plan for CTS DDTE certification activities and/or PCM execution as scoped and defined in the PWS. CAD models shall be provided in contractors CAD tool format or stp file format. Final DRD submission shall be coordinated with NASA.

Specifically, the Contractor shall provide data for the following areas:

(1) For ISS Integration and Stage Verification:

(a) Inputs as required per SSP 50964, *Visiting Vehicle ISS Integration Plan*, Appendix F, *Joint Verification Events List*.

(2) For Flight Mechanics and Guidance, Navigation & Control:

(b) GNC stability and performance analysis for all critical mission phases, including ascent, abort, entry, descent and landing.

Continued on next page...

Attachment J-02

Data Requirement Document (Continuation Sheet)

A. **DRD No.:** 114

B. **DRD Title:** CTS Data Input for NASA Integration and Independent Verification and Validation

F. **Data Requirements (continued):**

(2) For **Flight Mechanics and Guidance Navigation & Control:** (continued)

(c) Performance and trajectory analysis as a function of launch date and time (including appropriate abort cases).

(d) Performance capability, margins and reserves, including description of how performance reserve is calculated.

Typical supporting data includes:

- Guidance strategies and detailed algorithm description and/or source code or equivalent;

- Control strategies and detailed algorithm description and/or source code or equivalent;

- Navigation strategies and detailed algorithm description and/or source code or equivalent;

- Analysis/linearization assumptions by flight condition;

- Sequence of events and tracking coverage;

- Design reference trajectories and dispersed trajectories for all mission phases;

- Documentation and characterization of crew piloting interface, where crew piloting affects the flight mechanics, guidance, navigation, and control of the CTS;

- Spacecraft and Launch Vehicle mass, cg (center of gravity), moments and products of inertia including structural reference frames and any appropriate reserve quantities;

- Control effector characteristics (including dispersions) for thrusters, engines, separation mechanisms, parachutes, aero surfaces, actuators and throttles.

Continued on next page…

Attachment J-02

Data Requirement Document (Continuation Sheet)

A. **DRD No.:** 114

B. **DRD Title:** CTS Data Input for NASA Integration and Independent Verification and Validation

F. **Data Requirements (continued):**

(3) For **Loads and Structural Dynamics:**

(a) Coupled dynamic loads analysis including all flight/mission events and conditions that cause the greatest loads, deflections, and accelerations on the integrated vehicle.

(b) Forcing function derivation for conditions that cause the greatest loads, deflections, and accelerations on the integrated vehicle.

Typical supporting data includes:
- Models (FEM (Finite Element Model) and Craig-Bampton) and forcing functions used in loads analysis;

- Description of models, methodology and forcing functions used;

- Evidence supporting model validation via modal test and/or influence coefficient testing;

- The flight events and conditions that cause the greatest loads, accelerations, and deflections;

- Output from each flight event: maximum /minimum tables of payload selected Acceleration Transformation Matrices, interface forces, and internal Load Transformation Matrices;

- Derivation of and use of load indicators which serve as a means of selecting controlling load cases for delivery to structures/stress;

- Description/definition of day-of-launch loads process.

(4) For **Aerodynamics and Aerothermodynamics:**

(a) Aerodynamic analysis for all relevant mission phases.

(b) Aerothermal analysis for all relevant mission phases.

Continued on next page…

Attachment J-02

Data Requirement Document (Continuation Sheet)

A. DRD No.: 114

B. DRD Title: CTS Data Input for NASA Integration and Independent Verification and Validation

F. Data Requirements (continued):

(4) For **Aerodynamics and Aerothermodynamics:** (continued)

Typical supporting data includes:

- Integrated vehicle aerodynamic database and substantiation report;

- Spacecraft separation and free-flight aerodynamic database and substantiation report;

- Integrated vehicle aerothermal database and substantiation report;

- Spacecraft separation and free-flight aerothermal database and substantiation report;

- Wind tunnel test data;

- Integrated vehicle outer mold line Computer Aided Design (CAD) model;

- Spacecraft outer mold line CAD model.

Attachment J-02

Data Requirement Document
(Note: Please see DRL for Data Deliverable Type and Submission Frequency)

A. DRD No.: 201

B. DRD Title: Mission Integration and Operations Management Plan (MIOMP)

C. Date: 11/19/13

D. Purpose / Use:
To describe the various operations and processes, product delivery templates, and organizational interfaces necessary for the Contractor to implement the integration and operations (I&O) activities required for the Contractor's Post Certification Missions (PCMs) to the ISS.

E. Remarks:
For the purposes of this deliverable, "cargo" herein refers to cargo, payloads, and supplies.

F. Data Requirements:
The Contractor shall keep this document current with established processes, schedules, and interfaces throughout the contract period of performance. The document shall contain integrated text and graphics, as required, to describe and/or illustrate the various aspects of services provided, including process descriptions, schedule flows, facility and tool illustrations, and organizational hierarchies. As changes are made to the MIOMP, the Contractor shall submit updates for NASA review and concurrence according to the DRD type 2 definition. For DDTE, the Contractor shall propose a final submittal, consistent with the test flight to ISS.

The following information shall be included under the corresponding principal function material:

(1) For Mission Integration and Analysis Support:
The Contractor shall provide a functional breakdown and description of how it interfaces with NASA to:

    (a) ensure the timely provision of data required in support of mission integration and documentation.

    (b) incrementally mature the mission design (launch window, planned mission profile, back-up opportunities) and flight readiness.

    (c) provide the necessary data for NASA to determine pre-mission status and flight readiness including personnel training and certification, ground accommodation interfaces and service agreements.

    (d) define the procedures, timeline, and constraints associated with crew and cargo through handover for pre-launch and post-landing, including roles and responsibilities and interfaces associated with NASA personnel, equipment, and facilities.

Continued on next page…

Attachment J-02

Data Requirement Document (Continuation Sheet)

A. **DRD No.:** 201

B. **DRD Title:** Mission Integration and Operations Management Plan (MIOMP)

F. **Data Requirements (continued):**

(2) For Mission Operations Documentation:
The Contractor shall provide a functional breakdown and description of how the Contractor manages the preparation and utilization of joint operations products in conjunction with NASA.

(3) For Crew Transportation System (CTS) Systems and Commercial Cargo Operations Training:
The Contractor shall provide a functional breakdown and description of how it manages the training for CTS and commercial cargo for the flight crews, console operators, and instructors. This includes the approach to (1) development and maintenance of training plans, study materials, and hardware and software aids; (2) development of training requirements and schedules including personnel certification and certification maintenance; (3) development and utilization of training mockups.

(4) For Ground Facility Utilization:
The Contractor shall provide a functional breakdown and description of how it allocates facilities to be utilized during all phases of operations including pre-launch preparation, in flight execution, and post flight recovery.

(5) For Data Management:
The Contractor shall provide a functional breakdown and description of how it manages the CTS command and data. This includes: the approach to development of CTS and data requirements (including requirements for data processing, storage, and distribution); coordination of the method(s) by which this data is integrated into the standard ISS communication and data services; establishment of interfaces with NASA and non-NASA components of the air-to-ground communications network; and coordination of the Contractor's data management plan with NASA.

(6) For Simulations and Mission Operations Support:
The Contractor shall provide a functional breakdown and description of how it manages CTS support with the JSC Mission Control Center (MCC), ISS Management Center (IMC), and JSC Mission Evaluation Room (MER) facilities, personnel, and processes during all Joint Integrated Simulations and during real-time mission operations.

Continued on next page...

Attachment J-02

Data Requirement Document (Continuation Sheet)

A. DRD No.: 201

B. DRD Title: Mission Integration and Operations Management Plan (MIOMP)

F. Data Requirements (continued):

(7) For **Cargo Capabilities:**
The Contractor shall define its cargo capability and schedule flexibility in the following table:

Cargo Capabilities Table

Cargo Type	Maximum Mass	Maximum Volume	Turnover Schedule
Standard Internal Stow	TBP	TBP	L-TBP
Late Stow	TBP	TBP	L-TBP
Standard Internal Destow	TBP	TBP	Landing+TBP
Early Destow	TBP	TBP	Landing+TBP

TBP: To be Proposed
L-: Launch minus

(8) For **Cargo Manifesting and Integration Support:**
The Contractor shall provide a functional breakdown and description of how it works with the ISS Program Office, Commercial Crew Program (CCP), the Contracting Officer Representative (COR), and cargo hardware developers to establish a mission manifest within the capability of the spacecraft and based on the crew complement. The processes shall include: the collection and documentation of pertinent technical and operational data; establish mission manifests and execution; and physically integrate cargo into and out of the pressurized volume of the orbital spacecraft.

(9) For **Launch and Landing Processing:**
The Contractor shall provide a functional breakdown and description of the processes and schedule for ground processing of crew and cargo at the launch site, the landing site, and return facilities. This section shall include service and facility capabilities, ground safety processes, cargo and crew integration from handover to launch and from return to handover back to NASA, accommodation of NASA personnel (e.g., flight surgeons) and equipment, and high level processing schedule.

Attachment J-02

Data Requirement Document
(Note: Please see DRL for Data Deliverable Type and Submission Frequency)

A. DRD No.: 202

B. DRD Title: Post Certification Mission (PCM) Work Plan

C. Date: 11/19/13

D. Purpose / Use:

The Post Certification Mission Work Plan establishes the schedule milestones, payment milestones and completion criteria for each mission. The work plan is expected to be kept current to accommodate changes during PCM preparation and execution.

E. Remarks: None

F. Data Requirements:

The Contractor shall keep this document current to reflect the latest PCM planning and execution. When changes affecting the content of the PCM work plan, the Contractor shall submit an updated PCM Work Plan for NASA review and concurrence according to the DRD type 2 definition.

For each Post Certification Mission, the Contractor shall submit a PCM Work Plan that reflects the Contract Performance Work Statement and contains:

(a) Milestones, by name and description of the milestones, corresponding to the payment number;

(b) Number of months prior to (L-) launch;

(c) The targeted launch date and associated back-up opportunities;

(d) An acceptance criteria narrative (i.e., describes progress in terms of activities completed prior to the payment event) and any proposed changes from the Contract PWS;

(e) The review process, location, deliverables, delivery dates, means and timing for which data will be made available to NASA, and other logistics related information;

(f) Identification of any critical linkage to Certification and previous mission authorization(s) activities that may impacts planned activities.

Attachment J-02

Data Requirement Document
(Note: Please see DRL for Data Deliverable Type and Submission Frequency)

A. DRD No.: 203

B. DRD Title: Vehicle Interface Definition Document (IDD)

C. Date: 11/19/13

D. Purpose / Use:
To provide NASA with an understanding of the Contractor's CTS environments (launch, on-orbit, and landing) so that NASA can perform end item certification on crew interfaces and individual cargo items to ensure survivability.

E. Remarks:
For the purposes of this deliverable, "cargo" herein refers to cargo, payloads, and supplies.

F. Data Requirements:
The Contractor shall provide a Vehicle IDD that includes allowable crew and cargo mass properties, mechanical interfaces (i.e., mount, ducting), electrical interface, data interface (including command capability), handling, and any spacecraft specific constraint.

The environments shall include: quasi-static load, low frequency loads, random vibration loads, acoustic loads, thermal loads, pressure loads, shock, atmospheric gas concentration, allowable gas release, relative humidity, radiation, electromagnetic, and any other environment constraints deemed necessary. Environments shall be defined as the maximum environments that cargo may be exposed to during ground processing, launch, on-orbit, reentry, and recovery.

The Contractor shall provide an instrumentation plan including translation of data from flight instrumentation to the crew and cargo interface of interest. The plan shall include location and type of sensors, sampling rate, and downlink method and bandwidth for each mission phase.

Launch and landing load factors and rotational accelerations shall be provided in the following reference frame: $N_x(g)$, $N_y(g)$, $N_z(g)$,
$R_x(rad/sec^2)$, $R_y(rad/sec^2)$, $R_z(rad/sec^2)$

X: The longitudinal axis of the spacecraft. Positive x axis extends from the base or bottom of the spacecraft to the nose of the cargo spacecraft.

Y: Y axis is perpendicular to the x axis.

Z: Z axis is perpendicular to the x and y axes and completes the right-handed coordinate system.

Continued on next page…

Attachment J-02

Data Requirement Document (Continuation Sheet)

A. DRD No.: 203

B. DRD Title: Vehicle Interface Definition Document (IDD)

F. Data Requirements (continued):

Random vibration environments shall be provided in each axis from 20-2000 Hz at the crew and cargo interface to the spacecraft. The overall grms (root mean square acceleration) values shall be reported. The duration of the excitation shall be reported.

Acoustic environments shall be provided 1/3-octave band format, starting from a 31.5 Hz center frequency and extending to a 2500 Hz center frequency, at the cargo/payload interface. The overall acoustic environment shall also be provided. A reference sound pressure level of 2×10^{-5} N/m^2 shall be used to report the acoustic environment in terms of decibels.

Shock environments shall be provided from 10-10000 Hz at the cargo/payload interface. The response shall be reported in units of peak acceleration.

Load spectrums shall be provided which cover the expected loading events for one flight (launch, free-flight, berthing) at the cargo interface. The spectrum shall be divided by a minimum of 10% amplitude tiers.

Pressure and thermal environments for crew and cargo interfaces in the orbital spacecraft shall be provided.

Attachment J-02

Data Requirement Document
(Note: Please see DRL for Data Deliverable Type and Submission Frequency)

A. DRD No.: 204

B. DRD Title: Mission Resource Allocation Document (MRAD)

C. Date: 12/20/13

D. Purpose / Use:
To establish the allocation of resources and technical data requirements needed for Post Certification Missions. The associated data will provide the required assessment to confirm compatibility with the spacecraft environments defined in the Vehicle IDD and compatibility with SSP 50808 *ISS to Commercial Orbital Transportation Services (COTS) Interface Requirements Document (IRD)*, and CCT-REQ-1130, *ISS Crew Transportation and Services Requirements Document*.

E. Remarks:
For the purposes of this deliverable cargo herein refers to cargo, payloads, and supplies.

F. Data Requirements:
The Contractor's format will be acceptable, except for those sections concerned with stowage and labeling data for cargo. The format for stowage and labeling data for cargo shall be compatible with the ISS Inventory Management System (IMS).

The report shall be generated and updated based on progressive maturity of the mission definition and crew and cargo complement. The cargo complement will be defined by NASA at launch minus thirteen (L-13) months, L-5 months, and L-6 weeks. The MRAD shall be delivered at launch minus ten (10) months, launch minus three (3) months, and launch minus one (1) month. The Contractor shall submit any changes or additions to NASA, in a timely manner, for the execution of joint analysis and stage verification. The final MRAD delivery shall be coordinated with NASA. For DDTE, the Contractor shall propose a final submittal, consistent with the test flight to ISS.

The Contractor's response (this MRAD) shall address specific technical and operational issues pertaining to each proposed cargo item and contain recommendations for combining the proposed cargo items into an optimized crew/ cargo configuration. Any technical or operational issues that could not be resolved shall be documented in the report with a recommended forward action plan.

The MRAD shall be the source of accurate data pertaining to the mission-unique mass, volume and other resources allocated to each crew/cargo item. All data shall be updated with the latest crew/cargo complement.
Continued on next page…

Attachment J-02

Data Requirement Document (Continuation Sheet)

A. **DRD No.:** 204

B. **DRD Title:** Mission Resource Allocation Document (MRAD)

F. **Data Requirements (continued):**

The following requirements shall be included in the MRAD:

(a) Mission physical configuration of the spacecraft pressurized module including ascent, on-orbit, and return stowage configurations (crew and cargo layouts including bag-level IMS bar code/serial number);

(b) Mission propulsion and power resources and margins for all mission phases;

(c) Consumables and cargo/supplies for the crew for all mission phases;

(d) Command and data requirements for cargo;

(e) Crew and Cargo thermal/environmental assessment;

(f) Spacecraft vehicle dynamics;

(g) Spacecraft mass properties. The final mass properties delivery within L-6 weeks is expected to be a weighed, final spacecraft configuration;

(h) Spacecraft structural math model and thermal math model;

(i) Spacecraft thruster plume and firing history, propellant types;

(j) Verification Loads Analysis. This report shall include:

    (1) Sensitivity of crew and cargo response to spacecraft configuration (location and mass);

    (2) Expected crew and cargo environment during all phases of flight and associated margins against NASA-provided environmental limits;

(k) Plan for late access and/or early retrieval;

(l) Mission-unique hardware and Government furnished equipment (GFE);

Continued on next page…

Attachment J-02

Data Requirement Document (Continuation Sheet)
A. **DRD No.:** 204

B. **DRD Title:** Mission Resource Allocation Document (MRAD)

F. **Data Requirements (continued):**

(m) Flight operations support, standards for console time, and plan for Certification Status of support personnel;

(n) Crew Equipment Interface Test Date(s);

(o) Any design changes that may affect the requirements in CCT-REQ-1130 and SSP 50808 and associated analytical products necessary for the Contractor's spacecraft;

(p) Trajectory data to be delivered for assessments: within one month and again within one week of launch; within one month and again within one week of departure; and near real-time updates during flight for key events such as maneuvers monitoring. This shall include:

  (1) Timeline of free-flight activities (e.g., launch insertion, appendage configuration, jettisons, major mode changes);

  (2) Spacecraft maneuver plan. For each maneuver, insertion through entry, includes inertial and relative state vector, attitude at time of burn, burn components by axis, spacecraft mass at time of burn, and time of burn;

(q) Spacecraft ephemeris including time, position, velocity, and covariance.

(r) Atmospheric and drag characteristics for the ISS and Spacecraft that are used in the analysis.

Attachment J-02

Data Requirement Document
(Note: Please see DRL for Data Deliverable Type and Submission Frequency)

A. DRD No.: 205

B. DRD Title: Spacecraft Computer-Aided Design (CAD) Models

C. Date: 11/19/13

(a) **Purpose / Use:**

The three-dimensional (3-D) CAD models will be accurate geometrical depictions of the exterior and interior of the spacecraft. The CAD models will be used to support mission design, procedure development, clearance analysis, cargo integration, Extra-vehicular worksite analysis (if required), solar array shadowing, Aerodynamics/Mass Properties Data Book development, and Neutral Buoyancy Lab reconfiguration. The CAD models will also be used to validate hardware interfaces, to ensure hardware will mate on-orbit with International Space Station and performing Intra-Vehicular analysis. .

E. Remarks: None.

F. Data Requirements:
For DDTE, the Contractor shall propose a final submittal, consistent with the test flight to ISS.

The 3-D CAD models shall be of sufficient detail that the external and internal geometry shows an accurate depiction of the spacecraft. 3-D CAD models are required of the end items up to the major assembly. The 3-D CAD models shall include:

(a) For Exterior CAD models
Examples of the required detail (but not limited to) for exterior CAD models are docking aids, antennae, cables, cable clamps, debris shields, Extravehicular Activity (EVA) aids, sensors, thrusters, handrails, vents, cameras, lights, targets. All objects that deploy rotate or otherwise move shall be appropriately modeled with location and limit parameters described.

(b) For Interior CAD models
CAD models of the interior of the spacecraft shall require the following (but not limited to) internal pressure shell, standoff, hatches, ports, stowage compartments, rack attachments, vents, lights, handrails, seat tracks, emergency equipment. All objects that deploy rotate or otherwise move shall be appropriately modeled with location and limit parameters described.

Continued on next page…

Attachment J-02

Data Requirement Document (Continuation Sheet)

A. **DRD No.:** 205

B. **DRD Title:** Spacecraft Computer-Aided Design (CAD) Models

F. **Data Requirements (continued):**

Format:
- Models shall be full scale in English (inches) units.
- Models shall be constructed to nominal dimensions.
- Models should be built with respect to element local coordinate system.
- Models shall be supplied in one of the following formats: Unigraphics (preferred), Computer-Aided Three-Dimensional Interactive Application (CATIA), PTC Pro-Engineer, Parasolid, Stereo Lithography (SLA), Virtual Reality Modeling Language (VRML), or Product Vision (JT).
- Solid Models Only—Models may be unparameterized "dumb solids" meaning tolerance data; model history, material properties, etc. need not be included.
- Model parts should be individual entities and not fused together. This will allow CAD team to update the model based on hardware measurements.
- Description on movement limits for any articulating items should be provided.
- As-designed and as-built (validated and final) models shall be delivered and validated for areas of close clearances to ISS and/or crew access.
- Interior models shall be delivered either separate from exterior models or as an appropriately documented assembly such that interior models can easily be separated leaving both interior and exterior features intact.
- Where interior subassemblies are supplied as separate models, sufficient documentation shall be provided to support correct geometrical integration of each subassembly into its larger interior element.
- A model tree shall be provided which documents the element model assembly architecture as well as model and subassembly titles.
- Models shall be under configuration management so that the pedigree and source of models are documented and retained.
- Models and associated assembly trees and configuration data shall be delivered electronically.

Maintenance
Updates to CAD models shall be delivered to NASA within seven (7) days of drawing release.

Attachment J-02

Data Requirement Document
(Note: Please see DRL for Data Deliverable Type and Submission Frequency)

A. DRD No.: 206

B. DRD Title: Internal Cargo Interface Control Agreement (ICA)

C. Date: 11/19/13

D. Purpose / Use:

The Internal Cargo Interface Control Agreement (ICA) is designed to provide the spacecraft to cargo item requirements definition and interface details. This is required for complex internal cargo, which are typically all except soft-bags. It defines the mission requirements and interfaces as they are known. The Internal Cargo ICA will evolve as mission requirements are identified.

E. Remarks:
For the purposes of this deliverable, "cargo" herein refers to cargo, payloads, and supplies.

F. Data Requirements:
For DDTE, the Contractor shall propose a final submittal, consistent with the test flight to ISS. The internal cargo ICA shall define, to the extent required by each specific complex internal cargo: the hardware interfaces and resource requirements; ground processing requirements; safety and interface verification requirements; and operational requirements of each complex internal cargo item identified for the Post Certification Mission. It shall also include any other Contractor-furnished hardware and services required, such as transportation or analytical support services. Depending on the complexity of the payload and its interfaces, two types of Internal Cargo ICAs shall be available. These are:

(1) Interface Control Document (ICD)
Cargo, such as active payloads or hard mounted Orbital Replacement Units (ORUs), that require crew operation or resources (e.g., power, cooling, command and data), shall utilize ICDs. Once baselined, each ICD shall be under configuration control. The ICD shall include all figures or the figures must be available for delivery, if requested.

(2) Stowage Interface Agreement (SIA)
Cargo, such as passive payloads, with ground handling constraints and/or verification requirements, shall utilize SIAs. Once baselined, each SIA shall be under configuration control. The SIA shall include all figures (if any) or the figures must be available for delivery, if requested.

Maintenance
Cargo-specific Internal Cargo ICAs shall be maintained throughout the mission preparation and execution.

Attachment J-02

Data Requirement Document
(Note: Please see DRL for Data Deliverable Type and Submission Frequency)

A. **DRD No.: 207**

B. **DRD Title:** Integrated Cargo Phase III Hazard Report

C. **Date:** 11/19/13

D. **Purpose / Use:**

The ISS Safety Review Panel (SRP) will use the Integrated Hazard Reports and System Description to assess the design and operation of ISS element hardware configuration for preflight assessments.

A. **Remarks:** None

F. **Data Requirements:**

(a) Submittals shall consist of Integrated Hazard Reports and System Descriptions for all crew equipment and cargo that will be integrated into the spacecraft.

(b) Hazard Reports and System Descriptions shall be provided in accordance with SSP 30309, *Safety Analysis and Risk Assessment Requirements*.

(c) System Description: The Contractor shall provide a description of the launch and on-orbit configuration of the hardware in accordance with SSP 30599, *Safety Review Process*. Functional diagrams shall be submitted and supplemented with descriptions of interfaces and operations.

Attachment J-02

Data Requirement Document
(Note: Please see DRL for Data Deliverable Type and Submission Frequency)

A. DRD No.: 208

B. DRD Title: Flight Readiness Review (FRR) Data Package

C. Date: 11/19/13

D. Purpose / Use:

The FRR data package establishes the data required for NASA to evaluate readiness and provide approval to conduct crewed missions.

E. Remarks: None

F. Data Requirements:

The Contractor shall provide to NASA:

(a) Flight Readiness Review Data Package per CCT-PLN-1120, *Crew Transportation Technical Management Processes*, Appendix F, *CTS FTRR/FRR Milestone Data*.

(b) Documentation showing all acceptance, checkout and integration testing has been completed.

(c) Status of all Review Item Dispositions (RIDs), actions, and open work from Mission Review Milestones.

(d) Documentation that Mission support team is defined, has been trained, and is in place.

(e) Evidence that all operational supporting and enabling capabilities necessary for nominal and contingency operations have been tested and delivered/installed at the site(s).

(f) Plans, procedures, and training for nominal and contingency operations for the Crew Transportation System (CTS) have been completed.

(g) Evidence that systems, hardware, software, personnel, and procedures are in place.

(h) Plan and schedule of preplanned forward work.

Attachment J-02

Data Requirement Document
(Note: Please see DRL for Data Deliverable Type and Submission Frequency)

A. DRD No.: 209

B. DRD Title: Post Flight Assessment Report

C. Date: 11/19/13

D. Purpose / Use:

This report provides NASA a comprehensive post-flight summary of the Crew Transportation System (CTS). This post flight assessment report will support the NASA Contracting Officer's mission success determination.

E. Remarks: None

F. Data Requirements:
For DDTE, the Contractor shall propose a final submittal, consistent with the test flight to ISS.

After each launch, the Contractor shall deliver a Post Flight Assessment (PFA) report no later than (NLT) fourteen (14) days after docking with ISS, an updated PFA report NLT fourteen (14) days after landing and a final PFA report NLT sixty (60) days after landing. This report shall provide a comprehensive post-flight summary of the Crew Transportation System (CTS).

The Post Flight Assessment Report shall provide the following data as it pertains to the CTS:

(a) Predicted and actual vehicle system, subsystem, and component performance data;

(b) Comprehensive flight reconstructions, to include predicted and actual trajectories and communication coverage;

(c) Determination of actual flight environments;

(d) Explanation of significant differences between the predicted and actual flight environments;

(e) When applicable, mishap investigation and resolution documentation, responses and implementations to the mishap board's recommendations and return to flight activities;

(f) Problem identification, anomalies, and malfunctions from post Flight Readiness Review (FRR) through landing and recovery; their impact on the CTS, crew, cargo, and the overall mission.

Continued on next page…

Attachment J-02

Data Requirement Document (Continuation Sheet)

A. DRD No.: 209

B. DRD Title: Post Flight Assessment Report

F. Data Requirements (continued):

(g) Status of corrective actions and anomaly resolutions. This would include model and predicted environment updates due to collected flight data.

(h) Assessment of the adequacy of training, both for flight and ground personnel.

(i) Analysis demonstrating that the Mission Success Criteria has been met.

Attachment J-02

Data Requirement Document
(Note: Please see DRL for Data Deliverable Type and Submission Frequency)

A. DRD No.: 210

B. DRD Title: Imagery and Associated Cataloging

C. Date: 11/19/13

D. Purpose / Use:
To provide imagery of docking interfaces, crew interfaces, connectors, Extravehicular Activity (EVA) and Extravehicular Robotic (EVR) interfaces of the spacecraft vehicle. Also, to capture all ISS interfaces on the spacecraft and cargo transported to the ISS.

E. Remarks:

For the purposes of this deliverable, "cargo" herein refers to cargo, payloads, and supplies

F. Data Requirements:
For DDTE, the Contractor shall propose a final submittal, consistent with the test flight to ISS.

(1) Preflight Imagery Plan (PFIP) (Data Type 2)
A Contractor provided Pre-Flight Imagery Plan (PFIP) shall be constructed as described in SSP 50502, *ISS Hardware Preflight Imagery Requirements,* to facilitate Contractor planning and submittal of imagery. The PFIP shall define imagery requirements for the "before integration", "during integration", and "after integration" phases of the integration. The PFIP shall be submitted to NASA for review and approval. The imagery plan shall specify the imagery to be captured by the Contractor. The PFIP shall also be used for evaluation purposes to approve Contractor imagery submittals. The final PFIP shall be submitted to NASA at launch minus six (L-6) months.

The Contractor PFIP shall include the following imagery:

- Docking/ berthing interfaces

- Connectors (cables and fluid) between the spacecraft and the ISS including clocking and pin configuration

- Extravehicular Activity (EVA) interfaces

- Extravehicular Robotic (EVR) interfaces

- Intravehicular Activity (IVA) interfaces as related to cargo operations

Continued on next page…

Attachment J-02

Data Requirement Document (Continuation Sheet)

A. DRD No.: 210

B. DRD Title: Imagery and Associated Cataloging

F. Data Requirements (continued):

(1) Preflight Imagery Plan (PFIP) (continued):
Complex payload hardware, installed or mounted in the orbital vehicle pressurized module, shall require imagery of ISS attach points, connectors, fluid lines, and crew interfaces. The PFIP shall list all hardware to be imaged, the type of view (close up, normal, wide view) and the integration stage of the hardware (before, during or after integration onto the module and/or carrier).

(2) Imagery Requirements (Data Type 3)
The Contractor shall provide imagery of docking interfaces, crew interfaces, connectors, Extravehicular Activity (EVA) and Extravehicular Robotic (EVR) interfaces of the spacecraft vehicle. This imagery shall capture all ISS interfaces on the spacecraft and cargo transported to the ISS. The two (2) categories of imagery that comprise this task are Spacecraft Imagery and Pressurized Cargo Imagery. Within these two (2) categories, the imagery shall provide for:

    (a) Spacecraft Imagery
    Potential problems during on-orbit operations require imagery of all spacecraft to ISS interfaces. For docking interfaces, detailed close up and overall wide view imagery documenting ISS interfaces are required. Cable and fluid lines that connect to the ISS after docking require final configuration imagery of the connectors. This imagery shall provide the clocking and pin configuration of all ISS connections. This imagery shall be included in the PFIP.

    (b) Pressurized Cargo Imagery
    Pressurized cargo imagery shall be taken to support cargo unloading and loading operations and crew training. All Flight Support Equipment (FSE) attach points, connectors and crew interfaces shall be imaged before, during and after integration. This imagery shall be included in the PFIP to ensure requirements are defined and communicated to the integrator.

(3) Imagery Submittals (Data Type 3)
The minimum resolution for the PFIP digital still imagery shall be no less than six (6) megapixels. Images downloaded from the camera shall be native or raw format for maximum image resolution. Final imagery shall be submitted to NASA nominally at L-2 months but no later than launch. Image cataloging data with enough detail to support subsequent retrieval shall be submitted for incorporation into the NASA-JSC Digital Imagery Management System (DIMS) database. The preferred submittal method consists of submitting the imagery and data on Compact Disk – Read Only Memory (CD-ROM) or Digital Video Disc (DVD).

Attachment J-03
Contract Performance Work Statement

Attachment J-03

Table of Contents

1 **PERFORMANCE WORK STATEMENT** 7
   1.1 Introduction 7
   1.2 Background and Objective 7
   1.3 PWS Organization and Structure 7

2 **REFERENCE DOCUMENTS** 9
   2.1 Military Standards, Specifications, and Other Government Documents – Mandatory Compliance 9
   2.2 Military Standards, Handbooks, and Other Government Documents – Guidance Only 10

3 **REQUIREMENTS** 11
   3.1 CCtCap Program Management (All CLINs) 11
      3.1.1 Program Management 11
         3.1.1.1 Program Integration 11
         3.1.1.2 Program Management Reviews (PMRs) 11
         3.1.1.3 Program Support 12
         3.1.1.4 Government Insight 13
         3.1.1.5 Independent Verification and Validation (IV&V) 13
      3.1.2 Business Management 13
      3.1.3 Supplier Management 14
      3.1.4 Information Technology (IT) 14
      3.1.5 Risk Management 14
      3.1.6 Configuration and Data Management 15
         3.1.6.1 Configuration Management 15
         3.1.6.2 Data Management 15
   3.2 Design, Development, Test and Evaluation (DDTE)/Certification (CLIN 001) 16
      3.2.1 System Engineering and Integration (SE&I) 16
         3.2.1.1 System Engineering 16
            3.2.1.1.1 Requirements and Verification and Validation 17
            3.2.1.1.2 Interface Management 18
         3.2.1.2 Milestone/Technical Reviews 19

Attachment J-03

      3.2.1.2.1 Certification Baseline Review (CBR) [Mandatory Government Interim Milestone] 19
      3.2.1.2.2 ISS Design Certification Review (DCR) [Mandatory Government Delivery Milestone] 19
      3.2.1.2.3 Orbital Flight Test Flight Test Readiness Review (OFT FTRR) [Mandatory Government Interim Milestone] 20
      3.2.1.2.4 Crewed Flight Test Flight Test Readiness Review (CFT FTRR) [Mandatory Government Interim Milestone] 20
      3.2.1.2.5 Operations Readiness Review (ORR) [Mandatory Government Interim Milestone] 20
      3.2.1.2.6 Certification Review (CR) [Mandatory Government Delivery Milestone] 21
    3.2.1.3 System Analysis 21
    3.2.1.4 System Integration and Certification 22
    3.2.1.5 Specialty Engineering 24
  3.2.2 Safety, Reliability and Quality Assurance 25
    3.2.2.1 System Safety 25
    3.2.2.2 Environmental, Industrial, Launch Site and Range Safety 27
    3.2.2.3 Reliability, Maintainability and Availability 27
    3.2.2.4 Quality Assurance 27
    3.2.2.5 Software Safety and Assurance 28
  3.2.3 Production Control 28
  3.2.4 Vehicle (CST-100 and LV) 28
    3.2.4.1 Flight Hardware 28
    3.2.4.2 Flight Software 28

██

  3.2.5 Ground Systems 32
    3.2.5.1 Assembly Integration and Test (AIT) Facility and Systems 32
    3.2.5.2 Ground Communication Systems 33
    3.2.5.3 Cargo Handling Operations, Facilities and Systems 33
    3.2.5.4 Recovery Systems and Operations 33
    3.2.5.5 Logistics and Logistic Systems 33
    3.2.5.6 Pre-Flight and Launch Site Infrastructure 33
    3.2.5.7 Ground Segment Test and Checkout 33
  3.2.6 Crew and Mission Operations (CMO) 33
    3.2.6.1 Mission Planning and Analyses 34
    3.2.6.2 Training 34
    3.2.6.3 Flight Operations 34
    3.2.6.4 Cargo Operations 34

Attachment J-03

- 3.2.7 Test and Evaluation 34
    - 3.2.7.1 Test Planning and Integration 35
    - 3.2.7.2 Ground Test 35
    - 3.2.7.3 Flight Test 35
- 3.2.8 Incorporation of NASA Disposition of CPC products 37
    - 3.2.8.1 Alternate Standards (Reference PWS Section 3.2.1.1) 37
    - 3.2.8.2 Hazard Reports (Reference PWS Section 3.2.2.1) 54
    - 3.2.8.3 Variances (Reference PWS Section 3.2.1.1.1) 54
    - 3.2.8.4 Verification and Validation Plan (Reference PWS Section 3.2.1.4) 71
    - 3.2.8.5 Certification Plan (Reference PWS Section 3.2.1.4) 71
- 3.3 Post Certification Missions (PCMs) Services (CLIN 002) 72
    - 3.3.1 Key PCM Milestones/Reviews 72
        - 3.3.1.1 Vehicle Baseline Review (VBR) (At no later than 18 months prior to launch (L-18 mo)) 72
        - 3.3.1.2 Mission Integration Review (MIR) (At no later than 13 months prior to launch(L-13 mo)) 73
        - 3.3.1.3 Mission Certification Review (MCR) (After Certification has been granted, and no later than 4 months prior to launch) 73
        - 3.3.1.4 ISS Stage Operational Readiness Review (SORR) (Approximately 3 weeks prior to launch) 75
        - 3.3.1.5 Flight Readiness Review (FRR) (Approximately 2 weeks prior to launch) 75
        - 3.3.1.6 Undocking Readiness (Approximately two (2) weeks prior to landing) 75
        - 3.3.1.7 Post Flight Review (PFR) (Approximately 2.5 weeks after landing) 75
    - 3.3.2 PCM Vehicle Integration 76
        - 3.3.2.1 Launch Vehicle (LV) and Crew Vehicle (CV) Integration 76
        - 3.3.2.2 Safety, Reliability and Quality Engineering 76
    - 3.3.3 PCM Mission Integration 77
        - 3.3.3.1 PCM Approach 78
        - 3.3.3.2 PCM Initiation 78
        - 3.3.3.3 Mission Definition and Documentation 78
        - 3.3.3.4 PCM Certification Maintenance 79
        - 3.3.3.5 Safety and Mission Assurance 79
        - 3.3.3.6 Analytical Integration 80
        - 3.3.3.7 ISS Integration 80
        - 3.3.3.8 Licenses and Permits 80
        - 3.3.3.9 Range Safety 80

3.3.4 Crew and Mission Operations 80
   3.3.4.1 Mission Planning and Analysis 80
   3.3.4.2 Training 81
   3.3.4.3 Flight Operations 81
      3.3.4.3.1 Flight Operations 81
      3.3.4.3.2 Emergency Crew Search and Rescue Interface 81
   3.3.4.4 Ground Systems 81
      3.3.4.4.1 Assembly Integration and Test (AIT) Facility and System 82
   3.3.4.5 Ground Communication Systems 82
   3.3.4.6 Recovery Systems and Operations 82
   3.3.4.7 Logistics and Logistic Systems 82
   3.3.4.8 Ground Segment Test and Checkout 82
3.3.5 PCM Cargo Integration 82
   3.3.5.1 Cargo Integration 83
   3.3.5.2 Return Cargo 83
3.3.6 Inherent Capabilities 83
   3.3.6.1 Contractor System Inherent Capabilities 83
   3.3.6.2 Coordination of Inherent Capabilities 85

3.4 Special Studies (CLIN 003) 86

Appendix A   Milestone Acceptance Criteria and Payment Schedule .... 1 of 63

Appendix B   Post Certification Mission (PCM) Milestone Acceptance Criteria and Payment Schedule .... 1 of 28

Attachment J-03

List Of Tables

Table 1.3-1.	PWS Layout	8
Table 3.2.1.1.1-1.	Definitions	17
Table 3.2.1.1.1-2.	CCtCap Applicable Documents	18
Table 3.2.4.3-1.	Products developed during Phase I & II that will be provided to NASA for review, comment and approval	30
Table 3.2.4.3-2.	Programmatic and Technical Reviews to be executed during Alternate Launch Vehicle Integration Phases I and II	31
Table 3.2.7.3-1.	PCM Task Performed during CLIN 001 for Crewed Flight Test to ISS	36
Table 3.2.8.1-1	Tasks for Alternate Standards based on CPC Disposition Letters	38
Table 3.2.8.3-1	Tasks for Variances based on CPC Disposition Letters	55
Table 3.3.6.1-1.	Inherent Capabilities	84

Attachment J-03

1 PERFORMANCE WORK STATEMENT

1.1 Introduction

The Performance Work Statement describes the scope of work to be performed by the Contractor under the Commercial Crew Transportation Capability (CCtCap) contract.

1.2 Background and Objective

The CCtCap effort is the second phase of a two-phased Commercial Crew Program (CCP) procurement strategy to develop a U.S. commercial crew space transportation capability with the goal of achieving safe, reliable and cost effective access to and from low earth orbit (LEO) including the International Space Station (ISS) with a goal of no later than 2017.

The primary objective of Phase 1, Certification Products Contract (CPC), is the delivery, technical interchange, and National Aeronautics and Space Administration (NASA) disposition of early lifecycle certification products that address Crew Transportation System (CTS) compliance with NASA standards and requirements for an International Space Station (ISS) Design Reference Mission (DRM) within the CCT-DRM-1110, Crew Transportation Design Reference Missions.

The overall objective of Phase 2 (CCtCap) is focused on the final Design, Development, Test, and Evaluation (DDTE) activities necessary to achieve NASA certification of a CTS for the ISS DRM within the CCT-DRM-1110, Crew Transportation Design Reference Missions (DRM), culminating with execution of post certification missions (PCMs) to the ISS. Successful conclusion of the Certification Phase of CCtCap means that the Contractor's CTS meets NASA safety requirements for transporting NASA crew to the ISS (reference CLIN 001). Once the capability is achieved and available to the Government, the Commercial Crew provider will be eligible to provide services to and from the ISS. NASA intends to purchase transportation services to meet its ISS crew rotation and emergency return obligations defined under the Inter-Governmental Agreement as part of the PCM or Services Phase of CCtCap (reference CLIN 002).

The objective of this PWS is to document the requirements documented in Attachment J-01, Integrated Crew Transportation System Requirements, and J-02, Data Requirements Deliverables.

1.3 PWS Organization and Structure

The PWS is comprised of two parts, the basic document which details the work scope required to execute the entire contract and appendices which provide specific requirements for the unique milestone reviews required for DDTE/Certification CLIN 001 and for each Post Certification Missions (PCM) CLIN 002 respectively (Table 1.3-1). The body of the PWS is segregated by the individual contract line item (CLINs). This PWS covers all three work scope areas/CLINs. This PWS is organized to align with the three CLINs with one additional section that is applicable to all CLINs (Table 1.3-1). Each of the PWS sections 3.2, 3.3, and 3.4 describes the unique efforts required to complete the scope of the required CLIN and are considered additive to PWS Section 3.1.

Attachment J-03

Table 1.3-1. PWS Layout

PWS Section	CLIN	Description
1.0		Introduction
2.0		Reference Documents
3.0		Requirements
3.1	All CLINs	CCtCap Program Management
3.2	CLIN 001	DDTE/Certification
3.3	CLIN 002	Post Certification Missions (PCM)
3.4	CLIN 003	Special Studies
Appendix A	CLIN 001	Milestone Acceptance Criteria and Payment Schedule
Appendix B	CLIN 002	PCM Milestone Acceptance Criteria and Payment Schedule

Section 3.1 (All CLINs): This section defines the work applicable to all CLINs and is associated with the tasks required to manage and lead the CCtCap contract.

Section 3.2 (CLIN 001 – DDTE/Certification (core contract)): This section defines the work necessary to:

(a) Complete DDTE activities and certify the CTS to NASA requirements that comply with CCT-REQ-1130, ISS Crew Transportation and Services Requirements Document, and SSP 50808, ISS to Commercial Orbital Transportation Services (COTS) Interface Requirements Document (IRD), for safely transporting NASA crew to the ISS.

(b) Define, manage, and implement technical management plans and processes associated with achieving and maintaining NASA certification throughout the CTS lifecycle in accordance with CCT-PLN-1120, Crew Transportation Technical Management Processes.

(c) Demonstrate long term operational plans to produce and operate CTS such that flight and ground articles are manufactured, assembled, and integrated, in a repeatable manner that satisfies NASA requirements.

Section 3.3 (CLIN 002) – Post Certification Missions (PCM): This section defines the work necessary to perform PCMs to the ISS.

Section 3.4 (CLIN 003 – Special Studies): This section defines the work necessary to perform risk reduction activities that may be performed as special studies as requested by NASA.

Attachment J-03

2 REFERENCE DOCUMENTS

2.1 Military Standards, Specifications, and Other Government Documents – Mandatory Compliance

Document Number	Date/Version	Document Title
AS9100	Rev. C, 15-Jan-2009	Quality Management Systems – Requirements for Aviation, Space and Defense Organizations
AFSPC MAN91-710	Jul-2004	Air Force Space Command Range Safety User Requirements Manual
CCT-PLN-1100	Rev. B-1, 23-May-2013	Crew Transportation Plan
CCT-DRM-1110	Rev. Basic-1, 8-Dec-2011	Crew Transportation System Design Reference Missions
CCT-PLN-1120	Rev. C, 25-Oct-2013	Crew Transportation Technical Management Processes
CCT-REQ-1130	Rev. C, 12-Nov-2013	ISS Crew Transportation and Services Requirements Document
CCT-STD-1140	Rev. A-1, 23-May-2013	Crew Transportation Standards and Processes Criteria
CCT-STD-1150	Rev. A-1, 16-Jul-2013	Crew Transportation Operations Standards
CCT-PLN-2000	Draft	NASA Crew Transportation and Services Certification Plan
JSC 35089	12-Jul-2012	Visiting Vehicle Operations Annex
NASA-STD-8739.8	With Change 1, 28-Jul-2004	Software Assurance Standard
NASA-STD-8719.13	Rev. C, 7-May-2013	Software Safety Standard
NPR 8715.3	Rev. C Chg-6, 3-Feb-2011	NASA General Safety Program Requirements
SSP 30234	Rev. B, Not 1 9-Sep-1992	Instructions for Preparation of Failure Modes and Effects Analysis and Critical Items List Requirements for International Space Station
SSP 30309	Rev. E, 28-Oct-1994	Safety Analysis and Risk Assessment Requirements Document
SSP 30599	Rev. B, 13-Feb-2000	ISS Safety Review Process
SSP 41170	Rev. A, 22-Jun-2000	ISS Configuration Management Requirements
SSP 50108	Rev. C, Nov-2006	ISS Certification of Flight Readiness Process Document

Attachment J-03

Document Number	Date/Version	Document Title
SSP 50260	Rev. B, 15-May-2003	ISS Medical Operations Requirements Document (MORD)
SSP 50667	Mar-2004	Medical Evaluation Document (MED)
SSP 50808	Rev. E, 20-Sep-2013 plus DCNs 0135B, 0146A*, 0149*, 0151*, 0152*, 0153*	International Space Station (ISS) to Commercial Orbital Transportation Services (COTS) Interface Requirements Document (IRD) * indicates draft version
SSP 50964	Baseline, 9-Sep-2013	Visiting Vehicle ISS Integration Plan

2.2 **Military Standards, Handbooks, and Other Government Documents – Guidance Only**

Document Number	Date/Version	Document Title
CCT-REF-1121	Rev. A-1, 5-Nov-2012	Probabilistic Safety Analysis (PSA) Methodology Guide
DA8-13-193	31-Oct-2013	Notional Training Template for ISS Crew members

Attachment J-03

3 REQUIREMENTS

3.1 CCtCap Program Management (All CLINs)

The following work statements are applicable to all CLINs related to this contract.

3.1.1 Program Management

3.1.1.1 Program Integration

The Contractor shall maintain a program management system to direct and control all elements of the Commercial Crew Transportation Capability (CCtCap) program. The system shall include planning, controlling, and monitoring the cost, schedule, risk, and technical objectives of the development, certification, and production efforts associated with this PWS.

The Contractor shall update existing program management plans that were developed and executed to in the prior phases of the CTS program, if required, to ensure processes associated with achieving and maintaining NASA certification throughout the CTS lifecycle are included in accordance with CCT-PLN-1120, Crew Transportation Technical Management Processes. The contractor's program plans shall contain sufficient detail to convey the approach for accomplishing program objectives (J-01 1120 3.0). The contractor shall ensure that the CCTS Program Management Plan (PMP), DCC1-00124-01, provides a roadmap for executing, monitoring and controlling the CCtCap program and spans the entire CTS lifecycle (J-01 1120 3.1.1). The CCTS PMP shall be delivered as part of DRD 102, Certification Baseline Review (CBR) Data Package, in support of Certification Baseline Review (CBR). The contractor shall develop, utilize, and maintain the tools to enable management of CCtCap (J-01 1120 3.1).

The Contractor shall ensure that other processes and management approaches not addressed in the PMP are documented in other program plans. The contractor shall ensure these plans are updated to address the entire lifecycle of the CTS (J-01 1120 3.1.1). The contractor shall provide these existing program management plans to NASA in support of the first milestone review for re-baselining for CCtCap at that review. The contractor shall execute, implement, and manage the CCtCap program in accordance with these program management plans.

3.1.1.2 Program Management Reviews (PMRs)

The Contractor shall conduct Quarterly Program status and management Reviews (QPRs) covering all CCtCap program matters with NASA. The contractor shall host these face-to-face meetings/reviews at the contractor's facilities associated with CCtCap execution or other mutually agreed to location. The contractor top level organizational and technical leadership shall chair these reviews/meetings. The agenda for the PMR meeting shall at a minimum address the contractor's progress in Certification and Post Certification Mission of the CTS and various areas to include technical/systems/safety engineering, testing, integrated logistics support, configuration management, manufacturing, fabrication and/or quality assurance issues, and other areas identified as high risk. As part of this meeting, the Contractor shall also present production progress material which includes: critical build status, manufacturing progress vs. plan, parts availability and shortages including Government Furnished items, quality issues impacting production, engineering actions needed by production, problem recovery plans, and delivery schedules. Status shall include discussion of the relationship between DDTE/Certification work and all authorized Post Certification Missions. The contractor shall include a discussion on program cost, schedule and technical risks to include status of previous identified issues including mitigations and resolutions. Cost updates shall be provided for expected costs through

Attachment J-03

Certification (CLIN 001) and the PCMs, and may include cost variations due to technical issues, schedules delays, corporate commitment progress and impacts to lifecycle cost estimates. The contractor shall identify cost growth and potential growth items with emphasis on changes since the last QPR. Additionally, the contractor shall present the Integrated Master Schedule highlighting updates/changes from previous Quarterly Program Reviews and readiness status of upcoming program milestones/reviews (with emphasis on milestones in the next six months) to ensure progression through performance milestones in compliance with established completion criteria. The contractor shall develop and deliver a QPR briefing package, DRD 005 Quarterly Program Review (QPR) Briefing Package, and provide to NASA prior to every QPR. Additionally, the contractor shall provide NASA a final package with action items and closure plans within five working days after the conclusion of the meeting.

3.1.1.3 Program Support

The Contractor shall support government program meetings/reviews by providing technical and programmatic subject matter expertise to participate and provide program data for NASA CCP decisions, perform evaluations and review of performance milestone deliverables and/or support other programmatic activities as requested/invited by NASA to include participating on Government Boards and Forums. NASA CCP Program Boards/Forums are defined in CCT-PLN-1100, Crew Transportation Plan include:

a) Technical Review Board

b) Program Control Board

c) ISS Program (ISSP) Transportation Integration Control Board

d) Space Station Program Control Board

e) Joint Program Requirements Control Board (JPRCB) for requirements issues that are shared between CCP and ISSP

f) NASA Program Boards - in support of issues related to Crew Transportation System (CTS) Certification, the Contractor may attend and support as invited. The Contractor may also request a NASA Program Board to be convened in support of issues related to CTS Certification.

g) Operational forums (e.g., Joint Operations Panel (JOP) and Flight Operations Review (FOR)) to support the analyses and data delivered to NASA for the development of joint NASA operations products, analyses and tools

h) Visiting Vehicle Integration Manager forums (VVIM) for joint development of ISS integration products and execution of joint processes

i) NASA Independent Verification and Validation activities associated with contract data provided with Verification Closure Notices (VCNs)

j) Integrated Safety Review process defined in CCT-PLN-1120, Crew Transportation Technical Management Processes. The contractor's participation shall include Phase Safety Reviews of Hazard Reports.

k) The Contractor shall participate in NASA/Federal Aviation Administration (FAA)/Range trilateral discussions representing its recommendations when crew safety and public safety risk considerations are assessed

Attachment J-03

3.1.1.4 Government Insight

The Contractor shall allow Government to actively participate in CCtCap coordination and/or planning forums, briefings, meetings, boards, readiness reviews/milestones, simulations, hardware or operational demonstrations, tests, and other events consistent with the model in CCT-PLN-1100, Crew Transportation Plan, Section 3.2 CCP Insight/Oversight and Appendix C, Insight Areas, and Contract Clause H.15 Government Insight. The contractor shall expand the existing insight provided through the Partner Integration Team (PIT) and extend Government participation into operations certification efforts with the Joint Test Team (JTT) approach. This approach allows the Government to assess the contractor's progress towards CTS certification in CLIN 001 and the execution of PCM flights in CLIN 002. The contractor shall document and deliver these approaches in an Insight Implementation Plan, DRD 001, in accordance with Clause H.15 Government Insight, and execute in accordance with the plan. The contractor shall ensure the requirements of Contract Clause H.15 Government Insight flow down to subcontractors and/or other business entities performing or supporting any critical work associated with this contract. Consistent with this insight approach, all Boeing products and activities developed outside of the CCtCap contract for the CTS program shall be updated, as required, and delivered to NASA in accordance with the applicable DRD's or made available to NASA in support of CCtCap in accordance with DRD 001, Insight Implementation Plan.

The contractor shall execute and perform in accordance with the Insight Implementation Plan delivered with the proposal from program start until DRD 001 is formally delivered and dispositioned.

3.1.1.5 Independent Verification and Validation (IV&V)

The Contractor shall upon request and as necessary support the Government's IV&V efforts. The contractor shall develop and deliver CTS data to support verification and validation and input to NASA for integration and IV&V in accordance with DRD 114, Crew Transportation System (CTS) Data Input for NASA Integration and Independent Verification and Validation (IV&V). Types of data shall include existing CTS developed environments data, test data, CAD model data (in the contractor's format or .stp file) of vehicle OML and interfaces to ISS and cargo, mission trajectories and mission plans/events (nominal and aborts), analysis results and analytical models (executable code). The contractor shall support discussions, technical interchanges with the Government on development of provided data, ground rules, assumptions and limitations of data and analysis models, and interpretation of contractor's analytical results.

3.1.2 Business Management

The Contractor shall implement the necessary business management functions to ensure all budget and schedule constraints are met and shall provide necessary contract, schedule, financial, and other program progress reporting for all CLINs under this contract. The contractor shall ensure the collecting and reporting of cost performance, and related data is accomplished in a disciplined manner so an integrated uniform cost database exists.

The Contractor shall develop and implement plans to support successful execution of all work projects and programs. The Contractor shall develop and deliver an Integrated Master Plan (IMP) in accordance with DRD 002, Integrated Master Plan and Integrated Master Schedule. The contractor's IMP may be an update to or amendment of the CCTS IMP, DCC1-00003-01. The IMP shall describe the significant accomplishments with the associated success criteria as

Attachment J-03

derived from the Contract Performance Work Statement (Attachment J-03, Contract PWS), DRDs, and other contract requirements.

The contractor shall develop, update, maintain, manage, and deliver a CCtCap Certification and Post Certification Missions Integrated Master Schedule (IMS) in accordance with DRD 002, Integrated Master Plan and Integrated Master Schedule. The IMS shall be an integrated logically linked schedule that captures the accomplishments described in the IMP and the lower level work necessary to support each of the IMP accomplishments. The IMS shall include all contract milestones, activities and tasks leading to the proposed date for CTS certification and all post certification mission development, integration and execution activities. The IMS shall identify priorities of tasks, order and sequence of tasks, primary and secondary critical path, schedule margin, and dependencies and relationships among tasks. The IMS shall identify tasks at the system level for major activities or products associated with design, development, integration, testing, certification, manufacturing, assembly and operations.

The Contractor shall provide a single point of contact (POC) for contract management. The duties of this Contracts Management POC shall coordinate any contract changes as they may arise, ensure compliance with applicable Federal, state and local regulations, laws, ordnances, directives and statutes regarding exports and imports and manages Government Furnished Property (GFP) per terms of the contract. The contractor shall develop and deliver the CCTS Export Control Plan in accordance with DRD 006, Export Control Plan, to encompass the CCtCap program and contract requirements.

3.1.3 Supplier Management

The Contractor shall monitor and control subcontractors and shall ensure proper flowdown of requirements. The contractor shall report subcontractor problems affecting schedule, quality, and performance at quarterly program reviews. The contractor shall ensure the government can participate in significant/major subcontractor reviews and meetings. The contractor shall notify the Government designee of supplier technical meetings, control boards, reviews, tests, and areas identified for Government Quality Assurance in the mutually agreed timeframe in accordance with the Insight Implementation Plan (reference DRD 001) and the risk based analysis (RBA) for safety critical items (per Contract Clause H.15 Government Insight) to permit meaningful Government participation through the entire event.

3.1.4 Information Technology (IT)

The Contractor shall implement and maintain throughout the lifecycle of the CCtCap program information systems, tools, and processes to ensure effective security, management and utilization of program data. The contractor shall develop and deliver an Information Technology (IT) Security Management Plan, DRD 003, and an IT Security Plan, DRD 004, in accordance with Contract Clause I.2 NFS 1852.204-76 Security Requirements for Unclassified Information Technology Resources. Responsibilities include implementation of effective information security protocols and file sharing protocols with customers. The Contractor shall document the processes and procedures that will be followed to ensure appropriate security of information technology (IT) resources are deployed, processed and used under this contract.

3.1.5 Risk Management

The Contractor shall execute program risk and opportunity management by identifying, assessing, and ensuring mitigation of program risks for items that are unique to CCtCap (J-01

Attachment J-03

1120 3.3). The risk management process shall be executed across teams, products, services and phases of the program and it shall address cost, schedule, and technical risks in accordance with the CCTS Risk Management Plan (RMP), DCC1-00250-01. The Contractor shall ensure that the RMP addresses the full CTS lifecycle (J-01 1120 3.3.1). The CCTS RMP shall be delivered as part of DRD 102, Certification Baseline Review (CBR) Data Package, in support of Certification Baseline Review (CBR). The RMP shall address risk identification, risk characterization, mitigation and elevation, risk controls and contingency and residual risk planning (J-01 1120 3.3.2). The risk process shall determine and mitigate safety risk to the lowest achievable level throughout the lifecycle. In addition, the RMP shall include opportunity management to identify opportunities to improve vehicle safety, improve operational efficiencies and reduce lifecycle costs across the entire program lifecycle. A status of the contractor risk assessment shall be discussed for the high risks and opportunities during the quarterly PMRs.

3.1.6 Configuration and Data Management

3.1.6.1 Configuration Management

The Contractor shall plan and implement a Configuration Management (CM) system consistent with the policies, procedures and processes established in the CCTS Configuration Management Plan (CMP), DCC1-00009-01. The CCTS CMP shall be delivered as part of DRD 102, Certification Baseline Review (CBR) Data Package, in support of Certification Baseline Review (CBR). The contractor shall own and maintain configuration control over requirements, specifications, flight products, numerical models, and drawings that govern the development and baseline configuration of the CTS. The CMP shall define the tools and techniques to manage and document the integrated and approved CTS configuration including systems, equipment, and operations products (configuration control); control, record, and report changes (change management); variance and constraint handling, nonconformance reporting and disposition, and audit the systems and items to verify conformance (J-01 1120 3.2, 3.2.1).

3.1.6.2 Data Management

The Contractor shall develop and implement data management (DM) processes and systems that address the needs of CCtCap program. The contractor shall establish a means for sharing, reporting, collecting, recording and accessing CCtCap program information, product information, performance data, and technical data unless otherwise detailed in this PWS or DRDs.

3.2 Design, Development, Test and Evaluation (DDTE)/Certification (CLIN 001)

This PWS section contains the specific work scope associated with the activities required to perform CLIN 001 in addition to the work scope defined in PWS Section 3.1.

The Contractor shall obtain NASA certification of a CTS that meets or exceeds with CCT-REQ-1130, ISS Crew Transportation and Services Requirements Document, and SSP 50808, ISS to Commercial Orbital Transportation Services (COTS) Interface Requirements Document (IRD). The contractor shall demonstrate compliance to the technical requirements by designing, developing, testing and evaluating an end-to-end system culminating in a review for approval to grant NASA certification, including certification to technical requirements associated with all inherent capabilities of the CTS (reference 3.2.1.4, 3.3.6). The contractor shall assure that the CTS is developed, produced, and operated in a repeatable manner throughout the lifecycle of the system.

3.2.1 System Engineering and Integration (SE&I)

3.2.1.1 System Engineering

The Contractor systems engineering organization shall own, manage, and control the design and safety analysis approach and processes for producing a design that meets requirements, as well as identifying, understanding, eliminating, and controlling hazards and risks to safety (J-01 1120 4.0). The systems engineering team efforts include architecture and requirements development and verification, program configuration and data management, and safety/reliability and quality assurance.

The Contractor shall update existing technical management plans that were developed and executed to in prior phases of the CTS program, if required, to ensure processes associated with achieving and maintaining NASA certification throughout the CTS lifecycle are included in that lifecycle in accordance with CCT-PLN-1120, Crew Transportation Technical Management Processes. The contractor shall provide these existing technical management plans to NASA in support of the first milestone review for re-baselining for CCtCap at that review. The contractor shall execute, implement, and manage the CCtCap program in accordance with these technical management plans. Since the activities from the core certification effort (Reference PWS Section 3.2, CLIN 001) and the initial PCMs (Reference PWS Section 3.3, CLIN 002) can be conducted concurrently, the contractor shall ensure the interdependencies between the on-going core certification efforts and PCM objectives are addressed in development plans and mission execution planning.

The Contractor shall establish and utilize design, production, and operations Government standards or alternatives to NASA standards and CCT-REQ-1130, ISS Crew Transportation and Services Requirements Document, and CCT-STD-1140, Crew Transportation Standards and Processes Criteria, requirements as proposed and approved in CPC (J-01 1120 4.1) that result in safe, reliable and usable end items and an integrated certified CTS system.

The Contractor shall provide/request alternatives to meet the intent of requirements in CCT-REQ-1130, ISS Crew Transportation and Services Requirements Document, when usage of the NASA standard is prohibitive. Alternate standards will be reviewed and approved by the Government Program Control Board (PCB) (Reference PWS Section 3.1.1.3) (J-01 1120 4.1).

Attachment J-03

The Contractor shall implement changes to alternate standards submitted under CPC to provide compliance to the intent of documented NASA standards in accordance with Government disposition and CPC Final Technical Summary Report (reference PWS paragraph 3.2.8.1). Proposed changes to applicable Alternate Standards shall be presented for approval as part of the Certification Baseline Review (CBR) milestone.

3.2.1.1.1 Requirements and Verification and Validation

The Contractor shall develop, implement, and maintain a closed-loop requirements management process to ensure hardware, software, support equipment, ground systems processing (including facilities and ground support equipment for spacecraft assembly, integration and test; conduct planning, training and flight operations; and launch vehicle integration, test and launch operations for crewed and uncrewed), and configuration requirements are accounted for in the CTS configuration managed systems and equipment (J-01 1120 3.4). The contractor's requirements process shall address the process for architecture and requirements development, requirements management and control, requirements allocation and traceability (down to the module or component level including parent/child relationship and meet-the-intent requirements), requirements verification and validation planning, and variance and constraint handling (J-01 1120 3.4.2). The contractor shall document the requirements process in the CCTS Requirement Management Plan, DCC1-00422-01 (J-01 1120 3.4.1). The CCTS Requirements Management Plan shall be delivered as part of DRD 102, Certification Baseline Review (CBR) Data Package, in support of Certification Baseline Review (CBR). The contractor shall prepare and deliver one Verification Closure Notice per CCT-REQ-1130, ISS Crew Transportation and Services Requirements Document, SSP 50808, International Space Station (ISS) to Commercial Orbital Transportation Services (COTS) Interface Requirements Document (IRD) for all docked crewed and uncrewed requirements, and in accordance with DRD 111, Verification Closure Notices (VCN), as evidence of closure of each technical requirement.

The contractor shall provide the Government with access to all requirements, requirements products, requirements and the requirements management database. The contractor shall maintain a specification tree depicting requirements related products.

The Contractor shall process requests for variance (Table 3.2.1.1.1-1) (J-01 1120 3.4.3) to the requirements set defined in the Table 3.2.1.1.1-2 through the Government CCP Board (Reference PWS Section 3.1.1.3). Request for variance to SSP 50808, International Space Station (ISS) to Commercial Orbital Transportation Services (COTS) Interface Requirements Document (IRD), shall be processed in accordance with SSP 41170, ISS Configuration Management Requirements (J-01 1120 3.4.3).

Table 3.2.1.1.1-1. Definitions

Term	Definition
Variance	A formal request for relief from a requirement. Variances should be submitted as early in the lifecycle or workflow process as practical; a variance can be an exception, deviation or waiver.
• Exception	• A type of variance that authorizes permanent relief from a specific requirement and may be requested at any time during the lifecycle of the program

Term	Definition
• Deviation	• A type of variance that authorizes temporary relief in advance from a specific requirement and is requested during the formulation/planning/design stages of a program operation to address expected situations
• Waiver	• A type of variance that authorizes temporary relief from a specific requirement after the baseline system has been approved. Waivers are requested during the implementation of a program or operation to address situations that were unforeseen during design or advanced planning.

Table 3.2.1.1.1-2. CCtCap Applicable Documents

Document #	Document Title
CCT-PLN-1100	Crew Transportation Plan
CCT-DRM-1110	Crew Transportation System Design Reference Missions
CCT-PLN-1120	Crew Transportation Technical Management Processes
CCT-REQ-1130	ISS Crew Transportation and Services Requirements Document
CCT-STD-1140	Crew Transportation Standards and Processes Criteria
CCT-STD-1150	Crew Transportation Operations Standards
SSP 50808	International Space Station (ISS) to Commercial Orbital Transportation Services (COTS) Interface Requirements Document (IRD)

The Contractor shall continue to refine and implement changes to the variances submitted under CPC to provide compliance to the intent of documented NASA requirements in accordance with Government disposition and Final CPC product Technical Summary (reference PWS paragraph 3.2.8.3). Proposed changes to applicable variances shall be presented for approval as part of the Certification Baseline Review (CBR) milestone. The Contractor shall implement changes to its CTS requirements, appropriate hardware design, operational processes and procedure for variances to the CCT-REQ-1130, ISS Crew Transportation and Services Requirements Document, and SSP 50808, ISS to Commercial Orbital Transportation Services (COTS) Interface Requirements Document (IRD), Government requirements that were submitted under the CPC contract where Government disposition and Final CPC product Technical Summary resulted in a disapproved submitted variance. Proposed changes (or plans to implement required changes) to mitigate disapproved variance(s) shall be presented for approval as part of the Certification Baseline Review (CBR) milestone. For variances identified after the start of CCtCap and disapproved by the Government, the Contractor shall implement required changes to the CCTS design, processes and procedures to bring the system into compliance with the Government requirements or sufficiently reduce the risk to allow Government acceptance of the variance.

3.2.1.1.2 Interface Management

The Contractor shall establish procedures, practices, and agreements to ensure proper interface identification, definition, documentation, and compliance throughout the CTS lifecycle

Attachment J-03

(J-01 1120 3.5) for internal and external interfaces including operational (spacecraft to ISS, FAA, Range/Launch sites) (J-01 1120 3.5.1).

3.2.1.2 Milestone/Technical Reviews

The Contractor shall conduct milestone reviews/events to formally evaluate progress towards CTS certification which shall include, at a minimum, those identified in PWS sections 3.2.1.2.1 through 3.2.1.2.6 (J-01 1120 3.7). The contractor shall define additional interim reviews/events the contractor deems necessary to supplement the mandatory Government delivery/interim milestones. These events are structured to chart the maturity of the program in achieving certification. These reviews and the contractor defined interim reviews and events associated with progress payments shall be detailed in PWS Appendix A, Milestone Acceptance Criteria and Payment Schedule. These events represent essential decision points to accurately measure the success of the preceding phase of work and an entry point for subsequent work efforts.

The contractor shall develop and deliver a Milestone Review Plan (MRP) in accordance with DRD 101, Milestone Review Plan. The purpose of the MRP shall be to document for each review, detailed in PWS Appendix A, Milestone Acceptance Criteria and Payment Schedule: the review process, entrance criteria/readiness deliverables to address the milestone review objectives and timing by which data shall be made available to NASA for review, Technical Interchange Meetings (TIMs)/review meetings/applicable final RID boards, exit/success/acceptance criteria, and other logistics related information. The MRP shall define the specific data requirements required to successfully conduct each milestone review. The contractor shall implement, execute and perform in accordance with the Milestone Review Plan delivered with the proposal from program start until DRD 101 is formally delivered and dispositioned.

The MRP shall address requirements from the following:

a) Data Package DRDs 102, 103, 104, 105 and 106 data requirements for each milestone review

b) CCT-PLN-1120, Crew Transportation Technical Management Processes, Appendices F and H

c) PWS Appendix A, Milestone Acceptance Criteria and Payment Schedule

Upon NASA approval/concurrence of the Milestone Review Plan, the content of the plan will supersede the specific milestone review statements in b) above and shall be considered approved tailoring of the associated requirements. The milestone review Data Package DRD noted above (a) shall be utilized as the transmitting vehicle of those artifacts mutually agreed to in the MRP with exception of other CCtCap specific DRD requirements.

3.2.1.2.1 Certification Baseline Review (CBR) [Mandatory Government Interim Milestone]

The Contractor shall conduct a CBR and deliver the data described in DRD 102, Certification Baseline Review (CBR) Data Package, in support of the CBR. The contractor shall co-chair with NASA a CBR after award of contract. The purpose of the CBR is to establish the CTS design baseline, the contractor's certification plan, lifecycle costs, and schedules for CTS certification. (J-01 1120 3.7)

3.2.1.2.2 ISS Design Certification Review (DCR) [Mandatory Government Delivery Milestone]

Attachment J-03

The Contractor shall conduct an ISS DCR and deliver the data described in DRD 103, Design Certification Review (DCR) Data Package, in support of the DCR. Prior to the first low Earth orbit (LEO) test flight that docks to the ISS, the flight test readiness process shall include a DCR of applicable elements from completed CTS Certification Milestones (for an interim CTS certification) and a Flight Test Readiness Review. The ISS DCR formally documents the configuration baseline (hardware, software, and processes used in design, production, and operations) and the conditions under which the CTS is certified (performance, fabrication and operational environments, constraints). The ISS DCR verifies the CTS capability to safely approach, dock, mate, and depart from the ISS in applicable ISS visiting vehicle configurations. The ISS DCR also presents the current state of the verification and validation effort, including the overall status of all verification closures and any changes to the Verification and Validation (V&V) plan since CBR. (J-01 1120 3.7)

3.2.1.2.3 Orbital Flight Test Flight Test Readiness Review (OFT FTRR) [Mandatory Government Interim Milestone]

The Contractor shall conduct a Flight Test Readiness Review (FTRR) to assure procedure, process, flight hardware, facilities and personnel readiness to conduct the Orbital Flight Test and deliver the data described in DRD 104, Flight Test Readiness Review (FTRR) Data Package, in support of the OFT FTRR. The OFT FTRR examines tests, demonstrations, analyses, and audits that determine the system's readiness for a safe and successful flight/launch and for subsequent flight test operations. It also ensures that all flight and ground hardware, software, personnel, and procedures are operationally ready. The review will cover test objectives and requirements, verify required procedures are released, and verify flight hardware configuration and conformance to design requirements. Facility and support equipment readiness and personnel training will be verified. Program organizations will present certification of readiness to support the flight test. The review will be co-chaired by the Program Manager and the Contractor Mission Assurance lead. (J-01 1120 3.7)

3.2.1.2.4 Crewed Flight Test Flight Test Readiness Review (CFT FTRR) [Mandatory Government Interim Milestone]

The Contractor shall conduct a Flight Test Readiness Review (FTRR) to assure procedure, process, flight hardware, facilities and personnel readiness to conduct the Crewed Flight Test and deliver the data described in DRD 104, Flight Test Readiness Review (FTRR) Data Package, in support of the CFT FTRR. The CFT FTRR examines tests, demonstrations, analyses, and audits that determine the system's readiness for a safe and successful flight/launch and for subsequent flight test operations. It also ensures that all flight and ground hardware, software, personnel, and procedures are operationally ready. The review will cover test objectives and requirements, verify required procedures are released, and verify flight hardware configuration and conformance to design requirements. Facility and support equipment readiness and personnel training will be verified. Program organizations will present certification of readiness to support the flight test. The review will be co-chaired by the Program Manager and the Contractor Mission Assurance lead. (J-01 1120 3.7)

3.2.1.2.5 Operations Readiness Review (ORR) [Mandatory Government Interim Milestone]

Upon successful completion of the flight test phase of crewed flights, an Operational Readiness Review shall be conducted and deliver the data described in DRD 105, Operations Readiness Review (ORR) Data Package, in support of the ORR. The ORR occurs once during the program lifecycle or at the introduction of new or significantly modified systems/facilities. The Contractor shall demonstrate the actual CCTS Production and Ground Systems, Mission Operations systems and Launch Vehicle ground systems characteristics, facilities, equipment and procedures used in operations match the deployed state. The ORR evaluates all project and support (flight and ground) hardware, software, personnel, plans, processes, and procedures to ensure flight and associated ground systems are in compliance with program requirements and constraints during the sustaining phase. The Contractor shall demonstrate the actual CCTS Production and Ground Systems, Mission Operations systems and Launch Vehicle ground systems characteristics, facilities, equipment and procedures used in operations match the deployed state. This review is co-chaired by Boeing and NASA CCP. (J-01 1120 3.7)

3.2.1.2.6 Certification Review (CR) [Mandatory Government Delivery Milestone]

Upon successful completion of all flight tests, any delta DCRs, and the ORR, the Contractor shall conduct a Certification Review chaired by NASA. The contractor shall deliver the data described in DRD 106, Certification Review (CR) Milestone Data Package, in support of the CR. The CR determines that the CCTS meets CCT-DRM-1110, Crew Transportation System Design Reference Missions, for which it was developed. The CR will focus on System performance as validated from the end-to-end testing and flight test campaigns, closure of all verification and validation plans, and the Product Baseline to be used in Operations. (J-01 1120 3.7)

3.2.1.3 System Analysis

The Contractor shall perform technical and management efforts for directing and controlling the integrated engineering effort for the spacecraft. This effort includes the development, update and maintenance of simulations, drawings, and computer aided design (CAD) models.

The Contractor shall perform aerodynamic characterization of the vehicle through all phases of atmospheric flight including plume/flow field interactions and on-orbit rarefied flows within the aerodynamic environment of the vehicle forces, vehicle moments, related surface pressure, and related shear forces.

The Contractor shall provide aero thermodynamic characterization of the vehicle through all phases of atmospheric flight including plume/flow field interactions and on-orbit rarefied flows. The aero thermodynamic environment includes heat transfer to the vehicle surface.

The Contractor shall provide loads and dynamics analysis of the vehicle as part of the overall design analysis cycle process.

The Contractor shall provide definition of requirements for the specific dynamic environments and induced environments that the CTS must operate within and for which it must be qualified, encompassing all phases of production, testing and operation in all modes through disposal in accordance with the Natural and Induced Environments.

The Contractor shall provide identification and conduct of contractor-initiated trade studies and affordability analyses to ensure realistic options and alternatives are assessed for key CTS requirements and design decisions throughout the contract period of performance.

The Contractor shall collect spacecraft items mass properties, center of gravity, mass moments of inertia and mass products of inertia with respect to a reference coordinate system within the vehicle.

The Contractor shall develop an integrated vehicle performance and design margin allocation strategy, and implement it through a detailed set of vehicle stage, system, subsystem, and component performance requirements and specifications. The contractor's strategy shall identify and define the appropriate levels of design or performance margin needed at the vehicle stage, system, subsystem, and/or component level, and address uncertainties and the expected variations in vehicle manufacturing, operational performance, and/or operational environments. The contractor shall update the CCTS Margin Management Plan (MMP), DCC1-00424-01, that (J-01 1120 4.9, 4.9.1):

a) Identifies the set of critical system resources (e.g., mass, propellant, power) that need to be managed in order for the design to meet its requirements

b) Defines how margin is calculated for each resource

c) Provides process to assess operating margin, growth allowance, and program manager's reserve for each parameter

d) Documents the process for the margin specification required for each milestone review

e) Defines Margin management report content requirement for each milestone review

The CCTS MMP shall be delivered as part of DRD 102, Certification Baseline Review (CBR) Data Package, in support of Certification Baseline Review (CBR).

The contractor shall decompose and flow down higher-level CTS requirements and shall implement the strategy by clearly identifying and allocating the appropriate amount of margin into the approved stage, system, subsystem, and/or component requirements for the respective hardware and software designs (J-01 1120 4.9).

3.2.1.4 System Integration and Certification

The Contractor shall design, develop, test, and evaluate the interfaces between the CST-100 and LV and the integrated performance of the CST-100 and LV for nominal and abort design cases. The contractor shall perform analyses and tests and provide reports and engineering data supporting integration and operation of CST-100 and LV, such as: structural models and analyses for static, dynamic and coupled loads analyses; mass properties, dimensions and physical (material, thermal, etc.) properties; abort mode design case trigger condition and implementation assessments; Integrated compatibility analyses (EMC, RF, etc.); Interface and integration drawings/models and build/test procedures.

The Contractor shall continue to refine, deliver and implement the Certification Plan, developed under the CPC contract, in accordance with DRD 107, Certification Plan, CPC Final Technical Summary Report findings, and the content defined in CCT-PLN-1120, Crew Transportation Technical Management Processes, which supports CCT-PLN-2000, NASA Crew Transportation and Services Certification Plan, and SSP 50964, Visiting Vehicle ISS Integration Plan, and execute the end-to-end certification plan. The Certification Plan shall define an integrated strategy for certification of the complete CTS and defines a structured and organized approach for implementing the strategy. The Certification Plan is a comprehensive development plan and approach that shall document the processes, products and schedule encompassing all effort to demonstrate that the integrated CTS design and the associated production and operation capabilities shall achieve a NASA Certification. Certification is a progressive process and sensitive to the order of execution, the certification strategy shall clearly define the order of execution, with a schedule and critical path clearly outlined. The Certification Plan shall define the verification and validation (V&V) methods for all CTS technical requirements, including the requirements which result from the necessary decomposition and flow down of higher level CTS requirements to the appropriate level (including those requirements established to control critical hazards). The certification plan shall provide the objective evidence necessary to verify compliance with design and performance requirements governing the capability and performance of critical systems, subsystems, and the integrated CTS by inspection, demonstration, analysis and test (J-01 1120 7.0).

The Contractor shall continue to refine, deliver and implement the Verification and Validation (V&V) Plan developed under the CPC contract in accordance with DRD 108, Verification and Validation (V&V) Plan, the content defined in CCT-PLN-1120, Crew Transportation Technical Management Processes. The V&V Plan shall include NASA technical requirements in CCT-REQ-1130, ISS Crew Transportation and Services Requirements Document, and SSP 50808, International Space Station (ISS) to Commercial Orbital Transportation Services (COTS) Interface Requirements Document (IRD), and contractor's decomposed or derived requirements (J-01 1120 7.0).

The Contractor shall implement changes to the CCTS Verification and Validation Plan, DCC1-00005-01, and the CCTS Certification Plan, DCC1-00443-01, submitted under CPC to provide compliance in accordance with Government disposition and CPC Final Technical Summary Report findings. Proposed changes to the Verification and Validation Plan, and Certification Plan shall be presented for approval as part of the Certification Baseline Review (CBR) milestone.

In accordance with the Technical Reviews (Reference PWS Section 3.2.1.2), the Contractor shall utilize Milestone Reviews to mark progress towards CTS certification. The contractor shall deliver a CTS Certification Data Package which collectively illustrates, with supporting evidence, that the system meets the technical requirements and is safe to carry NASA crew to and from the ISS (J-01 1120 7.0) in accordance with the content defined in CCT-PLN-1120, Crew Transportation Technical Management Processes, Table 7-1, CTS Certification Data Package Content and in accordance with DRD 112, Certification Data Package.

The Contractor shall establish human systems integration (HSI) strategy to ensure that humans and human needs, as well as human capabilities and limitations, are considered during the design, build, test, operation, and maintenance across nominal, emergency, and contingency operating conditions of the system (J-01 1120 4.8). The contractor shall document the HSI strategy (CCTS HSI Standard, DCC1-00013-01). The CCTS HIS Standard shall be delivered as part of DRD 102, Certification Baseline Review (CBR) Data Package, in support of Certification Baseline Review (CBR).

The Contractor shall provide:

a) a master task list including identification of nominal and critical tasks necessary for established mission objectives and concepts of operation

b) evaluations of functional allocation for manual and automated crew and system tasks; expected utilization of operator capabilities to execute the mission, prevent aborts, and prevent catastrophic events; and evaluations of the crew's ability to accomplish mission critical and volume driving tasks

c) crew workload and usability evaluations that demonstrate the impact of crew interface designs on human error and total human-system performance

d) Human-In-The-Loop Testing in support of planned human test and demonstration activities (J-01 1120 4.8.1)

The Contractor shall conduct a human error analysis (HEA) for all mission phases, to include nominal operations and those operations planned for response to system failures. The results shall be incorporated into design and operational procedures to minimize the likelihood and negative effects of human error (J-01 1120 4.7). The HEA shall qualitatively characterize how human error affects the system. The HEA shall manage potential hazards which could be caused by humans, identify inadvertent operator actions which would cause a catastrophic event and determine the appropriate level of tolerance, identify other human error that would cause catastrophic event, and ensure application of the appropriate error management (J-01 1120 4.7.1, 4.7.2).

The contractor shall implement requirements that document the "inherent capabilities" of the CCTS system design that are in excess of NASA requirements (ref. paragraph 3.3.6.1) for SM propellant, number of crew, amount of cargo and uncrewed mission to ISS.

3.2.1.5 Specialty Engineering

The Contractor shall apply crosscutting specialty engineering disciplines of materials and processes, electromagnetic compatibility, EEE parts, aerosciences, instrumentation, mass properties, Micrometeoroid and Orbital Debris (MMOD) analyses, and radiation analyses to the spacecraft design.

The Contractor shall ensure materials are selected, controlled, implemented and verified to be consistent with intended usage environments. The contractor shall select, treat, fabricate, inspect, test, and analyze materials of construction to ensure the safety and success of the CTS in accordance with the Materials and Processes (M&P) Selection, Implementation, and Control Plan, Material Usage Agreements (MUAs), and Material Identification Usage Lists (MIULs).

The Contractor shall develop, update, and implement an Electrical, Electronic and Electromechanical (EEE) Parts Management and Implementation Plan for the CTS. The contractor shall establish processes to control aspects of EEE parts from part selection through testing and hardware fabrication and part failure analysis.

The Contractor shall design, develop, and verify the CTS is electromagnetically compatible with internally generated electromagnetic energy, the external electromagnetic energy environments, and the ISS. The contractor shall implement and execute to the Electromagnetic Compatibility Control and Verification Document to design, construct, and verify the CTS System Electromagnetic Compatibility requirements. The contractor shall develop and design the

Attachment J-03

CTS to control and mitigate hardware malfunction and damage that can be caused by lightning in accordance with the Lightning Verification Plan/Report.

The Contractor shall provide Radiation Analyses to describe the internal CTS radiation environments that result from exposure to natural radiation background environments and events. The contractor shall use these analyses including crew radiation exposure analysis to certify that the spacecraft meets the CTS radiation requirements for the space radiation environments described in the Natural and Induced Environment Document (NIED).

The Contractor shall provide micrometeoroid and orbital debris (MMOD) analyses. The analyses shall include assessment of the risk to the spacecraft and crew resulting from damage or penetration from micrometeoroid and orbital debris impacts during the following mission phases: ascent to mating, mated, and separation to reentry.

3.2.2 Safety, Reliability and Quality Assurance

3.2.2.1 System Safety

The Contractor shall plan and implement a system safety program consistent with the policies, procedures and processes established in the CCTS System Safety and Reliability Plan, DCC1-00459-01. The plan shall describe how safety methodologies are integrated into the design process and used to identify and eliminate or control catastrophic or critical hazards and balance risks and trades. The System Safety and Reliability Plan shall be delivered as part of DRD 102, Certification Baseline Review (CBR) Data Package, in support of Certification Baseline Review (CBR). For software and safety items where ISS is identified as being an effected party and/or stakeholder, the plan shall address (1) the process for complying with SSP 30234, Instructions for Preparation of Failure Modes and Effects Analysis and Critical Items List Requirements for International Space Station, SSP 30309, Safety Analysis and Risk Assessment Requirements Document, NASA-STD-8739.8, NASA Technical Standard: Software Assurance Standard, Sections 6, 7.1, 7.2.4, 7.3 and 7.4, and NASA-STD-8719.13, NASA Technical Standard: Software Safety Standard, Chapter 17 (J-01 1120 4.2.1). The contractor shall put in place controls that reduce the risk to an acceptable level that ensures crew safety. The contractor's safety process shall provide an integrated, systematic, and comprehensive approach, which can be used to determine the need for design changes and safety measures. The safety process shall include (J-01 1120 4.2):

a) the evaluation of hardware and software capabilities, limitations, and interdependence, as well as environmental and human factors relevant to safety

b) the use of industry standard safety analyses (e.g. hazards probability of occurrence, severity and severity categories) throughout the CTS lifecycle

c) closed-loop tracking and verification of hazard controls

d) detailed plans for the communication and acceptance of risk to stakeholders and/or the appropriate control boards to ensure residual risk is appropriately managed

e) a plan for communication and approval of safety analyses

f) the safety review process

The Contractor shall conduct safety analyses that include an assessment of crew survival strategies for all mission phases and the system capabilities required to execute each strategy.

The scenarios shall include system failures and emergencies (such as fire, collision, toxic atmosphere, decreasing atmospheric pressure, and medical emergencies) with specific capabilities or proposed capabilities (such as abort, safe haven, rescue, emergency egress, emergency systems, and emergency medical equipment or access to emergency medical care) identified to protect the crew. (J-01 1120 4.2)

The Contractor shall provide, develop, and manage a Mishap Reporting and Investigation Plan and process (J-01 1120 3.8) that are in accordance with Contract Clause H.26 Mishap Reporting. When applicable, the Contractor shall support a Commission appointed by the President per 51 U.S.C Section 70701 et seq, (J-01 1120 3.8).

The Contractor shall conduct a probabilistic safety analysis (PSA) following the guidance in CCT-REF-1121, Probabilistic Safety Analysis (PSA) Methodology Guide. The contractor shall implement reasonable design and operational modifications to achieve best possible Loss of Crew and Loss of Mission levels. The contractor shall improve modeling approach as the design matures including level of redundancy, component reliability, MTBF (mean time between failure), and operational enhancements. The PSA shall be applied throughout the lifecycle in order to verify through analysis that the CTS meets established Loss of Crew (LOC) and Loss of Mission (LOM) requirements (J-01 1120 4.3).

The Contractor shall define a safety review process that allows for the systematic identification and review of hazards related to the design, operations, and functional capabilities of transportation systems developed in support of milestone reviews (Reference PWS Section 3.2.1.2). This methodology shall ensure that proper controls are identified and implemented for all hazard causes consistent with CCP certification processes and requirements. The safety review process also shall include reviews of hazards and controls performed by contractor subject matter experts in the form of a peer review to ensure hazards are identified and controls are adequate. At the milestone reviews, the associated hazard reports shall be segregated by stakeholders as follows (J-01 1120 4.5):

   a) Occupant safety throughout all mission phases, including docked operations as it relates to hazards created by the CTS vehicle (stakeholder: CCP).

   b) Integrated hazards created by the combined operations during the Rendezvous, Proximity Operations, Docking and Undocking (RPODU) phase (stakeholder: ISS).

The Contractor shall conduct Phase Safety Reviews. The goal of each Phase Safety Review is for the safety analysis to achieve the relevant Phase II or III approval from NASA, resulting in a product that meets the criteria in SSP 30599, ISS Safety Review Process. The contractor shall deliver CTS hazard reports in accordance with DRD 110, Hazard Reports, and CCT-PLN-1120, Crew Transportation Technical Management Processes. The Contractor shall implement hazard controls documented in the approved hazard reports. The Contractor shall implement changes to CTS requirements, appropriate hardware design, operational processes and procedures for hazard reports submitted under the CPC contract where Government disposition and Final CPC product Technical Summary disapproved the submitted hazard report. Proposed changes (or plans to implement required changes) to strengthen controls to mitigate hazards to acceptable levels shall be presented as part of the Certification Baseline Review (CBR) milestone.

The CCP will participate in the contractor's safety review process by performing insight functions (Reference PWS Section 3.1.1.4) and working in a collaborative environment to gain an understanding of the incremental safety process: focusing on the assurance that all hazard and hazard causes inherent in the design and operations are identified; evaluating the means employed to control hazards; and assessing methods identified to verify all hazard controls. Risks identified as a result of the hazard analysis that are deemed a CCP risk and shall be coordinated with the CCP Risk Management Process (J-01 1120 4.5).

For hazard reports where the ISS is identified as being an affected party and/or stakeholder, the Contractor shall coordinate with the CCP to prepare and deliver such items for approval to the ISS Safety Review Panel (reference SSP 30599, ISS Safety Review Process, and SSP 30309, Safety Analysis and Risk Assessment Requirements Document) (J-01 1120 4.5).

The Contractor shall be responsible for characterizing and reporting potential risks associated with a planned launch of radioactive materials into space on launch vehicles and spacecraft, during normal or abnormal flight conditions in accordance with NPR 8715.3, NASA General Safety Program Requirements, Chapter 6 (J-01 1120 4.6).

3.2.2.2 Environmental, Industrial, Launch Site and Range Safety

The Contractor shall implement a safety and health program which identifies, eliminates, mitigates and control hazards and risks in activities in accordance with the existing CTS Safety and Health Plan and document the plan in the safety program plan. The contractor shall perform a Ground Processing Safety Analysis to derive requirements for implementation into the ground support equipment design, processes and procedures including data to support a range safety flight termination system (FTS) determination analysis per ASPC Manual 91-710, Air Force Space Command Range Safety User Policies and Procedures. The contractor shall support the range safety analysis to meet local test range safety requirements including a list of hazardous operations to be performed. The contractor shall comply with all Range requirements and deliver DRD 113, Range Safety Documentation.

3.2.2.3 Reliability, Maintainability and Availability

The Contractor shall implement an integrated, systematic and comprehensive reliability approach into the design process to balance risk and trades (J-01 1120 4.2). The contractor shall update the CCTS System Safety and Reliability Plan, DCC1-00459-01, to document Failure Modes Effects Analyses/Critical Items Lists (FMEA/CIL) processes including the CCtCap System Probabilistic Safety Assessments to include the entire CTS lifecycle. The CCTS System Safety and Reliability Plan shall be delivered as part of DRD 102, Certification Baseline Review (CBR) Data Package, in support of Certification Baseline Review (CBR). The reliability program plan shall also include participation in Exchanging Parts, Materials, and Safety Problem Data utilizing the Government Industry Data Exchange Program (GIDEP) (J-01 1120 3.6.1).

3.2.2.4 Quality Assurance

The Contractor shall develop and execute a quality management system that assures quality requirements are flowed down from design into the manufacturing and operational processes and is compliant with the requirements of AS9100, Quality Management Systems – Requirements for Aviation, Space and Defense Organizations (J-01 1120 3.6). The contractor shall update the CCTS Quality Management Plan (QMP), DCC1-00455-01, to capture any processes and procedures that are unique to CTS program lifecycle. The CCTS QMP shall be delivered as part of DRD 102, Certification Baseline Review (CBR) Data Package, in support of Certification

Attachment J-03

Baseline Review (CBR). The Contractor shall flow down and ensure implementation of appropriate quality assurance requirements to applicable suppliers.

3.2.2.5 Software Safety and Assurance

The Contractor shall be responsible for the management of software safety throughout the CTS lifecycle for flight software, flight support software, ground support equipment (GSE) ground software, and hardware and software used in the design, development, test, verification, storage, maintenance of software, and ensures that software products obtained from any source meet the software assurance requirements. The contractor shall define a software safety plan (CCTS Software Quality Program Plan, DCC1-00415-01) to document safety-critical software determination processes, management, software development and analysis methods (including support of hazard analyses and production of hazard reports), implementation and test, and operational use (J-01 1120 4.4). The CCTS Software Quality Program Plan shall be delivered as part of DRD 102, Certification Baseline Review (CBR) Data Package, in support of Certification Baseline Review (CBR).

3.2.3 Production Control

The Contractor shall produce CTSs such that each first article and ground article, including software, is manufactured, assembled, and integrated in a repeatable manner. The contractor shall establish and implement production control and manufacturing processes for the production and assembly of CTS hardware. The production control process shall include: (a) manufacturing, fabrication, storage and transportation, (b) inventory control, (c) nonconformance identification, tracking, and corrective action (d) material review process for acceptance of hardware not fully meeting drawing requirements (e) procedures for use of tooling and equipment, and (f) metrology and other critical production support activities. The contractor shall document assembly/integration test plans/procedures and test results/reports at the subsystem, system, and vehicle levels (J-01 1120 6.0, 6.1.1).

3.2.4 Vehicle (CST-100 and LV)

3.2.4.1 Flight Hardware

The Contractor shall continue to finalize the CTS design, perform analyses; manufacture, assemble, produce; and build-up the CTS vehicle. The contractor shall perform subsystem integration, verification, end-to-end testing, qualification, acceptance test; and checkout of the CTS vehicle hardware and software subsystems (J-01 1120 5.0, 5.1.1, 5.2). The contractor shall document, as part of the qualification and acceptance testing process, test plans and procedures, test results/reports, requirements traceability, test configurations, environments data, and margins and deviations data (J-01 1120 5.1.1). The contractor shall document the test procedures for demonstrating that the design and performance requirements can be demonstrated for all CCtCap program requirements, including the range of projected environments and operating conditions anticipated over the service life. The contractor shall prepare and deliver one Verification Closure Notice (VCN), DRD 111, per CCT-REQ-1130, ISS Crew Transportation and Services Requirements Document, and SSP 50808, International Space Station (ISS) to Commercial Orbital Transportation Services (COTS) Interface Requirements Document (IRD) for all docked crewed and uncrewed requirements, as evidence of closure of each technical requirement.

3.2.4.2 Flight Software

Attachment J-03

The contractor shall continue to develop, design, integrate, test, verify, qualify, and certify flight software (J-01 1120 5.0) to include software for vehicle avionics functions, including systems management, Command and Data Handling (C&DH), Communication and Tracking (C&T), instrumentation, crew interfaces, external interfaces, and the application software for other subsystems in accordance with the CCTS Software Development Plans, DCC1-00006-01 (for Spacecraft Segment) and DCC1-00115-01 (for Ground Systems Segment) (J-01 1120 5.1.1). The CCTS software development plans shall be delivered as part of DRD 102, Certification Baseline Review (CBR) Data Package, in support of Certification Baseline Review (CBR). Also included is firmware and acquired software (e.g. operating systems, device drivers, etc.). This includes facility integration for hardware and software (J-01 1120 5.0, 5.1.1, 5.2). The contractor shall prepare and deliver one Verification Closure Notice (VCN), DRD 111, per CCT-REQ-1130, ISS Crew Transportation and Services Requirements Document, and SSP 50808, International Space Station (ISS) to Commercial Orbital Transportation Services (COTS) Interface Requirements Document (IRD) for all docked crewed and uncrewed requirements, as evidence of closure of each technical requirement.

The contractor shall design and build an Avionics System Integration Laboratory (ASIL) with integrated test equipment, rigs, infrastructure, and test environments for hardware and software integration, checkout and verification testing. (J-01 1120 5.2)

Attachment J-03

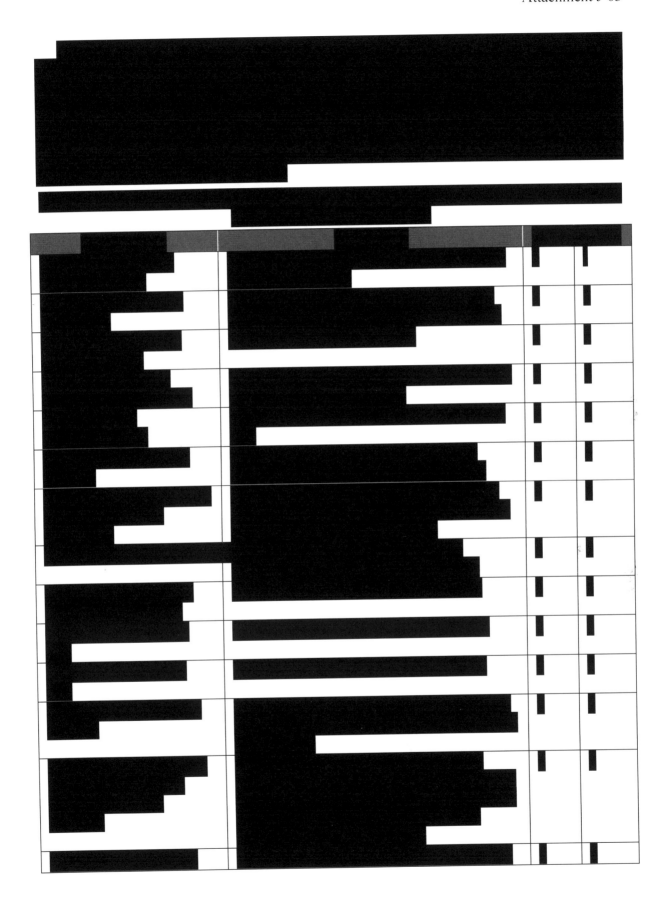

Attachment J-03

Attachment J-03

3.2.5 Ground Systems

The Contractor shall develop a ground processing process to support validation of the CTS. Ground processing shall include a process that tracks and resolves anomalies, captures potential process improvements, and lessons learned to improve and inform future ground operations and CTS design changes (J-01 1120 6.5.1). The Contractor shall provide Ground Systems (J-01 1120 5.0) supporting facilities, support equipment, and hardware and software required for ground and flight operations.

3.2.5.1 Assembly Integration and Test (AIT) Facilities and Systems

The Contractor shall perform vehicle (hardware and software) assembly, integration and end-to-end test (J-01 1120 5.2) at the contractor's facility or facilities.

The Contractor is responsible for providing all mechanical and electrical ground support equipment (GSE) required to support the AIT, vehicle integration, crew operations, and pre- and post-flight mission activities (e.g., fueling, cargo/crew loading, crew ingress/egress and crew/cargo recovery).

The Contractor is responsible for providing all tooling required to support refurbishment of the Spacecraft elements.

3.2.5.2 Ground Communication Systems

The Contractor shall provide a Ground Communications System that will encompass remotely operated ground stations to provide Space-to-Ground communications and recovery communications.

3.2.5.3 Cargo Handling Operations, Facilities and Systems

The Contractor shall provide Ground Support Equipment (GSE) for physical cargo integration including nominal stow cargo, late stow cargo and post mission cargo extraction, for early destow and nominal destow.

3.2.5.4 Recovery Systems and Operations

For a nominal land landing at a Primary Landing Site, the Contractor will provide all required services and equipment for the recovery of the crew, cargo and Crew Module (CM). For an emergency landing at an unsupported site, NASA will provide SAR support for the rescue and recovery of the crew. The Contractor shall provide Support Equipment (SE), training for the SAR provider, cargo and CM recovery.

3.2.5.5 Logistics and Logistic Systems

The Contractor shall provide ground segment logistics activities to include (1) databases for shipping/receiving, sparing analysis/tracking, ground maintenance planning/scheduling, and limited life items, (2) packaging, handling, storage, and transportation.

3.2.5.6 Pre-Flight and Launch Site Infrastructure

The Contractor shall provide pre-flight and launch site infrastructure required to successfully conduct launch operation. The infrastructure shall include an integration facility, crew access accommodations, and ground support equipment areas. The contractor shall provide crew and pre-flight operations support to successfully manage and coordinate crew operations and events.

The Contractor shall develop, design, and build a suitable access tower to allow crew, support personnel, and cargo, to ingress and egress from the CST-100. Emergency egress shall be available to provide evacuation of the flight crew and support personnel from the spacecraft access level to a suitable safe-haven. The launch-pad-to-CST-100 interface area and white room shall be designed to provide a controlled, clean environment for ingress/egress of the spacecraft habitable volume.

3.2.5.7 Ground Segment Test and Checkout

The Contractor shall conduct Ground Segment test and checkout. The integrated tests shall include the ▉▉▉▉▉ Mission Control Center (MCC), hardware and software integration facility, electrical GSE, ground communications networks, space communication networks, landing sites, ▉▉▉▉▉▉▉▉▉▉▉▉▉▉▉▉▉▉▉▉▉▉▉▉▉▉▉▉▉▉▉▉▉▉▉▉▉▉▉

3.2.6 Crew and Mission Operations (CMO)

The Contractor shall conduct mission planning and analysis; training; crew, flight and cargo operations; and mission systems/controls consistent with CCT-STD-1150, Crew Transportation Operations Standards, and SSP 50808, International Space Station (ISS) to Commercial Orbital Transportation Services (COTS) Interface Requirements Document (IRD). The planning activity

Attachment J-03

shall be based on an assumed flight rate of two (2) flights per year to the ISS. The Contractor shall develop real-time and post flight review process to support validation that the CTS is performing as predicted and operating within design limitations. Real-time review process shall analyze and assess in-flight anomalies and CTS performance such that mission execution can continue safely. The post flight review process shall include debriefing the flight crew and operations personnel (J-01 1120 6.5.1).

3.2.6.1 Mission Planning and Analysis

The Contractor shall develop operational processes and products for mission planning and execution. Operations processes shall define methods to develop, validate, and certify the operations products and facilities. Operations products shall include: mission manifesting; flight design; ground operations procedures supporting nominal and off-nominal operations, mission controller/flight crew procedures supporting nominal and off-nominal scenarios while in-flight, nomenclature definition, vehicle and crew timelines, ground monitoring/control systems, and flight rules (J-01 1120 6.2.1).

3.2.6.2 Training

The Contractor shall develop a training program for personnel having safety critical or mission critical roles. The Contractor shall jointly develop with NASA a crew training template that covers CTS and ISS training (Reference DA8-13-193, Notional Training Template for ISS Crew members, Dated October 31, 2013). This training program shall include simulation training for flight crew, mission controllers, pre-flight/launch operations, and crew support personnel that closely mimics the conditions that will be seen during flight and shall address nominal and off-nominal scenarios. Personnel with safety or mission critical roles include mission designers, assembly/integration/testing and launch engineers, technicians and quality control personnel, mission and ground controllers, all flight crew, launch site and landing recovery personnel (J-01 1120 6.3.1). The training program shall also define standards for non-critical roles.

3.2.6.3 Flight Operations

The Contractor shall develop a mission execution process addressing operational communication plans, operational management plans, real-time analyses, and contingency action plans (J-01 1120 6.4.1). For ISS integrated operations, the Contractor shall jointly develop with NASA the operational products and mission planning and joint execution.

3.2.6.4 Cargo Operations

The Contractor shall work with NASA to identify cargo capabilities and integrate cargo onto the CST-100 for OFT and CFT flight test missions. The cargo definition and integration activities shall follow the same process as outlined for the PCM missions PWS Section 3.3.5.

3.2.7 Test and Evaluation

The Contractor shall develop and implement a CCtCap test program as part of the verification and validation effort to include abort and flight tests (J-01 1120 5.3) and end-to-end integrated system qualification tests. The Contractor shall implement a Joint Test Team (JTT) for the planning and execution of flight test activities in order to leverage the joint knowledge and experience shared between the Government and the contractor.

The Contractor's test and evaluation program shall include conduct of site surveys, design and development and set-up of test instrumentation, simulators and test articles, performance of

Attachment J-03

applicable reviews and briefings, conduct of the test event(s), performance of data analysis and data reduction and preparation of test plans/procedures and result reports. The contractor shall prepare and deliver one Verification Closure Notice (VCN), DRD 111, per CCT-REQ-1130, ISS Crew Transportation and Services Requirements Document, and SSP 50808, International Space Station (ISS) to Commercial Orbital Transportation Services (COTS) Interface Requirements Document (IRD) for all docked crewed and uncrewed requirements, as evidence of closure of each technical requirement.

3.2.7.1 Test Planning and Integration

The Contractor shall conduct test planning for all CCtCap test and evaluation activities. The Contractor shall determine test requirements, procedures, and data requirements for development of test plans that describe the approach for conducting tests, document test objectives with linkage to the specific requirement that are verified by the test (J-01 1120 7.0), and analyzing the test results to show how the system will satisfy the requirements of the applicable design.

The Contractor shall maintain, deliver and implement a Flight Test Plan in accordance with DRD 109, Flight Test Plan, and the content defined in CCT-PLN-1120, Crew Transportation Technical Management Processes, and shall address the test objectives in CCT-PLN-1120 Table 7-1 (J-01 1120 5.3.1).

The Contractor shall conduct test readiness review(s) prior to conduct of an uncrewed or crewed flight test event to demonstrate readiness for flight (J-01 1120 7.0) and define the risk baseline for flight activities in accordance with PWS Section 3.2.1.2, and the following:

a) Flight Test Readiness Review (FTRR) Data Package, DRD 104

b) CCT-PLN-1120, Crew Transportation Technical Management Processes, Appendix F, CTS FTRR/FRR Milestone Data

c) PWS Appendix A, Milestone Acceptance Criteria and Payment Schedule

The Contractor shall be responsible for design and development of test instrumentation, test articles and simulators required to support the test program to include Development Flight Instrumentation (DFI), Pad Abort/Crewed Flight Test (PAT/CFT) Article Qualification Test Vehicle (QTV) Article, and Orbital Flight Test (OFT) Article instrumentation and mass simulators.

3.2.7.2 Ground Test

The Contractor shall conduct static loads testing, pressure cyclic testing, modal testing, and separation shock testing.

The Contractor shall conduct Performance testing, acoustic testing, Electromagnetic Interference/Electromagnetic Compatibility (EMI/EMC) testing and lightning testing.

3.2.7.3 Flight Test

The Contractor shall operate a CTS such that execution of the flight tests are within the constraints of the NASA certification and recurring ISS requirements.

The Contractor shall satisfy at least one of the following decision criteria when determining flight test objectives:

a) Ground testing is not sufficient to adequately test the objective
b) Significant risk exists after all ground testing and analysis is complete
c) Flight test is the only method to achieve validation of the objective

The Contractor's flight test program shall include an uncrewed orbital flight test to the ISS. The OFT shall include a CCTS that validates end-to-end connectivity, LV and CST-100 integration, launch and flight operations, automated rendezvous and proximity operations, and docking with the ISS, assuming ISS approval. ████████████████████████████

The Contractor's flight test program shall include a crewed flight test to the ISS. The crewed flight test shall include a NASA crew that docks with the ISS, remains docked for a sufficient duration to check-out ISS interfaces, and then return to a supported landing site (J-01 1120 5.3).

The following (Table 3.2.7.3-1) work statements from PWS Section 3.3, PCM (CLIN 002), shall apply to the OFT and CFT to ISS (except for the first sentence in paragraph 3.3.3.1 dealing with ATP).

Table 3.2.7.3-1. PCM Task Performed during CLIN 001 for Crewed Flight Test to ISS

Paragraph	Title	DRD
3.3.3.1	PCM Approach	DRD 201
3.3.3.3	Mission Definition and Documentation	DRD 204
3.3.3.4	PCM Certification Maintenance	DRD 110, DRD 111, DRD 112, DRD 205
3.3.3.7	ISS Integration	
3.3.3.9	Range Safety	DRD 113
3.3.4	Mission Operations	
3.3.5	PCM Cargo Integration	DRD 206
3.3.1.4	ISS Stage Operational Readiness Review	
3.3.1.6	Post launch Ascent Review	
3.3.1.7	Undocking Readiness Review	
3.3.1.8	Post Flight Review	DRD 209, DRD 210

The Contractor shall perform ISS integration activities in accordance with the intent of SSP 50964, Visiting Vehicle ISS Integration Plan, SSP 50808, ISS to Commercial Orbital Transportation Services (COTS) Interface Requirements Document (IRD), and associated ISS documents (e.g., JSC 35089, Visiting Vehicle Ops Annex, SSP 30599, ISS Safety Review Process, SSP 50108, ISS Certification of Flight Readiness Process Document). The ISS Program and the CCP will work with the Contractor to negotiate an ISS Visiting Vehicle Joint Integration, Verification, and Test Plan (JIVTP). This test plan will define the steps, planning agreements, and products to be completed for joint ISS Visiting Vehicle requirement verification, execution, and closure. It also identifies organizational roles, responsibilities, and verification ownership (J-01 1120 5.4).

The Contractor shall participate in two (2) Mission Management simulations for the first crewed flight to ISS that includes mission management, flight controllers and crew participation. NASA will conduct the simulations from the NASA-Johnson Space Center (JSC) Mission Control Center (MCC) and the ISS Management Center (IMC). Each of these simulations may last up to 48 hours.

3.2.8 Incorporation of NASA Disposition of CPC Products

The Contractor shall perform the tasks identified below (referenced in the columns titled "PWS Work Scope") and/or provide documentation for submittal to NASA in response to formal dispositions documented in the noted NASA disposition letters. Documentation may be provided in place of or in addition to the specific documents identified in the task descriptions, sufficient to allow NASA to definitively approve the subject CPC Product.

3.2.8.1 Alternate Standards (Reference PWS Section 3.2.1.1)

The Contractor shall continue to refine, deliver and update the Alternate Standards developed under the CPC contract in accordance with PWS Section 3.2.1.1, the specific disposition letters, and the CPC Final Technical Summary Report findings. The contractor shall provide documentation / data in place of or in addition to the specific documents identified in Table 3.2.8.1-1, sufficient to allow NASA to definitively approve the subject Alternate Standard. If a Variance is required to resolve Alternate Standards open items, the contractor shall document the Variance Request and submit to NASA for disposition.

3.2.8.4 Verification and Validation Plan (Reference PWS Section 3.2.1.4)

The Contractor shall continue to refine, deliver and update the CCTS Verification and Validation Plan (DCC1-00005-01) developed under the CPC contract in accordance with PWS Section 3.2.1.4, DRD 108 (Verification and Validation Plan), the specific disposition letters, and the CPC Final Technical Summary Report findings. The contractor shall provide documentation / data to allow NASA to definitively approve the Verification and Validation Plan.

3.2.8.5 Certification Plan (Reference PWS Section 3.2.1.4)

The Contractor shall continue to refine, deliver and update the CCTS Certification Plan (DCC1-00443-01) developed under the CPC contract in accordance with PWS Section 3.2.1.4, DRD 107 (Certification Plan), the specific disposition letters, and the CPC Final Technical Summary Report findings. The contractor shall provide documentation / data to allow NASA to definitively approve the Certification Plan.

3.3 Post Certification Missions (PCM) Services (CLIN 002)

This PWS section contains the specific work scope associated with conducting post certification missions (CLIN 002). The contractor's approach for post certification mission planning and execution shall be repeatable with the lowest achievable safety risk. A Post Certification Mission is defined as services provided by the Contractor, from Task Order Authority to Proceed, to Plan, Process, Train, Conduct Operations, Execute, Launch, On Orbit support, landing/recovery services through Contracting Officer Mission Success Determination and Acceptance as specified in Article H.21. Each PCM shall include all activities from mission planning through post flight assessment including unplanned events and inflight anomalies. For PCMs to ISS, the contractor shall support the objectives of CCT-STD-1150, Crew Transportation Operations Standards, and SSP 50808, International Space Station (ISS) to Commercial Orbital Transportation Services (COTS) Interface Requirements Document (IRD), which define preflight and mission planning and integration processes; standards; and products required to successfully complete the mission. The contractor processes defined in support of this objective shall satisfy CCT-PLN-1120, Crew Transportation Technical Management Processes, which defines mission integration rhythm, handover points, and roles of the contractor's team.

The efforts detailed in 3.3 are additive to the work scope defined in PWS Section 3.1. Since the activities from the core certification effort (Reference PWS Section 3.2, CLIN 001) and the initial PCMs (Reference PWS Section 3.3, CLIN 002) can be conducted concurrently, the contractor shall ensure the interdependencies between the on-going core certification efforts and PCM objectives are addressed in development plans and mission execution planning.

3.3.1 Key PCM Milestones/Reviews

The Contractor shall conduct reviews to prepare and execute each PCM in accordance with Contract Clause H-19 Post Certification Mission Payments Milestones and Authority to Proceed (ATP) Criteria. Each PCM shall include, at a minimum, the milestones/reviews identified in PWS sections 3.3.1.1 through 3.3.1.7. The contractor shall define additional interim reviews/events the contractor deems necessary to supplement the mandatory Government reviews and those associated with progress payments shall be detailed in PWS Appendix B, Post Certification Mission (PCM) Milestone Acceptance Criteria and Payment Schedule. These events represent essential decision points to accurately measure the success of the preceding phase of work and an entry point for control of subsequent work efforts. PWS Appendix B, Post Certification Mission (PCM) Acceptance Criteria and Payment Schedule, defines the success requirements to allow progress to next event for all payment milestones/reviews.

The PCM Work shall address the requirements from Attachment J-02, Data Requirements Deliverables; CCT-REQ-1130, ISS Crew Transportation and Services Requirements Document; and PWS Appendix B, Post Certification Mission (PCM) Acceptance Criteria and Payment Schedule.

3.3.1.1 Vehicle Baseline Review (VBR) (At no later than 18 months prior to launch (L-18 mo))

The Contractor shall co-chair a Vehicle Baseline Review (VBR) with NASA with the objective that establishes the integrated mission CTS configuration (launch vehicle, orbital vehicle, and ground systems) that accommodates NASA requirements for crew and cargo transportation. The intent of the VBR is to establish the baseline CTS for the mission and identifies any design or operations changes from the previous baseline and the corresponding plans for executing and verifying the changes. The content of the VBR shall include: A) Mission Baseline CTS and B) Design and Operation changes from prior mission baseline CTS which are detailed in PWS Appendix B, Post Certification Mission (PCM) Acceptance Criteria and Payment Schedule.

The VBR shall review updated versions, as required, of MIOMP, DRD 201, PCM Work Plan, DRD 202, and Vehicle IDD, DRD 203. The VBR shall be a payment milestone in accordance with Contract Clause H.19 Post Certification Mission Payments, Milestones and Authority to Proceed (ATP) Criteria and readiness and success criteria for this event shall be detailed in PWS Appendix B, Post Certification Mission (PCM) Acceptance Criteria and Payment Schedule.

3.3.1.2 Mission Integration Review (MIR) (At no later than 13 months prior to launch (L-13 mo))

The Contractor shall co-chair a Mission Integration Review (MIR) with NASA with a current mission integration status including specific mission hardware delivery schedules and vehicle layout arrangements. NASA and contractor will review and baseline the conditions and inputs for mission specific analytical assessments. The contractor shall demonstrate CTS operations and production activities in support of the launch date. A status of all open items presented at VBR shall be presented at this review. For open items, schedule plans for completion shall be presented. All milestones to this point shall have been met. The content for the MIR shall include: A) Mission Baseline CTS and B) Design and Operation changes from prior mission baseline CTS which are detailed in PWS Appendix B, Post Certification Mission (PCM) Acceptance Criteria and Payment Schedule.

The review data package shall include detailed design and associated analysis that implement and support the mission requirements. The MIR shall review updated versions, as required, of Hazard Reports, DRD 110, VCNs, DRD 111, MIOMP, DRD 201, Vehicle IDD, DRD 203, and MRAD, DRD 204, if updated since VBR. The review shall provide NASA with specific mission success determination criteria as well as overall mission integration status. Updated products and action closure from the VBR are presented. The intent of this review is to provide NASA the necessary information to determine if scheduled delivery dates can be achieved and if integration activities should continue as planned. The MIR establishes a 30-day window for the mission to ISS. The MIR shall be a payment milestone in accordance with Contract Clause H.19 Post Certification Mission Payments, Milestones and Authority to Proceed (ATP) Criteria and readiness and success criteria for this event shall be detailed in Appendix B, Post Certification Mission (PCM) Acceptance Criteria and Payment Schedule.

3.3.1.3 Mission Certification Review (MCR) (After Certification has been granted, and no later than 4 months prior to launch (L-4))

The Contractor shall co-chair with NASA a Mission Certification Review (MCR) that allows NASA to assess if the contractor has completed certification of all requirements (existing "generic" CCTS, mission specific and new requirements due to hardware, software and process changes), has completed ISS integration, has all infrastructure, facilities, personnel and services in place and will be ready for the mission and for crewed operations, included agreement on cargo turnover and crew handover. As status of all open items presented in both VBR and MIR shall be presented at this review. All mission unique design qualification and acceptance testing shall be completed. For open items, schedule plans for completion shall be presented. All milestones to this point shall have been met. The content of the MCR is detailed in PWS Appendix B, Post Certification Mission (PCM) Acceptance Criteria and Payment Schedule.

The contractor shall confirm agreements are in-place to support cargo turnover and flight crew handover. The contractor shall provide evidence that design; testing, qualification and acceptance of all mission-unique hardware have been completed. The MCR shall establish the final data and mission success determination criteria. The MCR shall review updated version, as required, of Vehicle IDD, DRD 203, if updated since MIR. The MCR shall be a payment milestone in accordance with Contract Clause H.19 Post Certification Mission Payments, Milestones and Authority to Proceed (ATP) Criteria and readiness and success criteria for this event shall be detailed in PWS Appendix B, Post Certification Mission (PCM) Acceptance Criteria and Payment Schedule.

3.3.1.4 ISS Stage Operational Readiness Review (SORR) (Approximately 3 weeks prior to launch)

At approximately three (3) weeks prior to launch, the Contractor shall support a pre-requisite review for the FRR and shall participate in the ISS Stage Operational Readiness Reviews (SORR). The contractor shall provide, at a minimum, the following data and presentation:

(a) Status of integration of CTS, cargo, and crew.

(b) Planned launch windows and available back-up opportunities; planned mission profile and activities including any special operations.

(c) CTS propellant and power budget (nominal and margins) and associated loiter capability.

(d) Crew consumables budget (nominal and margins) for free flight phases.

(e) Summary of all open work and closure plan.

(f) Summary of all risks or watch items including mitigation plans and/or acceptance rationales that may affect the crewmember(s) or commercial spacecraft's ability to complete the mission.

(g) Operations support readiness (facilities, tools, processes, products, personnel) for all phases of the mission.

3.3.1.5 Flight Readiness Review (FRR) (Approximately 2 weeks prior to launch)

The Contractor shall support a NASA Flight Readiness Review (FRR). The contractor shall provide a mission specific DRD 208, Flight Readiness Review Data Package, in support of FRR. The Contractor shall present a Certification of Flight Readiness endorsement for the upcoming flight including verification of all flight and ground systems readiness for launch, closure of previous review open items, review of documentation for residual risk items and plan showing completion of open work prior to launch. Launch Site, Range, FAA and Recovery forces ready to support mission. ISS program is ready to accept CCTS vehicle and crew. The FRR shall be a payment milestone in accordance with Contract Clause H.19 Post Certification Mission Payments, Milestones and Authority to Proceed (ATP) Criteria and readiness and success criteria for this event shall be detailed in Appendix B, Post Certification Mission (PCM) Acceptance Criteria and Payment Schedule.

3.3.1.6 Undocking Readiness (Approximately two (2) weeks prior to landing)

The Contractor shall participate in an Undocking Readiness Integrated Management Team (IMT) and, at a minimum, provide: (a) Planned landing windows, available backup opportunities, weather report, (b) Cargo to be returned, and (c) CTS resources margins.

3.3.1.7 Post Flight Review (PFR) (Approximately 2.5 weeks after landing)

The Contractor shall conduct Post Flight Reviews with NASA participation to assess mission success with supporting data in accordance with DRD 209, Post Flight Assessment Report. The PFR following each mission landing shall address CCTS system performance for ascent, rendezvous and docking; quiescent docked operations; undocking, entry and landing; post landing crew recovery. The review shall include a preliminary review of predicted vs. actual performance; evaluation of actual vs. predicted environments; a summary of any anomalies (flight hardware and ground systems) from start of LV tanking through crew recovery and the impacts on execution of the flight and preliminary assessment of flight crew and ground personnel training. The contractor shall present a determination of meeting the mission success criteria that was finalized at MCR. The Contractor shall conduct and deliver preliminary, updates, and final post flight assessment. The PFR shall be a payment milestone in accordance with Contract Clause H.19 Post Certification Mission Payments, Milestones and Authority to Proceed (ATP) Criteria and readiness and success criteria for this event shall be detailed in Appendix B, Post Certification Mission (PCM) Acceptance Criteria and Payment Schedule.

3.3.2 PCM Vehicle Integration

3.3.2.1 Launch Vehicle (LV) and Crew Vehicle (CV) Integration

The Contractor shall build, process, integrate and operate the CTS for the mission to the ISS. Integration shall include the physical integration of the CTS.

The Contractor shall define the necessary pre-launch testing such as Terminal Countdown Demonstration Test (TCDT) and Crew Equipment Interface Test (CEIT) that include flight controllers, crews, and required NASA and Contractor support personnel.

3.3.2.2 Safety, Reliability and Quality Engineering

The Contractor shall provide in-line system safety, reliability and quality engineering support.

The Contractor shall implement a system safety program consistent with the policies, procedures and processes established in the contractor's developed system safety program plan. The contractor's safety process shall provide an integrated, systematic, and comprehensive approach, which can be used to assess changes in risk resulting from design and operational changes, including anomaly resolutions. The safety process shall include:

a) the evaluation of hardware and software changes, operational changes, anomaly resolutions, as well as environmental and human factors relevant to safety

b) the use of industry standard safety analyses (e.g. hazards likelihood and severity categories) throughout the CTS lifecycle

c) closed-loop tracking and verification of mission unique hazard controls

d) detailed plans for the communication and acceptance of risk to stakeholders and/or the appropriate control boards to ensure mission unique residual risk is appropriately managed

e) the safety review process for communication and approval of updated safety analyses for flight readiness reviews

The Contractor shall provide and manage a Mishap Reporting and Investigation Plan and process that are in accordance with Contract Clause H.26 Mishap Reporting. When applicable, the Contractor shall support a Commission appointed by the President per 51 U.S.C Section 70701 et seq.

The Contractor shall conduct a safety review process that allows for the systematic identification and review of hazards related to the design, operations, and anomaly resolutions in support of PCM flight readiness reviews. This methodology shall ensure that proper controls are maintained for all hazard causes consistent with CCP certification processes and requirements. Risks identified as a result of the hazard analysis that are deemed a CCP risk shall be coordinated with the CCP Risk Management Process (J-01 1120 4.5). For hazard reports where the ISS is identified as being an affected party and/or stakeholder, the Contractor shall coordinate with the CCP to prepare and deliver such items for approval to the ISS Safety Review Panel (reference SSP 30599, ISS Safety Review Process, and SSP 30309, Safety Analysis and Risk Assessment Requirements Document) (J-01 1120 4.5).

The Contractor shall implement a safety and health program which identifies, eliminates, mitigates and control hazards and risks in activities in accordance with the existing CTS Safety and Health Plan. The contractor shall support the range safety analysis to meet local test range safety requirements including a list of hazardous operations to be performed. The contractor shall deliver Range Safety Documentation.

The Contractor shall implement its reliability program plan to update Failure Modes Effects Analyses/Critical Items Lists (FMEA/CIL), including the CCtCap System Probabilistic Safety Assessments, to reflect any changes in risk. The reliability program plan shall also include participation in Exchanging Parts, Materials, and Safety Problem Data utilizing the Government Industry Data Exchange Program (GIDEP).

The Contractor shall develop and execute a quality management system that assures quality requirements are flowed down from design into the manufacturing and operational processes and is compliant with the requirements of AS9100, Quality Management Systems – Requirements for Aviation, Space and Defense Organizations. The Contractor shall implement a quality function for inspection, material review, supplier quality control, quality investigations and manufacturing support, and software quality metrics. The Contractor shall flow down and ensure implementation of appropriate quality assurance requirements to applicable suppliers.

The Contractor shall be responsible for the management of software safety throughout the CTS lifecycle for flight software, flight support software, ground support equipment (GSE) ground software, and hardware and software used in the design, development, test, verification, storage, maintenance of software, and ensures that software products obtained from any source meet the software assurance requirements. The contractor shall maintain the software safety plan to document safety-critical software determination processes, management, software development and analysis methods (including support of hazard analyses and maintenance of hazard reports), implementation and test, and operational use.

3.3.3 PCM Mission Integration

The Contractor shall ensure the safe integration and transport of crew and cargo to and from the ISS. The Contractor shall put in place and support integration and operations process for all Post Certification Missions. The Contractor shall integrate the crew and cargo complement, and at the vehicle level, perform analysis and integration to safely execute the flight to and from the ISS including cargo turnover and crew handover.

Attachment J-03

[REDACTED]

If there is contractor crew(s) or commercial passenger(s) on a mission to ISS, the Contractor shall define and implement a process that complies with SSP 50260, ISS Medical Operations Requirements Document, and SSP 50667, Medical Evaluation Document, Volumes A-C.

3.3.3.1 PCM Approach

Upon receipt of Authorization to Proceed (ATP), the Contractor shall initiate initial mission planning work. The Contractor shall prepare and deliver a Mission Integration and Operations Management Plan (MIOMP), DRD 201, that details the contractor's approach to PCM mission integration including coordination with Government for mission planning and execution. The MIOMP shall outline the key aspects of mission integration activities, describe operations and processes, product delivery templates, and organization interfaces necessary for the contractor to implement integration and operations activities for the PCM to the ISS.

3.3.3.2 PCM Initiation

The Contractor shall prepare and deliver a Post Certification Mission Work Plan (PCM WP), DRD 202, that establishes for each milestone, including interim payment milestones/reviews leading up to the mandatory Government delivery milestones: the review process, the sequence of all reviews/milestones, anticipated schedule, entrance criteria/readiness deliverables to address the milestone review objectives and timing by which data will be made available to NASA for review, boards, exit/success/acceptance criteria, and other logistics related information. The PCM WP shall define the specific data requirements required to successfully conduct each review. The PCM Work Plan is a template that shall be updated and tailored to the unique requirements of each PCM.

3.3.3.3 Mission Definition and Documentation

The Contractor shall document mission requirements and definition for each flight, from which all other planning data is derived, in a Mission Requirements Document, Launch Vehicle (LV) Interface Control Document (ICD), Mission Resource allocation Document (MRAD), DRD 204, and Vehicle Interface Definition Document (VIDD), DRD 203. The contractor shall utilize these documents as the starting point for deriving all other mission products. The Mission Requirements Document shall be an internally controlled document and through Government insight the document shall be collaboratively prepared to include applicable ISS Interface Requirements Document (IRD), software load, vehicle number and configuration, crew complement, cargo complement/powered, launch/landing date, launch vehicle configuration and special mission requirements. [REDACTED] The contractor shall complete required mission specific analysis to ensure mission safety and success and deliver for each flight a Mission Resource Allocation Document (MRAD) in accordance with DRD 204, Mission Resource Allocation Document (MRAD. NASA and the Contractor will utilize the data from the MRAD in the mission analysis, mission procedures/ training, and crew/cargo integration. The MRAD establishes the allocation of resources and technical data requirements needed for each PCM. The contractor shall prepare and deliver a VIDD. The VIDD shall include specific mission interfaces for each flight and address the topics of environments and sensor information. The associated data shall provide the required assessment to confirm compatibility with the spacecraft environments defined in the Vehicle IDD (reference DRD 203) and compatibility with SSP 50808, ISS to Commercial Orbital Transportation Services (COTS) Interface Requirements Document (IRD), and CCT-REQ-1130, ISS Crew Transportation and Services Requirements Document.

The Contractor shall measure and provide telemetry data confirming the required launch, entry, and orbit conditions and cargo environments were met as stated in DRD 203, Vehicle Interface Definition Document (IDD). This shall include a detailed listing and description of all measurements and calibration coefficients.

The Contractor shall submit spacecraft Engineering Computer Aided Design models and CTS imagery plan and associated cataloging in accordance with DRD 205, Spacecraft Computer Aided Design (CAD) Models, and DRD 210, Imagery Plan and Associated Cataloging.

3.3.3.4 PCM Certification Maintenance

The Contractor shall maintain the product baselines and perform the mission and analytical integration for each flight. The contractor shall review and evaluate design, production, or operational changes from the NASA certification baseline for compliance to the requirements of CCT-REQ-1130, ISS Crew Transportation and Services Requirements Document, and SSP 50808, ISS to Commercial Orbital Transportation Services (COTS) Interface Requirements Document (IRD). The contractor shall maintain NASA certification for the CTS for all PCMs. Additionally, system performance from previous production, operation or flights shall be reviewed for potential impacts to the NASA certification. The contractor shall ensure that post flight inspections and test results are reviewed, nonconforming hardware is isolated and dispositioned. For changes to vehicle design, reference missions, or operational environments that require re-verification/certification, the contractor shall update and deliver CTS Hazard Reports in accordance with CCT-PLN-1120, Crew Transportation Technical Management Processes, and DRD 110, Hazard Reports, Verification Closure Notices (VCNs), DRD 111, and Certification Data Package, DRD 112 as required in support of MCR.

3.3.3.5 Safety and Mission Assurance

The Contractor shall implement a safety and mission assurance program consistent with the policies, procedures and processes established in the contractor's developed mission assurance plan. The contractor shall provide safety assessments of the mission as part of the Flight Readiness Review in support of mission planning. The contractor shall conduct mission assurance activities that assure product integrity and mission success focusing on issue prevention with Mission Assurance Independent Reviews (MAIRs) and Technical Independent Reviews (TIRs), independent risk assessment, and technical integrity verification. The contractor shall provide an independent evaluation of program and S&MA readiness assessments, including defining success criteria for the assessments. The contractor shall proactively identify the need for independent assessments (including technical, execution, cultural, and other issues) and facilitate independent reviews. The contractor shall monitor activities and process trends to ensure process discipline is maintained, review engineering products throughout maturation to ensure technical integrity, and independently assess the level of technical risk incurred and quality of mitigation plans. In cases where anomalies or unfavorable technical trends emerge or mishaps occur, the contractor shall ensure appropriate engineering root-cause analysis activities are conducted and that effective corrective actions are implemented, to include documentation of

Attachment J-03

lessons learned and procedural updates. The contractor mission assurance discipline shall participate in the CCTS Risk process, and attends the program risk board meetings to ensure the program maintains the necessary rigor in the identification and disposition of program level and lower level risks. The Contractor shall annually review the mission assurance plan for updates with the objective of strengthening the mission assurance program and incorporating applicable lessons learned. The contractor shall provide input to critical Go-No-Go calls during critical mission events including the launch countdown polls, undocking, and deorbit burn maneuvers.

3.3.3.6 Analytical Integration

The Contractor shall perform pre- and post flight analyses as required to support the PCM Mission Milestones and Reviews defined in PWS Section 3.3.1, Appendix B, Post Certification Mission (PCM) Milestone Acceptance Criteria and Payment Schedule and other appropriate contractor internally conducted reviews.

3.3.3.7 ISS Integration

The Contractor shall perform ISS integration activities in accordance with the intent of SSP 50964, Visiting Vehicle ISS Integration Plan, SSP 50808, ISS to Commercial Orbital Transportation Services (COTS) Interface Requirements Document (IRD), and associated ISS documents (e.g. JSC 35089, Visiting Vehicle Ops Annex, SSP 30599, ISS Safety Review Process, and SSP 50108, ISS Certification of Flight Readiness Process Document).

3.3.3.8 Licenses and Permits

The Contractor shall obtain the support services, permits and licenses to complete the mission to ISS such as Federal Communications Commission (FCC) and NASA frequency use agreements for the CV telecommunications. The contractor shall secure a Federal Aviation Administration (FAA) license for all post certification missions in accordance with Contract Clause H.18 Licenses, Permits, and Other Authorizations for a Launch or Reentry Service Operator.

3.3.3.9 Range Safety

The Contractor shall comply with applicable Launch Site Range Safety regulatory requirements (ASPC Manual 91-710, Air Force Space Command Range Safety User Policies and Procedures) and deliver Range Safety Documentation DRD 113, Range Safety Documentation.

3.3.4 Crew and Mission Operations

3.3.4.1 Mission Planning and Analysis

The Contractor shall perform mission planning, management and execution activities. The Contractor shall perform mission planning prior to all CLIN 002 PCMs. Operations products developed during the planning process shall include Timelines, Trajectories, Flight Crew and Ground Procedures, Flight Rules, Launch Commit Criteria, Operations Handbooks, Console Notes and other tools necessary to define and execute the PCM. These operations products shall be reviewed at key milestones during the PCM planning flow and culminate in a Flight Operations Review (FOR). The contractor shall certify that all operations products are complete and ready for flight for each PCM at the FRR. The contractor shall provide real-time re-planning in the event the mission plan changes during the flight due to inflight anomalies with either the CTS or ISS.

Attachment J-03

3.3.4.2 Training

The Contractor shall perform training of NASA Flight Crews, Boeing Flight Controllers, and Trainers, as well as key operations personnel supporting launch and landing. The contractor-developed Training System shall provide mission preparation in the form of CTS systems training and mission simulations including stand-alone, joint, and joint-integrated training with the ISS and MCC-CST. The contractor shall develop syllabi which reflect the experience level of the trainee and shall maintain appropriate training certifications consistent with CCT-STD-1150, Crew Transportation Operations Standards, and JSC 35089, Visiting Vehicle Operations Document. The contractor training syllabus shall be developed jointly with NASA's ISSP to ensure the timeline is consistent with the ISS training flow, and records of training shall be maintained in a Learning Management repository which shall be used to reflect personal training certifications. In addition to operations personnel, the contractor shall provide training events to develop Mission Management Team decision making skills.

The Contractor shall provide the required high fidelity CTS and ground facilities hardware, software, and data for interfacing with NASA, Software Development Integration Laboratory, and JSC Mission Control Center (MCC) to execute Joint spacecraft-ISS testing and Joint Multi-Segment Simulation Trainings (JMSTs).

The Contractor shall participate in Joint Multi-Segment Simulation Training (JMST) that includes flight controllers and crews participation and maintain the Training system to ensure that it meets the reliability needs of NASA.

3.3.4.3 Flight Operations

3.3.4.3.1 Flight Operations

The Contractor shall provide end-to-end real-time flight operations necessary to support the CTS mission to ISS. The contractor shall provide the Mission Control facility (MCC-CST), ground software tools, and mission systems necessary to execute spaceflight operations. ▉▉▉▉▉▉▉▉▉▉▉▉▉▉▉▉▉▉▉▉▉▉▉▉▉▉▉▉▉▉▉▉ The contractor shall provide continuous flight following from the MCC-CST during non-quiescent operations to ensure mission success and address in-flight anomalies which are beyond the capabilities of the flight crew to resolve. During quiescent docked operations, the contractor shall provide on-call support to address issues and anomalies which arise, as well as support ISS anomalies which may lead to unscheduled operations (i.e. safe haven operations). The contractor shall provide all landing operations support (excluding off-nominal landings outside of nominal landing area) including CST systems or weather-based landing, i.e. go-no go decisions.

3.3.4.3.2 Emergency Crew Search and Rescue Interface

The Contractor shall provide an operational interface and coordinate with the Government in the planning for emergency crew search and rescue services.

3.3.4.4 Ground Systems

The Contractor shall provide the ground operational resources necessary to support the CTS mission to ISS. The contractor shall build, process, integrate and operate the CTS for the mission to the ISS. The contractor shall provide Ground Systems supporting facilities, support equipment, hardware, and software required for ground and flight operations. The contractor shall participate in Joint Multi-Segment Simulation Training (JMST) that includes flight controllers, flight crews, ground crews, and landing sites.

3.3.4.4.1 Assembly Integration and Test (AIT) Facility and System

The Contractor shall perform vehicle (hardware and software) assembly, integration and end-to-end test at the contractor's facility or facilities. ███████████████

The Contractor shall maintain and operate all mechanical and electrical ground support equipment (GSE) required supporting the AIT. The contractor shall perform vehicle integration and pre- and post-flight mission activities (e.g., fueling, cargo/crew loading, and recovery).

The Contractor shall provide all tooling required to support refurbishment of the Spacecraft elements. ███████████████

3.3.4.5 Ground Communication Systems

The Contractor shall maintain and operate a Ground Communications System that provides Space-to-Ground communications to the spacecraft from launch through landing. The contractor shall provide ground communications capability between recovery ground crews, flight crew, and mission control.

3.3.4.6 Recovery Systems and Operations

The Contractor shall provide GSE, services, and equipment for nominal landing crew and crew module recovery. Services include: medevac evacuation, metrology forecasting, landing site maintenance, and landing site air traffic control/radar tracking.

3.3.4.7 Logistics and Logistic Systems

The Contractor shall provide ground segment logistics activities to include (1) databases for shipping/receiving, sparing analysis/tracking, ground maintenance planning/scheduling, and limited life items, (2) packaging, handling, storage, and transportation.

3.3.4.8 Ground Segment Test and Checkout

The Contractor shall conduct Ground Segment test and checkout. The integrated tests shall include the contractor's Mission Control Center (MCC), software integration facility, electrical GSE, ground communications networks, space communication networks, landing sites, Launch Control Center (LCC), and ISS Mission Control interfaces.

3.3.5 PCM Cargo Integration

The Contractor shall safely integrate cargo into the spacecraft. The Contractor shall maintain and operate Ground Support Equipment (GSE) for physical cargo integration including nominal stow cargo, late stow cargo and post mission cargo extraction, for early destow and nominal destow.

3.3.5.1 Cargo Integration

The Contractor shall develop an internal cargo interface control agreement (ICA) in accordance with DRD 206, Internal Cargo Interface Control Agreement (ICA), for middeck lockers and for items planned to be hard-mounted in the spacecraft volume per DRD 204 MRAD.

The Contractor shall provide a spacecraft pressurized module physical configuration per DRD 204, MRAD, and any constraints related to manifest and return flexibility.

The Contractor shall document the cargo ground handling procedures and constraints.

The Contractor shall document discrepancies to hardware turned over to the Contractor and report those discrepancies to NASA within forty-eight (48) hours of identifying the discrepancy.

The Contractor shall affix bar code labels per the ISS Inventory Management System (IMS) standard to Commercial cargo that will be transferred from the spacecraft to the ISS and shall correlate IMS bar code numbers to stowage location data for all cargo flown and provide this data to NASA in accordance with the final DRD 204, MRAD.

The Contractor shall conduct power/data testing for all first time flown powered middeck lockers to ensure interface compliance.

The Contractor shall prepare and submit Integrated Cargo Phase III Hazard Report, DRD 207, per SSP 30599, ISS Safety Review Process, at L-4 months, to ensure the hazards associated with the packaging of the cargo complement have sufficient controls. The Contractor shall submit, as required, a delta Integrated Cargo Phase III Hazard Report, DRD 207, that represents the final integrated cargo hazard assessment. .

3.3.5.2 Return Cargo

The Contractor shall identify constraints to the on-orbit packing of cargo for return per the final DRD 204, MRAD. NASA will plan cargo transfers with Contractor coordination and in accordance with identified constraints while the spacecraft remains docked to the ISS. NASA will maintain the capability to adjust the return cargo complement within the identified constraints while the spacecraft remains mated to the ISS.

3.3.6 Inherent Capabilities

3.3.6.1 Contractor System Inherent Capabilities

The Contractor's inherent capabilities beyond the requirements in Attachment J-01, Integrated Crew Transportation System (CTS) Requirements that are added value to the Government as a result of the unique contractor's robust design and/or operational concept that enhances operational flexibility and/or mission performance are described in Table 3.3.6.1-1 The contractor shall perform the required planning and analyses to define the inherent capabilities in excess of requirements to accomplish each PCM and provide these capabilities to NASA in the MRAD, DRD 204, and update in accordance with Table 3.3.6.1-1.

3.4 Special Studies (CLIN 003)

The Contractor shall provide engineering, logistics and related technical support functions for the CCtCap program as detailed and in accordance with the task ordering procedures in this contract, B.5 Special Studies Services (Indefinite Delivery Indefinite - IDIQ) (CLIN 003). Contractor shall perform special studies in support of this (CCtCap) contract/program as initiated by written direction from the Contracting Officer. These activities provide technical support to include but are not limited to:

a) research, analysis and recommendations of Government provided what-if exercises;

b) design, development, and test investigations/modeling/analyses/trade studies to provide further confidence and understanding of robustness of design, advance planning, or feasibility for development and certification activities;

c) assessment of new/additional requirements/systems, software, or product improvements and impacts on the Contractor's design, schedule and cost as it relates to the CCtCap or lifecycle activities;

d) new Training Aids, Devices, or training products development;

e) analyses in support of change requirements to authorized missions;

f) development, fabrication, and test of hardware or software to support planning studies, special tests, or mission-unique studies

g) development, fabrication, test, certification and integration for unique cargo configurations, mounting equipment and support equipment

Appendix A to Attachment J-03, Milestone Acceptance Criteria and Payment Schedule

Attachment J-03, Appendix A

1.0 INTRODUCTION

The Milestone Acceptance Criteria and Payment Schedule provided in Section 3.0 details all the milestones, reviews and/or payment events which mark progress towards completion of CLIN 001 activities and is provided in response to and supports:

Section	Description
B.3	Design, Development, Test and Evaluation (DDTE) / Certification (Core Contract) (CLIN 001)
G.8	Submission of Invoices for Payment
H.31	Interim Performance-Based Milestone Payments (Applicable to CLIN 001)
I.11	52.232-32 Performance-Based Payments (Apr 2012) (Deviation), (Applicable to Interim Performance-Based Payments Events)
L.21	Instructions for Milestones, Milestone Acceptance Criteria and Payment Schedule (Applicable to CLIN 001)
Attachment J-03, Section 3.2	Performance Work Statement
Attachment J-03, Appendix A	Milestone Acceptance Criteria and Payment Schedule

2.0 MILESTONE REVIEW PLAN (DRD 101)

The Contractor shall utilize the Milestone Review Plan (MRP), DRD 101, to describe for each mandatory Government and Contractor proposed payment milestone and interim review for CLIN 001 defined in Section 3.0 the following:

- the review process
- schedule
- location
- deliverables
- delivery dates
- method and timing by which data will be made available to NASA
- document review requirements
- presentation meetings
- pre-boards
- other logistics-related information

In advance of the each milestone, the Contractor shall collaborate with NASA to detail the mutually agreed to readiness indicators (also known as entrance criteria) and acceptance criteria (also called exit or success criteria) for that milestone/review in the MRP document. At a minimum, the team shall draw from the following requirements set and any other tools available at that time to refine and tailor the entrance and exit criteria to the specific milestone/review/event:

a) CCT-PLN-1120, Crew Transportation Technical Management Processes Document, Appendix H, CCP Milestone Review Data

b) This document, Appendix A to Attachment J-03, Milestone Acceptance Criteria and Payment Schedule

c) Applicable milestone/interim review Data Package DRD Data Requirements section (CBR-DRD 102, DCR-DRD 103, FTRR,-DRD 104, ORR-DRD 105, and CR-DRD 106)

d) NASA Systems Engineering Processes and Requirements, NPR 7123.1A

The Contractor shall submit the MRP detailing the agreed to specifics for the next milestone review(s) / event(s) to allow sufficient time for NASA approval of the MRP. The MRP shall be updated in accordance with the MRP submittal schedule provided in the MRP (reference DCC1-00773-01 Milestone Review Plan, Table 1.3-1). Once NASA approves the MRP, the plan shall supersede the associated contract milestone review requirements in (a) above, and will be considered tailoring of those requirements.

3.0 MILESTONE ACCEPTANCE CRITERIA AND PAYMENT SCHEDULE

The Milestone Acceptance Criteria and Payment Schedule includes mandatory Government milestones, readiness and success criteria provided by the Government in RFP Attachment J-03 and is supplemented with additional Contractor defined interim payment milestones/events.

The following legend is used to easily recognize the milestones, reviews and events.

Legend:
Mandatory Government Interim Milestone
Contractor Proposed Interim Milestone
Mandatory Government Delivery Milestone
IAW = in accordance with

Certification Baseline Review (CBR) Interim Milestone	Planned Start Date and Completion Date (mo/yr):	Amount:
(As proposed, interim NASA milestone in support of DCR) DCR Interim Milestone 01A.1	Sep - Oct/2014 No Final RID Board	

Objective:

At a NASA and Contractor co-chaired Certification Baseline Review (CBR) completed within ninety (90) days of contract start, the Contractor shall:

a) Identify the Baseline requirements, including the allocation to the Elements and Subsystems of the CTS, incorporating the results of NASA's guidance provided under Certification Products Contract (CPC) (if applicable), which meet NASA's requirements defined in CCT-REQ-1130, ISS Crew Transportation and Services Requirements Document and SSP 50808, International Space Station (ISS) to Commercial Orbital Transportation Services (COTS) Interface Requirements Document.

b) Identify the current Crew Transportation System (CTS) design baseline.

c) Document management plans and products incorporating the results of NASA's disposition provided under Certification Products Contract (CPC) (if applicable), to meet requirements in the CCT-PLN-1120, Crew Transportation Technical Management Processes.

d) Define the plan and schedule to complete Design, Development, Test, and Evaluation (DDTE) and certification for the CTS design, production, and operations.

e) Define top safety, technical, cost and schedule risks based on most current CTS design. (Att J-03 PWS Apx A)

Indicators of Milestone Readiness: (Att J-03 PWS Apx A)	Data / DRDs to be provided:	Delivery of Data/DRDs (mo/yr)
The Contractor has completed the following and provided to NASA:		
a) The requirements, including the allocation to the Elements and Subsystems of the CTS, incorporating the results of NASA's disposition under CPC (if applicable) which meet NASA's requirements defined in CCT-REQ-1130 and SSP 50808 including but not limited to:	Data to be transmitted via DRD 102	Aug/2014

Attachment J-03, Appendix A

Certification Baseline Review (CBR) Interim Milestone (As proposed, interim NASA milestone in support of DCR) DCR Interim Milestone 01A.1	Planned Start Date and Completion Date (mo/yr): Sep - Oct/2014 No Final RID Board	Amount: ■
1) Documentation of previously approved variances and alternate standards incorporated or tailored in requirements.	Data to be transmitted via DRD 102	Aug/2014
2) Provide joint ISS integration products (Interface Control Documents (ICDs), Joint Integrated Verification Test Plan (JiVTP), Bi-lateral Data Exchange Agreement List and Schedule (BDEALS), Bi-lateral Hardware Software Exchange Agreement List and Schedule (BHSEALS)) identified in SSP 50964, Visiting Vehicle ISS Integration Plan.	Data to be transmitted via DRD 102	Aug/2014
b) Documentation of the current CTS design baseline as defined in DRD 102 Certification Baseline Review (CBR) Data Package.	Data to be transmitted via DRD 102	Aug/2014
c) The management plans and products as defined in DRD 102 Certification Baseline Review (CBR) Data Package.	Data to be transmitted via DRD 102	Aug/2014
d) The DRD 108 Verification and Validation (V&V) Plan.	Data to be transmitted via DRD 108	Aug/2014
e) The DRD 107 Certification Plan.	Data to be transmitted via DRD 107	Aug/2014
f) The DRD 002 Integrated Master Plan and Integrated Master Schedule for CTS Certification activities.	Data to be transmitted via DRD 002	Aug/2014

Attachment J-03, Appendix A

Certification Baseline Review (CBR) Interim Milestone	Planned Start Date and Completion Date (mo/yr): Sep - Oct/2014 No Final RID Board	Amount:
(As proposed, interim NASA milestone in support of DCR) DCR Interim Milestone 01A.1		
g) An assessment of the top safety, technical, cost, and schedule risks to CTS Certification, and documentation of the approach to manage and accept risk with CTS Certification	Data to be transmitted via DRD 102	Aug/2014
h) DRD 001 Insight Implementation Plan and documentation of the organizational interaction and personnel interfaces to achieve the objectives of the Insight Implementation Plan and Insight Clause.	Data to be transmitted via DRD 001	Aug/2014
i) DRD 101 Milestone Review Plan.	Data to be transmitted via DRD 101	Aug/2014
j) DRD 109 Flight Test Plan.	Data to be transmitted via DRD 109	Aug/2014
Acceptance Criteria: (Att J-03 PWS Apx A)		
a) Requirements are baselined and controlled. The allocation of requirements to the CTS design baseline is complete.	Data dispositioned to the level required per DRD 102	
1) Requirements are traceable to CCT-REQ-1130 and SSP 50808.	Data dispositioned to the level required per DRD 102	
2) Variances and alternate standards have been incorporated and appropriately tailored into the Contractor's requirements.	Data dispositioned to the level required per DRD 102	
3) Technical coordination is complete for joint ISS integration products (ICDs, JiVTP, BDEALS, BHSEALS) identified in SSP 50964, and products are ready for ISS to baseline post CBR review.	Data dispositioned to the level required per DRD 102	

Attachment J-03, Appendix A

Certification Baseline Review (CBR) Interim Milestone (As proposed, interim NASA milestone in support of DCR) DCR Interim Milestone 01A.1	Planned Start Date and Completion Date (mo/yr): Sep - Oct/2014 No Final RID Board	Amount:
4) The Concept of Operations has been baselined.	Data dispositioned to the level required per DRD 102	
5) The CTS design definition products identified in the DRD 102 Certification Baseline Review (CBR) Data Package identify the current design baseline.	Data dispositioned to the level required per DRD 102	
6) Integrated vehicle performance and design margin is appropriate and supports completion of development.	Data dispositioned to the level required per DRD 102	
7) Management plans and products identified in the DRD 102 Certification Baseline Review (CBR) Data Package are in place, controlled and are being implemented. The plans and products identified in the CBR Data Package as type 2 have been approved.	Data dispositioned to the level required per DRD 102	
8) The DRD 108 V&V Plan has been Baselined.	Data dispositioned per DRD 108	
9) The DRD 107 Certification Plan has been Baselined.	Data dispositioned per DRD 107	
10) An DRD 002 Integrated Master Plan and Integrated Master Schedule (IMP/IMS) is baselined.	Data dispositioned per DRD 002	
11) The top safety, technical, cost and schedule risks are identified, assessed, mitigation plans identified and clearly documented in BORIS. Risk & Opportunity Management plan is released to effectively manage the risks.	Data dispositioned to the level required per DRD 102	

Attachment J-03, Appendix A

Certification Baseline Review (CBR) Interim Milestone (As proposed, interim NASA milestone in support of DCR) DCR Interim Milestone 01A.1	Planned Start Date and Completion Date (mo/yr): Sep - Oct/2014 No Final RID Board	Amount: ■
12) DRD 001 Insight Implementation Plan has been approved. The organizational interaction and personnel interfaces to achieve the objectives of the Insight Implementation Plan and Insight Clause have been documented.	Data dispositioned per DRD 001	
13) DRD 101 Milestone Review Plan in accordance with the Data Requirement List (DRL) and DRD has been approved.	Data dispositioned per DRD 101 MRP	
14) DRD 109 Flight Test Plan in accordance with the DRL and DRD has been approved.	Data dispositioned per DRD 109	
15) A plan and schedule have been defined for the resolution of all actions and open items resulting from the CBR. All To be Determined (TBD) and To be Resolved (TBR) items are clearly identified with acceptable plans and schedules for their disposition.		

Attachment J-03, Appendix A

Ground Segment Critical Design Review (CDR) Interim Milestone (As proposed, interim Contractor milestone in support of DCR) DCR Interim Milestone 01A.2	Planned Start Date and Completion Date (mo/yr): CMO CDR: Oct/2014 Grnd Sys CDR: Oct/2014 Combined Final RID Board Nov/2014	Amount: ■

Objective:

Contractor chaired. Perform (1) a Critical Design Review (CDR) of Crew & Mission Operations systems designs and processes for Mission Operations, Training Systems and Processes and Cargo Integration Processes; (2) a CDR of Ground Systems used for spacecraft AI&T, Space-to-Ground Comm, Landing and CM recovery ground systems; and (3) review of VAC-1 execution plan and schedule.

a) Baseline tailored requirements, incorporating the results of NASA's guidance provided under CPC (if applicable), which meet NASA's requirements;

b) Baseline most current CTS CMO design;

c) Baseline Ground systems designs for AI&T, Space-to-Ground communications and post landing CM recovery, present summary updates to launch site facilities and pre-flight systems designs;

d) Define schedule; and

e) Define top safety, technical, cost and schedule risks.

Indicators of Milestone Readiness:	Data / DRDs to be provided:	Delivery of Data/DRDs (mo/yr)
For CMO CDR the Contractor has completed the following:		
a) Tailored requirements incorporating the results of NASA's guidance under CPC (if applicable) which meet NASA's requirements defined in CCT-STD-1150 Crew Transportation Operations Standards	Data to be transmitted IAW DRD 101 MRP Appendix B	Sep/2014
b) Mission Operations Plan, Train and Fly CDR technical work products for both hardware and software system elements for Mission Planning and Analysis, Flight Training, Flight Operations, Crew and Cargo Integration and Missions Systems have been made available to include:	Data to be transmitted IAW DRD 101 MRP Appendix B	Sep/2014

Attachment J-03, Appendix A

Ground Segment Critical Design Review (CDR) Interim Milestone	Planned Start Date and Completion Date (mo/yr): CMO CDR: Oct/2014 Grnd Sys CDR: Oct/2014 Combined Final RID Board Nov/2014	Amount:
(As proposed, interim Contractor milestone in support of DCR) DCR Interim Milestone 01A.2		
1) Product specifications for each hardware and software configuration item	Data to be transmitted IAW DRD 101 MRP Appendix B	Sep/2014
2) Fabrication, Assembly, integration and test plans and procedures	Data to be transmitted IAW DRD 101 MRP Appendix B	Sep/2014
3) Interface control documents	Data to be transmitted IAW DRD 101 MRP Appendix B	Sep/2014
4) Operations limits and constraints	Data to be transmitted IAW DRD 101 MRP Appendix B	Sep/2014
5) Technical resource utilization estimates and margins	Data to be transmitted IAW DRD 101 MRP Appendix B	Sep/2014
6) Command and telemetry lists	Data to be transmitted IAW DRD 101 MRP Appendix B	Sep/2014
7) Verification and Validation plan(s)	Data to be transmitted IAW DRD 101 MRP Appendix B	Sep/2014
8) Software design document(s) including interface design document(s)	Data to be transmitted IAW DRD 101 MRP Appendix B	Sep/2014
9) Training documentation (e.g. plans, curriculum, schedules)	Data to be transmitted IAW DRD 101 MRP Appendix B	Sep/2014
10) Safety analyses	Data to be transmitted IAW DRD 101 MRP Appendix B	Sep/2014
11) Certification plans and requirements (as needed)	Data to be transmitted IAW DRD 101 MRP Appendix B	Sep/2014

Attachment J-03, Appendix A

Ground Segment Critical Design Review (CDR) Interim Milestone (As proposed, interim Contractor milestone in support of DCR) DCR Interim Milestone 01A.2	Planned Start Date and Completion Date (mo/yr): CMO CDR: Oct/2014 Grnd Sys CDR: Oct/2014 Combined Final RID Board Nov/2014	Amount: ■
c) CMO schedule elements as part of the Integration Master Schedule (DRD 002) for CTS Certification activities.	Data to be provided at meeting IAW DRD 002	Oct/2014
d) An assessment of the top safety, technical, cost, and schedule risks to CMO and documentation of the approach to manage and accept risks.	Data to be provided at meeting IAW DRD 101 MRP Appendix B	Oct/2014
For Ground Systems CDR the Contractor has completed the following:		
a) Tailored requirements incorporating the results of NASA's guidance under CPC (if applicable) which meet NASA's requirements defined in CCT-REQ-1130.	Data to be transmitted IAW DRD 101 MRP Appendix B	Sep/2014
b) CDR technical work products for both hardware and software system elements for Ground Systems used for spacecraft AI&T, Space-to-Ground Communication, Landing and CM recovery ground systems have been made available to include:	Data to be transmitted IAW DRD 101 MRP Appendix B	Sep/2014
1) Updated baselined documents, as required	Data to be transmitted IAW DRD 101 MRP Appendix B	Sep/2014
2) Product specifications for each hardware and software configuration item	Data to be transmitted IAW DRD 101 MRP Appendix B	Sep/2014
3) Spacecraft Fabrication, Assembly, integration and test plans and procedures	Data to be transmitted IAW DRD 101 MRP Appendix B	Sep/2014
4) Interface control documents	Data to be transmitted IAW DRD 101 MRP Appendix B	Sep/2014

Attachment J-03, Appendix A

Ground Segment Critical Design Review (CDR) Interim Milestone (As proposed, interim Contractor milestone in support of DCR) DCR Interim Milestone 01A.2	Planned Start Date and Completion Date (mo/yr): CMO CDR: Oct/2014 Grnd Sys CDR: Oct/2014 Combined Final RID Board Nov/2014	Amount: ■
5) Operations limits and constraints	Data to be transmitted IAW DRD 101 MRP Appendix B	Sep/2014
6) Technical resource utilization estimates and margins	Data to be transmitted IAW DRD 101 MRP Appendix B	Sep/2014
7) Command and telemetry lists	Data to be transmitted IAW DRD 101 MRP Appendix B	Sep/2014
8) Verification and Validation plan(s)	Data to be transmitted IAW DRD 101 MRP Appendix B	Sep/2014
9) Software design document(s) including interface design document(s)	Data to be transmitted IAW DRD 101 MRP Appendix B	Sep/2014
10) Safety analyses	Data to be transmitted IAW DRD 101 MRP Appendix B	Sep/2014
11) Certification plans and requirements (as needed)	Data to be transmitted IAW DRD 101 MRP Appendix B	Sep/2014
c) Ground Systems schedule elements as part of the Integration Master Schedule (DRD 002) for CTS Certification activities.	Data to be transmitted IAW DRD 002	Oct/2014
d) An assessment of the top safety, technical, cost, and schedule risks to Ground Systems and documentation of the approach to manage and accept risks.	Data to be provided at meeting IAW DRD 101 MRP Appendix B	Oct/2014
Draft VAC-1 execution plan and schedule provided.	Data to be provided at meeting IAW DRD 101 MRP Appendix B	Oct/2014

Attachment J-03, Appendix A

Ground Segment Critical Design Review (CDR) Interim Milestone (As proposed, interim Contractor milestone in support of DCR) DCR Interim Milestone 01A.2	Planned Start Date and Completion Date (mo/yr): CMO CDR: Oct/2014 Grnd Sys CDR: Oct/2014 Combined Final RID Board Nov/2014	Amount: ■
Acceptance Criteria:		
a) For both CMO and Ground Systems CDRs the following apply:		
1) Top-level requirements are agreed upon, finalized, stated clearly and consistent with the final design	Data dispositioned to the level required per DRD 101 MRP Appendix B	
2) The flow down of verifiable requirements is complete and proper or, if not, an adequate plan exists for timely resolution of open items. Requirements are traceable to mission goals and objectives.	Data dispositioned to the level required per DRD 101 MRP Appendix B	
3) The final design is expected to meet the requirements at an acceptable level of risk	Data dispositioned to the level required per DRD 101 MRP Appendix B	
4) Definition of technical interfaces are consistent with the overall technical maturity and provides an acceptable level of risk	Data dispositioned to the level required per DRD 101 MRP Appendix B	
5) Adequate technical margins exist with respect to the TPMs or, if not, an adequate plan exists for timely resolution of open items	Data dispositioned to the level required per DRD 101 MRP Appendix B	
6) Project risks are understood and have been assess, and plans, a process, and resources exist to effectively manage them	Data dispositioned to the level required per DRD 101 MRP Appendix B	
7) The operational concept is technically sound, incorporates human factors considerations (as appropriate) and includes flow down of requirements for its execution	Data dispositioned to the level required per DRD 101 MRP Appendix B	

Attachment J-03, Appendix A

Ground Segment Critical Design Review (CDR) Interim Milestone (As proposed, interim Contractor milestone in support of DCR) DCR Interim Milestone 01A.2	Planned Start Date and Completion Date (mo/yr): CMO CDR: Oct/2014 Grnd Sys CDR: Oct/2014 Combined Final RID Board Nov/2014	Amount: ■
8) Completion of review per Milestone Review Plan (DRD 101)	Data dispositioned to the level required per DRD 101 MRP Appendix B	
b) VAC-1 plan and schedule reviewed. VAC products provide integrated assessment of system performance against applicable CCTS requirements and are consistent with the V&V plan. Schedule inter-dependencies are correctly identified. Risks to execution are identified and mitigation plans documented.	Data dispositioned to the level required per DRD 101 MRP Appendix B	

Attachment J-03, Appendix A

Phase II Safety Review - Part B (Integrated System) Interim Milestone	Planned Start Date and Completion Date (mo/yr): Dec/2014 No Final RID Board	Amount: ▮
(As proposed, interim Contractor milestone in support of DCR) DCR Interim Milestone 01A.3		

Objective:

▮. Prepare and conduct a Phase II Safety Review of the integrated Contractor CCTS system for CDR level requirements, system architecture and design, and associated safety products to assess conformance with CCTS Certification process (based on CDR maturity level). Focus is to review updates to hazard reports/analyses including cause identification, development of controls and specific safety verification methods. Review status of open actions from Phase II Part A review on CST-100 safety products.

Indicators of Milestone Readiness:	Data / DRDs to be provided:	Delivery of Data/DRDs (mo/yr)
The following technical products are available:		
a) Hazard Reports reflecting the final equipment design and operations, and documented the status and results of all completed hazard verification work.	Data to be transmitted IAW DRD 101 MRP Appendix C	Oct/2014
b) Hazard Reports shall be signed by the responsible safety and engineering managers or a representative where applicable before submittal.	Data to be transmitted IAW DRD 101 MRP Appendix C	Oct/2014
c) All open hazard verifications are listed on a safety verification tracking log.	Data to be transmitted IAW DRD 101 MRP Appendix C	Oct/2014
d) Final overview description of the design and operations of the hardware being addressed in the review to assist in understanding hazards.	Data to be transmitted IAW DRD 101 MRP Appendix C	Oct/2014
e) Identification and resolution of open safety items and noncompliances.	Data to be transmitted IAW DRD 101 MRP Appendix C	Oct/2014
f) Closure of action items assigned during previous Safety Review(s).	Data to be provided at meeting IAW DRD 101 MRP Appendix C	Dec/2014

Attachment J-03, Appendix A

Phase II Safety Review - Part B (Integrated System) Interim Milestone	Planned Start Date and Completion Date (mo/yr):	Amount:
(As proposed, interim Contractor milestone in support of DCR) DCR Interim Milestone 01A.3	Dec/2014 No Final RID Board	
Acceptance Criteria:		
a) Hazard Reports have been completed such that: all hazards and hazard causes have been identified; hazard controls have been defined and specific safety verification methods have been documented. Contractor approval for flight of Hazard Reports.	Data dispositioned to the level required per DRD 101 MRP Appendix C	
b) Open standard safety verification items are documented on the safety verification tracking log. Note: This log allows the safety review panel to sign the Hazard Reports indicating completion of the safety analyses, but with the understanding that approval for flight or corresponding ground operations will be withheld until all applicable verification activity is complete.	Data dispositioned to the level required per DRD 101 MRP Appendix C	
c) Noncompliances have been approved for flight or have a documented resolution plan with scheduled closeout prior to DCR or FRR.	Data dispositioned to the level required per DRD 101 MRP Appendix C	
d) Completion of review per Milestone Review Plan (DRD 101).	Data dispositioned to the level required per DRD 101 MRP Appendix C	

Attachment J-03, Appendix A

Delta Integrated Critical Design Review (I-CDR) (As proposed, interim Contractor milestone in support of DCR) DCR Interim Milestone 01A.4	Planned Start Date and Completion Date (mo/yr): Jan/2015 Final RID Board Jan/2015	Amount: ■

Objective:

A NASA and Contractor Co-Chaired Review.
The Contractor shall prepare and conduct a Delta I-CDR reviewing the baseline design established and reviewed during the I-CDR (during CCiCap) and any additional design content to demonstrate that the integrated design across Launch Segment, Spacecraft Segment and Ground Segment including hardware, software, facilities, support equipment and plans satisfy CCTS System level, Segment level and module level requirements. The contractor will provide closed RIDs and Actions and status of all open RIDs and Actions from the I-CDR and any segment and subsystem CDRs since the I-CDR. The Delta I-CDR demonstrates that the design maturity is appropriate to proceed to assembly, integration and test activities.

Indicators of Milestone Readiness:	Data / DRDs to be provided:	Delivery of Data/DRDs (mo/yr)
a) At least 90 days prior to the review, the MRP has been updated to include all details of the delta I-CDR and has been submitted to NASA for approval	Data to be transmitted IAW DRD 101 MRP Appendix V	Oct/2014
b) CDR Agenda and charge to the board have been agreed to by Boeing Program Management and Review Chair	Data to be transmitted IAW DRD 101 MRP Appendix V	Dec/2014

Attachment J-03, Appendix A

Delta Integrated Critical Design Review (I-CDR) (As proposed, interim Contractor milestone in support of DCR)	Planned Start Date and Completion Date (mo/yr):	Amount:
DCR Interim Milestone 01A.4	Jan/2015 Final RID Board Jan/2015	

Attachment J-03, Appendix A

Delta Integrated Critical Design Review (I-CDR) (As proposed, interim Contractor milestone in support of DCR) DCR Interim Milestone 01A.4	Planned Start Date and Completion Date (mo/yr): Jan/2015 Final RID Board Jan/2015	Amount:

Acceptance Criteria:

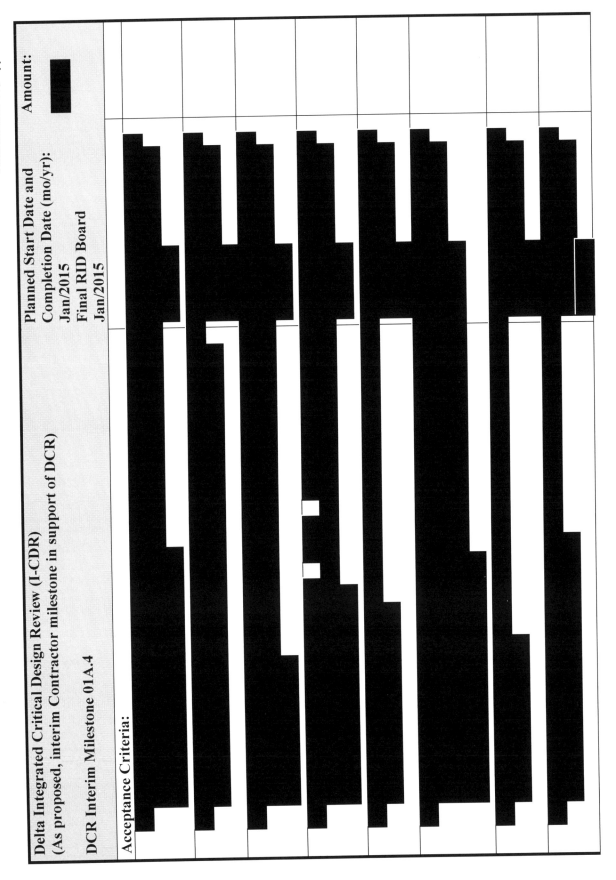

Attachment J-03, Appendix A

Delta Integrated Critical Design Review (I-CDR) (As proposed, interim Contractor milestone in support of DCR)	Planned Start Date and Completion Date (mo/yr): Jan/2015 Final RID Board Jan/2015	Amount: 
DCR Interim Milestone 01A.4		

Attachment J-03, Appendix A

Qualification Test Vehicle (QTV) Production Readiness Review (PRR) Interim Milestone (As proposed, interim Contractor milestone in support of DCR) DCR Interim Milestone 01A.5	Planned Start Date and Completion Date (mo/yr): Mar/2015 No Final RID Board	Amount: ■

Objective:

Indicators of Milestone Readiness:	Data / DRDs to be provided:	Delivery of Data/DRDs (mo/yr)
a) The significant production engineering problems encountered during development are resolved.	Data to be transmitted IAW DRD 101 MRP Appendix D	Mar/2015
b) The design documentation is adequate to support production.	Data to be transmitted IAW DRD 101 MRP Appendix D	Mar/2015
c) The production plans, procedures and preparation are adequate to begin fabrication.	Data to be transmitted IAW DRD 101 MRP Appendix D	Mar/2015
d) The production-enabling products and adequate resources are available, have been allocated, and are ready to support end product production.	Data to be transmitted IAW DRD 101 MRP Appendix D	Mar/2015

Acceptance Criteria:

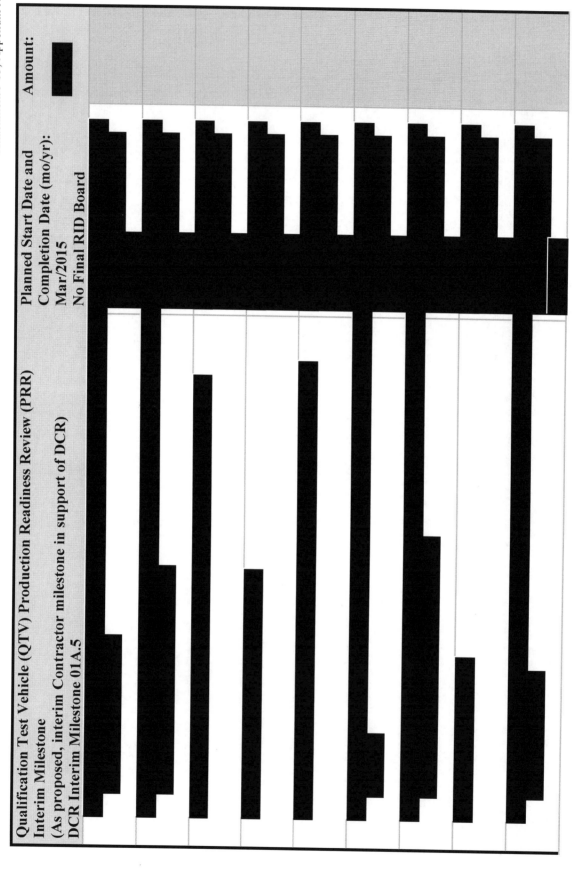

Attachment J-03, Appendix A

Interim Milestone	Planned Start Date and Completion Date (mo/yr):	Amount:
Qualification Test Vehicle (QTV) Production Readiness Review (PRR) (As proposed, interim Contractor milestone in support of DCR) DCR Interim Milestone 01A.5	Mar/2015 No Final RID Board	▮

Attachment J-03, Appendix A

STA Test Readiness Review (TRR) Interim Milestone	Planned Start Date and Completion Date (mo/yr):	Amount:
(As proposed, interim Contractor milestone in support of DCR) DCR Interim Milestone 01A.6	Apr/2015 No Final RID Board	

Objective: ▆▆▆. Conduct a Test Readiness Review (TRR) to ensure readiness to start testing of the STA. Verify all requirements changes are complete, verify test article as-built configuration, test procedures are complete and approved, facilities and support equipment readiness to support test (including any required software), all personnel supporting test have complete required training and review of test based hazards to ensure proper controls are incorporated into the test design and test procedures.

Indicators of Milestone Readiness:	Data / DRDs to be provided:	Delivery of Data/DRDs (mo/yr)
a) The test objectives are clearly defined and documented, and all of the test plans, procedures, environments, and configuration end items support those objectives.	Data to be transmitted IAW DRD 101 MRP Appendix E	Mar/2015
b) Configuration of the system under test has been defined and agreed to. Interfaces have been placed under configuration management or have been defined in accordance with an agreed to plan, and a version description document has been made available.	Data to be transmitted IAW DRD 101 MRP Appendix E	Mar/2015
c) Applicable functional, unit-level, subsystem, system, and qualification testing has been conducted successfully.	Data to be transmitted IAW DRD 101 MRP Appendix E	Mar/2015
d) TRR-specific materials such as test plans, test cases, and procedures are available.	Data to be transmitted IAW DRD 101 MRP Appendix E	Mar/2015
e) Known system discrepancies have been identified and disposed in accordance with agreed-upon plan.	Data to be transmitted IAW DRD 101 MRP Appendix E	Mar/2015
f) Previous design review success criteria and key issues have been satisfied in accordance with an agreed-upon plan.	Data to be transmitted IAW DRD 101 MRP Appendix E	Mar/2015

Attachment J-03, Appendix A

STA Test Readiness Review (TRR) Interim Milestone	Planned Start Date and Completion Date (mo/yr):	Amount:
(As proposed, interim Contractor milestone in support of DCR) **DCR Interim Milestone 01A.6**	Apr/2015 No Final RID Board	■
g) Required test personnel are certified (including a designated test director) and facilities, test articles, test instrumentation, and other test enabling products have been identified, calibration current for expected duration of test, facilities and data acquisition systems capabilities satisfy test requirements, and are available to support required tests.	Data to be transmitted IAW DRD 101 MRP Appendix E	Mar/2015
h) Roles and responsibilities of all test participants are defined and agreed to.	Data to be transmitted IAW DRD 101 MRP Appendix E	Mar/2015
i) Test contingency planning has been accomplished, and all personnel have been trained.	Data to be transmitted IAW DRD 101 MRP Appendix E	Mar/2015

Attachment J-03, Appendix A

STA Test Readiness Review (TRR) Interim Milestone	Planned Start Date and Completion Date (mo/yr):	Amount:
(As proposed, interim Contractor milestone in support of DCR) DCR Interim Milestone 01A.6	Apr/2015 No Final RID Board	

Attachment J-03, Appendix A

CCCS Activation/Validation Tests Complete Interim Milestone	Planned Start Date and Completion Date (mo/yr): Jul/2015 No Final RID Board	Amount: ■
(As proposed, interim Contractor milestone in support of DCR) DCR Interim Milestone 01A.7		

Objective:

Indicators of Milestone Readiness:	Data / DRDs to be provided:	Delivery of Data/DRDs (mo/yr)
a) Completed execution of CCCS activation test per approved test procedure.		
b) Review test results, discrepancy reports and test deviations	Data to be transmitted IAW DRD 101 MRP Appendix F	Jul/2015

Acceptance Criteria:

a) Completion of post test data review and acceptance of discrepancies and deviations.	Data dispositioned to the level required per DRD 101 MRP Appendix F	
b) Test results support the certification plan with a disposition of remaining or open items from the test.	Data dispositioned to the level required per DRD 101 MRP Appendix F	
c) Preparation of quick-look summary test briefing to document test results.	Data dispositioned to the level required per DRD 101 MRP Appendix F	

Attachment J-03, Appendix A

QTV Integrated Readiness Review (IRR) Interim Milestone	Planned Start Date and Completion Date (mo/yr):	Amount:
(As proposed, interim Contractor milestone in support of DCR) DCR Interim Milestone 01A.8	Aug/2015 No Final RID Board	▮

Objective: ▮. Conduct an Integrated Readiness Review for the QTV to ensure test hardware, test plans, procedures, facilities, support equipment and any required test support software are progressing in development to support planned test activities. The review will evaluate test plans and draft procedures against test objectives and requirements, test hardware build and delivery status, test equipment and facility build-up, validation and preparations are progressing, a review of identified test hazards and associated controls, and, training requirements have been identified and planned for all critical personnel.

Indicators of Milestone Readiness:	Data / DRDs to be provided:	Delivery of Data/DRDs (mo/yr)
a) Integration plans have been completed and released, draft procedures are available for review	Data to be transmitted IAW DRD 101 MRP Appendix G	Jul/2015
b) Segments and/or components are available for integration.	Data to be transmitted IAW DRD 101 MRP Appendix G	Jul/2015
c) Mechanical and electrical interfaces have been verified against the interface control documentation.	Data to be transmitted IAW DRD 101 MRP Appendix G	Jul/2015
d) Applicable functional, unit-level, subsystem, and qualification testing have been conducted successfully or planned to support test schedule.	Data to be transmitted IAW DRD 101 MRP Appendix G	Jul/2015
f) Support personnel trained has been identified and planned to support assembly and test activities.	Data to be transmitted IAW DRD 101 MRP Appendix G	Jul/2015
g) Handling and safety requirements have been documented.	Data to be transmitted IAW DRD 101 MRP Appendix G	Jul/2015

Attachment J-03, Appendix A

QTV Integrated Readiness Review (IRR) Interim Milestone	Planned Start Date and Completion Date (mo/yr):	Amount:
(As proposed, interim Contractor milestone in support of DCR) DCR Interim Milestone 01A.8	Aug/2015 No Final RID Board	
j) Quality control organization is ready to support integration effort.	Data to be transmitted IAW DRD 101 MRP Appendix G	Jul/2015
Acceptance Criteria:		

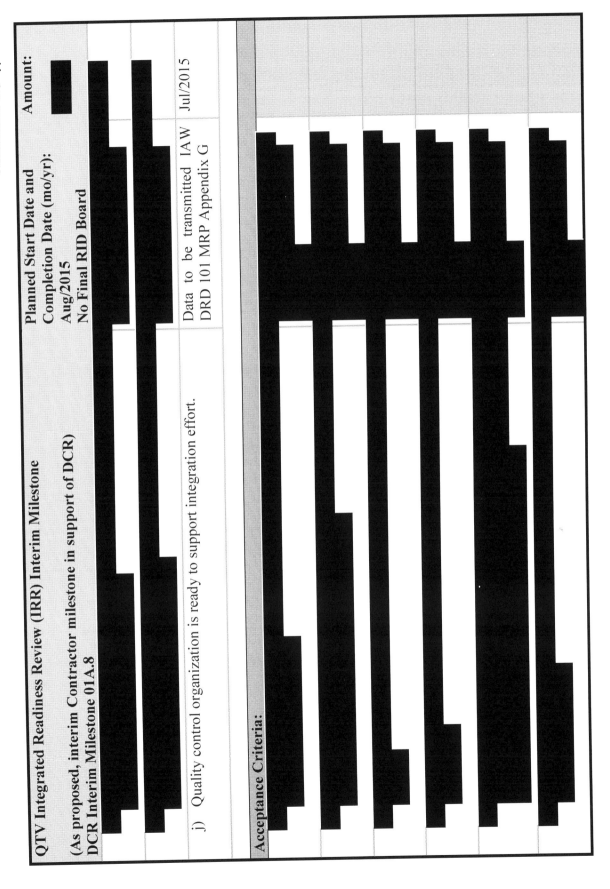

Attachment J-03, Appendix A

Milestone	Planned Start Date and Completion Date (mo/yr):	Amount:
FSW Demonstration Nominal Launch, Docking and De-Orbit Interim (As proposed, interim Contractor milestone in support of DCR) DCR Interim Milestone 01A.9	Oct/2015 No Final RID Board	

Objective:

Indicators of Milestone Readiness:	Data / DRDs to be provided:	Delivery of Data/DRDs (mo/yr)
a) Test Plan has been developed consisting of key objectives, auxiliary objectives, configuration of unit under test, test conditions and environment, differences between baselines design configuration and test (if applicable), and definition of information in quick-look report and approved by Boeing Program Management.	Data to be transmitted IAW DRD 101 MRP Appendix H	Sep/2015
b) Required demonstration personnel are certified and facilities, units under test (including software version) and other demonstration enabling products have been identified, are ready and available to support the demonstration.	Data to be transmitted IAW DRD 101 MRP Appendix H	Sep/2015

Acceptance Criteria:

a) Completion of test per approved test plan.	Data dispositioned to the level required per DRD 101 MRP Appendix H	
b) Presentation of quick-look summary results briefing and demonstration results.	Data dispositioned to the level required per DRD 101 MRP Appendix H	

Attachment J-03, Appendix A

OFT Configuration Performance & Weight Status Report (CPWSR) Review Interim Milestone (As proposed, interim Contractor milestone in support of DCR) DCR Interim Milestone 01.A.10	Planned Start Date and Completion Date (mo/yr): Dec/2015 No Final RID Board	Amount: ■
Objective: ■		
Indicators of Milestone Readiness:	**Data / DRDs to be provided:**	**Delivery of Data/DRDs (mo/yr)**
a) Definition of LV and spacecraft configuration for the OFT mission, including preliminary (predicted) mass properties and preliminary ascent trajectories	Data to be transmitted IAW DRD 101 MRP Appendix I	Nov/2015
b) Completion of analyses and documentation of performance margins for OFT mission	Data to be transmitted IAW DRD 101 MRP Appendix I	Nov/2015
Acceptance Criteria:		

Attachment J-03, Appendix A

MCC Integrated Simulation System Acceptance Review (SAR) Interim Milestone (As proposed, interim Contractor milestone in support of DCR) DCR Interim Milestone 01A.11	Planned Start Date and Completion Date (mo/yr): Jan/2016 No Final RID Board	Amount:
Objective: Evaluate summary of Primary Mission Control Center (MCC) system validation test results, anomalies and open work plan needed to achieve operational readiness to support training and integrated simulations.		
Indicators of Milestone Readiness:	**Data / DRDs to be provided:**	**Delivery of Data/DRDs (mo/yr)**

Attachment J-03, Appendix A

MCC Integrated Simulation System Acceptance Review (SAR) Interim Milestone (As proposed, interim Contractor milestone in support of DCR) DCR Interim Milestone 01A.11	Planned Start Date and Completion Date (mo/yr): Jan/2016 No Final RID Board	Amount:

Acceptance Criteria:

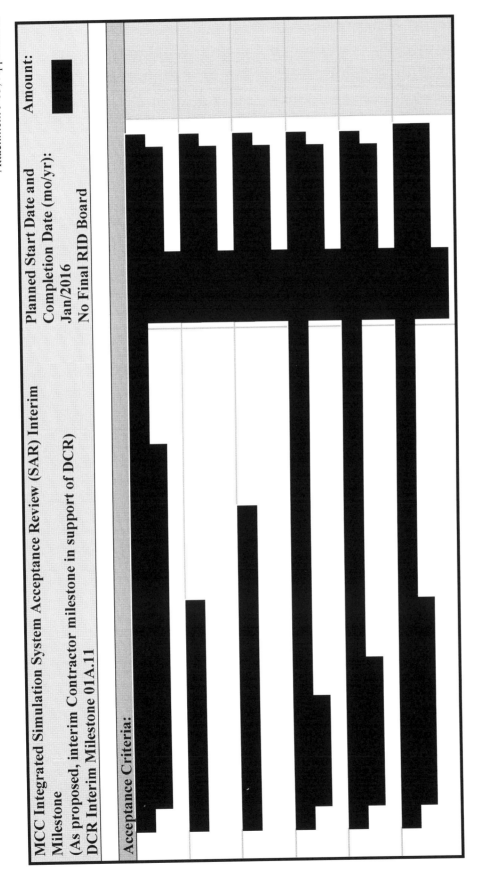

Attachment J-03, Appendix A

QTV Test Readiness Review (TRR) Interim Milestone	Planned Start Date and Completion Date (mo/yr): Apr/2016 No Final RID Board	Amount: ■
(As proposed, interim Contractor milestone in support of DCR) DCR Interim Milestone 01A.12		

Objective: ■. Conduct a Test Readiness Review (TRR) to ensure readiness to start testing of the QTV Testing. Verify all requirements changes are complete, verify test article as-built configuration, test procedures are complete and approved, facilities and support equipment readiness to support test (including any required software), all personnel supporting test have complete required training and review of test based hazards to ensure proper controls are incorporated into the test design and test procedures.

Indicators of Milestone Readiness:	Data / DRDs to be provided:	Delivery of Data/DRDs (mo/yr)
a) The test objectives are clearly defined and documented, and all of the test plans, procedures, environments, and configuration of the end items support those objectives.	Data to be transmitted IAW DRD 101 MRP Appendix K	Apr/2016
b) Configuration of the system under test has been defined and agreed to. Interfaces have been placed under configuration management or have been defined in accordance with an agreed to plan, and a version description document has been made available.	Data to be transmitted IAW DRD 101 MRP Appendix K	Apr/2016
c) Applicable functional, unit-level, subsystem, system, and qualification testing has been conducted successfully.	Data to be transmitted IAW DRD 101 MRP Appendix K	Apr/2016
d) TRR-specific materials such as test plans, test cases, and procedures are available.	Data to be transmitted IAW DRD 101 MRP Appendix K	Apr/2016
e) Known system discrepancies have been identified and disposed in accordance with agreed-upon plan.	Data to be transmitted IAW DRD 101 MRP Appendix K	Apr/2016
f) Previous design review success criteria and key issues have been satisfied in accordance with an agreed-upon plan.	Data to be transmitted IAW DRD 101 MRP Appendix K	Apr/2016

Attachment J-03, Appendix A

QTV Test Readiness Review (TRR) Interim Milestone	Planned Start Date and Completion Date (mo/yr): Apr/2016 No Final RID Board	Amount:
(As proposed, interim Contractor milestone in support of DCR) DCR Interim Milestone 01A.12		
g) Required test personnel are certified (including a designated test director), and facilities, test articles, test instrumentation, and other test enabling products have been identified, calibration current for expected duration of test, facilities and data acquisition systems capability satisfy test requirements, and are available to support required tests.	Data to be transmitted IAW DRD 101 MRP Appendix K	Apr/2016
h) Roles and responsibilities of all test participants are defined and agreed to.	Data to be transmitted IAW DRD 101 MRP Appendix K	Apr/2016
i) Test contingency planning has been accomplished, and all personnel have been trained.	Data to be transmitted IAW DRD 101 MRP Appendix K	Apr/2016
Acceptance Criteria:		
a) Adequate test plans are completed and approved for the system under test.	Data dispositioned to the level required per DRD 101 MRP Appendix K	
b) Adequate identification and coordination of required test resources are completed.	Data dispositioned to the level required per DRD 101 MRP Appendix K	
c) Previous component, subsystem, and system test results form a satisfactory basis for proceeding into planned tests.	Data dispositioned to the level required per DRD 101 MRP Appendix K	
d) Risk level is identified and accepted by program / competency leadership are required	Data dispositioned to the level required per DRD 101 MRP Appendix K	
e) Plans to capture any lessons learned from the test program are documented.	Data dispositioned to the level required per DRD 101 MRP Appendix K	

Attachment J-03, Appendix A

QTV Test Readiness Review (TRR) Interim Milestone (As proposed, interim Contractor milestone in support of DCR) **DCR Interim Milestone 01A.12**	Planned Start Date and Completion Date (mo/yr): Apr/2016 **No Final RID Board**	Amount: ■
f) The test objectives have been clearly defined and documented, and the review of all the test plans, as well as the procedures, environments, and configuration of the end items, provides a reasonable expectation that objectives can be met.	Data dispositioned to the level required per DRD 101 MRP Appendix K	
g) The test cases have been reviewed and analyzed for expected results, and the results are consistent with the test plans and objectives.	Data dispositioned to the level required per DRD 101 MRP Appendix K	
h) Test personnel have received appropriate training in test operation and safety procedures.	Data dispositioned to the level required per DRD 101 MRP Appendix K	
i) Open actions are identified, corrective actions defined and scheduled, and constraints are in-place to ensure all required actions are implemented prior to the first applicable work activity.	Data dispositioned to the level required per DRD 101 MRP Appendix K	

Attachment J-03, Appendix A

Integrated Parachute System Drop Tests 1 & 2 Complete Interim Milestone	Planned Start Date and Completion Date (mo/yr): Jun/2016 No Final RID Board	Amount:
(As proposed, interim Contractor milestone in support of DCR) DCR Interim Milestone 01A.13		

Objective:

Indicators of Milestone Readiness:	Data / DRDs to be provided:	Delivery of Data/DRDs (mo/yr)
a) Test Plan has been developed consisting of key objectives, auxiliary objectives, configuration of unit under test, test conditions and environment, differences between baselines design configuration and test (if applicable), and definition of information in quick-look report and approved by Boeing Program Management.	Data to be transmitted IAW DRD 101 MRP Appendix L	Jun/2016

Acceptance Criteria:

a) Completion of test per approved test plan.	Data dispositioned to the level required per DRD 101 MRP Appendix L	
b) Preparation of quick-look summary test briefing to document test results.	Data dispositioned to the level required per DRD 101 MRP Appendix L	

Attachment J-03, Appendix A

SM Hot Fire Launch Abort Test Complete Interim Milestone

(As proposed, interim Contractor milestone in support of DCR)
DCR Interim Milestone 01A.14

	Planned Start Date and Completion Date (mo/yr): Sep/2016 No Final RID Board	Amount:

Objective:

Indicators of Milestone Readiness:	Data / DRDs to be provided:	Delivery of Data/DRDs (mo/yr)
a) Test Plan has been developed consisting of key objectives, auxiliary objectives, configuration of unit under test, test conditions and environment, differences between baselines design configuration and test (if applicable), and definition of information in quick-look report and approved by Boeing Program Management.	Data to be transmitted IAW DRD 101 MRP Appendix N	Sep/2016

Acceptance Criteria:

a) Completion of test per approved test plan.	Data dispositioned to the level required per DRD 101 MRP Appendix N	
b) Preparation of quick-look summary test briefing to document test results.	Data dispositioned to the level required per DRD 101 MRP Appendix N	

Attachment J-03, Appendix A

ISS Design Certification Review (DCR) Delivery Milestone	Planned Start Date and Completion Date (mo/yr):	Amount:
(As proposed, NASA Delivery milestone) DCR Delivery Milestone 01A	Nov/2016 Final RID Board Nov/2016	

Objective:

DCR acceptance criteria shall be met prior to any crewed test flights.
At a NASA and Contractor co-chaired DCR, the Contractor shall:

a) Demonstrate that the Crew Transportation System (CTS) and operations meet all applicable requirements (exceptions must be preapproved by the Commercial Crew Program/ISS Program (CCP/ISSP)), as defined in CCT-REQ-1130, ISS Crew Transportation and Services Requirements Document, and SSP 50808, ISS to Commercial Orbital Transportation Services (COTS) Interface Requirements Document (IRD) in order to meet the ISS Design Reference Mission (DRM) within CCT-DRM-1110, CTS DRM.

  1) Exceptions will be prepared and submitted to CCP/ISSP for approval for each open and partially completed VCN

b) Provide evidence that it has met all applicable requirements (exceptions must be preapproved by the CCP/ISSP) through the implementation of its baselined management and certification plans and processes required in CCT-PLN-1120, Crew Transportation Technical Management Processes.

c) Demonstrate schedule performance in accordance with the DRD 002 Integrated Master Plan and Integrated Master Schedule.

d) Define top safety, technical, cost, and schedule risks. (Att J-03 PWS Apx A)

Indicators of Milestone Readiness: (Att J-03 PWS Apx A)	Data / DRDs to be provided:	Delivery of Data/DRDs (mo/yr)
The Contractor has completed the following and provided to NASA:		
a) The DRD 103 Design Certification Review Data Package.	Data to be transmitted IAW DRD 103	Oct/2016
b) The DRD 112 Certification Data Package including but not limited to:	Data to be transmitted IAW DRD 112	Oct/2016

Attachment J-03, Appendix A

ISS Design Certification Review (DCR) Delivery Milestone (As proposed, NASA Delivery milestone) DCR Delivery Milestone 01A	Planned Start Date and Completion Date (mo/yr): Nov/2016 Final RID Board Nov/2016	Amount: ▮
1) All DRD 111 Verification Closure Notices (VCNs) demonstrating that the CTS requirements have been met. (All VCNs shall be closed unless exceptions are preapproved by the CCP/ISSP).	Data to be transmitted IAW DRD 111	Oct/2016
a) Open and partially completed VCNs submitted as exceptions will document a plan to complete open work, estimated completion dates, and risk to program milestones between ISS DCR and CFT FTRR.		

Attachment J-03, Appendix A

ISS Design Certification Review (DCR) Delivery Milestone (As proposed, NASA Delivery milestone) DCR Delivery Milestone 01A	Planned Start Date and Completion Date (mo/yr): Nov/2016 Final RID Board Nov/2016	Amount:
2) The hazard analysis and DRD 110 Hazard Reports have been approved by NASA.	Data to be transmitted IAW DRD 110	Oct/2016
c) All management and certification plans and processes required in CCT-PLN-1120 have been completed.	Data to be transmitted IAW DRD 103	Oct/2016
d) ISS Integration per SSP 50964, Visiting Vehicle ISS Integration Plan, including the Flight Operations Review and the ISS Phase III Safety Review have been completed. Forward work is scheduled and approved by NASA.	Data to be transmitted IAW DRD 103	Oct/2016
e) The DRD 002 Integrated Master Plan and Integrated Master Schedule.	Data to be transmitted IAW DRD 002	Oct/2016
f) The DRD 113 Range Safety Data Documentation.	Data to be transmitted IAW DRD 113	Oct/2016
g) The DRD 203 Vehicle Interface Definition Document (IDD).	Data to be transmitted IAW DRD 203	Oct/2016
h) An assessment of the top safety risks and documentation of the management and acceptance of risk including, but not limited to:		Oct/2016
1) Most recent results of the Probabilistic Safety Analysis (PSA) that identify the integrated safety and mission assurance risk of the baseline design, and individually identifies top risk contributors.	Data to be transmitted IAW DRD 103	Oct/2016
2) An assessment of crew survival capability of the baseline design in accordance with CCT-PLN-1120.	Data to be transmitted IAW DRD 103	Oct/2016
i) The top programmatic risks have been identified and assessed.	Data to be transmitted IAW DRD 103	Oct/2016

Attachment J-03, Appendix A

ISS Design Certification Review (DCR) Delivery Milestone (As proposed, NASA Delivery milestone) DCR Delivery Milestone 01A	Planned Start Date and Completion Date (mo/yr): Nov/2016 Final RID Board Nov/2016	Amount:
j) Documentation substantiating all Review Item Dispositions (RIDs) and actions from design reviews, verification reviews, and Certification Baseline Review (CBR) are closed or opened items are dispositioned with rationale for acceptance and updated plans for closure.	Data to be transmitted IAW DRD 103	Oct/2016

Acceptance Criteria: (Att J-03 PWS Apx A)

a) The DRD 112 Certification Data Package has been approved by NASA.	Data dispositioned per DRD 112
1) All applicable DRD 111 VCNs have been approved by NASA. (All VCNs relevant to crewed flight test will be approved by NASA with acceptable open work).	Data dispositioned per DRD 111
2) The design provides crew survival capability.	Data dispositioned to the level required per DRD 103
3) Operational limits and constraints have been implemented and verified.	Data dispositioned to the level required per DRD 103
4) Operational roles and procedures have been defined for crew, mission team and mission management.	Data dispositioned to the level required per DRD 103
b) An DRD 002 Integrated Master Plan and Integrated Master Schedule has been approved.	Data dispositioned per DRD 002
c) The top safety risks are identified, assessed, and clearly communicated. Plans, processes, and appropriate resources necessary to effectively manage the risks are in place.	Data dispositioned to the level required per DRD 103

Attachment J-03, Appendix A

ISS Design Certification Review (DCR) Delivery Milestone (As proposed, NASA Delivery milestone) DCR Delivery Milestone 01A	Planned Start Date and Completion Date (mo/yr): Nov/2016 Final RID Board Nov/2016	Amount: ■
1) Major risks to crew safety and mission success have been identified, quantified, and integrated in a PSA.	Data dispositioned to the level required per DRD 103	
2) Risk mitigation strategies associated with the CTS design baseline, cost and schedule have been identified and agreed upon by NASA.	Data dispositioned to the level required per DRD 103	
d) The top programmatic risks have been identified. Plans, processes, and appropriate resources necessary to effectively manage the risks are in place.	Data dispositioned to the level required per DRD 103	
e) All RIDs and actions from design reviews, verification reviews and CBR are closed. All To Be Determined (TBD) and To Be Resolved (TBR) items are clearly identified with acceptable plans and schedules for their disposition and have been submitted.		
f) A plan and schedule have been defined for the resolution of all actions and open items resulting from the DCR. All TBD and TBR items are clearly identified with acceptable plans and schedules for their disposition.		

Attachment J-03, Appendix A

OFT Flight Operations Review (FOR) Interim Milestone	Planned Start Date and Completion Date (mo/yr): Aug/2016 No Final RID Board	Amount:
(As proposed, interim Contractor milestone in support of CR) CR Interim Milestone 01B.1		
Objective: Conduct readiness review of CCTS CMO element for readiness to support the OFT. This is a precursor to the OFT FTRR. The objective of the FOR is to evaluate and baseline flight operations products to ensure the safe and accurate implementation of mission requirements.		
Indicators of Milestone Readiness:	**Data / DRDs to be provided:**	**Delivery of Data/DRDs (mo/yr)**

Attachment J-03, Appendix A

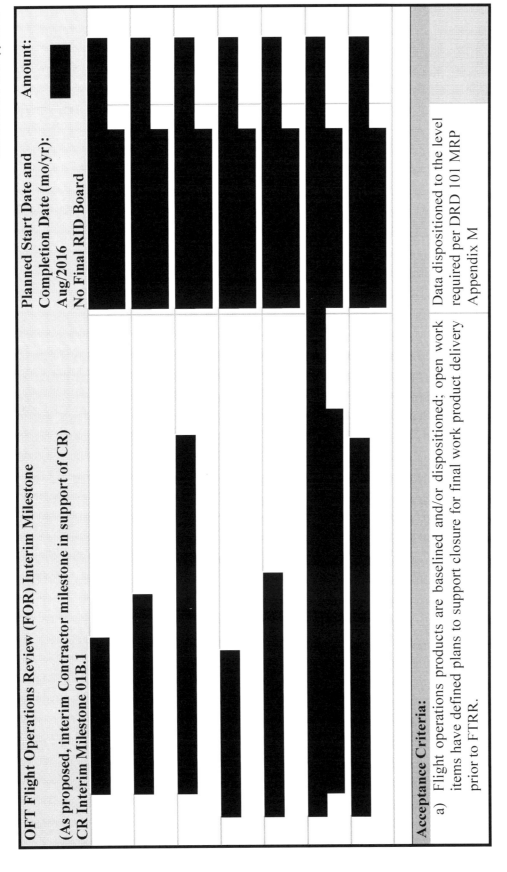

OFT Flight Operations Review (FOR) Interim Milestone	Planned Start Date and Completion Date (mo/yr):	Amount:
(As proposed, interim Contractor milestone in support of CR) CR Interim Milestone 01B.1	Aug/2016 No Final RID Board	
Acceptance Criteria: a) Flight operations products are baselined and/or dispositioned; open work items have defined plans to support closure for final work product delivery prior to FTRR.	Data dispositioned to the level required per DRD 101 MRP Appendix M	

Attachment J-03, Appendix A

Spacecraft Servicing Operational Readiness Review (ORR) Interim Milestone	Planned Start Date and Completion Date (mo/yr): Nov/2016 No Final RID Board	Amount:
(As proposed, interim Contractor milestone in support of CR) CR Interim Milestone 01B.2		

Objective:

Indicators of Milestone Readiness:	Data / DRDs to be provided:	Delivery of Data/DRDs (mo/yr)
a) Propellant fueling and servicing equipment is ready for servicing	Data to be transmitted IAW DRD 101 MRP Appendix P	
b) Propellant fueling and servicing procedures ready	Data to be transmitted IAW DRD 101 MRP Appendix P	Oct/2016
c) Contingency plans documented	Data to be transmitted IAW DRD 101 MRP Appendix P	Oct/2016
d) Servicing facilities and equipment validation tests complete	Data to be transmitted IAW DRD 101 MRP Appendix P	Nov/2016

Acceptance Criteria:

a) Plans, processes, resources and personnel are in place and baselined and ready for execution. Anomalies from validation test have been reviewed, dispositioned and required corrective actions are planned prior to CST-100 servicing.	Data dispositioned to the level required per DRD 101 MRP Appendix P

Attachment J-03, Appendix A

Pad Abort Test Complete Interim Milestone	Planned Start Date and Completion Date (mo/yr): Dec/2016 No Final RID Board	Amount: ■

(As proposed, interim Contractor milestone in support of CR)
CR Interim Milestone 01B.3

Objective:

■ . Review of quick look report on completion of Pad Abort Test (PA + 2 weeks)

Indicators of Milestone Readiness:	Data / DRDs to be provided:	Delivery of Data/DRDs (mo/yr)
a) Test Plan has been developed consisting of key objectives, auxiliary objectives, configuration of unit under test, test conditions and environment, differences between baselines design configuration and test (if applicable), and definition of information in quick-look report and approved by Boeing Program Management.	Data to be transmitted IAW DRD 101 MRP Appendix Q	Nov/2016
b) Completion of test per approved test plan.	Data to be transmitted per DRD 101 MRP Appendix Q	

Acceptance Criteria:

a) Presentation of quick-look summary test briefing and test results.	Data dispositioned to the level required per DRD 101 MRP Appendix Q	

Attachment J-03, Appendix A

Orbital Flight Test (OFT) Flight Test Readiness Review (FTRR) Interim Milestone (As proposed, interim NASA milestone in support of CR) CR Interim Milestone 01B.4	Planned Start Date and Completion Date (mo/yr): Jan/2017 No Final RID Board	Amount: ▉
Objective: Contractor and NASA co-chaired. Contractor shall conduct an FTRR that demonstrates readiness to conduct an uncrewed Orbital Flight Test and defines a risk baseline for flight test activities. (Att J-03 PWS Apx A)		

Indicators of Milestone Readiness: (Att J-03 PWS Apx A)	Data / DRDs to be provided:	Delivery of Data/DRDs (mo/yr)
The Contractor has completed the following and provided to NASA:		
a) All data and documentation identified in CCT-PLN-1120, Crew Transportation Technical Management Processes, Appendix F, CTS FRR Milestone Data, as the DRD 104 FTRR Data Package.	Data to be transmitted IAW DRD 104	Jan/2017
1) Approval of any new, open or changes to applicable DRD 111 Verification Closure Notices (VCNs), DRD 110 Hazard Reports, and DRD 112 Certification Data Package.	Data to be transmitted IAW DRD 110, 111, and 112	Jan/2017
2) Documentation that all acceptance, checkout and integration testing has been completed.	Data to be transmitted IAW DRD 104	Jan/2017
3) Documentation of flight specific products.	Data to be transmitted IAW DRD 104	Jan/2017
4) Documentation that the launch site, Range, recovery and tracking and data support resources have committed to launch.	Data to be transmitted IAW DRD 104	Jan/2017
5) Documentation that landing site recovery support and resources have committed to landing.	Data to be transmitted IAW DRD 104	Jan/2017

Attachment J-03, Appendix A

Orbital Flight Test (OFT) Flight Test Readiness Review (FTRR) Interim Milestone (As proposed, interim NASA milestone in support of CR) CR Interim Milestone 01B.4	Planned Start Date and Completion Date (mo/yr): Jan/2017 No Final RID Board	Amount: ▇
6) Documentation that all operational supporting and enabling capabilities (e.g., facilities, equipment, documents, updated databases) necessary for nominal and contingency operations have been tested and delivered/installed at the site(s) necessary to support operations.	Data to be transmitted IAW DRD 104	Jan/2017
7) Documentation that plans, processes, procedures and training for nominal and contingency operations for the Crew Transportation System (CTS) have been completed to support operations.	Data to be transmitted IAW DRD 104	Jan/2017
8) Documentation that systems hardware, software, personnel, processes and procedures are in place to support operations.	Data to be transmitted IAW DRD 104	Jan/2017
b) The Contractor, its subcontractors, suppliers and team members have provided flight readiness endorsements demonstrating that they have met requirements in accordance with the Contractor's management processes.	Data to be transmitted IAW DRD 104	Jan/2017
c) International Space Station (ISS) Stage Operational Readiness Review (SORR) has been completed and the ISS is ready to accept the Visiting Vehicle.	Data to be transmitted IAW DRD 104	Jan/2017
1) Documentation of residual mission risks and related analyses for acceptance.	Data to be transmitted IAW DRD 104	Jan/2017
d) All open actions from Design Certification review (DCR) and SORR have been closed.	Data to be transmitted IAW DRD 104	Jan/2017
Acceptance Criteria: (Att J-03 PWS Apx A)		
a) The DRD 104 FTRR Data Package has been presented and accepted by NASA.	Data dispositioned to the level required per DRD 104	

Attachment J-03, Appendix A

Orbital Flight Test (OFT) Flight Test Readiness Review (FTRR) Interim Milestone (As proposed, interim NASA milestone in support of CR) CR Interim Milestone 01B.4	Planned Start Date and Completion Date (mo/yr): Jan/2017 No Final RID Board	Amount:
b) All changes, modifications and anomalies since DCR have been resolved and resolutions have been accepted by NASA	Data dispositioned to the level required per DRD 104	
c) Mission management team, crew, and mission support team have been identified, have been trained, and are in place.	Data dispositioned to the level required per DRD 104	
d) The plan and schedule of preplanned forward work has been accepted by NASA.	Data dispositioned to the level required per DRD 104	
e) Any open work or constraints to launch are identified and closeout plans and schedules are in place and supportable.	Data dispositioned to the level required per DRD 104	
f) NASA has accepted the flight specific products.	Data dispositioned to the level required per DRD 104	
g) Launch Site, Range, and recovery support organizations have committed to launch.	Data dispositioned to the level required per DRD 104	
h) Landing site support and resources have committed to landing.	Data dispositioned to the level required per DRD 104	
i) NASA has accepted residual flight test risks.	Data dispositioned to the level required per DRD 104	

Attachment J-03, Appendix A

CFT DCR Interim Milestone	Planned Start Date and Completion Date (mo/yr):	Amount:
(As proposed, interim Contractor milestone in support of CR) CR Interim Milestone 01B.5	Mar/2017 Final RID Board Mar/2017	■

Objective:

As part of the CFT FTRR process the contractor shall conduct a CFT DCR prior to the crewed test flight. The contractor shall conduct the CFT DCR in the same manner as the ISS DCR and deliver data as described in DRD 103 (DCR Data Package), DRD 110 (Hazards Reports), DRD 111 (Verification Closure Notices) and DRD 112 (Certification Data Package). The purpose of the NASA and Contractor co-chaired CFT DCR is to review the final system qualification performance and associated analyses to support VCN closures that were exceptions at the ISS DCR and review all open actions from the previous ISS DCR.

Indicators of Milestone Readiness: (Att J-03 PWS Apx A)	Data / DRDs to be provided:	Delivery of Data/DRDs (mo/yr)
The Contractor has completed the following and provided to NASA updates since ISS DCR for the following:		
j) The DRD 103 Design Certification Review Data Package.	Data to be transmitted IAW DRD 103	Feb/2017
k) The DRD 112 Certification Data Package including but not limited to:	Data to be transmitted IAW DRD 112	Feb/2017

Attachment J-03, Appendix A

CFT DCR Interim Milestone (As proposed, interim Contractor milestone in support of CR) CR Interim Milestone 01B.5	Planned Start Date and Completion Date (mo/yr): Mar/2017 Final RID Board Mar/2017	Amount:
2) All DRD 111 Verification Closure Notices (VCNs) demonstrating that the CTS requirements have been met. (All VCNs shall be closed unless exceptions are preapproved by the CCP/ISSP).	Data to be transmitted IAW DRD 111	Feb/2017
b) Open and partially completed VCNs submitted as exceptions will document a plan to complete open work, estimated completion dates, and risk to program milestones between ISS DCR and CFT FTRR.		
3) The hazard analysis and DRD 110 Hazard Reports have been approved by NASA.	Data to be transmitted IAW DRD 110	Feb/2017
l) All management and certification plans and processes required in CCT-PLN-1120 have been completed.	Data to be transmitted IAW DRD 103	Feb/2017
m) ISS Integration per SSP 50964, Visiting Vehicle ISS Integration Plan, including the Flight Operations Review and the ISS Phase III Safety Review have been completed. Forward work is scheduled and approved by NASA.	Data to be transmitted IAW DRD 103	Feb/2017
n) The DRD 002 Integrated Master Plan and Integrated Master Schedule.	Data to be transmitted IAW DRD 002	Feb/2017
o) The DRD 113 Range Safety Data Documentation.	Data to be transmitted IAW DRD 113	Feb/2017
p) The DRD 203 Vehicle Interface Definition Document (IDD).	Data to be transmitted IAW DRD 203	Feb/2017

Attachment J-03, Appendix A

CFT DCR Interim Milestone	Planned Start Date and Completion Date (mo/yr): Mar/2017 Final RID Board Mar/2017	Amount:
(As proposed, interim Contractor milestone in support of CR) CR Interim Milestone 01B.5		
q) An assessment of the top safety risks and documentation of the management and acceptance of risk including, but not limited to:		Feb/2017
4) Most recent results of the Probabilistic Safety Analysis (PSA) that identify the integrated safety and mission assurance risk of the baseline design, and individually identifies top risk contributors.	Data to be transmitted IAW DRD 103	Feb/2017
5) An assessment of crew survival capability of the baseline design in accordance with CCT-PLN-1120.	Data to be transmitted IAW DRD 103	Feb/2017
r) The top programmatic risks have been identified and assessed.	Data to be transmitted IAW DRD 103	Feb/2017
s) Documentation substantiating all Review Item Dispositions (RIDs) and actions from design reviews, verification reviews, and Certification Baseline Review (CBR) are closed or opened items are dispositioned with rationale for acceptance and updated plans for closure.	Data to be transmitted IAW DRD 103	Feb/2017

Acceptance Criteria: (Att J-03 PWS Apx A)		
t) The DRD 112 Certification Data Package has been approved by NASA.	Data dispositioned per DRD 112	
6) All applicable DRD 111 VCNs have been approved by NASA. (All VCNs relevant to crewed flight test will be approved by NASA with acceptable open work).	Data dispositioned per DRD 111	
7) The design provides crew survival capability.	Data dispositioned to the level required per DRD 103	
8) Operational limits and constraints have been implemented and verified.	Data dispositioned to the level required per DRD 103	

Attachment J-03, Appendix A

CFT DCR Interim Milestone	Planned Start Date and Completion Date (mo/yr): Mar/2017 Final RID Board Mar/2017	Amount:
(As proposed, interim Contractor milestone in support of CR) CR Interim Milestone 01B.5		
9) Operational roles and procedures have been defined for crew, mission team and mission management.	Data dispositioned to the level required per DRD 103	
u) An DRD 002 Integrated Master Plan and Integrated Master Schedule has been approved.	Data dispositioned per DRD 002	
v) The top safety risks are identified, assessed, and clearly communicated. Plans, processes, and appropriate resources necessary to effectively manage the risks are in place.	Data dispositioned to the level required per DRD 103	
10) Major risks to crew safety and mission success have been identified, quantified, and integrated in a PSA.	Data dispositioned to the level required per DRD 103	
11) Risk mitigation strategies associated with the CTS design baseline, cost and schedule have been identified and agreed upon by NASA.	Data dispositioned to the level required per DRD 103	
w) The top programmatic risks have been identified. Plans, processes, and appropriate resources necessary to effectively manage the risks are in place.	Data dispositioned to the level required per DRD 103	
x) All RIDs and actions from design reviews, verification reviews and CBR are closed. All To Be Determined (TBD) and To Be Resolved (TBR) items are clearly identified with acceptable plans and schedules for their disposition and have been submitted.		
y) A plan and schedule have been defined for the resolution of all actions and open items resulting from the DCR. All TBD and TBR items are clearly identified with acceptable plans and schedules for their disposition.		

Attachment J-03, Appendix A

Crewed Flight Test (CFT) Flight Test Readiness Review (FTRR) Interim Milestone	Planned Start Date and Completion Date (mo/yr): Apr/2017 No Final RID Board	Amount:
(As proposed, interim NASA milestone in support of CR) CR Interim Milestone 01B.6		

Objective:

Contractor and NASA co-chaired. For each crewed flight test(s), the Contractor shall conduct an FTRR that demonstrates readiness to conduct a crewed flight test and defines a risk baseline for crewed flight test activities. (Att J-03 PWS Apx A)

Indicators of Milestone Readiness: (Att J-03 PWS Apx A)	Data / DRDs to be provided:	Delivery of Data/DRDs (mo/yr)
The Contractor has completed the following and provided to NASA:		
a) All data and documentation identified in CCT-PLN-1120, Crew Transportation Technical Management Processes, Appendix F, CTS FRR Milestone Data, as the DRD 104 FTRR Data Package.	Data to be transmitted IAW DRD 104	Apr/2017
1) Approval of any new, open or changes to applicable DRD 111 Verification Closure Notices (VCNs), DRD 110 Hazard Reports, and DRD 112 Certification Data Package.	Data to be transmitted IAW DRD 110, 111 and 112	Apr/2017
2) Documentation that all acceptance, checkout and integration testing has been completed.	Data to be transmitted IAW DRD 104	Apr/2017
3) Documentation of flight specific products.	Data to be transmitted IAW DRD 104	Apr/2017
4) Documentation that the launch site, Range, recovery and tracking and data support resources have committed to launch.	Data to be transmitted IAW DRD 104	Apr/2017
5) Documentation that landing site recovery support and resources have committed to landing.	Data to be transmitted IAW DRD 104	Apr/2017

Attachment J-03, Appendix A

Crewed Flight Test (CFT) Flight Test Readiness Review (FTRR) Interim Milestone (As proposed, interim NASA milestone in support of CR) CR Interim Milestone 01B.6	Planned Start Date and Completion Date (mo/yr): Apr/2017 No Final RID Board	Amount: ▇
6) Documentation that all operational supporting and enabling capabilities (e.g., facilities, equipment, documents, updated databases) necessary for nominal and contingency operations have been tested and delivered/installed at the site(s) necessary to support operations.	Data to be transmitted IAW DRD 104	Apr/2017
7) Documentation that plans, processes, procedures and training for nominal and contingency operations for the Crew Transportation System (CTS) have been completed to support operations.	Data to be transmitted IAW DRD 104	Apr/2017
8) Documentation that systems hardware, software, personnel, processes and procedures are in place to support operations.	Data to be transmitted IAW DRD 104	Apr/2017
b) The Contractor, its subcontractors, suppliers and team members have provided flight readiness endorsements demonstrating that they have met requirements in accordance with the Contractor's management processes.	Data to be transmitted IAW DRD 104	Apr/2017
c) International Space Station (ISS) Stage Operational Readiness Review (SORR) has been completed and the ISS is ready to accept the Visiting Vehicle and crew for flight tests to ISS.	Data to be transmitted IAW DRD 104	Apr/2017
1) Documentation of residual mission risks and related analyses for acceptance.	Data to be transmitted IAW DRD 104	Apr/2017
d) All open actions from Design Certification review (DCR) and SORR have been closed.	Data to be transmitted IAW DRD 104	Apr/2017
e) Conduct CFT DCR	Data to be transmitted IAW DRD 103	
Acceptance Criteria: (Att J-03 PWS Apx A)		
a) The DRD 104 FTRR Data Package has been presented and accepted by NASA.	Data dispositioned to the level required per DRD 104	

Attachment J-03, Appendix A

Crewed Flight Test (CFT) Flight Test Readiness Review (FTRR) Interim Milestone (As proposed, interim NASA milestone in support of CR) CR Interim Milestone 01B.6	Planned Start Date and Completion Date (mo/yr): Apr/2017 No Final RID Board	Amount: ■
b) All changes, modifications and anomalies since DCR have been resolved and resolutions have been accepted by NASA	Data dispositioned to the level required per DRD 104	
c) Mission management team, crew, and mission support team have been identified, have been trained, and are in place.	Data dispositioned to the level required per DRD 104	
d) The plan and schedule of preplanned forward work has been accepted by NASA.	Data dispositioned to the level required per DRD 104	
e) Any open work or constraints to launch are identified and closeout plans and schedules are in place and supportable.	Data dispositioned to the level required per DRD 104	
f) NASA has accepted the flight specific products.	Data dispositioned to the level required per DRD 104	
g) Launch Site, Range, and recovery support organizations have committed to launch.	Data dispositioned to the level required per DRD 104	
h) Landing site support and resources have committed to landing.	Data dispositioned to the level required per DRD 104	
i) NASA has accepted residual flight test risks.	Data dispositioned to the level required per DRD 104	

Attachment J-03, Appendix A

Operational Readiness Review (ORR) Interim Milestone	Planned Start Date and Completion Date (mo/yr):	Amount:
(As proposed, interim NASA milestone in support of CR) CR Interim Milestone 01B.7	Jul/2017 Final RID Board Jul/2017	

Objective:

At a NASA and Contractor co-chaired Operations Readiness Review (ORR), the Contractor shall demonstrate that the actual Crew Transportation System (CTS) system characteristics and the procedures used in operations reflect the deployed state of the CTS. The ORR evaluates all project and support (flight and ground) hardware, software, personnel, and procedures to ensure flight and associated ground systems are in compliance with program requirements and constraints.

An ORR occurs upon successful completion of the crewed test flight to International Space Station (ISS). Upon meeting the ORR Acceptance Criteria defined below, NASA will accept operations readiness of the system for Post Certification Missions (PCMs). (Att J-03 PWS Apx A)

Indicators of Milestone Readiness: (Att J-03 PWS Apx A)	Data / DRDs to be provided:	Delivery of Data/DRDs (mo/yr)
The Contractor has completed the following and provided to NASA:		
a) The DRD 105 Operations Readiness Review (ORR) Data Package.	Data to be transmitted IAW DRD 105	Jun/2017
b) Any updates to the DRD 112 Certification Data Package.	Data to be transmitted IAW DRD 112	Jun/2017
c) Any new, open or changed DRD 111 Verification Closure Notices (VCNs) and DRD 110 Hazard Reports.	Data to be transmitted IAW DRD 110 and 111	Jun/2017
d) Approval of closure of action items from Flight Test Readiness Review(s) (FTRR(s)), Design Certification Review(s) (DCR(s)) and previous reviews.	Data to be transmitted IAW DRD 105	Jun/2017
e) Documentation substantiating that all validation testing has been completed.	Data to be transmitted IAW DRD 105	Jun/2017
f) Documentation providing evidence that failures and anomalies have been resolved and the results incorporated.	Data to be transmitted IAW DRD 105	Jun/2017

Attachment J-03, Appendix A

Operational Readiness Review (ORR) Interim Milestone (As proposed, interim NASA milestone in support of CR) CR Interim Milestone 01B.7	Planned Start Date and Completion Date (mo/yr): Jul/2017 Final RID Board Jul/2017	Amount:
g) Documentation that all operational supporting and enabling capabilities (e.g., facilities, equipment, documents, updated databases) necessary for nominal and contingency operations have been tested and delivered/installed at the site(s) necessary to support recurring operations.	Data to be transmitted IAW DRD 105	Jun/2017
h) Documentation that plans, procedures and training for nominal and contingency operations for the CTS have been completed to support recurring operations.	Data to be transmitted IAW DRD 105	Jun/2017
i) Documentation that systems hardware, software, personnel, and procedures are in place to support recurring operations.	Data to be transmitted IAW DRD 105	Jun/2017
j) An assessment of the top safety risks and documentation of the management and acceptance of risk including but not limited to:		Jun/2017
1) Most recent results of the Probabilistic Safety Analysis (PSA) that identify the integrated safety and mission assurance risk of the baseline design, and individually identifies top risk contributors.	Data to be transmitted IAW DRD 105	Jun/2017
2) An assessment of crew survival capability of the baseline design in accordance with CCT-PLN-1120, Crew Transportation Technical Management Processes.	Data to be transmitted IAW DRD 105	Jun/2017
k) The top programmatic risks have been identified and assessed.	Data to be transmitted IAW DRD 105	Jun/2017
l) Documentation substantiating all Review Item Dispositions (RIDs) and actions from design reviews, verification reviews, DCR(s), and FTRR(s) are closed.	Data to be transmitted IAW DRD 105	Jun/2017

Attachment J-03, Appendix A

Operational Readiness Review (ORR) Interim Milestone	Planned Start Date and Completion Date (mo/yr):	Amount:
(As proposed, interim NASA milestone in support of CR) CR Interim Milestone 01B.7	Jul/2017 Final RID Board Jul/2017	
Acceptance Criteria: (Att J-03 PWS Apx A)		
a) The CTS, including any enabling products, is determined to be ready to be placed in a recurring operations status.		
1) NASA has approved the updated DRD 112 Certification Data Package including any remaining open DRD 111 Verification Closure Notices and DRD 110 Hazard Reports.	Data dispositioned per DRD 110, 111 and 112	
2) NASA has approved closure of action items from DCR and previous reviews.	Data dispositioned per DRD 105	
3) NASA has accepted documentation as evidence that all validation testing has been completed.	Data dispositioned per DRD 105	
4) NASA has accepted documentation as evidence that failures and anomalies have been resolved and the results incorporated.	Data dispositioned per DRD 105	
5) NASA has accepted documentation that all operational supporting and enabling capabilities (e.g., facilities, equipment, documents, updated databases) necessary for nominal and contingency operations have been tested and delivered/installed at the site(s) necessary to support sustaining operations.	Data dispositioned per DRD 105	
6) NASA has accepted documentation that all plans, procedures and training for nominal and contingency operations for the CTS have been completed to support sustaining operations.	Data dispositioned per DRD 105	
7) NASA has accepted documentation that systems hardware, software, personnel, and procedures are in place to support operations.	Data dispositioned per DRD 105	

Attachment J-03, Appendix A

Operational Readiness Review (ORR) Interim Milestone	Planned Start Date and Completion Date (mo/yr): Jul/2017 Final RID Board Jul/2017	Amount: ■
(As proposed, interim NASA milestone in support of CR) CR Interim Milestone 01B.7		
b) The top safety risks for Post Certification Missions are identified, assessed, and clearly communicated. Plans, processes, and appropriate resources necessary to effectively manage the risks are in place.	Data dispositioned per DRD 105	
c) Major risks to crew safety and mission success have been identified, quantified, and integrated in a PSA.	Data dispositioned per DRD 105	
1) Risk mitigation strategies associated with the CTS design baseline, cost and schedule have been identified and agreed upon by NASA.	Data dispositioned per DRD 105	
2) The top programmatic risks have been identified. Plans, processes, and appropriate resources necessary to effectively manage the risks are in place.	Data dispositioned per DRD 105	
d) A plan and schedule have been defined for the resolution of all actions and open items resulting from the ORR. All To be Determined (TBD) and To be Resolved (TBR) items are clearly identified with acceptable plans and schedules for their disposition.	Data dispositioned per DRD 105	

Attachment J-03, Appendix A

Certification Review (CR) Delivery Milestone (As proposed, NASA Delivery milestone) CR Delivery Milestone 01B	Planned Start Date and Completion Date (mo/yr): Aug/2017 Final RID Board Aug/2017	Amount: ■
Objective: At a NASA chaired review, the Contractor shall provide evidence that the CTS has met all NASA requirements identified in Attachment J-01, Integrated Crew Transportation System (CTS) Requirements. The Contractor shall also provide documentation of the crew safety and mission assurance risks associated with the CTS. (Att J-03 PWS Apx A)		

Indicators of Milestone Readiness: (Att J-03 PWS Apx A)	Data / DRDs to be provided:	Delivery of Data/DRDs (mo/yr)
The Contractor has completed the following and provided to NASA:		
a) The DRD 106 Certification Review Milestone Data Package	Data to be transmitted IAW DRD 106	Jun/2017
b) The DRD 112 Certification Data Package.	Data to be transmitted IAW DRD 112	Jun/2017
c) Documentation of results from all flight tests, Operations Readiness Review (ORR), production acceptance testing and closure of any open requirements from Design Certification Review(s) (DCR(s)).	Data to be transmitted IAW DRD 106	Jun/2017 update Jul/2017
d) An assessment of the top safety risks and documentation of the management and acceptance of risk including but not limited to:	Data to be transmitted IAW DRD 106	Jun/2017
e) Most recent results of the Probabilistic Safety Analysis (PSA) that identify the integrated safety and mission assurance risk of the baseline design, and individually identifies top risk contributors.	Data to be transmitted IAW DRD 106	Jun/2017
f) An assessment of crew survival capability of the baseline design.	Data to be transmitted IAW DRD 106	Jun/2017

Attachment J-03, Appendix A

Certification Review (CR) Delivery Milestone (As proposed, NASA Delivery milestone) CR Delivery Milestone 01B	Planned Start Date and Completion Date (mo/yr): Aug/2017 Final RID Board Aug/2017	Amount: ■
g) The top programmatic risks have been identified and assessed.	Data to be transmitted IAW DRD 106	Jun/2017
h) Documentation substantiating all Review Item Dispositions (RIDs) and actions from design reviews, verification reviews, DCR(s), Flight Test Readiness Review(s) (FTRR(s)) and ORR are closed.	Data to be transmitted IAW DRD 106	Jun/2017
Acceptance Criteria: (Att J-03 PWS Apx A)		
a) CTS Certification recommendation has been approved including DRD 112 Certification Data Package.	Data dispositioned per DRD 112	
b) Results from risk assessment have been accepted by NASA.	Data dispositioned per DRD 106	
c) Closure of all open actions from previous reviews have been approved by NASA or NASA approval of closure plan prior to applicable PCM milestone	Data dispositioned per DRD 106	

Appendix B to Attachment J-03, Post Certification Mission (PCM) Milestone Acceptance Criteria and Payment Schedule

Attachment J-03, Appendix B

1.0 INTRODUCTION

The PCM Milestone Acceptance Criteria and Payment Schedule provided in Section 3.0 details all the milestones, reviews and/or payment events which mark progress towards completion of CLIN 002 activities and is provided in response to and supports:

Section	Description
B.4	Post Certification Missions (IDIQ) CLIN 002)
G.8	Submission of Invoices for Payment
H.19	Post Certification Mission Payments, Milestones and Authority to Proceed (ATP) Criteria
H.21	Post Certification Mission Success Determination
I.11	52.232-32 Performance-Based Payments (Apr 2012) (Deviation), (Applicable to Interim Performance-Based Payments Events)
L-02	Draft Performance Work Statement, Section 4.0 Mission Review Milestones
Attachment J-03, Section 3.3	Performance Work Statement

2.0 POST CERTIFICATION MISSION (PCM) WORK PLAN (DRD 202)

The Contractor shall utilize the Post Certification Mission (PCM) Work Plan (WP), DRD 202, to describe for each milestone review and interim milestones:

- the review process
- schedule
- location
- deliverables
- delivery dates
- method and timing by which data will be made available to NASA
- document review requirements
- presentation meetings
- pre-boards
- other logistics related information

In advance of the each milestone, the Contractor shall collaborate with NASA and document the mutually agreed to readiness indicators (also known as entrance criteria) and acceptance criteria (also called exit or success criteria) for the review in the PCM Work Plan document. The Contractor shall draw from the following requirements document set at a minimum to define the applicable milestone entrance and exit criteria:

Attachment J-03, Appendix B

a) This document, Appendix B to Attachment J-03, PCM Readiness Indicators and Success Criteria
b) NASA Systems Engineering Processes and Requirements, NPR 7123.1A
c) Certification Plan, DCC1-00443-01

The Contractor shall submit the PCM Work Plan detailing the specifics for the next major event at the preceding interim milestone/milestone review to allow sufficient time for NASA approval of the PCM WP and subsequent execution of the plan detailed in the PCM Work Plan.

3.0 PCM MILESTONE ACCEPTANCE CRITERIA AND PAYMENT SCHEDULE

Legend:
Mandatory Government Interim Milestone
Contractor Proposed Interim Milestone
Mandatory Government Delivery Milestone

Attachment J-03, Appendix B

Vehicle Baseline Review (VBR) Interim Milestone for PCM-1

Planned Start Date and Completion Date (mo/yr): ▮

(As proposed, interim NASA milestone in support of PFR)
PFR Interim Milestone 02A.1

No Final RID Board

Objective:

At no later than 18 months prior to launch (L-18 mo), the Contractor shall co-chair a Vehicle Baseline Review (VBR) with NASA that establishes the integrated mission CTS configuration (launch vehicle, orbital vehicle, and ground systems) that accommodates NASA requirements for crew and cargo transportation. The intent of the VBR is to establish the baseline CTS for the mission and identify any design or operation changes from the previous and the corresponding plans for executing and verifying these changes. The content for the VBR shall include:

Indicators of Milestone Readiness:	Data / DRDs to be provided:	Delivery of Data/DRDs (mo/yr)
The Contractor shall, at this review: Mission Baseline CTS:		
a) Baseline the post certification mission objectives, to include crew and cargo complement, and associated baseline CTS configuration, including ground accommodation specific interfaces and service agreements, so that mission integration efforts have definite configuration, environments and performance capabilities identified.	Data to be transmitted IAW DRD 202 PCM WP	▮
b) Reconfirm the launch window as defined per Clause H.20, Adjustments to Post Certification Mission Schedule.	Data to be transmitted IAW DRD 202 PCM WP	▮
c) Provide, if necessary, an updated DRD 201, Mission Integration and Operations Management Plan (MIOMP), and if necessary, an updated DRD 202, Post Certification Mission (PCM) Work Plan.	(MIOMP) Data to be transmitted IAW DRD 201 (PCM WP) Data to be transmitted IAW DRD 202 PCM WP.	▮

Vehicle Baseline Review (VBR) Interim Milestone for PCM-1 (As proposed, interim NASA milestone in support of PFR) PFR Interim Milestone 02A.1	Planned Start Date and Completion Date (mo/yr): ▮ No Final RID Board
d) Provide, as required, an update to the mission specific instrumentation plan and the Vehicle Interface Definition Document (IDD) in accordance with DRD 203, Vehicle Interface Definition Document (IDD).	Data to be transmitted IAW DRD 203 — IAW DRD 203
Design And Operation Changes From Prior Mission Baseline CTS: The Contractor shall, at this review, identify any design and operation changes from the previous mission baseline CTS.	
a) Identify all CCT-1100 series and SSP 50808, ISS to Commercial Orbital Transportation Services (COTS) Interface Requirements Document(IRD), requirements that require re-verification and have been allocated to the appropriate system, subsystem and/or component level. Demonstrate requirements flow down is adequate to verify compliance with CCT-1100 series and SSP 50808.	Data to be transmitted IAW DRD 202 PCM WP — ▮
b) Identify any hazards, controls, or verifications that are affected by design changes.	Data to be transmitted IAW DRD 202 PCM WP — ▮
c) Discuss analyses and tests to be performed to execute these designs and operation changes and include their methodology, assumptions and results, along with comparisons to any similar proven designs.	Data to be transmitted IAW DRD 202 PCM WP — ▮
d) Show how these changes affect performance, reliability and environments and associated risks.	Data to be transmitted IAW DRD 202 PCM WP — ▮
e) Discuss how previous In-Flight Anomaly (IFA) and previous production non-conformances affect the mission baseline.	Data to be transmitted IAW DRD 202 PCM WP — ▮
f) Present the status or results of any mission unique or special study task assessments requested by NASA.	Data to be transmitted IAW DRD 202 PCM WP — ▮

Attachment J-03, Appendix B

Vehicle Baseline Review (VBR) Interim Milestone for PCM-1	Planned Start Date and Completion Date (mo/yr):
(As proposed, interim NASA milestone in support of PFR) PFR Interim Milestone 02A.1	No Final RID Board
g) Provide a schedule to complete all work required to accomplish the design changes and close requirement verifications prior to Mission Certification Review (MCR).	Data to be transmitted IAW DRD 002
h) Provide updates to design margins (spacecraft and launch vehicle) if margins changed.	Data to be transmitted IAW DRD 202 PCM WP
i) Identify updates to the overall system architecture including ground accommodation specific interfaces and service agreements.	Data to be transmitted IAW DRD 202 PCM WP
j) Identify any mission unique and unproven processes, risks and mitigation plans.	Data to be provided at meeting IAW DRD 202 PCM WP
k) Present the operations concept to satisfy mission objectives.	Data to be provided at meeting IAW DRD 202 PCM WP
l) Identify updates to operational products, personnel certification, facilities changes, and provide any scope and/or schedule changes for crew training.	Data to be provided at meeting IAW DRD 202 PCM WP
m) Status crew related items to be proposed by the Contractor in the MIOMP.	Data to be provided at meeting IAW DRD 202 PCM WP

Acceptance Criteria:

Attachment J-03, Appendix B

Mission Integration Review (MIR) Interim Milestone for PCM-1	Planned Start Date and Completion Date (mo/yr):
(As proposed, interim NASA milestone in support of PFR) PFR Interim Milestone 02A.2	No Final RID Board

Objective:

At no later than (NLT) thirteen (13) months prior to launch (L-13 mo), the Contractor shall co-chair a Mission Integration Review (MIR) with NASA with a current mission integration status. NASA and Contractor will review and baseline the conditions and inputs for mission specific analytical assessments. The Contractor shall demonstrate CTS operations and production activities support the launch date. A status of all open items presented at VBR shall be presented at this review. For open items, schedule plans for completion shall be presented. All milestones to this point shall have been met. The content for the MIR shall include:

Indicators of Milestone Readiness:	Data / DRDs to be provided:	Delivery of Data/DRDs (mo/yr)
A. Mission Baseline CTS:: The Contractor shall, at this review:		
a) Reconfirm the launch window as defined in Table H.20.1, Launch Windows for PCM ATP Prior to ISS DCR, or defined in Table H.20.2, Launch Windows for PCM ATP After ISS DCR, per Clause H.20, Adjustments to Post Certification Mission Schedule.	Data to be transmitted IAW DRD 202 PCM WP	
b) Provide, as required, an update to DRD 203 Vehicle Interface Definition Document (IDD) and an update to the mission specific instrumentation plan for the Vehicle Interface Definition Document (IDD).	Data to be transmitted via DRD 203	
c) Provide initial data and parameters for Mission Success Determination per Clause H.21, Post Certification Mission Success Determination.	Data to be transmitted IAW DRD 202 PCM WP	
d) Provide, if necessary, an updated DRD 201 Mission Integration and Operations Management Plan (MIOMP) and if necessary, an updated DRD 202 Post Certification Mission PCM Work Plan.	Data to be transmitted via DRD 201	

Mission Integration Review (MIR) Interim Milestone for PCM-1	Planned Start Date and Completion Date (mo/yr):
(As proposed, interim NASA milestone in support of PFR) PFR Interim Milestone 02A.2	▮ No Final RID Board
e) Provide initial DRD 204 MRAD	Data to be transmitted via DRD 204 IAW DRD 204
B. Design Changes From Prior Mission Baseline CTS: The Contractor shall:	
a) Present designs and their supporting analyses that implement mission unique requirements.	Data to be transmitted IAW DRD 202 PCM WP ▮
b) Present progress in manufacturing and lay out remaining milestones and risks to accomplishing them.	Data to be transmitted IAW DRD 202 PCM WP ▮
c) Present progress towards closure of CCT-1100 series and SSP 50808 requirements, and lay out remaining milestones and risks to accomplishing them.	Data to be transmitted via DRD 002 ▮
d) Present progress of ISS integration and integrated safety hazard assessments. Integrated safety analysis identifying any remaining hazards and proposed resolution per CCT-PLN-1120, Section 4.5, Integrated Safety Review Process.	Data to be transmitted via DRD 110 and DRD 111 IAW DRD 110 and 111
e) Present progress for changes identified at VBR for:	
(1) The overall system architecture including ground accommodation specific interfaces and service agreements.	Data to be provided at meeting IAW DRD 202 PCM WP ▮
(2) Mission unique and unproven processes, risks and mitigation plans.	Data to be provided at meeting IAW DRD 202 PCM WP ▮

Attachment J-03, Appendix B

Mission Integration Review (MIR) Interim Milestone for PCM-1	Planned Start Date and Completion Date (mo/yr):
(As proposed, interim NASA milestone in support of PFR) PFR Interim Milestone 02A.2	No Final RID Board
(3) Operational products, including personnel certification, facilities and crew training.	Data to be provided at meeting IAW DRD 202 PCM WP
f) Discuss how technical problems and anomalies have been resolved and effects of design changes on system performance, reliability and safety...	Data to be provided at meeting IAW DRD 202 PCM WP
g) Discuss how simulations and prototyping results for CTS do not present any potential mission risks.	Data to be provided at meeting IAW DRD 202 PCM WP
h) Present defined test plans for CTS.	Data to be provided at meeting IAW DRD 202 PCM WP
i) Status crew related items to be proposed by the Contractor in the MIOMP.	Data to be provided IAW DRD 201

Acceptance Criteria:

Attachment J-03, Appendix B

Mission Certification Review (MCR) Interim Milestone for PCM-1	Planned Start Date and Completion Date (mo/yr):
(As proposed, interim NASA milestone in support of PFR) PFR Interim Milestone 02A.3	No Final RID Board

Objective:

After NASA Certification has been granted, and no later than four (4) months prior to launch (L-4 mo), the Contractor shall co-chair with NASA a Mission Certification Review (MCR) that allows NASA to assess if the Contractor has completed certification of all requirements, has completed ISS integration, has all infrastructure, facilities, personnel, and services in place, and will be ready for the mission and for crewed operations, including agreement on cargo turnover and crew handover. A status of all open items presented in both the VBR and MIR shall be presented at this review. All mission unique design qualification and acceptance testing shall be complete. For open items, schedule plans for completion shall be presented. All milestones to this point shall have been met. The content for the MCR shall include:

Indicators of Milestone Readiness:	Data / DRDs to be provided:	Delivery of Data/DRDs (mo/yr)
The Contractor shall, at this review:		
a) Reconfirm the launch window as defined in table H.20.1, Launch Windows for PCM ATP Prior to ISS DCR, or defined in Table H.20.2, Launch Windows for PCM ATP after ISS DCR, per clause H.20, Adjustments to Post Certification Mission Schedule.	Data to be transmitted IAW DRD 202 PCM WP	
b) Provide the final specific mission instrumentation plan and an update, as required, to DRD 203 Vehicle Interface Definition Document (IDD).	Data to be transmitted IAW DRD 203	IAW DRD 203
c) Present evidence of verification closures for mission unique designs and requirements.	Data to be transmitted IAW DRD 111	IAW DRD 111
d) Present evidence of verification closures for all open CCT-1100 series and SSP 50808 requirements.	Data to be transmitted IAW DRD 111	IAW DRD 111

Attachment J-03, Appendix B

Mission Certification Review (MCR) Interim Milestone for PCM-1 (As proposed, interim NASA milestone in support of PFR) PFR Interim Milestone 02A.3	Planned Start Date and Completion Date (mo/yr): ▇▇▇▇ No Final RID Board
e) Provide all analytical assessments that show the compatibility of crew and cargo mass, when applicable, with the launch and spacecraft such as integrated loads, Launch to Activation thermal assessments, electromagnetic interference (EMI), propellant resources and power.	Data to be transmitted IAW DRD 204 — IAW DRD 204
f) Present status of all anomalies and associated corrective actions showing low-risk closure plans in place to completion prior to ISS Stage Operational Readiness Reviews (SORR) / Flight Readiness Review (FRR).	Data to be provided at meeting IAW DRD 202 PCM WP — ▇▇▇
g) Present evidence that all Safety Assessments have been approved by NASA.	Data to be transmitted IAW DRD 110, 113 and 207 — IAW DRD 110, 113 and 207
h) Present evidence that all open items in both the VBR and MIR have been closed or present plans showing low risk to completion prior to SORR/ FRR.	Data to be provided at meeting IAW DRD 202 PCM WP — ▇▇▇
i) Provide final data and parameters for mission success determination.	Data to be transmitted IAW DRD 204 — IAW DRD 204
j) Reach agreement on NASA identified Launch Commit Criteria (LCC) constraints concerning CTS, ISS, crew, and cargo.	Data to be provided at meeting IAW DRD 202 PCM WP — ▇▇▇
k) Present evidence that all operational products, plans, processes and training are complete or present plans showing low risk to completion prior to SORR/ FRR.	Data to be provided at meeting IAW DRD 202 PCM WP — ▇▇▇
l) Define the post flight data for review.	Data to be provided at meeting IAW DRD 202 PCM WP — ▇▇▇
m) Present status of crew related items to be proposed by the Contractor in the MIOMP.	Data to be provided at meeting IAW DRD 202 PCM WP — ▇▇▇

Attachment J-03, Appendix B

Mission Certification Review (MCR) Interim Milestone for PCM-1	Planned Start Date and Completion Date (mo/yr):
(As proposed, interim NASA milestone in support of PFR) PFR Interim Milestone 02A.3	▬ No Final RID Board
n) Present status of acceptance testing (launch vehicle and spacecraft).	Data to be provided at meeting IAW DRD 202 PCM WP

Acceptance Criteria:

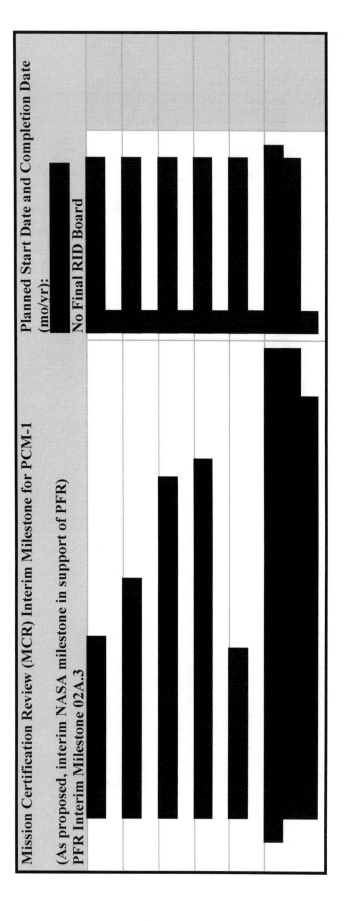

Attachment J-03, Appendix B

Flight Readiness Review (FRR) Interim Milestone for PCM-1	Planned Start Date and Completion Date (mo/yr):
(As proposed, interim NASA milestone in support of PFR) PFR Interim Milestone 02A.4	▓▓▓ No Final RID Board

Objective:

At approximately two (2) weeks prior to launch, (4.62) the Contractor shall support the NASA Flight Readiness Reviews (FRRs). The Contractor shall provide a mission specific DRD 208, Flight Readiness Review Data Package in support of the FRR. The support will confirm the following.

Indicators of Milestone Readiness:	Data / DRDs to be provided:	Delivery of Data/DRDs (mo/yr)
a) All critical items required to proceed into final launch countdown are ready.	Data to be transmitted IAW DRD 208	▓▓▓
b) All CTS systems have been verified for launch.	Data to be transmitted IAW DRD 111	IAW DRD 111
c) All previously held Contractor readiness review actions have been closed or resolved.	Data to be transmitted IAW DRD 208	▓▓▓
d) Launch Site, Range, FAA, and recovery support organizations have committed to launch.	Data to be transmitted IAW DRD 208	▓▓▓
e) Tracking and data support resources have committed to launch.	Data to be transmitted IAW DRD 208	▓▓▓
f) Any open work or constraints to launch are identified and closeout plans and schedules are in place and supportable.	Data to be transmitted IAW DRD 002	▓▓▓
g) Residual mission risks are known, documented, and presented for acceptance.	Data to be transmitted IAW DRD 208	▓▓▓

Attachment J-03, Appendix B

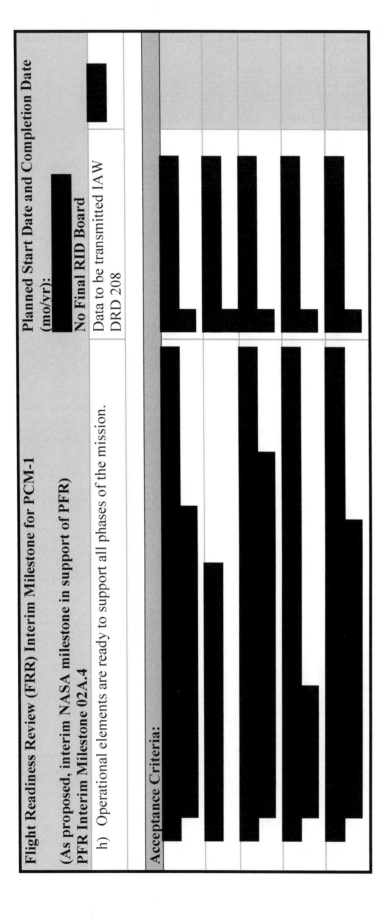

Flight Readiness Review (FRR) Interim Milestone for PCM-1 | Planned Start Date and Completion Date (mo/yr):

(As proposed, interim NASA milestone in support of PFR)
PFR Interim Milestone 02A.4

No Final RID Board

h) Operational elements are ready to support all phases of the mission. | Data to be transmitted IAW DRD 208

Acceptance Criteria:

Attachment J-03, Appendix B

Post Flight Review Delivery Milestone for PCM-1

(As proposed, NASA delivery milestone) Delivery Milestone 02A.5	Planned Start Date and Completion Date (mo/yr): ▇▇▇ No Final RID Board

Objective:

The Contractor shall conduct Post Flight Reviews with NASA participation to assess mission success supporting data in accordance with DRD 209 Post Flight Assessment Report. Following landing, the contractor shall assess CCTS system performance for ascent, rendezvous and docking; quiescent docked operations; undocking, entry and landing; post landing crew recovery. The review shall include a preliminary review of predicted vs. actual performance; evaluation of actual vs. predicted environments; a summary of any anomalies (flight hardware and ground systems) from start of LV tanking through crew recovery and their impacts on execution of the flight and preliminary assessment of flight crew and ground personnel training.

Indicators of Milestone Readiness:	Data / DRDs to be provided:	Delivery of Data/DRDs (mo/yr)
The Contractor shall, at this review: a) Landing completed b) Provide updated quick-look report in accordance with DRD 209, Post Flight Assessment Report. The contractor shall present their determination of meeting the mission success criteria that was finalized at MCR. A final written DRD 209 post flight report shall be provided NLT 60 days following landing, but submittal of that report is not a constraint on closure of this milestone. c) The contractor shall present their determination of meeting the mission success criteria that was finalized at MCR.	Data to be transmitted IAW DRD 209 Data to be provided at review IAW DRD 202 PCM WP	▇▇▇ ▇▇▇
Acceptance Criteria:		

Attachment J-03, Appendix B

The following table details the planned dates for the identical milestones/reviews for PCM-2.

Table 4.0-1 Planned PCM-2 Dates

Milestone Number	Milestone / Review	Date	Review Doc Delivery
02B.1	PCM-2 Vehicle Baseline Review (VBR)		
02B.2	PCM-2 Mission Integration Review (MIR)		
02B.3	PCM-2 Mission Certification Review (MCR)		
02B.4	PCM-2 FRR		
02B.5	PCM-2 Post Flight Review		

Attachment J-05
Acronym List

Attachment J-05

Acronym List

Acronym	Definition
3-D	Three Dimensional
3DCS	Three Dimensional Control Systems
5S	Sort, Simplify, Sweep, Standardize and Self-Discipline
A&OSP	Assembly and Operations Support Plan
A&SW	Avionics and Software
A/R	As Required
AA	Ascent Abort
ABCL	As-Built Configuration List
ABU	Accounting Business Unit
AC	Accomplishment Criteria
AC	Ascent Cover
ACC	Alternation Control Center
ACT-VAL	Activation and Validation
ACQ	Astronaut Crew Quarters
ACT	Activated
ADDIE	Analyze, Design, Develop, Implement and Evaluate
ADMC	Aerospace Defense Manufacturing Center
ADP	Acceptance Data Package
AE	Approach Ellipsoid
AF	Air Force
AFB	Air Force Base
AFRCC	Air Force Rescue Coordination Center
AFRSI	Advanced Flexible Reusable Surface Insulation
AFSPC	Air Force Space Command
AFSPCMAN	Air Force Space Command Manual
AHA	Agency Honor Awards
AI	Affordability Initiative
AI	Approach Initiation
AIA	Aerospace Industries Association
AIAA	American Institute of Aeronautics and Astronautics
AIT	Assembly, Integration and Test
AIV	Abort Isolation Valve
ALERT	Acute Launch Emergency Reliability Tip
ALTV	Approach and Landing Test Vehicle
AMS	Alpha Magnetic Spectrometer
AMVER	Automated Mutual-assistance Vessel Rescue System

Acronym	Definition
ANSI	American National Standards Institute
APAS	Androgynous Peripheral Attach System
■	■
APU	Auxiliary Power Unit
AR	Anomaly Report
■	■
AR&D	Automated Rendezvous and Docking
ARD	Abort Region Determinator
ARES	Accelerated Receiving Execution System
■	■
ARS	Air Revitalization System
ARS	Atmospheric Revitalization Subsystem
ARS	Automated Requisition System
ASAP	Automated Source Activity Planning
ASC	Advanced Scientific Concepts
ASIF	Avionics Systems Integration Facility
ASIL	Avionics Systems Integration Laboratory
ASIM	Avionics and Software Integration Meeting
ASOC	Atlas Spaceflight Operations Center
ASP	Astronaut Support Personnel
ASPEN	Automated Scheduling and Planning Environment
ASTM	American Society for Testing and Materials
ASTP	Apollo–Soyuz Test Project
ATCS	Active Thermal Control Subsystem
ATF	Bureau of Alcohol, Tobacco, Firearms and Explosives
■	■
ATM	Ascent Trajectory Model
ATO	Abort to Orbit
ATP	Authority to Proceed
ATRD	Acceptance Test Requirements Document
ATV	All-Terrain Vehicle
AUPP	Average Unit Production Price
B	Benefit
■	■
■	■
■	■

Attachment J-05

Acronym	Definition
BCB	Baseline Change Board
BCC	Backup Control Center
BCMT	Boeing Cargo Manifest Tool
BD	Business Development
BDA	Blast Danger Area
BDEAL	Bi-lateral Data Exchange Agreement List
BDEALS	Bi-lateral Data Exchange Agreement List and Schedule
BDS	Boeing Defense, Space and Security
BES	Boeing Engineering Simulator
BEST	Boeing Enterprise Supplier Tool
BFPR	Basic Flight Product Review
BHS	Base Heat Shield
BHSEALS	Bilateral Hardware / Software Exchange Agreement List and Schedule
BIT	Built-In Test
BLA	Boeing Lightweight Ablator
BMCC	Boeing Mission Control Center
BMS	Boeing Mission Simulator
BOE	Basis of Estimate
BOM	Bill of Materials
BORIS	Boeing Opportunity, Risk and Issue System
BPF	Boeing Processing Facility
BPG	Business Process Guide
BPI	Business Process Instruction
BRAIDSS	Boeing Recurring and Independent Demand Scheduling System
BRID	Boeing Review Item Discrepancy Tool
■	■
BtCC	Breaking the Cost Curve
BTP	Build-to/Buy-to Package
BTU	Basic Task Unit
BURS	Boeing Usability Scale
BWS	Bedford Work Scale
C	Consequence
C&DH	Command and Data Handling
C&T	Communication and Tracking
C&W	Caution and Warning
C2V2	Common Communications for Visiting Vehicles

Attachment J-05

Acronym	Definition
C3PF	Commercial Crew and Cargo Processing Facility
CAA	Crew Access Arm
CAC	Common Access Card
CAD	Computer-Aided Design
CAM	Cost Account Manager
CAP	Corrective Action Plan
CAP	Contractor-Acquired Property
CAPA	Corrective and Preventive Action
CAPP	Computer Aided Process Planning
CAPPS	Checkout, Assembly and Payload Processing Services
CAR	Certification Assessment Report
CAS	Cost Accounting Standards
CAS	Compliant Accounting System
CASIS	Center for the Advancement of Science in Space
CASPER	Continuous Activity Scheduling Planning Execution and Replanning
CAT	Crew Access Tower
CATIA	Computer-Aided Three-Dimensional Interactive Application
CB	Certification Body
CBA	Collective Bargaining Agreement
CBR	Certification Baseline Review
CCAFS	Cape Canaveral Air Force Station
CCB	Change Control Board
CCB	Configuration Control Board
CCCS	CST-100 Checkout and Control System
CCDev	Commercial Crew Development
CCDev2	Commercial Crew Development 2
CCDL	Cross Channel Data Link
CCiCap	Commercial Crew Integrated Capability
CCIDC	Commercial Crew Integrated Design Contract
CCP	Commercial Crew Program
CCPO	Commercial Crew Program Office
CCR	Cargo Compatibility Review
CCR	Central Contractor Registry
CCS	Communications Checkout System
CCSDS	Consultative Committee for Space Data Systems
CCtCap	Commercial Crew Transportation Capability

Attachment J-05

Acronym	Definition
CCTS	Commercial Crew Transportation System
CCTSdb	Commercial Crew Transportation System Data Base
CD-ROM	Compact Disk – Read Only Memory
CDP	Certification Data Package
CDR	Critical Design Review
CDRL	Contract Data Requirements List
CDT	Count Down Time
CeIL	Certification Indenture Listing
CEIT	Crew Equipment Interface Test
CEO	Chief Executive Officer
CER	Cost Estimating Relationship
CERR	Critical Events Readiness Review
CEV	Crew Exploration Vehicle
CFD	Computational Fluid Dynamics
CFT	Crewed Flight Test
CG or c.g.	Center of Gravity
CHS	Capital Harness System
CI	Configuration Item
CIAO	Central Industry Assistance Office
CID	Cargo Interface Definition
CIL	Critical Item List
CIR	Cargo Integration Review
CIS	Crew Information System
CISO	Chief Information Security Officer
CL	Certification Lead
CLA	Coupled Loads Analysis
CLIN	Contract Line Item Number
CLS	Contractor Logistics Support
CLSA	Commercial Space Launch Act
CLSRB	Current Launch Schedule Review Board
CM	Crew Module
CM	Configuration Management
CM/DM	Configuration Management/Data Management
CM/SM	Crew Module/Service Module
CMD	Command
CMIS	Common Metrology Information System

Attachment J-05

Acronym	Definition
CMMI	Capability Maturity Model Integration
CMO	Crew and Mission Operations
CMP	Configuration Management Plan
CO	Contracting Officer
CoD	Certification of Design
CoFR	Certification of Flight Readiness
CoFTR	Certification of Flight Test Readiness
COI	Conflict of Interest
COLA	Collision Avoidance
COMSEC	Communications Security
CONOPS	Concept of Operations
CONUS	Continental United States
COPV	Composite Overwrapped Pressure Vessel
COR	Contracting Officer Representative
COTR	Contracting Officer Technical Representative
COTS	Commercial off the Shelf
COTS	Commercial Orbital Transportation Services
CP	Commercial Program
CPAR	Contractor Performance Assessment Report
CPAS	Crew Exploration Vehicle (CEV) Parachute Assembly System
CPC	Certification Products Contract
CPI	Cost Performance Index
CPS	Common Pricing System
CPU	Central Processing Unit
CPWSR	Configuration Performance and Weight Status Report
CR	Certification Review
CR	Change Request
CRS	Commercial Resupply Services
CSAS	Configuration Status Accounting System
CSC	Computer Software Component
CSCI	Computer Software Configuration Item
CSCS	Contingency Spacecraft Crew Support
CSDT	Customer and Supplier Data Transmittal
CSLA	Commercial Space Launch Act
CSPR	Cost, Schedule, Planning and Reporting
CST	Commercial Space Transporter

Attachment J-05

Acronym	Definition
CSTSP	Commercial Space Transportation Strategic Partnership
CTB	Cargo Transfer Bag
CTM	Crew Transfer Mission
CTS	Crew Transportation System
CUM	Cumulative
CV	Cargo Variant
CVCC	Commercial Vehicle Control Center
CVDR	Cargo Vehicle Departure Review
CY	Calendar Year
D&C	Displays and Controls
DAC	Design Analysis Cycle
DACS	Divert and Attitude Control System
DAEZ	Downrange Abort Exclusion Zone
DCAA	Defense Contract Audit Agency
DCLA	Design Coupled Loads Analysis
DCMA	Defense Contracts Management Agency
DCN	Document Change Notice
DCR	Design Certification Review
DCR	Designated Customer Representative
DDL	Data Downlink
DDTE	Design, Development, Test, and Evaluation
DEC	Dual Engine Centaur
DELMIA	Digital Enterprise Lean Manufacturing Interactive Application
DER	Design Equivalency Review
DFI	Development Flight Instrumentation
DFMA	Design For Manufacturing and Assembly
DFMR	Design For Minimum Risk
DFOS	Design For Operations and Supportability
DFV	Design For Value
DGWY	Dugway
DI	Detailed Instruction
DIL	Deliverable Items List
DIMS	Digital Imagery Management System
DM	Data Management
DM	Documentation Management
DMC	Display Management Computer

Attachment J-05

Acronym	Definition
DMS	Display Management Software
DN	Discrepancy Notice
DOD	Department of Defense
DOE	Department of Energy
DOF	Degrees of Freedom
DOL	Day of Launch
DOLWG	Day of Launch Working Group
DOORS	Dynamic Object Oriented Requirements System
DOR	Demonstration Objectives Report
DOSC	Denver Operations Support Center
DOT	Department of Transportation
DPE	Development Program Excellence
■■■	■■■
DPM	Deputy Program Manager
DQA	Data Quality Assurance
DR	Data Requirements
DR	Decommissioning Review
DRD	Data Requirements Deliverable
DRL	Data Requirements List
DRM	Data Recorder Module
DRM	Design Reference Mission
DTA	Debris Transport Analysis
DUNS	Data Universal Numbering System
DVD	Digital Video Disk
DVR	Detailed Verification Requirements
DXL	DOORS Extension Language
EAC	Estimate at Completion
EAFB	Edwards Air Force Base
EAS	Enterprise Accounting System
EBBET	Excel Based Basic Task Unit (BTU) Estimating Tool
EBOM	Engineering Bill of Materials
Ec	Expected Number of Casualties
ECAT	Engineering Control Analysis Tool
ECB	Engineering Change Board
ECB	Engineering Control Board
ECD	Estimated Completion Date

Acronym	Definition
ECF	Environmental Correction Factor
ECL	Engineering Configuration List
ECLS	Environmental Control Life Support
ECLSS	Environmental Control Life Support System
EDIS	Estimating and Data Information System
EDL	Entry, Descent, Landing
ECP	Export Control Plan
EDRS	Engineering Design and Release System
EDS	Emergency Detection System
EDU	Engineering Development Unit
EE	Engineering Estimate
EEE	Electrical, Electronic and Electromechanical
EELV	Extended Expendable Launch Vehicle
EES	Emergency Egress System
EGSE	Electrical Ground Support Equipment
ELS	Exploration Launch Systems
ELSA	Emergency Life Support Apparatus
ELV	Expendable Launch Vehicle
EMA	Electromechanical Actuator
EMC	Electromagnetic Compatibility
EMD	Engineering Manufacturing Development
EME	Electromagnetic Effects
EMI	Electromagnetic Interference
EMU	Extravehicular Mobility Unit
EO	Engineering Order
EOM	End of Mission
EP	Equivalent People
EPA	Environmental Protection Agency
EPS	Electrical Power System
EQI	Early Quality Involvement
ER	Engineering Release
ERB	Engineering Review Board
ERD	Equipment Requirements Description
ERP	Enterprise Resource Planning
ERS	Emergency Recommendation System
ERS	Emergency Re-pressurization System
ERU	Engineering Release Unit

Attachment J-05

Acronym	Definition
ES	Environmental Seal
ESGP	Enterprise Standard Gated Process
ESM	Ethernet Switch Module
eSRS	Electronic Subcontracting Reporting System
ET	External Tank
ETE	End-to-End
ETRIP	Expedition Training Requirements Integration Panel
EV	Earned Value
EVA	Extravehicular Activity
EVM	Earned Value Management
EVMS	Earned Value Management System
EVR	Extravehicular Robotics
EWR	Eastern and Western Range
FAA	Federal Aviation Administration
FAI	First Article Inspection
FAR	Federal Acquisition Regulations
FAWG	Flight Analysis Working Group
FCA	Functional Configuration Audit
FCC	Federal Communications Commission
FCCOM	Facilities Capital Cost of Money
FCOD	Flight Crew Operations Directorate
FCOH	Flight Controller's Operational Handbook
FCR	Flight Control Room
FCS	Flow Control Subassembly
FCS	Future Combat System
FCT	Flight Control Team
FCV	Flow Control Valve
FD	Flight Director
FDIR	Failure, Detection, Isolation and Recovery
FDR	Facility Design Review
FDS	Fire Detection System
FEM	Finite Element Model
FEM	Federal Information Processing Standards (FIPS) Encryption Model
FEMA	Federal Emergency Management Agency
FET	Flight Execution Team
FEU	Functional Equivalent Unit

Attachment J-05

Acronym	Definition
FFP	Firm Fixed Price
FHS	Forward Heat Shield
FIM	Flight Integration Meeting
FIPS	Federal Information Processing Standards
FLT	Flight
FMC	Flight Management Computer
FMD	Financial Management Division
FMEA	Failure Modes and Effects Analysis
FMECA	Failure Mode, Effects and Criticality Analysis
FMS	Flight Management System
FOC	Full Operational Capability
FOD	Foreign Object Debris
FOR	Flight Operations Review
FPR	Final Proposal Revision
FPRP	Forward Pricing Rate Proposal
FQT	Formal Qualification Test
FRAM	Flight Releasable Attachment Mechanism
FRCB	Flight Rules Control Board
FRD	Flight Requirements Document
FRM	Fault Response Matrix
FRR	Flight Readiness Review
FRS	Failure Response System
FSE	Flight Support Equipment
FSS	Fire Suppression System
FSW	Flight Software
FTA	Fault Tree Analysis
FTAR	Flight Test Article Review
FTINU	Fault Tolerant Inertial Navigation Unit
FTO	Flight Test Objectives
FTRR	Flight Test Readiness Review
FTS	Flight Termination System
FTSR	Final Technical Summary Report
FTT	Full Task Trainer
FTU	Functional Test Unit
FU	Flight Unit
FY	Fiscal Year
FYI	For Your Information

Attachment J-05

Acronym	Definition
GAAP	Generally Accepted Accounting Principles
GAO	Government Accountability Office
GBL	Generation Breakdown List
■■■	■■■
GFE	Government Furnished Equipment
GFP	Government Furnished Property
GFPS	Government Furnished Property and Services
GFS	Government Furnished Services
GFY	Government Fiscal Year
GIDEP	Government-Industry Data Exchange Program
GLOW	Gross Lift-Off Weight
GLS	Ground Launch Sequencer
GMD	Ground-based Midcourse Defense
GN&C	Guidance, Navigation and Control
GOES-R	Geostationary Operational Environmental Satellite
GOTS	Government off the Shelf
GPA	General Performance Assessment
GPS	Global Positioning System
GQA	Government Quality Assurance
GR&C	Ground Rules and Constraints
GRS	Gate Review System
GS	Ground Segment
GSCB	Ground Segment Control Board
GSE	Ground Support Equipment
GSFC	Goddard Space Flight Center
GST	Ground System Test
GSW	Ground Software
GTM	Go-To-Market
GUI	Graphical User Interface
GVAN	Ground Van
H&S	Health and Status
HA	Hazard Analysis
HAR	Hazard Analysis Report
HazOps	Critical and Hazardous Operations
HB	Huntington Beach
HBCU/MI	Historically Black Colleges and Universities / Minority Institutions

Attachment J-05

Acronym	Definition
HBZ	HUB Zone
HCS	Humidity Control Subsystem
HDD	High Definition Data
HDR	High Data Rate
He	Helium
HEA	Human Error Analysis
HFPRVA	High Flow Pressure Regulation Valve Array
HFT	Hot Fire Test
HFTA	Hot Fire Test Article
HIM	Horizontal Integration Meeting
HITL	Human in the Loop
HLA	High Level Architecture
HQ	Headquarters
HR	Hazard Report
HRR	Human Rating Requirement
HSF	Human Space Flight
HSI	Hardware/Software Integration
HSI	Human System Integration
HTV	High Velocity Transfer Vehicle
HUB/HUBZone	Historically Underutilized Business Zone
HW	Hardware
I&CP	Instrumentation and Control Panel
I&O	Integration and Operations
I/O	Input/Output
IAD	Interface Analysis Document
IAD	Integrated Architecture Drawing
IAGP	Installation Accountable Government Property
IAQG	International Aerospace Quality Group
IAW	In Accordance With
ICA	Independent Cost Assessment
ICA	Interface Control Agreement
ICD	Interface Control Document
ICD	Interface Control Drawing
ICDR	Integrated Critical Design Review
ICE	Independent Cost Estimate
ICLS	Incremental Capability Launch Service

Attachment J-05

Acronym	Definition
ICLS	Integrated Contractor Logistics Support
ID	Identification
ID	Instructional Developers
IDA	International Docking Adapter
IDD	Interface Definition Document
IDD	Interface Description Document
IDD	Interface Design Document
IDIQ	Indefinite Delivery Indefinite Quantity
IDR	Initial Design Review
IDWG	Interface Definition Working Group
IEA	Integrated Equipment Assembly
IEC	International Electro-Technical Commission
IFA	In Flight Anomaly
IGA	International Governmental Agreement
IHA	Integrated Hazard Analysis
IID	Incremental and Iterative Development
ILA	Intermediate Level of Assembly
ILC	Initial Launch Capability
ILV	Integrated Launch Vehicle
IMC	ISS Management Center
IMMT	ISS Mission Management Team
IMP	Integrated Master Plan
IMR	Integrated Mission Review
IMS	Integrated Master Schedule
IMS	Inventory Management System
IMU	Inertial Measurement Unit
IMV	Inter- (or Intra-) Module Ventilation
INCOSE	International Council on Systems Engineering
INKSNA	Iran, North Korea, Syria Non-proliferation Act
IOC	Initial Operational Capability
IOS	Instructor Operator Station
IOS	Integrated Operational Scenario
IOZ	Industrial Operations Zone
IP	International Partner
IP/P	International Partners/Participants
IPC	Integrated Propulsion Controller

Attachment J-05

Acronym	Definition
IPCL	Instrument Program and Command List
IPO	Industrial Property Officer
IPR	In Progress Review
IPT	Integrated Product Team
IQDS	Integrated Quality Data System
IR&D	Independent Research and Development
IRD	Interface Requirements Document
IRIG	Inter-Range Instrumentation Group
IRR	Integration Readiness Review
IRR	Internal Rate of Return
ISIS	Integrated Supplier Information System
ISO	International Organization for Standardization
ISP	Individual Subcontracting Plan
ISR	Individual Subcontracting Report
ISR	Integrated Systems Review
ISS	International Space Station
ISSP	International Space Station Program
IST	Integrated Systems Test
ISVT	Integrated System Verification Testing
IT	Information Technology
ITA	Independent Technical Authority
ITAR	International Traffic in Arms Regulations
ITSMP	Information Technology Security Management Plan
ITSP	Information Technology Security Plan
ITSSP	Information Technology System Security Plan
IUA	Instrument Unit Avionics
IV&V	Independent Verification and Validation
IVA	Intravehicular Activity
IVT	Interface Verification Test
IVT	Integrated Verification Test
IWA	Inter-Organizational Work Authorization
IWT	Inter-Organizational Work Transaction
JAXA	Japan Aerospace Exploration Agency
JCB	Joint Control Board
JIVTP	Joint Integration Verification Test Plan
JMICB	Joint Mission Integration Control Board

Attachment J-05

Acronym	Definition
JMM	Joint Management Meeting
JMST	Joint Multi-segment Simulation Training
JOIP	Joint Operations Interface Plan
JON	Job Order Number
JOP	Joint Operations Panel
JPL	Jet Propulsion Laboratory
JPRCB	Joint Program Requirements Control Board
JSA	Job Safety Analysis
JSC	Johnson Space Center
JSL	Joint Station Local Area Network
JSPOC	Joint Space Operations Center
JTT	Joint Test Team
JV	Joint Venture
kg	Kilogram
KOS	Keep-Out Sphere
KPP	Key Performance Parameter
KSC	Kennedy Space Center
L	Likelihood
L&D	Landing and Deceleration
L&R	Landing and Recovery
L/D	Lift-to-Drag Ratio
L/D	Length-to-Diameter
LAA	Low Altitude Abort
LADAR	Laser Detection and Ranging
LAE	Launch Abort Engines
LAN	Local Area Network
LaRC	Langley Research Center
LAS	Launch Abort System
LB	Large Business
LCC	Launch Commit Criteria
LCC	Launch Control Center
LCC	Life Cycle Cost
LCD	Launch Configuration Drawing
LCM	Learning Content Management
LCROSS	Lunar Crater Observation and Sensing Satellite
LD	Launch Director

Attachment J-05

Acronym	Definition
LDB	Loads Data Book
LDCM	Landsat Data Continuity Mission
LDD	Loss, Damage, Destruction
LDR	Low Data Rate
LEO	Low Earth Orbit
LIDAR	Light Detection and Ranging
LIF	Load Image File
Li-ion	Lithium-ion
LLC	Limited Liability Company
LMS	Learning Management System
LO2	Liquid Oxygen
LOC	Loss of Crew
LOM	Loss of Mission
LOx	Liquid Oxygen
LPRR	Launch Processing Readiness Review
LRO	Lunar Reconnaissance Orbiter
LRS	Landing and Recovery System
LRU	Line Replaceable Unit
LS	Launch Services
LS	Launch Segment
LSA	Launch Site Accommodations
LSI	Launch Segment Integration
LSIM	Launch System Integration Manager
LSP	Launch Services Program
LSS	Launch Support Specification
LT	Launch Time
LTA	Launch to Activation
LV	Launch Vehicle
LVA	Launch Vehicle Adapter
LVCC	Launch Vehicle Control Center
LVDS	Low Voltage Differential Signaling
LVI	Launch Vehicle Integration
LVOS	Launch Vehicle on Stand
LVP	Launch Vehicle Provider
LWIR	Long Wave Infrared
LxC	Likelihood (multiplied by) Consequence

Acronym	Definition
M&FS	Mass and Frequency Simulator
M&P	Materials and Processes
MBD	Model-Based Development
MBE	Model-Based Engineering
MBI	Model-Based Instruction
MBOM	Manufacturing Bill of Material
MCA	Mission Complement Analysis
MCAS	Marine Corps Air Station
MCC	Mission Control Center
MCC21	21st Century Mission Control Center
MCC-H	Mission Control Center Houston
MCCS	Mission Control Center Systems
MCO	Mission Contract Objectives
MCR	Mission Certification Review
MDCT	Market Driven Target Cost
MDL	Mission Data Load
MDR	Mission Data Reduction
MECO	Main Engine Cut-off
MEDEVAC	Medical Evacuation
MEL	Master Equipment List
MEP	Manufacturing Extension Partnership
MEP	Mission Execution Plan
MER	Mission Execution Readiness
MER	Mission Evaluation Room
MES	Manufacturing Execution System
MET	Management Emphasis Tracking
MET	Mission Execution Team
MGA	Mass Growth Allowance
MGSE	Mechanical Ground Support Equipment
MI	Minority Institution
MI&O	Mission Integration and Operations
MIL-STD	Military Standard
MIOCB	Mission Integration and Operations Control Board
MIOMP	Mission Integration and Operations Management Plan
MIP	Mandatory Inspection Point
MIPL	Mission Integration Project Lead

Attachment J-05

Acronym	Definition
MIR	Mission Integration Review
MIR	Most Important Requirement
MIS	Management Information System
MIT	Massachusetts Institute of Technology
MIUL	Material Identification Usage List
MLE	Middeck Locker Equivalent
MLI	Multi-layer Insulation
MLP	Mobile Launch Platform
MMH	Monomethyl Hydrazine
MMIOC	Multi-Mission Integration and Operations Contract
MMOD	Micro-Meteoroid On-orbit Debris
MMRTG	Multi-Mission Radioisotope Thermal Generator
MMT	Mission Management Team
MOC	Morrell Operations Center
MOD	Mission Operations Directorate
MODEAR	Mission Operations Directorate Enterprise Architecture Repository
MON	Mixed Oxides of Nitrogen
MOS	Measure of Suitability
MOS	Mission Operations Directorate (MOD) Operations Services
MOWG	Mission Operations Working Group
MP	Manufacturing Plan
MPA	Manufacturing Process Assessment
MPA	Mission Planning and Analysis
MPAR	Mission Planning and Analysis Report
MPCP	Mishap Preparedness and Contingency Plan
MPCV	Multi Purpose Crew Vehicle
MPDB	Mass Properties Data Base
MPL	Maximum Possible Loss
MPLM	Multi-Purpose Logistics Module
MPSR	Mass Properties Status Report
MRAD	Mission Resource Allocation Document
MRAP	Mine-Resistant, Ambush Protected
MRB	Material Review Board
MRD	Mission Requirements Document
MRL	Material Requirements List
MRL	Manufacturing Readiness Level

Attachment J-05

Acronym	Definition
MRO	Mars Reconnaissance Orbiter
MRO	Medical Review Officer
MRP	Manufacturing Resource Planning
MRP	Material Requirements Planning
MRP	Milestone Review Plan
MRR	Mission Requirements Review
MS	Microsoft
MS	Mass Simulator
msec	Millisecond
MSFC	Marshall Space Flight Center
MSL	Mars Science Laboratory
MSP	Master Subcontracting Plan
MSPSP	Missile System Pre-launch Safety Package
MSR	Mission Support Room
MST	Mission Sequence Test
MSTP	Mission Specific Training Plan
MUA	Material Usage Agreement
MUOS	Mobile User Objective System
MVP	Master Verification Plan
N&SS	Network and Space Systems
N/A or NA	Not Applicable
NAFCOM	NASA/Air Force Cost Model
NAICS	North American Industry Classification System
NASA	National Aeronautics and Space Administration
NASA LaRC	NASA Langley Research Center
NASTRAN	NASA Stress Analysis Program
NAWBO	National Association of Women Business Owners
NBL	Neutral Buoyancy Laboratory
NCAIED	National Center for American Indian Enterprise Development
NCM	Nonconformance Management
NCR	Noncompliance Report
NDA	Non-Disclosure Agreement
NDE	Non-Destructive Evaluation
NDS	NASA Docking System
NDSB1	NASA Docking System Block 1
NDSP	NASA Docking System Program

Attachment J-05

Acronym	Definition
NDT	Non-Destructive Test
NEOM	Nominal End of Mission
NEPA	National Environmental Policy Act
NF	NASA Form
NFS	NASA Federal Acquisition Regulations (FAR) Supplement
NFTE	Non-Real-Time Flight Software Test Environment
NIED	Natural and Induced Environments Document
NISN	NASA Integrated Services Network
NIT	NASA Insight Team
NLS	NASA Launch Services
NLT	No Later Than
nm	Nautical Mile
NMC	NASA Management Center
NMSDC	National Minority Supplier Development Council
NMT	Not More Than
NPR	NASA Procedural Requirement
NPV	Net Present Value
NR	Not Required
NRO	National Reconnaissance Office
NROL	National Reconnaissance Office Launch
NSF	National Science Foundation
NSI	National Standard Initiator
NSS	National Security Space
NSTS	National Space Transportation System
NTO	Nitrogen Tetroxide
NWP	Networks Procurement
O&M	Operations and Maintenance
O&SHA	Operations and Support Hazard Analysis
OBT	Onboard Trainer
OCAD	Operational Control Agreement Database
OCI	Organizational Conflict of Interest
ODC	Other Direct Cost
ODF	Operations Data File
ODFCB	Operational Data File Control Board
OEM	Original Equipment Manufacturer
OFM	Onboard Flight Manager
OFT	Orbital Flight Test

Attachment J-05

Acronym	Definition
OFTRR	Orbital Flight Test Readiness Review
OIG	Office of Internal Governance
OIP	Operational Interface Procedure
OIS	Operational Intercom System
OJT	On-the-Job Training
OLV	Orbital Launch Vehicle
OMAC	Orbital Maneuvering and Attitude Control
OMB	Office of Management and Budget
OML	Outer Mold Line
OMRS	Operations Maintenance Requirements Specifications
OMRSD	Operations Maintenance Requirements and Specifications Document
OMS	Orbital Maneuvering System
OPF	Orbiter Processing Facility
OPF3	Orbiter Processing Facility 3
OPT	Organizational Process Training
OR	Operating Rhythm
ORBITS	Online Rocket Build Inspection and Test System
ORCA	Online Representations and Certifications Application
ORI	Operational Readiness Inspection
ORR	Operational Readiness Review
ORSAT	Object Re-entry Survival Analysis Tool
ORT	Operational Readiness Test
ORU	Orbital Replacement Unit
OS	Operating System
OSA	Open Systems Architecture
OSC	Orbital Space Complex
OSHA	Occupational Safety and Health Administration
██████	██
OSMci	Operational and Supplier Management Common Image
OV	Orbital Vehicle
OVS	Operational Voice System
P&GP	Production and Ground Processing
P&GS	Production and Ground Systems
P2C2	Post-Production Crew Checklist
P2SR	Phase II Safety Review

Attachment J-05

Acronym	Definition
P3SR	Phase III Safety Review
PA	Pad Abort
PA	Product Audit
PA	Purchasing Agent
PAF	Pad Abort Facility
PAO	Public Affairs Office
PAT	Pad Abort Test
PATRAN	A finite element analysis software tool
PBA	Probabilistic Safety Analysis
PBOM	Priced Bill of Material
PBS	Product Breakdown Structure
PCA	Physical Configuration Audit
PCA	Power Controller Assembly
PCB	Program Control Board
PCC	Processing Control Center
PCDTV	Parachute Compartment Drop Test Vehicle
PCM	Post Certification Mission
PCS	Portable Computer System
PCS	Pressure Control Subsystem
PCS	Property Control System
PCSA	Property Control System Analysis
PCU	Power Control Unit
PCU	Power Converter Unit
PDF	Portable Document Format
PDM	Product Data Management
PDR	Preliminary Design Review
PE	Program Event
PEG	Powered Explicit Guidance
PEL	Power Equipment List
PEM	Product Exchange Matrix
PEP	Program Execution Plan
PERA	Public Entry Risk Assessment
PFA	Post-Flight Assessment
PFAR	Post-Flight Assessment Report
PFIP	Pre-Flight Imagery Plan
PFR	Post Flight Review

Acronym	Definition
PSFP	Private Space Flight Participants
PGS	Production and Ground Systems
PGUID	Pointing Guidance
PHA	Preliminary Hazard Analysis
PHL	Preliminary Hazard List
PI	Physical Inventory
PI	Program Instruction
PI	Program Integration
PIA	Proprietary Information Agreement
PICB	Payload Integration Control Board
PIO	Provisioning Item Order
PIRR	Program Introduction Readiness Review
PISCES	Platform Independent Software Component for the Exploration of Space
PIT	Partner Integration Team
PIT	Program Integration Team
PLAR	Post-Launch Assessment Review
PLCU	Payload DC Converter Unit
PLM	Product Lifecycle Management
PLS	Primary Landing Site
PM	Program Manager
PM	Project/Program Management
PM	Property Management
PM	Pump Module
PMA2	Pressurized Mating Adapter 2
PMBP	Program Management Best Practices
PMC	Project Management Contractor
PMP	Program/Project Management Plan
PMR	Program Management Review
PO	Purchase Order
POC	Point of Contact
POD	Point of Departure
PQR	Post Qualification Review
PR	Problem Report
PRA	Probabilistic Risk Assessment
PRO	Professional
PRO	Procedure

Attachment J-05

Acronym	Definition
PRR	Production Readiness Review
PSA	Probabilistic Safety Analysis
PSA	Probabilistic Safety Assessment
psia	Pounds per Square Inch Absolute
PSR	Phase Safety Review
PSR	Program Status Review
PSS	Platform Services System
PTA	Parachute Test Article
PTAC	Procurement Technical Assistance Center
PTCS	Passive Thermal Control System
PTF	Plan-Train-Fly
PTT	Part Task Trainer
PVAN	Phase Vocoder Analysis
PWP	PCM Work Plan
PWS	Performance Work Statement
QA	Quality Assurance
QD	Quick Disconnect
QE	Quality Engineering
QFT	Qualification Flight Test
QMS	Quality Management System
QPA	Quality Process Assessment
QPR	Quarterly Program Review
QRR	Quality Requirement Review
QSP	Quality Surveillance Plan
QSR	Quality Source Representative
QT	Qualification Test
QTP	Qualification Test Procedure
QTV	Qualification Test Vehicle
QVT	Qualification Verification Test
R&D	Research and Development
R&M	Reliability and Maintainability
R&O	Risk and Opportunity
R&U	Redistribution and Utilization
R/I	Receipt and Issue
RAA	Responsibility, Authority, and Accountability
RAIU	Remote Analog Interface Unit

Attachment J-05

Acronym	Definition
RAM	Requirements Allocation Matrix
RAM	Resource Allocation Matrix
RBA	Risk-Based Analysis
RBAC	Role Based Access Control
RBSP	Radiation Belt Storm Probes
RCC	Reinforced Carbon-Carbon
RCC	Rescue Coordination Center
RCS	Reaction Control System
RCV	Return Cargo Vehicle
REBR	Re-entry Breakup Recorder
RF	Radio Frequency
RFI	Request for Information
RFP	Request for Proposal
RFQ	Request for Quote
RHC	Rotational Hand Controller
RI	Receive and Inspection
RID	Review Item Discrepancy
RID	Review Item Disposition
RIMS	Records Identification Management System
RIP	Requirements Integration Panel
RLV	Reusable Launch Vehicle
RM	Requirements Management
RMP	Risk Management Plan
ROM	Rough Order of Magnitude
RoS	Relief of Stewardship
RP-1	Rocket Propellant-1 Kerosene
RPODU	Rendezvous, Proximity Operations, Docking and Undocking
RQM	Requirement Quality Metric
RS	Range Safety
RTC	Real Time Command
RTDA	Real Time Data Analysis
RTF	Return to Flight
S&H	Safety and Health
S&MA	Safety and Mission Assurance
S/W	Software

Attachment J-05

Acronym	Definition
S2S	Space-to-Space
SA	Significant Accomplishment
SA	Solar Array
SAA	Space Act Agreement
SAC	Solar Array Controller
SAE	Society of Automotive Engineers
SAIL	Shuttle Avionics Integration Laboratory
SAM	System for Award Management
SAP	Systems, Application and Products in Data Processing
SAR	Search and Rescue
SAR	System Acceptance Review
SARJ	Solar Alpha Rotary Joint
SARR	Spacecraft Assembly Readiness Review
SARSAT	Search and Rescue Satellite Aided Tracking
SAS	Special Aerospace Services LLC
SAT	System Acceptance Test
SB	Small Business
SBA	Small Business Administration
SBC	Single Board Computer
SBDC	Small Business Development Center
SBDS	Small Business Dynamic Search
SBIR	Small Business Innovation Research
SBLO	Small Business Liaison Officer
SC	Spacecraft
SCA	Service Contract Act
SCA	Statistical Composite Average
SCaN	Space Communications and Navigation
SCAPE	Self-Contained Atmospheric Protective Ensemble
SCCB	Software Configuration Control Board
SCCM	Systems Center Configuration Management
SCE	Senior Chief Engineer
SCLS	Space Coast Launch Services
SCM	Software Configuration Management
SCM	Specification Compliance Matrix
SCP	Supplier Change Proposal
SCTF	Sonny Carter Training Facility

Attachment J-05

Acronym	Definition
SDB	Small Disadvantaged Business
SDD	System Design and Development
SDD	System Development and Demonstration
SDN	Supplier Diversity Network
SDO	Solar Dynamics Observatory
SDP	Safety Data Package
SDP	Software Development Plan
SDP	Supplier Diversity Program
SDR	System Definition Review
SDR	System Design Review
SDRL	Supplier Data Requirements List
SDVET	Small Disadvantaged Veteran-Owned
SDVOSB	Service-Disabled Veteran-Owned Small Business
SE	Space Exploration
SE	Support Equipment
SE	Systems Engineering
SE&I	Systems Engineering and Integration
SEB	Source Evaluation Board
SEC	Securities and Exchange Commission
SEER	System Evaluations and Estimation of Resources
SEIT	Systems Engineering Integration and Test
SEM	Software Estimation Model
SEMO	Supply and Equipment Management Officer
SEMP	Systems Engineering Management Plan
SEPORT	Solicitation Enterprise PRO-70 Online Roster Tool
SER	System Engineering Review
SETA	Systems Engineering and Technical Analysis
SFM	Shop Floor Management
SFOC	Space Flight Operations Contract
SFR	Spacecraft Flow Review
SGLT	Space-Ground Link Terminal
SHA	Safety Hazard Analysis
SHCS	Side Hatch Counterbalance Strut
SHEA	Safety, Health and Environmental Affairs
SHO	Space-to-Ground Handover
SIA	Stowage Interface Agreement

Attachment J-05

Acronym	Definition
SIGI	Space Integrated GPS and Inertial Navigation System
SIL	Systems Integration Laboratory
SIM	Simulation
SINC	Supplier Insight Control
SIOP	Systems Integration and Operations Panel
SIR	System Integration Review
SIT	Spacecraft Insertion Team
SLAN	Spacecraft Local Area Network
SLC-41	Space Launch Complex 41
SLS	Space Launch System
SM	Service Module
SM	Supplier Management
SM&P	Supplier Management and Procurement
SMA	Safety and Mission Assurance
SMC	System Management Computer
SME	Subject Matter Expert
SMG	Spaceflight Meteorological Group
SMHFT	Service Module Hot Fire Test
SMP	Supplier Management Plan
SMS	Systems Management System
SMT	Supplier Management Team
SNC	Sierra Nevada Corporation
SOC	Security Operations Center
SOO	Statement of Objectives
SOOT	Significantly Out of Tolerance
SOP	Standard Operating Procedure
SORR	Stage Operational Readiness Review
SOW	Statement of Work
SPA	Supporting Property Administrator
SPI	Schedule Performance Index
SPM	Supplier Program Manager
SPMR	Supplier Program Management Review
SPOC	Space Program Operations Contract
SPR	Supplier Performance Review
SPRT	Subsystem Problem Resolution Team
SQ	Supplier Quality

Attachment J-05

Acronym	Definition
SQR	Supplier Quality Representative
SQS	Supplier Quality Surveillance
SR	Service Request
SR&QA	Safety, Reliability and Quality Assurance; equal to S&MA, SRQ&MA
SR&QE	Safety, Reliability and Quality Engineering
SRA	Schedule Risk Analysis
SRB	Software Review Board
SRB	Solid Rocket Booster
SRP	Safety Review Panel
SRQ&MA	Safety, Reliability, Quality and Mission Assurance; equal to S&MA, SR&QA
SRR	System Requirements Review
SRS	Software Requirement Specification
SRT	System Readiness Test
SRVR	Subcontract Requirements Validation Review
SSHA	Subsystem Hazard Analysis
SSORR	Spacecraft Servicing Operational Readiness Review
SSOW	Supplier Statement of Work
SSP	Software Safety Plan
SSP	Space Station Program
SSPCB	Space Station Program Change Board
SSPCB	Space Station Program Control Board
SSPCM	Solid State Power Control Module
SSQ	Space Station Quality
SSR	Summary Subcontractor Report
SSTF	Space Station Training Facility
STA	Structural Test Article
STCB	Spaceflight Training Control Board
STD	Standard
STEM	Science, Technology, Engineering and Mathematics
STEP	Science, Technology, Engineering and Production
STG	Space-to-Ground
STP	Short Term Plan
STR	Structure
STS	Space Transportation System
STS	Space-to-Space

Attachment J-05

Acronym	Definition
STTR	Small Business Technology Transfer
SUM	Software User Manual
SUS	System Usability Scale
SVMF	Space Vehicle Mockup Facility
SVTL	Safety Verification Tracking Log
SW	Software
SWLPV	Split, Weld-Less Pressure Vessel
SWO	Small Woman-Owned
T&C	Terms and Conditions
T&M	Time and Materials
T&V	Test and Verification
T&VCP	Test and Verification Control Panel
T&VWG	Test and Verification Working Group
TA	Test Article
TAYO	Test-As-You-Operate
TBD	To Be Determined
TBP	To Be Proposed
TBR	To Be Resolved
TC	Teamcenter
TCB	Technical Control Board
TCD	Test Control Drawing
TCDT	Terminal Countdown Demonstration Test
TcMfg	Teamcenter Manufacturing
TCS	Thermal Control System
TcSE	Teamcenter Systems Engineering
TCV	Total Contract Value
TDAD	Trailing Deployable Aerodynamic Decelerator
TDDP	Trajectory Design Data Pack
TDP	Trajectory Data Pack
TDR	Test Design Review
TDRS	Tracking and Data Relay Satellite
TDRS-K	Tracking and Data Relay Satellite
TDRSS	Tracking and Data Relay Satellite System
TDS	Task Description Sheet
TE	Test Equipment
TECS	Thermal Environment Control System
TF	Technical Fellows

Acronym	Definition
TGUID	Translation Guidance
THAAD	Terminal High Altitude Area Defense
THC	Translational Hand Controller
TI	Test Instruments
TICB	Test Infrastructure Control Board
TICB	Transportation Integration Control Board
TIM	Technical Interchange Meeting
TIO	Transportation Integration Office
TIPQA	TIP Technologies, Inc Quality Assurance
TLM	Telemetry
TLYF	Test-Like-You-Fly
TM	Telemetry
TNA	Training Needs Analysis
TO	Task Order
TPM	Technical Performance Measure
TPS	Thermal Protection System
TRB	Technical Review Board
TRL	Technology Readiness Level
TRR	Test Readiness Review
TS	Training System
TS21	21st Century Training System
TSGS	Training Systems and Government Services
TSS	Training Systems and Services
TSWG	Training System Working Group
TV	Television
TVC	Thrust Vector Control
TVCB	Test and Verification Control Board
U.S., US	United States
UAS	User Application System
UAT	User Acceptance Test
UAV	Unmanned Aerial Vehicle
UCS	Universal Camera Site
UDA	Umbilical Deployment Actuator
UHF	Ultra High Frequency
UID	Unique Identification

Attachment J-05

Acronym	Definition
UOP	Utility Outlet Panel
URL	Uniform Resource Locator
US	Upper Stage
USA	United Space Alliance
USAF	United States Air Force
USC	United States Code
USG	United States Government
USOS	United States On-orbit Segment
USP	Upper Stage Program
USSTRATCOM	United States Strategic Command
UTAS	United Technologies Aerospace Systems
UTC	Coordinated Universal Time
V&V	Verification and Validation
V&VP	Verification and Validation Plan
VA	Verification Activity
VAC	Verification Analysis Cycle
VAL	Validated
VAR	Vehicle Assessment Review
VBR	Vehicle Baseline Review
VCN	Verification Closure Notice
VCRI	Verification Cross Reference Index
VCRM	Verification Cross Reference Matrix
■■■	■■■
VESTA	Vision-based Electro-optical Sensor Tracking Assembly
■■■	■■■
VHF	Very High Frequency
VIDD	Vehicle Interface Definition Document
VIF	Vertical Integration Facility
VIP	VESTA Image Processor
VIS	Vision
VIT	Vehicle Integration Test
VITA	VMEbus International Trade Association
VITT	Vehicle Integration Test Team
VLA	Verification Loads Analysis
VME	Virtual Memory Extension
VOS	Vehicle on Stand

Acronym	Definition
VOSB	Veteran Owned Small Business
VP	Vice President
VPP	Voluntary Protection Program
VR	Verification Requirement
VS	Verification Strategy
VSE	Vehicle Systems Engineer
VSM	Value Stream Mapping
VTL	Verification Tracking Log
VV	Visiting Vehicle
VVDOR	Visiting Vehicle Demonstration Objectives Report
VVIM	Visiting Vehicle Integration Manager
VVV	Visiting Vehicle Verification
WAN	Wide-Area Network
WBENC	Women's Business Enterprise National Council
WBS	Work Breakdown Structure
WC	Work Center
WDR	Wet Dress Rehearsal
■	■
WOSB	Woman-Owned Small Business
WP	Work Plan
WR	White Room
WRDT	Water Recovery Development Test
■	■
■	■
■	■
WTT	Wind Tunnel Test
XTA	Expansion Tube Assembly
■	■

Attachment J-06
Personal Identity Verification (PIV) Card Issuance Procedure

Attachment J-06

PERSONAL IDENTITY VERIFICATION (PIV)

PIV Card Issuance Procedures in accordance with FAR clause 52.204-9, *Personal Identity Verification of Contractor Personnel*

FIPS 201 Appendix A, *PIV Process*, graphically displays the following procedure for the issuance of a PIV credential.

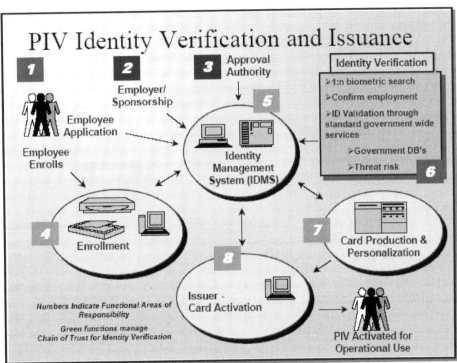

Figure A-1, FIPS 201, Appendix A, PIV Identity Verification and Issuance

The following steps describe the procedures for the NASA Personal Identity Verification Card Issuance (PCI) of a PIV credential:

Step 1:
The Contractor's Corporate Security Officer (CSO), Program Manager (PM), or Facility Security Officer (FSO) submits a formal letter that provides a list of contract employees (applicant) names requesting access to the NASA Contracting Officer's Representative (COR). In the case of a foreign national applicant, approval through the NASA Foreign National Management System (NFNMS) must be obtained for the visit or assignment before any processing for a PIV credential can take place. Further, if the foreign national is not under a contract where a COR has been officially designated, the foreign national will provide the information directly to their visit/assignment host, and the host sponsor will fulfill the duties of the COR mentioned herein. In each case, the letter shall provide notification of the contract or foreign national employee's (hereafter the "applicant") full name (first, middle and last), social security number (SSN) or NASA Foreign National Management System Visitor Number if the foreign national does not

Attachment J-06

have a SSN, and date of birth. If the contract employee has a current satisfactorily completed National Agency Check with Inquiries (NACI) or an equivalent or higher degree of background investigation, the letter shall indicate the type of investigation, the agency completing the investigation, and date the investigation was completed. Further, the letter shall also acknowledge that contract employees may be denied access to NASA information or information systems based on an unsatisfactory background investigation/adjudication.

After reviewing the letter for completeness the COR/host must forward the letter to the Center Chief of Security (CCS). The CCS shall review the OPM databases (e.g., Defense Clearance Investigations Index [DCII], PIP, et al.), and take appropriate steps to validate the applicant's investigation status. Requirements for a NACI or other investigation shall be initiated only if necessary.

Applicants who do not currently possess the required level of background investigation shall be directed to the Electronic Questionnaires for Investigations Processing (e-QIP) web site to complete the necessary background investigation forms online. The CCS shall provide to the COR/host information and instructions on how to access the e-QIP for each contract or foreign national employee requiring access.

Step 2:
Upon acceptance of the letter/background information, the applicant will be advised that in order to complete the investigative process, he or she must appear in-person before the authorized PIV registrar and submit two forms of identity source documents in original form. The identity source documents must come from the list of acceptable documents included in Form I-9, *Employment Eligibility Verification*, one which must be a Federal[1] or State issued picture identification. Fingerprints will be taken at this time. The applicant must appear **no later than** the entry on duty date.

When the applicant appears, the registrar will electronically scan the submitted documents; any document that appears invalid will be rejected by the registrar. The registrar will capture electronically both a facial image and fingerprints of the applicant. The information submitted by the applicant will be used to create or update the applicant identity record in the Identity Management System (IDMS).

Step 3:
Upon the applicant's completion of the investigative document, the CCS reviews the information, and resolves discrepancies with the applicant as necessary. When the applicant has appeared in person and completed fingerprints, the package is electronically submitted to initiate the NACI. The CCS includes a request for feedback on the NAC portion of the NACI at the time the request is submitted.

---

[1] A non-PIV government identification badge, including the NASA Photo Identification Badge, <u>MAY NOT BE USED</u> for the original issuance of a PIV vetted credential

Attachment J-06

Step 4:
Prior to authorizing physical access of a contractor employee to a federally-controlled facility or access to a Federal information system, the CCS will ensure that a check has been performed with the National Crime Information Center (NCIC) and Interstate Identification Index. In the case of a foreign national, a national check of the Bureau of Immigration and Customs Enforcement (BICE) database will be performed for each applicant. If this process yields negative information, the CCS will immediately notify the COR/host of the determination regarding access made by the CCS.

Step 5:
Upon receipt of the completed NAC, the CCS will update IDMS from the NAC portion of the NACI and indicate the result of the suitability determination. If an unsatisfactory suitability determination is rendered, the COR will advise the contractor that the employee is being denied physical access to all federally-controlled facilities and Federal information systems.

Based on a favorable NAC and NCIC/III or BICE check, the CCS will authorize the issuance of a PIV federal credential in the Physical Access Control System (PACS) database. The CCS, based on information provided by the COR/host, will determine what physical access the applicant should be granted once the PIV issues the credential.

Step 6:
Using the information provided by the applicant during his or her in-person appearance, the PIV card production facility creates and instantiates the approved PIV card for the applicant with an activation date commensurate with the applicant's start date.

Step 7:
The applicant proceeds to the credential issuance facility to begin processing for receipt of his/her federal credential.

The applicant provides to the credential issuing operator proof of identity with documentation that meets the requirements of FIPS 201 (*Department of Homeland Security (DHS) Employment Eligibility Verification (Form I-9)*) documents. These documents **must** be the same documents submitted for registration.

The credential issuing operator will verify that the facial image, and optionally reference finger print, matches the enrollment data used to produce the card. Upon verification of identity, the operator will locate the employee's record in the PACS database, and modify the record to indicate the PIV card has been issued. The applicant will select a personal identification number (PIN) for use with his or her new PIV card. Although root data is inaccessible to the operator, certain fields (hair color, eye color, et al.) may be modified to more accurately record the employee's information.

Attachment J-06

The applicant proceeds to a kiosk or other workstation to complete activation of the PIV card using the initial PIN entered at card issuance.

ALTERNATIVE FOR APPLICANTS WHO DO NOT HAVE A COMPLETED AND ADJUDICATED NAC AT THE TIME OF ENTRANCE ON DUTY

Steps 1 through 4 shall be accomplished for all applicants in accordance with the process described above. If the applicant is unable to appear in person until the time of entry on duty, or does not, for any other reason, have a completed and adjudicated NAC portion of the NACI at the time of entrance on duty, the following interim procedures shall apply:

1. If the documents required to submit the NACI have not been completed prior to entrance on duty (EOD), the applicant will be instructed to complete all remaining requirements for submission of the investigation request. This includes presentation of I-9, *Employment Eligibility Verification*, documents and completion of fingerprints, if not already accomplished. If the applicant fails to complete these activities as prescribed in NPR 1600.4, *Identity and Credential Management*, it may be considered as failure to meet the conditions required for physical access to a federally-controlled facility or access to a Federal information system, and result in denial of such access.

2. Based on favorable results of the NCIC, the applicant shall be issued a temporary NASA identification card for a period not-to-exceed six months. If at the end of the six (6) month period the NAC results have not been returned, the agency will at that time make a determination if an additional extension will be granted for the temporary identification card.

3. Upon return of the completed NAC, the process will continue from Step 5.

Modification 001

H.3 NFS 1852.223-72 SAFETY AND HEALTH (SHORT FORM). (APR 2002)

(a) Safety is the freedom from those conditions that can cause death, injury, occupational illness; damage to or loss of equipment or property, or damage to the environment. NASA's safety priority is to protect: (1) the public, (2) astronauts and pilots, (3) the NASA workforce (including Contractor employees working on NASA contracts), and (4) high-value equipment and property.

(b) The Contractor shall take all reasonable safety and occupational health measures consistent with standard industry practice in performing this contract. The Contractor shall comply with all Federal, State, and local laws applicable to safety and occupational health and with the safety and occupational health standards, specifications, reporting requirements, and any other relevant requirements of this contract.

(c) The Contractor shall take, or cause to be taken, any other safety, and occupational health measures the Contracting Officer may reasonably direct. To the extent that the Contractor may be entitled to an equitable adjustment for those measures under the terms and conditions of this contract, the equitable adjustment shall be determined pursuant to the procedures of the Changes clause of this contract; provided, that no adjustment shall be made under this Safety and Health clause for any change for which an equitable adjustment is expressly provided under any other clause of the contract.

(d) The Contracting Officer may notify the Contractor in writing of any noncompliance with this clause and specify corrective actions to be taken. In situations where the Contracting Officer becomes aware of noncompliance that may pose a serious or imminent danger to safety and health of the public, astronauts and pilots, the NASA workforce (including Contractor employees working on NASA contracts), or high value mission critical equipment or property, the Contracting Officer shall notify the Contractor orally, with written confirmation. The Contractor shall promptly take and report any necessary corrective action. The Government may pursue appropriate remedies in the event the Contractor fails to promptly take the necessary corrective action.

(e) The Contractor (or subcontractor or supplier) shall insert the substance of this clause, including this paragraph (e) and any applicable Schedule provisions, with appropriate changes of designations of the parties, in subcontracts of every tier that exceed the micro-purchase threshold.

(End of Clause)

H.4 NFS 1852.232-77 LIMITATION OF FUNDS (FIXED- PRICE CONTRACT). (MAR 1989)

(a) Of the total price of all CLIN items identified in Section B, the sum of $320,075,675 is presently available for payment and allotted to this contract. It is anticipated that from time to time additional funds will be allocated to the contract as required by the payment schedules in Attachment J-03, Appendix A, *Milestone Acceptance Criteria and Payment Schedule* and task

Modification 001

orders awarded under CLIN 002 and 003 (see table B.4.2 and B.5.2 respectively) until the total price of said items is allotted.

(b) The Contractor agrees to perform or have performed work on the items specified in paragraph (a) of this clause up to the point at which, if this contract is terminated pursuant to the Termination for Convenience of the Government clause of this contract, the total amount payable by the Government (including amounts payable for subcontracts and settlement costs) pursuant to paragraphs (f) and (g) of that clause would, in the exercise of reasonable judgment by the Contractor, approximate the total amount at the time allotted to the contract. The Contractor is not obligated to continue performance of the work beyond that point. The Government is not obligated in any event to pay or reimburse the Contractor more than the amount from time to time allotted to the contract, anything to the contrary in the Termination for Convenience of the Government clause notwithstanding.

(c) (1) It is contemplated that funds presently allotted to this contract will cover the work to be performed until December 13, 2014.

(2) If funds allotted are considered by the Contractor to be inadequate to cover the work to be performed until that date, or an agreed date substituted for it, the Contractor shall notify the Contracting Officer in writing when within the next 60 days the work will reach a point at which, if the contract is terminated pursuant to the Termination for Convenience of the Government clause of this contract, the total amount payable by the Government (including amounts payable for subcontracts and settlement costs) pursuant to paragraphs (f) and (g) of that clause will approximate 75 percent of the total amount then allotted to the contract.

(3) (i) The notice shall state the estimate when the point referred to in paragraph (c) (2) of this clause will be reached and the estimated amount of additional funds required to continue performance to the date specified in paragraph (c) (1) of this clause, or an agreed date substituted for it.

(ii) The Contractor shall, 60 days in advance of the date specified in paragraph (c) (1) of this clause, or an agreed date substituted for it, advise the Contracting Officer in writing as to the estimated amount of additional funds required for the timely performance of the contract for a further period as may be specified in the contract or otherwise agreed to by the parties.

(4) If, after the notification referred to in paragraph (c) (3) (ii) of this clause, additional funds are not allotted by the date specified in paragraph (c) (1) of this clause, or an agreed date substituted for it, the Contracting Officer shall, upon the Contractor's written request, terminate this contract on that date or on the date set forth in the request, whichever is later, pursuant to the Termination for Convenience of the Government clause.

(d) When additional funds are allotted from time to time for continued performance of the work under this contract, the parties shall agree on the applicable period of contract performance to be covered by these funds. The provisions of paragraphs (b) and (c) of this clause shall apply to

Modification 02   Attachment J-03, Appendix A

Certification Baseline Review (CBR) Interim Milestone	Planned Start Date and Completion Date (mo/yr):	Amount:
(As proposed, interim NASA milestone in support of DCR) DCR Interim Milestone 01A.1	Sep - Nov/2014 No Final RID Board	■

Objective:

At a NASA and Contractor co-chaired Certification Baseline Review (CBR) completed within ninety (90) days of contract start, the Contractor shall:

a) Identify the Baseline requirements, including the allocation to the Elements and Subsystems of the CTS, incorporating the results of NASA's guidance provided under Certification Products Contract (CPC) (if applicable), which meet NASA's requirements defined in CCT-REQ-1130, ISS Crew Transportation and Services Requirements Document and SSP 50808, International Space Station (ISS) to Commercial Orbital Transportation Services (COTS) Interface Requirements Document.

b) Identify the current Crew Transportation System (CTS) design baseline.

c) Document management plans and products incorporating the results of NASA's disposition provided under Certification Products Contract (CPC) (if applicable), to meet requirements in the CCT-PLN-1120, Crew Transportation Technical Management Processes.

d) Define the plan and schedule to complete Design, Development, Test, and Evaluation (DDTE) and certification for the CTS design, production, and operations.

e) Define top safety, technical, cost and schedule risks based on most current CTS design. (Att J-03 PWS Apx A)

Indicators of Milestone Readiness: (Att J-03 PWS Apx A)	Data / DRDs to be provided:	Delivery of Data/DRDs (mo/yr)
The Contractor has completed the following and provided to NASA: a) The requirements, including the allocation to the Elements and Subsystems of the CTS, incorporating the results of NASA's disposition under CPC (if applicable) which meet NASA's requirements defined in CCT-REQ-1130 and SSP 50808 including but not limited to:	Data to be transmitted via DRD 102	Sep/2014

Modification 02 — Attachment J-03, Appendix A

Certification Baseline Review (CBR) Interim Milestone (As proposed, interim NASA milestone in support of DCR) DCR Interim Milestone 01A.1	Planned Start Date and Completion Date (mo/yr): Sep - Nov/2014 No Final RID Board	Amount:
1) Documentation of previously approved variances and alternate standards incorporated or tailored in requirements.	Data to be transmitted via DRD 102	Sep/2014
2) Provide joint ISS integration products (Interface Control Documents (ICDs), Joint Integrated Verification Test Plan (JiVTP), Bi-lateral Data Exchange Agreement List and Schedule (BDEALS), Bi-lateral Hardware Software Exchange Agreement List and Schedule (BHSEALS)) identified in SSP 50964, Visiting Vehicle ISS Integration Plan..	Data to be transmitted via DRD 102	Sep/2014
b) Documentation of the current CTS design baseline as defined in DRD 102 Certification Baseline Review (CBR) Data Package.	Data to be transmitted via DRD 102	Sep/2014
c) The management plans and products as defined in DRD 102 Certification Baseline Review (CBR) Data Package.	Data to be transmitted via DRD 102	Sep/2014
d) The DRD 108 Verification and Validation (V&V) Plan.	Data to be transmitted via DRD 108	Sep/2014
e) The DRD 107 Certification Plan.	Data to be transmitted via DRD 107	Sep/2014
f) The DRD 002 Integrated Master Plan and Integrated Master Schedule for CTS Certification activities.	Data to be transmitted via DRD 002	Sep/2014

Modification 02   Attachment J-03, Appendix A

Certification Baseline Review (CBR) Interim Milestone (As proposed, interim NASA milestone in support of DCR) DCR Interim Milestone 01A.1	Planned Start Date and Completion Date (mo/yr): Sep – Nov/2014 No Final RID Board	Amount:
g) An assessment of the top safety, technical, cost, and schedule risks to CTS Certification, and documentation of the approach to manage and accept risk with CTS Certification	Data to be transmitted via DRD 102	Sep/2014
h) DRD 001 Insight Implementation Plan and documentation of the organizational interaction and personnel interfaces to achieve the objectives of the Insight Implementation Plan and Insight Clause.	Data to be transmitted via DRD 001	Sep/2014
i) DRD 101 Milestone Review Plan.	Data to be transmitted via DRD 101	Sep/2014
j) DRD 109 Flight Test Plan.	Data to be transmitted via DRD 109	Sep/2014
Acceptance Criteria: (Att J-03 PWS Apx A)		
a) Requirements are baselined and controlled. The allocation of requirements to the CTS design baseline is complete.	Data dispositioned to the level required per DRD 102	
1) Requirements are traceable to CCT-REQ-1130 and SSP 50808.	Data dispositioned to the level required per DRD 102	
2) Variances and alternate standards have been incorporated and appropriately tailored into the Contractor's requirements.	Data dispositioned to the level required per DRD 102	
3) Technical coordination is complete for joint ISS integration products (ICDs, JiVTP, BDEALS, BHSEALS) identified in SSP 50964, and products are ready for ISS to baseline post CBR review.	Data dispositioned to the level required per DRD 102	

Modification 02
Attachment J-03, Appendix A

Certification Baseline Review (CBR) Interim Milestone (As proposed, interim NASA milestone in support of DCR) DCR Interim Milestone 01A.1	Planned Start Date and Completion Date (mo/yr): Sep - Nov/2014 No Final RID Board	Amount:
4) The Concept of Operations has been baselined.	Data dispositioned to the level required per DRD 102	
5) The CTS design definition products identified in the DRD 102 Certification Baseline Review (CBR) Data Package identify the current design baseline.	Data dispositioned to the level required per DRD 102	
6) Integrated vehicle performance and design margin is appropriate and supports completion of development.	Data dispositioned to the level required per DRD 102	
7) Management plans and products identified in the DRD 102 Certification Baseline Review (CBR) Data Package are in place, controlled and are being implemented. The plans and products identified in the CBR Data Package as type 2 have been approved.	Data dispositioned to the level required per DRD 102	
8) The DRD 108 V&V Plan has been Baselined.	Data dispositioned per DRD 108	
9) The DRD 107 Certification Plan has been Baselined.	Data dispositioned per DRD 107	
10) An DRD 002 Integrated Master Plan and Integrated Master Schedule (IMP/IMS) is baselined.	Data dispositioned per DRD 002	
11) The top safety, technical, cost and schedule risks are identified, assessed, mitigation plans identified and clearly documented in BORIS. Risk & Opportunity Management plan is released to effectively manage the risks.	Data dispositioned to the level required per DRD 102	

Certification Baseline Review (CBR) Interim Milestone (As proposed, interim NASA milestone in support of DCR) DCR Interim Milestone 01A.1	Planned Start Date and Completion Date (mo/yr): Sep - Nov/2014 No Final RID Board	Amount:
12) DRD 001 Insight Implementation Plan has been approved. The organizational interaction and personnel interfaces to achieve the objectives of the Insight Implementation Plan and Insight Clause have been documented.	Data dispositioned per DRD 001	
13) DRD 101 Milestone Review Plan in accordance with the Data Requirement List (DRL) and DRD has been approved.	Data dispositioned per DRD 101 MRP	
14) DRD 109 Flight Test Plan in accordance with the DRL and DRD has been approved.	Data dispositioned per DRD 109	
15) A plan and schedule have been defined for the resolution of all actions and open items resulting from the CBR. All To be Determined (TBD) and To be Resolved (TBR) items are clearly identified with acceptable plans and schedules for their disposition.		

Modification 02   Attachment J-03, Appendix A

Ground Segment Critical Design Review (CDR) Interim Milestone (As proposed, interim Contractor milestone in support of DCR) DCR Interim Milestone 01A.2	Planned Start Date and Completion Date (mo/yr): CMO CDR: Oct/2014 Grnd Sys CDR: Nov/2014 Combined Final RID Board Dec/2014	Amount:

Objective:

Contractor chaired. Perform (1) a Critical Design Review (CDR) of Crew & Mission Operations systems designs and processes for Mission Operations, Training Systems and Processes and Cargo Integration Processes; (2) a CDR of Ground Systems used for spacecraft AI&T, Space-to-Ground Comm, Landing and CM recovery ground systems; and (3) review of VAC-1 execution plan and schedule.

    a) Baseline tailored requirements, incorporating the results of NASA's guidance provided under CPC (if applicable), which meet NASA's requirements;

    b) Baseline most current CTS CMO design;

    c) Baseline Ground systems designs for AI&T, Space-to-Ground communications and post landing CM recovery, present summary updates to launch site facilities and pre-flight systems designs;

    d) Define schedule; and

    e) Define top safety, technical, cost and schedule risks.

Indicators of Milestone Readiness:	Data / DRDs to be provided:	Delivery of Data/DRDs (mo/yr)
For CMO CDR the Contractor has completed the following:		
a) Tailored requirements incorporating the results of NASA's guidance under CPC (if applicable) which meet NASA's requirements defined in CCT-STD-1150 Crew Transportation Operations Standards	Data to be transmitted IAW DRD 101 MRP Appendix B	Oct/2014
b) Mission Operations Plan, Train and Fly CDR technical work products for both hardware and software system elements for Mission Planning and Analysis, Flight Training, Flight Operations, Crew and Cargo Integration and Missions Systems have been made available to include:	Data to be transmitted IAW DRD 101 MRP Appendix B	Oct/2014

Ground Segment Critical Design Review (CDR) Interim Milestone	Planned Start Date and Completion Date (mo/yr): CMO CDR: Oct/2014 Grnd Sys CDR: Nov/2014 Combined Final RID Board Dec/2014	Amount:
(As proposed, interim Contractor milestone in support of DCR) DCR Interim Milestone 01A.2		
1) Product specifications for each hardware and software configuration item	Data to be transmitted IAW DRD 101 MRP Appendix B	Oct/2014
2) Fabrication, Assembly, integration and test plans and procedures	Data to be transmitted IAW DRD 101 MRP Appendix B	Oct/2014
3) Interface control documents	Data to be transmitted IAW DRD 101 MRP Appendix B	Oct/2014
4) Operations limits and constraints	Data to be transmitted IAW DRD 101 MRP Appendix B	Oct/2014
5) Technical resource utilization estimates and margins	Data to be transmitted IAW DRD 101 MRP Appendix B	Oct/2014
6) Command and telemetry lists	Data to be transmitted IAW DRD 101 MRP Appendix B	Oct/2014
7) Verification and Validation plan(s)	Data to be transmitted IAW DRD 101 MRP Appendix B	Oct/2014
8) Software design document(s) including interface design document(s)	Data to be transmitted IAW DRD 101 MRP Appendix B	Oct/2014
9) Training documentation (e.g. plans, curriculum, schedules)	Data to be transmitted IAW DRD 101 MRP Appendix B	Oct/2014
10) Safety analyses	Data to be transmitted IAW DRD 101 MRP Appendix B	Oct/2014
11) Certification plans and requirements (as needed)	Data to be transmitted IAW DRD 101 MRP Appendix B	Oct/2014

Modification 02   Attachment J-03, Appendix A

Ground Segment Critical Design Review (CDR) Interim Milestone (As proposed, interim Contractor milestone in support of DCR) DCR Interim Milestone 01A.2	Planned Start Date and Completion Date (mo/yr): CMO CDR: Oct/2014 Grnd Sys CDR: Nov/2014 Combined Final RID Board Dec/2014	Amount: ▓▓▓
c) CMO schedule elements as part of the Integration Master Schedule (DRD 002) for CTS Certification activities.	Data to be provided at meeting IAW DRD 002	Oct/2014
d) An assessment of the top safety, technical, cost, and schedule risks to CMO and documentation of the approach to manage and accept risks.	Data to be provided at meeting IAW DRD 101 MRP Appendix B	Oct/2014
For Ground Systems CDR the Contractor has completed the following:		
a) Tailored requirements incorporating the results of NASA's guidance under CPC (if applicable) which meet NASA's requirements defined in CCT-REQ-1130.	Data to be transmitted IAW DRD 101 MRP Appendix B	Oct/2014
b) CDR technical work products for both hardware and software system elements for Ground Systems used for spacecraft AI&T, Space-to-Ground Communication, Landing and CM recovery ground systems have been made available to include:	Data to be transmitted IAW DRD 101 MRP Appendix B	Oct/2014
1) Updated baselined documents, as required	Data to be transmitted IAW DRD 101 MRP Appendix B	Oct/2014
2) Product specifications for each hardware and software configuration item	Data to be transmitted IAW DRD 101 MRP Appendix B	Oct/2014
3) Spacecraft Fabrication, Assembly, integration and test plans and procedures	Data to be transmitted IAW DRD 101 MRP Appendix B	Oct/2014
4) Interface control documents	Data to be transmitted IAW DRD 101 MRP Appendix B	Oct/2014

Modification 02
Attachment J-03, Appendix A

Ground Segment Critical Design Review (CDR) Interim Milestone (As proposed, interim Contractor milestone in support of DCR) DCR Interim Milestone 01A.2	Planned Start Date and Completion Date (mo/yr): CMO CDR: Oct/2014 Grnd Sys CDR: Nov/2014 Combined Final RID Board Dec/2014	Amount: ▉
5) Operations limits and constraints	Data to be transmitted IAW DRD 101 MRP Appendix B	Oct/2014
6) Technical resource utilization estimates and margins	Data to be transmitted IAW DRD 101 MRP Appendix B	Oct/2014
7) Command and telemetry lists	Data to be transmitted IAW DRD 101 MRP Appendix B	Oct/2014
8) Verification and Validation plan(s)	Data to be transmitted IAW DRD 101 MRP Appendix B	Oct/2014
9) Software design document(s) including interface design document(s)	Data to be transmitted IAW DRD 101 MRP Appendix B	Oct/2014
10) Safety analyses	Data to be transmitted IAW DRD 101 MRP Appendix B	Oct/2014
11) Certification plans and requirements (as needed)	Data to be transmitted IAW DRD 101 MRP Appendix B	Oct/2014
c) Ground Systems schedule elements as part of the Integration Master Schedule (DRD 002) for CTS Certification activities.	Data to be transmitted IAW DRD 002	Oct/2014
d) An assessment of the top safety, technical, cost, and schedule risks to Ground Systems and documentation of the approach to manage and accept risks.	Data to be provided at meeting IAW DRD 101 MRP Appendix B	Oct/2014
Draft VAC-1 execution plan and schedule provided.	Data to be provided at meeting IAW DRD 101 MRP Appendix B	Oct/2014

Modification 02   Attachment J-03, Appendix A

Ground Segment Critical Design Review (CDR) Interim Milestone (As proposed, interim Contractor milestone in support of DCR) DCR Interim Milestone 01A.2	Planned Start Date and Completion Date (mo/yr): CMO CDR: Oct/2014 Grnd Sys CDR: Nov/2014 Combined Final RID Board Dec/2014	Amount: ■
Acceptance Criteria:		
a) For both CMO and Ground Systems CDRs the following apply:		
1) Top-level requirements are agreed upon, finalized, stated clearly and consistent with the final design	Data dispositioned to the level required per DRD 101 MRP Appendix B	
2) The flow down of verifiable requirements is complete and proper or, if not, an adequate plan exists for timely resolution of open items. Requirements are traceable to mission goals and objectives.	Data dispositioned to the level required per DRD 101 MRP Appendix B	
3) The final design is expected to meet the requirements at an acceptable level of risk	Data dispositioned to the level required per DRD 101 MRP Appendix B	
4) Definition of technical interfaces are consistent with the overall technical maturity and provides an acceptable level of risk	Data dispositioned to the level required per DRD 101 MRP Appendix B	
5) Adequate technical margins exist with respect to the TPMs or, if not, an adequate plan exists for timely resolution of open items	Data dispositioned to the level required per DRD 101 MRP Appendix B	
6) Project risks are understood and have been assess, and plans, a process, and resources exist to effectively manage them	Data dispositioned to the level required per DRD 101 MRP Appendix B	
7) The operational concept is technically sound, incorporates human factors considerations (as appropriate) and includes flow down of requirements for its execution	Data dispositioned to the level required per DRD 101 MRP Appendix B	

Ground Segment Critical Design Review (CDR) Interim Milestone	Planned Start Date and Completion Date (mo/yr): CMO CDR: Oct/2014 Grnd Sys CDR: Nov/2014 Combined Final RID Board Dec/2014	Amount:
(As proposed, interim Contractor milestone in support of DCR) DCR Interim Milestone 01A.2		
8) Completion of review per Milestone Review Plan (DRD 101)	Data dispositioned to the level required per DRD 101 MRP Appendix B	
b) VAC-1 plan and schedule reviewed. VAC products provide integrated assessment of system performance against applicable CCTS requirements and are consistent with the V&V plan. Schedule inter-dependencies are correctly identified. Risks to execution are identified and mitigation plans documented.	Data dispositioned to the level required per DRD 101 MRP Appendix B	

Modification 003

H.3 NFS 1852.223-72 SAFETY AND HEALTH (SHORT FORM). (APR 2002)

(a) Safety is the freedom from those conditions that can cause death, injury, occupational illness; damage to or loss of equipment or property, or damage to the environment. NASA's safety priority is to protect: (1) the public, (2) astronauts and pilots, (3) the NASA workforce (including Contractor employees working on NASA contracts), and (4) high-value equipment and property.

(b) The Contractor shall take all reasonable safety and occupational health measures consistent with standard industry practice in performing this contract. The Contractor shall comply with all Federal, State, and local laws applicable to safety and occupational health and with the safety and occupational health standards, specifications, reporting requirements, and any other relevant requirements of this contract.

(c) The Contractor shall take, or cause to be taken, any other safety, and occupational health measures the Contracting Officer may reasonably direct. To the extent that the Contractor may be entitled to an equitable adjustment for those measures under the terms and conditions of this contract, the equitable adjustment shall be determined pursuant to the procedures of the Changes clause of this contract; provided, that no adjustment shall be made under this Safety and Health clause for any change for which an equitable adjustment is expressly provided under any other clause of the contract.

(d) The Contracting Officer may notify the Contractor in writing of any noncompliance with this clause and specify corrective actions to be taken. In situations where the Contracting Officer becomes aware of noncompliance that may pose a serious or imminent danger to safety and health of the public, astronauts and pilots, the NASA workforce (including Contractor employees working on NASA contracts), or high value mission critical equipment or property, the Contracting Officer shall notify the Contractor orally, with written confirmation. The Contractor shall promptly take and report any necessary corrective action. The Government may pursue appropriate remedies in the event the Contractor fails to promptly take the necessary corrective action.

(e) The Contractor (or subcontractor or supplier) shall insert the substance of this clause, including this paragraph (e) and any applicable Schedule provisions, with appropriate changes of designations of the parties, in subcontracts of every tier that exceed the micro-purchase threshold.

(End of Clause)

H.4 NFS 1852.232-77 LIMITATION OF FUNDS (FIXED- PRICE CONTRACT). (MAR 1989)

(a) Of the total price of all CLIN items identified in Section B, the sum of $439,575,675 is presently available for payment and allotted to this contract. It is anticipated that from time to time additional funds will be allocated to the contract as required by the payment schedules in Attachment J-03, Appendix A, *Milestone Acceptance Criteria and Payment Schedule* and task

Modification 003

orders awarded under CLIN 002 and 003 (see table B.4.2 and B.5.2 respectively) until the total price of said items is allotted.

(b) The Contractor agrees to perform or have performed work on the items specified in paragraph (a) of this clause up to the point at which, if this contract is terminated pursuant to the Termination for Convenience of the Government clause of this contract, the total amount payable by the Government (including amounts payable for subcontracts and settlement costs) pursuant to paragraphs (f) and (g) of that clause would, in the exercise of reasonable judgment by the Contractor, approximate the total amount at the time allotted to the contract. The Contractor is not obligated to continue performance of the work beyond that point. The Government is not obligated in any event to pay or reimburse the Contractor more than the amount from time to time allotted to the contract, anything to the contrary in the Termination for Convenience of the Government clause notwithstanding.

(c) (1) It is contemplated that funds presently allotted to this contract will cover the work to be performed until February 2, 2015.

(2) If funds allotted are considered by the Contractor to be inadequate to cover the work to be performed until that date, or an agreed date substituted for it, the Contractor shall notify the Contracting Officer in writing when within the next 60 days the work will reach a point at which, if the contract is terminated pursuant to the Termination for Convenience of the Government clause of this contract, the total amount payable by the Government (including amounts payable for subcontracts and settlement costs) pursuant to paragraphs (f) and (g) of that clause will approximate 75 percent of the total amount then allotted to the contract.

(3) (i) The notice shall state the estimate when the point referred to in paragraph (c) (2) of this clause will be reached and the estimated amount of additional funds required to continue performance to the date specified in paragraph (c) (1) of this clause, or an agreed date substituted for it.

(ii) The Contractor shall, 60 days in advance of the date specified in paragraph (c) (1) of this clause, or an agreed date substituted for it, advise the Contracting Officer in writing as to the estimated amount of additional funds required for the timely performance of the contract for a further period as may be specified in the contract or otherwise agreed to by the parties.

(4) If, after the notification referred to in paragraph (c) (3) (ii) of this clause, additional funds are not allotted by the date specified in paragraph (c) (1) of this clause, or an agreed date substituted for it, the Contracting Officer shall, upon the Contractor's written request, terminate this contract on that date or on the date set forth in the request, whichever is later, pursuant to the Termination for Convenience of the Government clause.

(d) When additional funds are allotted from time to time for continued performance of the work under this contract, the parties shall agree on the applicable period of contract performance to be covered by these funds. The provisions of paragraphs (b) and (c) of this clause shall apply to

Made in the USA
Columbia, SC
10 December 2022

73283068R00207